T0381628

"In his book, Devin O. 1   / phase of the trial. He provides an.   ....of the complex, lengthy legal and political machinations that preceded the trial, moves on to an exhaustive analysis of the actual courtroom proceedings and concludes with an assessment of German public reactions. The extremely detailed narrative will certainly satisfy readers who prefer encyclopedic rigor, although others might consider the book's reconstruction of the procedural maneuvers during the trial to be denser than necessary, despite the author's formidable lucidity. The impressive archival research on which the book is based is well reflected in its extensive citations, which Cambridge University Press admirably continues to print at the bottom of the page."

– *H-NET*

"Pendas is...scrupulous in analysing the reception of the trial.... [A] brilliant analysis of the trial's legal implications."

– *German History*

"Provides a meticulously detailed and comprehensive analysis: from the pretrial history to its public repercussions; from the courtroom proceedings to their wider political and legal contexts (the Cold War, the politics of the past in the Federal Republic, German criminal law, and so on)."

– *Journal of Genocide Research*

"Devin Pendas has written a major study of the largest and most important trial of Nazi perpetrators held in the Federal Republic of Germany. The book carefully reconstructs the preparations made for the trial, the course of the proceedings, public reactions, and the long-term impact of the event. Most crucially, Pendas provides a lucid and penetrating analysis of the manner in which the application of criminal law in general, and German criminal law specifically, to a trial concerned with genocide and set within a highly politicized domestic and international context set severe limits to the court's ability to make just and historically valid decisions."

– Omer Bartov, Brown University

"This excellent, landmark study engages the reader through the author's ability to apply his vast knowledge of German law and legal procedures, and through his equally astute grasp of the history of the Auschwitz camps and the crimes committed there, to a compelling narrative describing how these histories and the events in postwar West Germany led to the Auschwitz trial. The presiding judge, Hans Hofmeyer, insisted that the proceedings were not an Auschwitz trial but a criminal case against individual defendants whose personal guilt as murderers or accessories had to be proven beyond doubt, based on specific, documented, credible evidence. Given how Auschwitz functioned as a factory of mass murder, as the author masterfully demonstrates, these evidentiary burdens made the case inadequate to the moral expectations that the prosecutors, the German press, and much of the world had of the trial. Professor Pendas deftly places the trial within the context of the Cold War hostilities of the mid-1960s, as well as the international efforts to bring Nazi perpetrators to justice, and, in an especially absorbing chapter, details the reaction to the trial and its verdicts among the German public and press and the international community at large."

> – Charles W. Sydnor, Jr., President and CEO of Commonwealth
> Public Broadcasting

"Pendas has a talent for organizing his vast material systematically. All in all, Pendas' study is stylistically a well-balanced historical protocol of the trial."

> – *German Politics and Society*

"Displaying an impressive erudition in German criminal law, Pendas traverses not only the intricacies of homicide, but also the current of opinion in German law journals of the 1960s. He combines a historian's sensitivity to context with a jurist's appreciation of substantive and procedural criminal law. Pendas's important and stimulating work on *Vergangenhietsbewältigung* (coming to terms with the past) should provoke deep reflection on Holocaust representation in the postwar German trials."

> – *Holocaust and Genocide Studies*

The Frankfurt Auschwitz Trial, 1963–1965

Genocide, History, and the Limits of the Law

The Frankfurt Auschwitz trial was the largest, most public, and most important trial of Holocaust perpetrators conducted in West German courts. Drawing on a wide range of archival sources, Devin O. Pendas provides a comprehensive history of this momentous event. Situating the trial in a thorough analysis of West German criminal law, the book argues that in confronting systematic, state-sponsored genocide, the Frankfurt court ran up against the limits of law. Because many of the key categories of German criminal law were defined with direct reference to the specific motives of the defendants, the trial was unable to grasp adequately the deep social roots and systematic character of Nazi genocide. Much of the trial's significance came from the vast public attention it captured, and this book provides a compelling account of the divided response to the trial among the West German public.

Devin O. Pendas is an associate professor of history at Boston College. He received his Ph.D. from the University of Chicago and is the recipient of grants from the German Academic Exchange Service and the MacArthur Foundation. His articles have appeared in the *Yale Journal of Law and the Humanities* and *traverse: Zeitschrift für Geschichte/Revue d'histoire*, as well as in a number of edited volumes.

For my mother and grandmother and in memory of my grandfather

The Frankfurt Auschwitz Trial, 1963–1965

Genocide, History, and the Limits of the Law

DEVIN O. PENDAS

Boston College

CAMBRIDGE
UNIVERSITY PRESS

CAMBRIDGE UNIVERSITY PRESS
Cambridge, New York, Melbourne, Madrid, Cape Town,
Singapore, São Paulo, Delhi, Tokyo, Mexico City

Cambridge University Press
32 Avenue of the Americas, New York, NY 10013-2473, USA

www.cambridge.org
Information on this title: www.cambridge.org/9780521127981

First published 2006
First paperback edition 2010
Reprinted 2011

A catalog record for this publication is available from the British Library.

Library of Congress Cataloging in Publication Data

Pendas, Devin O. (Devin Owen)
The Frankfurt Auschwitz trial, 1963–1965 : genocide, history, and the limits of the law /
Devin O. Pendas.
   p. cm.
Includes bibliographical references and index.
ISBN 0-521-84406-1 (hardback : alk. paper)
1. Auschwitz Trial, Frankfurt am Main, Germany, 1963–1965. 2. War crime trials –
Germany – Frankfurt am Main. 3. Trials (Genocide) – Germany – Frankfurt am Main.
4. Auschwitz (Concentration camp) I. Title.
KK73.5.A98P46 2006
345.43´0238–dc22   2005006330

ISBN 978-0-521-84406-2 Hardback
ISBN 978-0-521-12798-1 Paperback

Contents

Illustrations and Tables

Illustrations

Tables

Acknowledgments

It is commonplace to note that any substantial scholarly work is more than simply the result of the author's own personal efforts, and this is certainly true of the present work. This is especially true of projects that, like this one, began their lives as dissertations, where the author is necessarily a novice. I would therefore like to thank especially my teachers at the University of Chicago for their constant, critical, and always helpful advice and guidance: Michael Geyer, who supervised the dissertation; Moishe Postone, who was in many ways its intellectual guiding light; and William Novak, who kept me honest about the law. Lawrence Douglas of Amherst College was kind enough to serve as an outside reader. I also received invaluable assistance from many people in the Federal Republic of Germany. I would like to thank especially the staff of the Fritz Bauer Institute in Frankfurt, who demonstrated admirable patience with a young scholar just finding his way around the complexities of archival research. I am particularly indebted to the institute's archivist, Werner Renz, who guided me to countless sources I would never have found on my own. In addition, the director of the institute at the time, Hanno Loewy, provided much useful feedback and advice both during my research in Frankfurt and afterward. The institute's staff historian, Irmtrud Wojak, was also very generous with her time and advice. Norbert Frei of Bochum University was also kind enough to meet with me and share his insights into the Auschwitz Trial and the politics of memory in the Federal Republic.

I would also like to thank the Justice Ministry of the Federal State of Hesse and the Frankfurt Prosecutor's Office for granting me access to the Auschwitz Trial files, without which this project would not have been possible. The staff of the Federal Archives in Koblenz and Berlin-Lichterfelde, as well as of the Hessisches Hauptarchiv in Wiesbaden, were also always helpful and willing to grant access to documents.

In addition, I would like to thank Axel Honneth and the members of his doctoral seminar at the J. W. Goethe University in Frankfurt for their

support and critical insight during my stay in Frankfurt. Simon Critchley,
Caitlin Dempsy, Christine Holbo, Mathias Iser, Jennifer Kolpakov, Eric
Oberle, David Strecker, and Rebecca Wittmann all helped to make my time
in Frankfurt intellectually stimulating and productive. In Chicago, I would
like to thank the members of the Modern European History Workshop and
the Social Theory Workshop for allowing me to present drafts of my work
in progress and for providing valuable feedback. Paul Townsend and Nicole
Jarnagin both read drafts of many of the chapters and provided countless
helpful comments. Till van Rahden read and critiqued the introduction.
Sean Gilsdorf, Erik Grimmer-Solem, Jeff Kilpatrick, H. Paul Manning, and
Amanda Seaman provided many hours of stimulating conversation on matters concerning this project. Finally, my colleagues at Boston College, James
Cronin and Franziska Seraphim in particular, were especially kind with their
suggestions in the closing phases of the project.

A project of this magnitude also requires considerable financial support. The German Academic Exchange Service provided generous financial support for my primary research in Germany in 1996 and 1997, and
the MacArthur Foundation provided me with a write-up grant for 1999–
2000 through the Center for Advanced Studies in Peace and International
Cooperation at the University of Chicago, without which it would have been
much more difficult to complete this project in a timely manner. Boston College enabled me to take one final research trip to Germany in the summer
of 2004 through a research expense grant. Lewis Bateman of Cambridge
University Press responded positively to this project and has been constantly
encouraging in bringing it to completion. I would also like to thank Stephanie
Sakson, who copyedited the manuscript.

I would like to thank several journals and publications for permission
to reprint material from the following articles: "The Historiography of
Horror: The Auschwitz Trial and the German Historical Imagination," in
Jeffrey Diefendorf, ed., *Lessons and Legacies VI: New Currents in Holocaust
Research* (Evanston: Northwestern University Press, 2004), 209–30; "Truth
and Its Consequences: Reflections on Political, Historical and Legal 'Truth' in
West German Holocaust Trials," *traverse: Zeitschrift für Geschichte/Revue
d'histoire* 11 (2004): 25–38; and "'I didn't know what Auschwitz was': The
Frankfurt Auschwitz Trial and the German Press, 1963–1965," *Yale Journal
of Law and the Humanities* 12 (June 2000): 387–446.

Finally, I would like to especially thank my family. My wife, Christine
McAllister, has shown boundless patience and never-ending support during
what must at times have seemed like an interminable project. My daughter,
Olivia, who arrived at the tail end of my work on this book, is a profound
reminder of the importance of history for the present. My mother and grand-
parents have been a constant inspiration and support for me in my historical
studies, and it is to them that I dedicate this book, in particular to my late
grandfather, Owen Rothman.

Abbreviations

AA	Auswärtige Amt
AWJD	*Allgemeine Wochenzeitung der Juden in Deutschland*
BAB	Bundesarchiv, Berlin-Lichterfelde
BAK	Bundesarchiv, Koblenz
BgF	Bundesminister für gesamtdeutsche Fragen
BGH	Bundesgerichtshof
BGHSt	*Entscheidungen des Bundesgerichtshofs in Strafsachen*
BK	Bundeskanzleramt
BMI	Bundesministerium des Innern
BMJ	Bundesministerium der Justiz
BPA	Presse- und Informationsamt der Bundesregierung
BVB	Bund für Volksbildung, Frankfurt
BVG	Bundesverfassungsgericht
CC	Allied Control Council
CIC	Comité International des Camps
DNZ	*Deutsche National-Zeitung und Soldaten-Zeitung*
FAZ	*Frankfurter Allgemeine Zeitung*
FBI	Fritz Bauer Institut
FBI SAP	Fritz Bauer Institut, Sammlung Auschwitz-Prozeß
FDP	Freie Demokratische Partei
FFStA	Frankfurt Staatsanwaltschaft
FFStA HA	Frankfurt Staatsanwaltschaft, Handakten
FNP	*Frankfurter Neue Presse*
FR	*Frankfurter Rundschau*
FRG	Federal Republic of Germany
GDR	German Democratic Republic
GVG	Gerichtsverfassungsgesetz
HHA	Hessisches Hauptarchiv
HMJ	Hessische Ministerium der Justiz
HVP	Hauptverhandlungsprotokoll

IAC	International Auschwitz Committee
IfZ	Institut für Zeitgeschichte
MDR	*Monatsschrift für Deutsches Recht*
MStGB	Militärstrafgesetzbuch
NDP	Nationaldemokratischen Partei Deutschlands
NJW	*Neue Juristische Wochenschrift*
OKW	Oberkommando der Wehrmacht
PA	Politische Abteilung
RG	Reichsgericht
RGSt	*Entscheidungen des Reichsgerichts in Strafsachen*
RSHA	Reichssichheitshauptamt
SAFF	Stadtsarchiv, Frankfurt am Main
SAPMO	Stiftung Archiv der Parteien und Massenorganizationen der DDR
SED	Sozialistische Einheitspartei Deutschlands
SPD	Sozialdemokratische Partei Deutschlands
StA	Staatsanwaltschaft
StGB	*Strafgesetzbuch*
StPO	*Strafprozeßordnung*
SZ	*Süddeutsche Zeitung*
TR	Tape Recording of Main Proceedings, Frankfurt Auschwitz Trial
UDWV	Union Deutscher Wiederstandskämpfer- und Verfolgtenverbände
UIRD	Union Internationale de la Résistance et de la Déportation
VFM	Verband für Freiheit und Menschenwürde
WJC	World Jewish Congress
ZK SED	Zentralkomitee der Sozialistische Einheitspartei Deutschlands

1 Court examination of Auschwitz I: Trial participants going through the entry gate. Lead prosecutor Dr. Hanns Großmann is in the foreground. Photo courtesy of the Fritz Bauer Institute.

2 Court examination of Auschwitz I: Civil counsel Henry Ormond (right) and Kazimierz Smolen, director of the Auschwitz Museum (foreground). Photo courtesy of the Fritz Bauer Institute.

3 Court examination of Auschwitz I: Photographers and journalists following the trial participants. Kazimierz Smolen is visible on the left, with the white roll of paper under his arm. Photo courtesy of the Fritz Bauer Institute.

4 Court examination of Auschwitz II: Civil counsel Friedrich Karl Kaul (middle), civil plaintiff Mieczyslaw Kieta (left), civil counsel Joachim Noack, Kaul's assistant (right). Photo courtesy of the Fritz Bauer Institute.

5 Court examination of Auschwitz II: Examination of the new ramp. Defendant Dr. Franz Lucas is in the foreground. In the background, the camp gate is visible. Photo courtesy of the Fritz Bauer Institute.

6 Court examination of Auschwitz II: Measuring distances on the new ramp. Bailiff Walter Lanz (first from left), Judge Walter Hotz (second from left), Defense Counsel Herbert W. Naumann (third from left), and defense counsel Eugen Gerhard (fourth from left). Photo courtesy of the Fritz Bauer Institute.

7 Court examination of Auschwitz: Trial participants waiting at the Warsaw airport. Photo courtesy of the Fritz Bauer Institute.

8 Court examination of Auschwitz I: Trial participants exiting the camp through the main gate. Defense counsel Georg Bürger (first from left), civil counsel Friedrich Karl Kaul (second from left), Polish representative Jan Sehn (third from left), Judge Walter Hotz (fifth from left), Kazimierz Smolen (sixth from left). Photo courtesy of dpa.

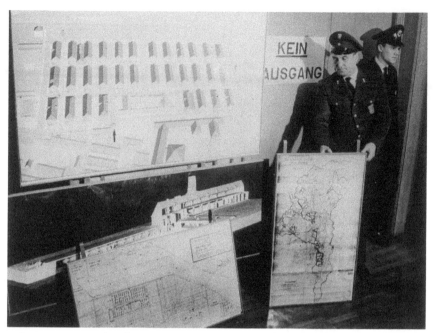

9 Court session in the plenary hall of the Frankfurt City Hall (Römer): On the wall is a map of Auschwitz I; in front is a model of a crematorium and a map of the entire Auschwitz complex. Photo courtesy of dpa.

10 Lead defendant Robert Mulka (left) speaking with an unknown reporter on the opening day of the trial. Photo courtesy of dpa.

11 Defendants Heinrich Bischoff, Herbert Scherpe, Josef Klehr, Robert Mulka, and Stefan Baetzki (from left to right). Photo courtesy of dpa.

12 In the courtroom, 32nd court session: Defense counsel Engelbert P. Joschko (right) and Karlheiz Staiger (middle) speaking with defendant Johann Schobert (left). Photo courtesy of dpa.

13 Opening day: Civil counsel Friedrich Karl Kaul talking to an unknown journalist. Photo courtesy of Keystone Press Service.

Introduction

This book is a history of the Frankfurt Auschwitz Trial (1963–65), the largest, most public, and most important Nazi trial to take place in West German courts after 1945. It was the most dramatic and politically resonant of the more than 6,000 such trials that took place in between 1945 and 1980.[1] Yet if the Auschwitz Trial was unusual among such trials in its drama and significance, in two other important respects it was quite typical. First, like all West German Nazi trials after the Federal Republic regained full legal autonomy in the early 1950s, the Auschwitz Trial was conducted under ordinary statutory (as opposed to international) law. Second, like most such trials after the late 1950s, the Auschwitz Trial was a Holocaust trial, concerned at its core with the Nazi genocide of the Jews.[2] This book is thus an examination of how the Federal Republic of Germany tried to grapple with genocide by means of ordinary criminal law. How did this effort work in detail? What were its strengths and weaknesses, its limits and boundaries? What were the legal, political, and cultural ramifications of using domestic law to prosecute one's own genocidal history?

This book chooses to address these questions by means of a detailed history of a single trial. Twenty-two defendants stood in the dock at the start of the Auschwitz Trial; twenty remained at the end.[3] Of these, seven were

---

[1] Adalbert Rückerl, *NS-Verbrechen vor Gericht: Versuch einer Vergangenheitsbewältigung* (Heidelberg: C. F. Müller, 1984), p. 329.

[2] Falko Kruse, "NS-Prozesse und Restauration: Zur justitiellen Verfolgung von NS-Gewaltverbrechen in der Bundesrepublik," in Redaktion Kritische Justiz, ed., *Der Unrechts-Staat: Recht und Justiz im Nationalsozialismus*, vol. 1 (Baden-Baden: Nomos Verlagsgesellschaft, 1983), pp. 180–82.

[3] Two – Gerhard Neubert and Heinrich Bischoff – had their cases suspended for health reasons. Neubert was subsequently a defendant in the so-called Second Frankfurt Auschwitz Trial from December 14, 1965, to September 16, 1966. Bischoff died before his case could be brought back to trial. In addition, Hans Nierzwicki's case was dropped from the proceedings prior to the trial's opening.

convicted of murder, and ten of accessory to murder, and three were acquitted. Sentences ranged from three and one-quarter years to life in prison. Over the course of twenty months and 183 trial sessions, over 350 witnesses testified, including 211 survivors of Auschwitz. Dozens of attorneys, representing the prosecution, the defense, and civil plaintiffs from around the world, argued about the nature and meaning of mass murder, torture, and genocide. In its final judgment – both oral and written – the court attempted to render justice for the crimes of Auschwitz within the limits allowed by the law.[4] And the West German public watched it all with a curious blend of macabre fascination, hostile indifference, and heartfelt shame and remorse.

In the Auschwitz Trial, the law came up against the limits of its capacity to deal adequately with systematic genocide. West German criminal law was designed to deal primarily with very different kinds of crimes: ordinary crimes, committed for the most part by individuals or small groups driven by personal motives. Yet the legal categories developed to differentiate defendants according to their subjective relationship to the crime became at best misleading when applied to a crime whose implementation did not depend wholly on the specific individual motivation of any one of its numerous perpetrators. The Holocaust was not merely massive in scale but also bureaucratically organized and state-directed. Consequently, the personal motives of any of the thousands of perpetrators became subsidiary factors in a process of mass murder that extended well beyond any one of them. Auschwitz would certainly not have been possible without the willing participation of perpetrators such as those on trial in Frankfurt, but its terrible reality cannot be explained simply as a composite of individual crimes committed for individual reasons. The whole is, as it were, greater than the sum of its parts. Yet it is precisely this exponential character of Nazi genocide that the Auschwitz Trial found so difficult to encompass within the terms of German law.

Furthermore, the Auschwitz Trial has to be understood as a political trial. This is not to claim that it was an illegitimate attempt to use legal forms to pursue extra-legal ends, but rather to point out that rendering justice on Auschwitz necessarily raised important contemporary political questions.[5] The Cold War was a constant presence in the courtroom, but so too were questions about the nature of West German democracy and the relationship

---

[4] The judgment is now available in a full, critical edition: Friedrich-Martin Balzer and Werner Renz, eds., *Das Urteil im Frankfurter Auschwitz-Prozess, 1963–1965* (Bonn: Pahl-Rugenstein, 2004). However, I have chosen to quote from the older published edition of the judgment because it remains more widely accessible. See C. F. Rüter et al., eds., *Justiz und NS-Verbrechen: Sammlung Deutscher Strafurteile wegen nationalsozialistischer Tötungsverbrechen, 1945–1966*, vol. 21 (Amsterdam: University Press Amsterdam, 1979).

[5] This is the classic understanding of political trials. See Otto Kirchheimer, *Political Justice: The Use of Legal Procedure for Political Ends* (Princeton: Princeton University Press, 1961). However, see Charles F. Abel and Frank H. Marsh, *In Defense of Political Trials* (Westport, Conn.: Greenwood Press, 1994).

between the German past and the German present. The trial was a political trial because Auschwitz was as much a contemporary political problem as it was a historical one.

The history of West German Nazi trials has to date been treated by scholars mostly at a quite general level. Broadly speaking, this historiography can be divided into three phases. In the 1960s, there were attempts to address the legal and political nature of contemporaneous Nazi trials.[6] Then, beginning in the 1980s, there were efforts at a preliminary overview, often either rather cursory or polemical.[7] Finally, in recent years there have been efforts at a more thorough, empirically grounded, and archivally researched analysis of such trials.[8] This most recent literature is particularly useful, demonstrating the full complexity – both political and legal – of the history of Nazi trials in the Federal Republic. It points out that one cannot properly speak of "Nazi trials" as a unitary whole but must rather consider them in all their variability and in their proper historical context.

---

[6] Reinhard Henkys, *Die nationalsozialistischen Gewaltverbrechen: Geschichte und Gericht*, ed. Dietrich Goldschmidt (Stuttgart: Kreuz Verlag, 1964); Hermann Langbein, *Im Namen des deutschen Volkes: Zwischenbilanz der Prozesse wegen nationalsozialistischer Verbrechen* (Vienna: Europa Verlag, 1963); Presse- und Informationsamt der Bundesregierung, *Die Verfolgung nationalsozialistischer Straftaten in der Bundesrepublik* (Flensburg: Christian Wolff, 1963); and Peter Schneider and Herman J. Meyer, eds., *Rechtliche und politische Aspekte der NS-Verbrecherprozesse: Gemeinschaftsvorlesung des studium generale Wintersemester 1966/67* (Mainz: Guttenberg-Universität Mainz, 1968).

[7] *Nationalsozialismus und Justiz: Die Aufarbeitung von Gewaltverbrechen damals und heute* (Münster: agenda Verlag, 1993); Volker Ducklau, "Die Befehlsproblematik bei NS-Tötungsverbrechen: Eine Untersuchung anhand von 900 Urteilen deutscher Gerichte von 1945 bis 1965," Ph.D. diss., Universität Freiburg, 1976; Jörg Friedrich, *Die kalte Amnestie: NS-Täter in der Bundesrepublik*, rev. ed. (Munich: Piper, 1994 [1984]); Albrecht Götz, *Bilanz der Verfolgung von NS-Straftaten* (Cologne: Bundesanzeiger Verlag, 1986); Bernd Hey, "NS-Prozesse: Versuch einer juristischen Vergangenheitsbewältigung," *Geschichte in Wissenschaft und Unterricht* 6 (1981): 51–70; Bernd Hey, "NS-Gewaltverbrechen: Wissenschaft und Öffentlichkeit. Anmerkungen zu einer interdisziplinären Tagung über die Vergangenheitsbewältigung," *Geschichte in Wissenschaft und Unterricht* 9 (1984): 86–91; Redaktion Kritische Justiz, ed., *Der Unrechts-Staat: Recht und Justiz im Nationalsozialismus*, 2 vols. (Baden-Baden: Nomos Verlag, 1983–84); Landeszentrale für Politische Bildung NRW, ed., *Vereint Vergessen? Justiz- und NS-Verbrechen in Deutschland* (Düsseldorf: Landeszentrale für Politische Bildung Nordrhein-Westfalen, 1993); Michael Ratz et al., *Die Justiz und die Nazis: Zur Strafverfolgung von Nazismus und Neonazismus seit 1945* (Frankfurt: Röderberg-Verlag, 1979); Rückerl, *NS-Verbrechen vor Gericht*; Julius H. Schoeps and Horst Hillerman, eds., *Justiz und Nationalsozialismus: Bewältigt-Verdrängt-Vergessen* (Stuttgart: Burg Verlag, 1987); Jürgen Weber and Peter Steinbach, eds., *Vergangenheitsbewältigung durch Strafverfahren? NS-Prozesse in der Bundesrepublik Deutschland* (Munich: Günter Olzog Verlag, 1984).

[8] Kerstin Freudiger, *Die juristische Aufarbeitung von NS-Verbrechen* (Tübingen: Mohr Siebeck, 2002); Michael Greve, *Der justitielle und rechtspolitische Umgang mit den NS-Gewaltverbrechen in den sechziger Jahren* (Frankfurt: Peter Lang, 2001); Friedrich Hoffmann, *Die Verfolgung der nationalsozialistischen Gewaltverbrechen in Hessen* (Baden-Baden: Nomos, 2001); and Marc von Miquel, *Ahnden oder amnestieren? Westdeutsche Justiz und Vergangenheitspolitik in den sechziger Jahren* (Göttingen: Wallstein, 2004).

Yet for all its value, what none of this literature does is provide a comprehensive, empirically grounded history of any given trial. If, however, it is necessary to recognize the variability of Nazi trials across time, as well as to situate them in their proper political and legal context, then such detailed individual histories are urgently needed. Because the Auschwitz Trial was both the most prominent Nazi trial in the history of the Federal Republic and also one that was utterly typical of the 1960s in its subject matter and in its application of ordinary law to Nazi crimes, it offers a particularly useful opportunity for such an analysis.

The importance of the trial was immediately recognized by contemporaries. In addition to the massive press coverage of the trial (see chapter 9), several classic books about the trial appeared shortly after its conclusion. Hermann Langbein's two-volume "documentation" of the trial contains brief reflections on the origin of the trial but consists primarily of extensive excerpts from witness testimony, which Langbein took down personally during the trial.[9] The book is organized typologically, according to the camp's own organization, thus making plain that the book's true interest is less the Auschwitz Trial than Auschwitz itself. The book is, in effect, a history of the camp as told by eyewitnesses during the trial. Bernd Naumann's *Auschwitz: A Report on the Proceedings against Robert Karl Ludwig Mulka and Others before the Court at Frankfurt* is a compendium of the author's reportage on the trial for the *Frankfurter Allgemeine Zeitung*.[10] With subtle irony and a novelist's eye for telling detail, Naumann paints a vivid portrait of the trial as a lived experience. What he lacks, however, is a thorough analysis of the legal foundations of the trial, as well as the historian's retroactive ability to glimpse behind the curtain of events to discover the behind-the-scenes actions that drove the public occurrences. Finally, Peter Weiss's play, *The Investigation: An Oratorio in 11 Cantos*, presents dialogue taken verbatim from the trial in a form deliberately modeled on Greek tragedy.[11] As important for the history of twentieth-century drama as his earlier avant-garde work,

[9] Hermann Langbein, *Der Auschwitz Prozeß: Eine Dokumentation*, 2 vols. (Frankfurt: Verlag Neue Kritik, 1995 [1965]).

[10] First published in 1965, the book went through several revised and abbreviated editions, as well as an English translation. See Bernd Naumann, *Auschwitz: Bericht über die Strafsache gegen Mulka und andere vor dem Schwurgericht Frankfurt* (Frankfurt: Athenäum Verlag, 1965); Naumann, *Auschwitz: Bericht über die Strafsache gegen Mulka und andere vor dem Schwurgericht Frankfurt*, abridged and revised by the author (Frankfurt: Fischer Bücherei, 1968). There is now a new German reissue of the 1968 edition: Naumann, *Auschwitz: Bericht über die Strafsache gegen Mulka und andere vor dem Schwurgericht Frankfurt* (Berlin: Philo Verlag, 2004). For the English translation, see Naumann, *Auschwitz: A Report on the Proceedings against Robert Karl Ludwig Mulka and Others before the Court at Frankfurt*, trans. Jean Steinberg (New York: Frederick A. Praeger, 1966).

[11] Peter Weiss, *Die Ermittlung: Oratorium in elf Gesängen* (Frankfurt: Suhrkamp, 1965). In English: Peter Weiss, *The Investigation: Oratorio in 11 Cantos*, trans. Alexander Gross (London: Caldar and Boyers, 1966).

Marat/Sade, The Investigation is less a history of the Auschwitz Trial than it is a dramatic representation of the tragic character of modernity itself.[12]

In recent years, the trial has begun to attract growing scholarly interest as well. The efforts of the Fritz Bauer Institute in Frankfurt am Main have been particularly significant in fostering this new attention.[13] In addition to its archival work, the institute organized a major public exhibition on the history of the trial in 2004 and has published two collections of articles on the trial.[14] Among those working on the trial, Irmtrud Wojak, assistant director of the Fritz Bauer Institute; Werner Renz, its archivist, and Canadian historian Rebecca Wittmann particularly stand out. All have produced significant insights into the nature and history of the trial.[15] Wojak has examined the central role played by Hessian Attorney General Fritz Bauer and has pointed out the significance of the trial for the political culture of the Federal Republic in the 1960s, though with perhaps too little attention to the ambiguity of that impact.[16] Renz has done more than any previous scholar to trace in exacting and precise detail the internal trajectory of the trial based on the original documents.[17] Wittmann has highlighted what she considers

---

[12] Robert Cohen, *Understanding Peter Weiss* (Columbia: University of South Carolina Press, 1993); James E. Young, *Writing and Rewriting the Holocaust: Narrative and the Consequences of Interpretation* (Bloomington: Indiana University Press, 1988), pp. 64–80. More broadly: Stephan Braese, ed., *Rechenschaften: Juristischer und literarischer Diskurs in der Auseinandersetzung mit den NS-Massenverbrechen* (Göttingen: Wallstein, 2004).

[13] The institute now holds virtually all trial related files. In addition to copies of the original trial files, these include the prosecution's internal files ("Handakten"), numerous private papers from various trial participants, and a voluminous press-clipping file. The institute has also undertaken the massive project of digitalizing and transcribing the tape recordings made of the proceedings. Selections of the original recordings, together with the complete transcripts and numerous additional documents, are to be released on DVD sometime in the near future. Unfortunately, much of this project was completed too late to be evaluated fully for this book.

[14] The exhibition opened in March 2004 in the Haus Gallus in Frankfurt where much of the trial took place as well. See the exhibition catalogue: Irmtrud Wojak, ed., *Auschwitz-Prozeß 4 Ks 2/63, Frankfurt am Main* (Cologne: Snoeck Verlagsgesellschaft, 2004). The two collections of articles are Irmtrud Wojak, ed., *"Gerichtstag halten über uns selbst...": Geschichte und Wirkung des ersten Frankfurter Auschwitz-Prozesses* (Frankfurt: Campus Verlag, 2001), and Irmtrud Wojak and Susanne Meinl, eds., *Im Labyrinth der Schuld: Täter–Opfer–Ankläger* (Frankfurt: Campus Verlag, 2003).

[15] Not surprisingly, given the overlap in the sources used, many of these authors come to empirical conclusions that are substantially similar to those found in this book. I have endeavored to indicate this where relevant in the text, without, however, indicating every occasion on which I used the same documents or sources as these authors.

[16] Irmtrud Wojak, "Im Labyrinth der Schuld: Fritz Bauer und die Aufarbeitung der NS-Verbrechen nach 1945," in Wojak and Meinl, eds., *Im Labyrinth der Schuld*, pp. 17–40, and Irmtrud Wojak, "'Die Mauer des Schweigens durchbrochen': Die Erste Frankfurter Auschwitz-Prozeß 1963–1965," in Wojak, ed., *Gerichtstag Halten*, pp. 21–42.

[17] Werner Renz, "Der erste Frankfurter Auschwitz-Prozeß: Völkermord als Strafsache," *1999: Zeitschrift für Sozialgeschichte des 20. und 21. Jahrhunderts* 15 (2000): 11–48; Renz,

to be the central paradox of the Auschwitz Trial: namely, that the prosecution had to rely on Nazi norms and regulations to demonstrate that the
defendants had exceeded these norms in the commission of their crimes.[18]
While she is certainly right that the issue of individual initiative was crucial
for the trial, I would argue that the prosecution's use of Nazi regulations
and norms was perhaps less paradoxical than Wittmann claims, since the
defendants were indicted (and convicted) both for exceeding and for obeying criminal orders. I would argue that the true paradox of the trial lies less
in the attempt to indict Nazi crimes according to Nazi norms than in the fact
that German law was oriented toward a radically different understanding
of crime and human agency than that revealed in the Holocaust. Wittmann
has also argued quite rightly for the centrality of survivor testimony for the
trial. This was, as she points out, the overwhelming source of evidence in the
trial.[19] She perhaps underestimates, however, the difficulties, both psychological and epistemological, confronting the witnesses in creating a coherent
narrative of Auschwitz as a place of systematic mass murder. Nonetheless,
these works, when taken together, enable us to begin to piece together the
history of the Frankfurt Auschwitz Trial and its significance for postwar West
German history. What remains necessary above all, however, is to begin to
embed these insights into a more comprehensive understanding of the nature
of German law and of the Federal Republic in the 1960s.[20]

   To understand the Auschwitz Trial properly, one must also understand
the role of Nazi trials in the Federal Republic more generally. The history
of the Federal Republic of Germany in the first decades after the Second
World War has been variously described as one of "democratization," "modernization," or "westernization."[21] Despite their differences in method and

   "Auschwitz als Augenscheinsobjekt: Anmerkungen zur Erforschung der Wahrheit im ersten
   Frankfurter Auschwitz-Prozess," *Mittelweg 36* 1 (2001): 63–72; Renz, "Tatort Auschwitz:
   Ortstermin im Auschwitz-Prozess," *Tribüne* 40 (2001): 132–44; and Renz, "Opfer und Täter:
   Zeugen der Shoah. Ein Tondbandmitschnitt vom ersten Frankfurter Auschwitz-Prozess als
   Geschichtsquelle," *Tribüne* 41 (2002): 126–36.
[18] Rebecca Elisabeth Wittmann, "Indicting Auschwitz? The Paradox of the Frankfurt
   Auschwitz Trial," *German History* 21 (2003): 506; Wittmann, "Holocaust on Trial? The
   Frankfurt Auschwitz Trial in Historical Perspective," Ph.D. diss., University of Toronto,
   2001, pp. 115–19.
[19] Rebecca Elisabeth Wittmann, "Telling the Story: Survivor Testimony and the Narration of
   the Frankfurt Auschwitz-Trial," *Bulletin of the German Historical Institute*, no. 32 (Spring
   2003): 93–101.
[20] Rebecca Wittmann's book appeared too late to be evaluated for this text, though it also strives
   for such a contextual analysis. See Rebecca Wittmann, *Beyond Justice: The Auschwitz Trial*
   (Cambridge: Harvard University Press, 2005).
[21] For an overview of all these different approaches, see Ulrich Herbert, "Liberalisierung
   als Lernprozeß: Die Bundesrepublik in der deutschen Geschichte – eine Skizze," in
   Ulrich Herbert, ed., *Wandlungsprozesse in Westdeutschland: Belastung, Integration, Liberalisierung, 1945–1980* (Göttingen: Wallstein, 2002), pp. 7–49. For democratization,
   see Moritz Scheibe, "Auf der Suche nach der demokratischen Gesellschaft," in Herbert,

emphasis, what all of these approaches agree on is that until well into the 1960s democracy and liberalism had found at best a somewhat precarious home in West Germany. While the risk of a full-fledged neo-fascist restoration may have been less than some contemporaries feared, the legacy of Nazism – institutional, political, intellectual, and personal – still weighed heavily on the fledgling democracy.[22] So too did older authoritarian traditions stretching back to the nineteenth century.[23] The early decades of the Federal Republic were marked not only by a rupture with the German past, but also by continuity. Democracy in West Germany, thus, has to be understood not as a fact, accomplished institutionally with the passage of the *Grundgesetz* (Basic Law) in 1949 but, in the words of Ulrich Herbert, as a "learning process."[24] One key question for this learning process was what to do about the continuities of German history, specifically, what to do about the legacy of Nazism. That criminal trials would become, especially from the late 1950s, one of the central responses to this problem was by no means a forgone conclusion from the perspective of 1949 or even 1955.

The notion that Nazi atrocities represented not just unavoidable horrors of war but rather "crimes" in the full sense of that term originated during World War II and became a centerpiece of Allied policy toward Germany.[25] Beginning with the founding of the United Nations War Crimes Commission (UNWCC) in October 1942 and culminating with the Moscow Declaration in November 1943, the Allies made clear their intention to prosecute criminally those responsible after the war.[26] Implicitly excluding crimes against German citizens or stateless persons, the Moscow Declaration distinguished

ed., *Wandlungsprozesse*, pp. 245–77; Oscar W. Gabriel, "Demokratiezufriedenheit und demokratische Einstellungen in der Bundesrepublik," *Aus Politik und Wissenschaft* 22 (1987): 32–45; and David P. Conradt, "Changing German Political Culture," in Gabriel A. Almond and Sidney Verba, eds., *The Civic Culture Revisited* (Boston: Little Brown, 1980), pp. 212–72. For modernization, see Axel Schildt and Arnold Sywottek, eds., *Modernisierung im Wiederaufbau: Die westdeutsche Gesellschaft in der 50er Jahre* (Bonn: Dietz, 1998). For westernization, see Anselm Doering-Manteuffel, "Dimensionen von Amerikanisierung der deutschen Gesellschaft," *Archiv für Sozialgeschichte* 35 (1995): 1–35, and Anselm Doering-Manteuffel, *Wie westlich sind die Deutschen? Amerikanisierung und Westernisierung im 20. Jahrhundert* (Göttingen: Vandenhoeck & Ruprecht, 1999). Finally, for an attempt to problematize the "happy ending" of the second half of the twentieth century in Germany, see Michael Geyer, "Germany, or, The Twentieth Century as History," *South Atlantic Quarterly* 96 (Fall 1997): 663–702.

[22] For the most prominent statement of such fears, see Karl Jaspers, *Wohin treibt die Bundesrepublik? Tatsachen, Gefahren, Chancen* (Munich: Piper, 1966).

[23] Herbert, "Liberalisierung als Lernprozeß," p. 17.

[24] Ibid., p. 13.

[25] Arieh J. Kochavi, *Prelude to Nuremberg: Allied War Crimes Policy and the Question of Punishment* (Chapel Hill: University of North Carolina Press, 1998).

[26] On the UNWCC, see Michel Fabréguet, "La Commission des Nations Unies pour les Crimes de Guerre et la Notion de Crimes contre l'Humanité (1943–1948)," *Revue d'Allemagne* 23 (Fall 1991): 519–53, and Kochavi, *Prelude*, pp. 54–62.

two categories of Nazi crimes: those committed in a specific locale and those committed by "principle criminals" whose crimes had no precise geographic boundaries. In the former case, the perpetrators were to be returned to the site of their crimes to stand trial under local jurisdiction; the fate of the latter was to be determined at war's end by a "joint decision of the Governments of the Allies."[27] Yet despite the promise of a joint decision on major war criminals, there remained considerable disagreement among the Allied leaders for the remainder of the war as to how exactly such principle criminals should be handled, whether through criminal trials or via summary executions.[28]

On June 26, 1945, the British government, in agreement with the United States, convened an Allied conference in London for the purpose of reaching an accord regarding the prosecution of the major war criminals in a court of law. After prolonged and difficult negotiations, marked by serious disagreements due to differences in legal tradition between the Anglo-Americans and their continental colleagues, as well as personal animosity between the chief U.S. and Soviet negotiators, the conference promulgated the so-called London Charter on August 8, 1945.[29] This provided the statutory basis for the International Military Tribunal that met at Nuremberg from October 29, 1945, to October 1, 1946, to try twenty-two leading Nazi officials.[30]

[27] Moscow Declaration, cited in Kochavi, *Prelude*, p. 57.

[28] At the Teheran Conference, Stalin proposed – perhaps facetiously – that 50,000 leading Nazis simply be shot. Churchill reacted with outrage, although he himself supported smaller scale summary executions. It was the Americans who pushed hardest for a formal legal prosecution, though here too there was considerable disagreement. Secretary of the Treasury Henry Morgenthau, Jr., supported summary executions in his famous plan for postwar Germany, while Secretary of War Henry Stimson argued decisively for criminal trials. In addition to Kochavi, *Prelude*, see the discussion in Warren F. Kimball, *Swords or Ploughshares? The Morgenthau Plan for Defeated Germany, 1943–1945* (Philadelphia: Lippincott, 1976), and Henri Meyrowitz, *La Répression par les Tribunaux Allemands des Crime contre L'Humanité et de L'Appartenance a une Organisation Criminelle en application de la Loi no. 10 du Conseil de Contrôle Allié* (Paris: Librarie Générale de Droit et de Jurisprudence, 1960), pp. 28–32.

[29] Kochavi, *Prelude*, pp. 222–30.

[30] There is an almost limitless literature on the Nuremberg Trial. The first source are the trial records themselves: International Military Tribunal, *The Trial of Major War Criminals before the International Military Tribunal, 14 November 1945–1 October 1946*, 42 vols.(Nuremberg: Secretariat of the Tribunal, 1947–49). Many of the participants in the trial have also left memoirs, the most valuable being: G. M. Gilbert, *Nuremberg Diary* (New York: Signet Books, 1947); Robert H. Jackson, *The Nuremberg Case* (New York: Cooper Square Publishers, 1971); and Telford Taylor, *The Anatomy of the Nuremberg Trials: A Personal Memoir* (New York: Knopf, 1992). Although not technically a memoir, the account by Whitney Harris benefits from his participation on the staff of the U.S. Chief of Counsel: Whitney R. Harris, *Tyranny on Trial: The Trial of the Major German War Criminals at the End of World War II at Nuremberg, Germany, 1945–1946* (Dallas: Southern Methodist University Press, 1999 [1954]). There are also a variety of narrative accounts, including Richard E. Conot, *Justice at Nuremberg* (New York: Carroll & Graf, 1984); Eugene Davidson, *The Trial of the Germans: An Account of the Twenty-two Defendants before the International*

The London Charter also formed the basis for Allied Control Council Law No. 10, issued on December 20, 1945, which provided statutory authority for subsequent Allied trials against Nazi criminals (the twelve so-called successor trials at Nuremberg and others), as well as for trials conducted in German courts during the occupation period. Altogether, according to official statistics compiled by the West German government in 1965, a total of 5,025 Germans were convicted in (Western) Allied courts inside Germany during the occupation period.[31]

In this context, two things are particularly relevant about the Allied "war crimes program," as it was somewhat inaccurately called.[32] The first was its legal innovation in creating the category of "crimes against humanity," one of three crimes defined by the London Charter and extended to subsequent proceedings by CC Law No. 10.[33] Crimes against humanity provided legal protection against "murder, extermination, enslavement, deportation, and other inhumane acts" to civilian populations "before or during the war," as well as against "persecutions on political, racial or religious grounds" when committed in connection with other crimes defined by the charter.[34]

Essentially a derivation from the older category of war crimes, the category of crimes against humanity was distinct in that it extended protection to German citizens and stateless persons, that is, to precisely those victims excluded by the territoriality principle of the Moscow Declaration.[35] The

Military Tribunal at Nuremberg (New York: Collier Books, 1966); Ann and John Tusa, *The Nuremberg Trial* (New York: Atheneum, 1986); and Joseph Persico, *Nuremberg: Infamy on Trial* (New York: Viking, 1994). Though highly critical, the best scholarly account of the trial remains Bradley F. Smith, *Reaching Judgment at Nuremberg* (New York: Basic Books, 1977). In recent years, other scholarly treatments have begun to emerge as well. See Donald Bloxham, *Genocide on Trial: War Crimes Trials and the Formation of Holocaust History and Memory* (Oxford: Oxford University Press, 2003); Lawrence Douglas, *The Memory of Judgment: Making Law and History in the Trials of the Holocaust* (New Haven: Yale University Press, 2001); and Peter Maguire, *Law and War: An American Story* (New York: Columbia University Press, 2001). The best introduction to the extensive legal commentary on the trial is provided in George Ginsburgs and V. N. Kudriavtsev, eds., *The Nuremberg Trials and International Law* (Dodrecht: M. Nijhoff, 1990). Finally, although it is extremely brief, the account by Michael R. Marrus is not to be missed: *The Nuremberg War Crimes Trial, 1945–46: A Documentary History* (Boston: Bedford Books, 1997).

[31] Bundesministerium der Justiz, *Die Verfolgung nationalsozialistischer Straftaten im Gebiet der Bundesrepublik Deutschland seit 1945* (Bundestagsdrucksache IV/3124), p. 37. Of these, 806 received death sentences, of which 486 were actually carried out.

[32] Frank M. Buscher, *The U.S. War Crimes Trial Program in Germany, 1945–1955* (New York: Greenwood Press, 1989), p. 4.

[33] The London Charter is reprinted in the documents section of M. Cheriff Bassiouni, *Crimes against Humanity in International Criminal Law* (Dodrecht: M. Nijhoff, 1992). The other crimes defined by the London Charter were crimes against peace, designed to cover the planning and implementation of the German war of aggression, and war crimes, essentially a codification and restatement of existing international laws of war.

[34] Ibid.

[35] Ibid., p. 7.

true innovation lay in the claim that some acts were so egregious that the traditional immunity provided by the doctrine of national sovereignty to acts of state in the domestic sphere did not apply.[36] Although Nazi genocide clearly fell under the definition of crimes against humanity, as a legal category, it was not conceptualized as a law of genocide, but as a more general category applying to a wide variety of state acts including but not limited to mass murder and extermination.[37]

The second significant aspect of the Nuremberg and other Allied war crimes trials for the subsequent history of West German Nazi trials is the way that the Allies – the Americans, in particular – tried to deploy such criminal trials as part of a broader project to "reorient" German society away from authoritarianism, militarism, and Nazism. Criminal trials formed one pillar, alongside Denazification and formal reeducation programs, of this project.[38] It was hoped not only that justice would prevail at Nuremberg but that truth would emerge as well. In 1950, General Lucius D. Clay, former head of the American Military Government in Germany, said of the Nuremberg Trials that by revealing the full extent of Nazi criminality, they "completed the destruction of Nazism in Germany."[39] Unfortunately, whatever the successes and failures of the Allied war crimes trials program may have been, Clay's optimistic assessment of their popular impact in Germany cannot be sustained. It may be true, as Donald Bloxham suggests, that "the trial records remained, indelible."[40] However, the immediate impact on the German understanding of Nazism was far less than the Allies may have hoped.

In fact, the Nuremberg trials were not generally well received by the Germans, either among professional jurists or among the general populace.[41] Even among Germans who felt that Nazi actions were crimes and demanded some form of punishment, there was considerable trepidation at the form

---

[36] Geoffrey Robertson, *Crimes against Humanity: The Struggle for Global Justice* (New York: New Press, 1999).

[37] Douglas, *The Memory of Judgment*, pp. 38–64, and Bloxham, *Genocide on Trial*, pp. 63–69. On the distinction between genocide as a legal category and crimes against humanity, see William A. Schabas, *Genocide in International Law* (Cambridge: Cambridge University Press, 2000), pp. 10–12.

[38] Bloxham, *Genocide on Trial*, pp. 137–45, and Buscher, *U.S. War Crimes Trials Program*, pp. 2–3.

[39] Lucius D. Clay, *Decision in Germany* (New York: Doubleday, 1950), p. 250. For a more positive assessment of German reactions to Nuremberg, see Stephen Breyer, "Crimes against Humanity: Nuremberg, 1946," *New York University Law Review* 71 (1996): 1161–63.

[40] Bloxham, *Genocide on Trial*, p. 223.

[41] Heribert Ostendorf, "Die – widersprüchlichen – Auswirkungen der Nürnberger Prozesse auf die westdeutsche Justiz," in Gerd Hankel and Gerhard Stuby, eds., *Strafgerichte gegen Menschheitsverbrechen: Zum Völkerstrafrecht 50 Jahre nach den Nürnberger Prozessen* (Hamburg: Hamburger Edition, 1995), pp. 73–95.

taken by the Allied trials. As one German jurist put it at the time: "That the defendants at Nuremberg were held responsible, condemned and punished, will seem to most of us initially as a kind of historical justice. However, no one who takes the question of guilt seriously, above all no responsibly thoughtful jurist, will be content with this sensibility nor should they be allowed to be. Justice is not served when the guilty parties are punished in any old way, even if this seems appropriate with regard to their measure of guilt. Justice is only served when the guilty are punished in a way that carefully and conscientiously considers their criminal errors according to the provisions of valid law under the jurisdiction of a legally appointed judge."[42] And it was precisely on these terms that a great many Germans felt that the Allied trials failed.

In a motion adopted by all defense counsel in the Nuremberg Trial, Göring's attorney Otto Strahmer declared two central objections to the proceedings. First, he argued that the "principles of a penal character contained in the [London] Charter are in contradiction with the maxim, '*Nulla Poena Sine Lege*' [no punishment without prior law]."[43] Second, he noted that "[t]he Judges have been appointed exclusively by states which were the one party in this war."[44] Strahmer felt that this meant that the prosecutors and judges were really on the same side, thus violating a further principle of legality, that of an impartial judiciary. The former objection to the trial, that it was based on ex post facto law, resonated quite strongly with German jurists in particular. So, while German legal scholars (and the drafters of the German Basic Law) acknowledged the basic validity of the principles contained in the London Charter for *future* crimes, they generally rejected its applicability to Nazi crimes.[45] But it was above all the second objection that found a popular resonance in Germany. It was widely believed, as the title of one well-known German history of the trial put it, that Nuremberg was a "tribunal of the victors."[46] "To a great many Germans, the results of the trials seemed to be a boundless over-stepping and whitewashing of an act of vengeance."[47] Indeed, one German defense attorney, Robert Servatius, went even further, proclaiming that "Nuremberg is a regression to barbarism."[48] Thus, the form that justice took at Nuremberg and in other

[42] Wilhelm Grewe, *Nürnberg als Rechtsfrage* (Stuttgart: Ernst Klett, 1947), p. 10.
[43] Otto Strahmer, "Motion Adopted by All Defense Counsel, 19 November 1945," in Wilbourn E. Benton and Georg Grimm, eds., *Nuremberg: German Views of the War Trials* (Dallas: Southern Methodist University Press, 1955), p. 29.
[44] Ibid., pp. 29–30.
[45] Bernd Hey, "Die NS-Prozesse – Probleme einer juristischen Vergangenheitsbewältigung," in Weber and Steinbach, eds., *Vergangenheitsbewältigung durch Strafverfahren*, pp. 56–57.
[46] Werner Maser, *Nürnberg: Tribunal der Sieger* (Düsseldorf: Econ Verlag, 1977).
[47] Ibid., p. 577.
[48] Cited in Frei, *Vergangenheitspolitik*, p. 163.

Allied trials precluded any widespread acceptance among Germans of the truth that emerged.[49]

Parallel to the Allied war crimes trials program, the overburdened occupation authorities also granted German courts authority to try Nazi crimes against German citizens or stateless persons under CC Law No. 10.[50] German courts were thus compelled to apply the charge of crimes against humanity even to actions that had not been criminal under German law at the time.[51] (Particularly controversial in this regard were cases of denunciation.) The cases thus prosecuted overwhelmingly involved either relatively minor crimes, such as assault and the like, or the various extra-judicial executions of the so-called end phase of the Third Reich, when local officers and officials sought to propel fanatical resistance through draconian punishment. Altogether, 5,228 persons were convicted of Nazi crimes in German courts in the territories of the eventual Federal Republic between 1945 and 1950.[52] Among the general public, these trials were frequently perceived as overtly political acts of vengeance because, in the absence of any systematic investigative effort, charges were usually brought by private individuals.[53] Many of the judges and prosecutors in charge of such cases were deeply resentful of the perceived violation of the prohibition on ex post facto law.[54]

The remarkably strong allegiance among postwar German jurists to the prohibition on ex post facto laws would itself be a topic worthy of further

---

[49] It is true that the German press reported extensively on the Nuremberg Trial, in part no doubt due to the considerable control exercised over the press by the Allied occupation authorities. The impact of that reportage is more difficult to measure, however. See Jürgen Wilke et al., *Holocaust und NS-Prozesse: Die Presseberichterstattung in Israel und Deutschland zwischen Aneignung und Abwehr* (Cologne: Böhlau Verlag, 1995). See also Steffen Radlmaier, ed., *Der Nürnberger Lernprozeß: Von Kriegsverbrechen und Starreportern* (Frankfurt: Eichborn Verlag, 2001). Given the extent to which Germans were predisposed to view themselves as victims after the war, it seems unlikely that even the most extensive coverage of the Nuremberg could have changed their minds. See Robert G. Moeller, *War Stories: The Search for a Usable Past in the Federal Republic of Germany* (Berkeley: University of California Press, 2001).

[50] Rückerl, *NS-Verbrechen*, pp. 107–11.

[51] German courts were allowed to apply German law to cases, mostly ordinary criminal cases, where the charges were not covered by CC Law No. 10 (i.e., were not war crimes or crimes against humanity). See Rückerl, *NS-Verbrechen vor Gericht*, p. 108. The states of Bavaria, Bremen, Hesse, and Württemberg-Baden passed substantively identical laws for dealing with such cases. See Bundesministerium der Justiz, *Die Verfolgung nationalsozialistischer Straftaten*, p. 40.

[52] Rückerl, *NS-Verbrechen*, p. 329.

[53] Alfred Streim, "Die Verfolgung von NS-Gewaltverbrechen in der Bundesrepublik Deutschland," in *Nationalsozialismus und Justiz: Die Aufarbeitung von Gewaltverbrechen damals und heute* (Münster: agenda Verlag, 1993), p. 18.

[54] Martin Broszat, "Siegerjustiz oder strafrechtliche 'Selbstreinigung' – Vergangenheitsbewältigung der Justiz, 1945–1949," *Vierteljahrshefte für Zeitgeschichte* 4 (1981): 477–544.

investigation. Although one cannot dismiss out of hand the possibility that it was motivated by genuine conviction or by the desire not to repeat the sins of the past by doing unto Nazis as the Nazis themselves had done unto others by applying so-called *Sondergesetze* (special laws applying only to certain groups or applied retroactively), there is much to cast doubt on such self-justifying explanations. In particular, the strong continuity of personnel among German judges and prosecutors makes it likely that many were reluctant to pursue Nazi crimes vigorously, given their own far from unimpeachable professional biographies.[55]

Given this hostility to the charge of crimes against humanity in Nazi cases, it is hardly surprising that German courts promptly ceased prosecuting Nazi crimes under the provisions of CC Law No. 10 as soon as they were able and began to apply ordinary German criminal statutes. In January 1950, CC Law No. 13 granted German courts jurisdiction over crimes against Allied nationals, which were then tried on the basis of German law. On August 31, 1951, the British withdrew the authority for German courts in their zone to prosecute on the basis of CC Law No. 10, effectively freeing the courts to prosecute on the basis of ordinary statutory law. Finally, on May 5, 1955, Law A-37 of the Allied High Commission lifted the last remaining constraints on German courts contained in CC Laws 10 and 13, granting German courts full legal autonomy. Thenceforth, all Nazi crimes tried in West German courts were prosecuted under statutory law.

At about the same time, what one observer has called "amnesty fever" broke out among the Allied authorities.[56] Indeed, in the early 1950s, there was a highly organized campaign to win amnesty for convicted "war criminals" in the Federal Republic.[57] Often led by former high-ranking Nazis, such as Werner Best, this campaign was designed not only to bring to a close the threat of further prosecutions but to overturn the results of prior convictions as well.[58] For instance, under strong German pressure, the Allies commuted the sentences of a great many Nazi defendants, including not just military officers convicted of war crimes, but also defendants convicted of crimes against humanity for their role in Nazi genocide.[59]

---

[55] Ingo Müller, *Furchtbare Juristen: Die unbewältigte Vergangenheit unserer Justiz* (Munich: Kindler Verlag, 1987), and von Miquel, *Ahnden oder amnestieren*, pp. 23–142.

[56] Robert Kempner, speaking during a colloquium on Nazi trials at the Gutenberg University in Mainz on November 10, 1966. "Kolloquim über die Bedeutung der Nürnberg Prozesse für die NS-Verbrecherprozesse," in Schneider and Meyer, eds., *Aspekte der NS-Verbrecherprozesse*, p. 14.

[57] Buscher, *U.S. War Crimes Trial Program*, pp. 91–114; Frei, *Vergangenheitspolitik*, pp. 163–308.

[58] Ulrich Herbert, *Best: Biographische Studien über Radikalismus, Weltanschauung und Vernunft, 1903–1989*, 2nd ed. (Bonn: Dietz Verlag, 1996), pp. 437–43, 451–60.

[59] See, e.g., the figures given for the defendants in the Nuremberg *Einsatzgruppen* Trial in Kruse, "NS-Prozesse und Restauration," p. 174.

Once the German judiciary was freed of Allied supervision in 1950–55, they were free to prosecute Nazi crimes in any manner they saw fit. Given the antipathy among German jurists to the perceived violation of the prohibition on ex post facto law by both the London Charter and CC Law No. 10, it is hardly surprising that on May 30, 1956, the Bundestag formally annulled both the criminal categories, including especially crimes against humanity, as well as the sentencing guidelines (e.g., the death penalty) contained therein (*"1. Gesetz zur Aufhebung des Besatzungsrechts"*). Indeed, while the German Basic Law contains provisions acknowledging the supremacy of international law (Article 25), it also contains an explicit prohibition on ex post facto prosecutions (Article 103).[60] Therefore, the Basic Law ensures that the crime of "genocide" (*Volkermord*), as codified in the German penal code (§220 StGB), was to be applied only to *future* infractions, not against Nazi atrocities. This corresponds to German statutory law as well, which further specifies that the type and degree of punishment for any crime must correspond to that in effect at the time of its commission (§2 StGB).

The 1950s were marked by a sharp decline in Nazi investigations and trials in West German courts.[61] From 1945 to 1949, there were a total of 4,419 convictions in German courts for Nazi crimes, although only fifteen of these were for crimes committed in the camps.[62] In contrast, the second period of Nazi prosecutions, from 1950 to 1958, was marked by what one historian has called a "half-hearted judicial processing of the Nazi past."[63] After 1950, when the German courts de facto regained their legal autonomy, the rate of investigation, prosecution, and conviction for Nazi crimes dropped precipitously. Thus, in the peak year of 1948, there had been 1,819 guilty verdicts handed down in German courts for defendants charged with

---

[60] Karl-Heinz Seifert and Dieter Hömig, eds., *Grundgesetz für die Bundesrepublik Deutschland: Taschenkommentar*, 4th ed. (Baden-Baden: Nomos Verlag, 1991), pp. 200–202, 464–67. Although Article 25 accords international law primacy over German domestic law, it subordinates it to the German constitution. Since the prohibition on ex post facto law is enshrined in the constitution, international law does not trump this prohibition.

[61] Not all of this decline can necessarily be blamed on the structure of German law itself. At least some of it was probably due to a disinclination by some (if not many) German officials to treat such crimes harshly. Wolfgang Schulze-Allen, "Die Praxis der Verhinderung von Verurteilungen und Strafverbüßungen," in Michael Ratz et al., eds., *Die Justiz und die Nazis: Zur Strafverfolgung von Nazismus und Neonazismus seit 1945* (Frankfurt: Röderberg-Verlag, 1979), p. 95.

[62] The total comes from Rückerl, *NS-Verbrechen.*, p. 329. The number of convictions for crimes committed in concentration camps is cited in Kruse, "NS-Prozesse," p. 180.

[63] Gotthard Jasper, "Wiedergutmachung und Westintegration: Die halbherzige justizielle Aufarbeitung der NS-Vergangenheit in der frühen Bundesrepublik," in Ludolf Herbst, ed., *Westdeutschland, 1945–1955: Unterwerfung, Kontrolle, Integration* (Munich: R. Oldenbourg Verlag, 1986), p. 183.

Nazi crimes (though only twenty-five of these involved homicide).[64] In 1949 there were still 1,523 convictions. In 1950, however, there were only 809 convictions, falling even more dramatically the following year to 259 and declining steadily to a mere twenty-one in 1955.[65] The number of investigations dropped equally precipitously, from 2,495 in 1950 to 467 in 1952 and only 183 in 1957.[66]

The early and mid-1950s were not, in general, a happy time for prosecutors and judges concerned with prosecuting Nazi crimes. According to the longtime director of the Central Office for the Investigation of Nazi Crimes, Adalbert Rückerl, they were hampered by three main factors.[67] First, they suffered from chronic shortages of personnel and the inadequacy of their own legal training, which ill-prepared them for the kind of intensive historical/documentary investigative work required. Second, they were further hampered by the complexities of German jurisdictional requirements. Since the majority of Nazi crimes were committed outside Germany, German courts generally had jurisdiction only when the alleged perpetrator either lived or was arrested in their locale. This, in turn, presupposed that prosecutors were looking for such defendants in the first place. In the absence of any systematic investigation of Nazi crimes at either the national or local level, this meant that prosecutors almost always sought after alleged perpetrators only on the basis of specific allegations brought to their attention by private citizens. Finally, there was a general political climate in the 1950s that viewed the "war criminals" problem as a thing of the past, an unfortunate legacy of the occupation period best left behind.[68]

Indeed, the political atmosphere in West Germany in the 1950s was extremely hostile to further Nazi trials, and it would be a mistake, therefore, to lay all the blame for the precipitous decline in Nazi prosecutions at the feet of the judiciary. Fritz Bauer, Attorney General for Hesse and the guiding force behind the Auschwitz Trial, later noted that in the 1950s, judges and prosecutors "felt they could infer that the legislature (parliament) and executive (government) viewed the judicial mastering of the past as over."[69] Whatever practical difficulties may have stood in the way of a more vigorous

---

[64] The total number comes from Rückerl, *NS-Verbrechen*, p. 329; the number of homicide convictions comes from Kruse, "NS-Prozesse," p. 180.

[65] See the statistical appendix in Rückerl, *NS-Verbrechen*, p. 329. For the period 1950 to 1957, there were a total of 1,513 convictions in German courts for Nazi crimes.

[66] Adalbert Rückerl, *Die Strafverfolgung von NS-Verbrechen, 1945–1978: Eine Dokumentation* (Heidelberg: C. F. Müller, 1979), p. 125.

[67] Ibid., pp. 127–30.

[68] Frei, *Vergangenheitspolitik*, pp. 266–302; Herbert, *Best*, pp. 457–61.

[69] Fritz Bauer, "Im Namen des Volkes: Die strafrechtliche Bewältigung der Vergangenheit," in Fritz Bauer, *Die Humanität der Rechtsordnung: Ausgewählte Schriften*, ed. Joachim Perels and Irmtrud Wojak (Frankfurt: Campus Verlag, 1998), p. 85.

or systematic prosecution of Nazi crimes in the 1950s, this was also a political problem.[70]

During negotiations for a return of German sovereignty, Chancellor Konrad Adenauer was able to sidestep calls for a general amnesty for German "war criminals" by insisting that while indeed most of those convicted in Allied courts were the victims of political persecution and should be amnestied, there were a handful of real criminals among them who deserved their sentences.[71] This was part of Adenauer's successful effort to stake out a middle ground between those who rejected any criminalization of former Nazis (e.g., the resurgent nationalist right or the nationalist wing of the Free Democratic Party) and the occupation authorities who were trying to salvage some remnant of their war crimes trials program.[72] Preserving the principle that there were in fact some, though very few, genuine Nazi criminals opened up a political space vis-à-vis the allies for Adenauer's government to pursue a generous rehabilitation policy with respect to the vast majority of former Nazis. Whether in the form of the partial but generous amnesty for minor Nazi crimes in 1949 or in the formal rehabilitation and reinstatement of Nazi civil servants and police officers via the so-called Law 131 in 1951, the Adenauer government pursued a strategy that Jeffrey Herf has called "democratization via integration."[73] This was aided by Adenauer's equally successful effort to internationalize the problem of the Nazi past via reparations to the state of Israel and to non-Israeli Nazi victims.[74]

Hermann Lübbe has interpreted this "silence" regarding the Nazi past as a functional prerequisite for the stabilization of democracy in the Federal Republic.[75] Although other authors have argued, apologetically, that the 1950s were actually less silent about the Nazi past than generally assumed,

---

[70] Ulrich Brochhagen, *Nach Nürnberg: Vergangenheitsbewältigung und Westintegration in der Ära Adenauer* (Hamburg: Junius Verlag, 1994).

[71] Buscher, *U.S. War Crimes Trials Program*, pp. 136–37; Frei, *Vergangenheitspolitik*, pp. 234–64; Herbert, *Best*, pp. 455–57.

[72] Brochhagen, *Nach Nürnberg*, pp. 46–50.

[73] Herf, *Divided Memory*, p. 289.

[74] Ibid., pp. 280–88. On German-Israeli relations, see Lily Gardner Feldman, *The Special Relationship between West Germany and Israel* (Boston: George Allen & Unwin, 1984), and George Lavy, *Germany and Israel: Moral Debt and National Interest* (London: Frank Cass, 1996). On reparations more generally, see Ludolf Herbst, *Wiedergutmachung in der Bundesrepublik Deutschland* (Munich: R. Oldenbourg, 1989); Hans Günter Hockerts and Christiane Kuller, eds., *Nach der Verfolgung: Widergutmachung nationalsozialistischen Unrechts in Deutschland?* (Göttingen: Wallstein, 2003); and Susanna Schrafstetter, "The Diplomacy of *Wiedergutmachung*: Memory, the Cold War, and the Western European Victims of Nazism, 1956–1964," *Holocaust and Genocide Studies* 17 (Winter 2003): 459–79.

[75] Hermann Lübbe, "Der Nationalsozialismus im politischen Bewußtsein der Gegenwart," *Historische Zeitschrift* 236 (1983): 579–99. Cf. Hermann Lübbe, "Verdrängung? Über eine Kategorie zur Kritik des deutschen Vergangenheitsverhältnisses," in Hans-Hermann Weibe, ed., *Die Gegenwart der Vergangenheit: Historikerstreit und Erinnerungsarbeit* (Bad Segeberg: C. H. Wässer, 1989), pp. 94–106.

the fact remains that in comparison to both the late 1940s and the 1960s and '70s, the 1950s have to be seen as an era of conservative retrenchment regarding the Nazi past.[76] As Mary Fulbrook has noted, "[w]hat is perhaps most striking about the first two decades of the Federal Republic's existence is not only the relative high degree of continuity in personnel in the higher reaches of many areas of West German life, but also the extraordinary degree of toleration and indeed elevation to high office of men who, if not exactly guilty of war crimes, were at best political opportunists and immoral trimmers."[77] However, as Norbert Frei has rightly pointed out, the 1950s have to be seen in a more differentiated way, as marked both by the political and social rehabilitation of former Nazis, including those guilty of the most serious crimes, and by a widespread public rejection of Nazi ideology and a cautious embrace of the newly democratic state.[78] In this regard, the early years of the Federal Republic can be understood as neither a full-fledged restoration of the old regime nor as a radical democratic rupture, a genuine "zero hour." While obviously far from perfect, the Federal Republic's efforts to deal with the legacy of the Nazi past in the 1950s have to be seen as comparatively reasonable and energetic.[79]

By the late 1950s, the strategy of democratization via integration was beginning to break down in the face of mounting scandals concerning former

[76] Christa Hoffmann, "Die justitielle 'Vergangenheitsbewältigung' in der Bundesrepublik Deutschland: Tatsachen und Legenden," in Uwe Backes, Eckhard Jesse, and Rainer Zitelmann, eds., *Die Schatten der Vergangenheit: Impulse zur Historisierung des Nationalsozialismus* (Frankfurt: Ullstein, 1992); Christa Hoffmann, *Stunden Null? Vergangenheitsbewältigung in Deutschland 1945 und 1989* (Bonn: Bouvier, 1992); and Manfred Kittel, *Die Legende von der "Zweiten Schuld": Vergangenheitsbewältigung in der Ära Adenauer* (Berlin: Ullstein, 1993).
[77] Mary Fulbrook, *German National Identity after the Holocaust* (Cambridge: Polity Press, 1999), p. 61. For other, even more critical evaluations of the treatment of the Nazi past in the Federal Republic, see Heinz Bude, *Bilanz der Nachfolge: Die Bundesrepublik und der Nationalsozialismus* (Frankfurt: Suhrkamp, 1992); Ralph Giordano, *Die zweite Schuld oder Von der Last Deutscher zu sein* (Hamburg: Rasch und Röhring Verlag, 1987); and Gesine Schwan, *Politik und Schuld: Die zerstörerische Macht des Schweigens* (Frankfurt: Fischer Verlag, 1997). For a general overview, see Werner Bergmann, "Die Reaktion auf den Holocaust in Westdeutschland von 1945 bis 1989," *Geschichte in Wissenschaft und Unterricht* 21 (1992): 327–50.
[78] Frei, *Vergangenheitspolitik*, p. 14.
[79] While overly optimistic about West Germany and correspondingly overcritical of Japan, Ian Buruma's main point that West Germany's efforts to deal with the Nazi past have to be considered relatively successful in comparison with other such efforts is not without some merit. Ian Buruma, *The Wages of Guilt: Memories of War in Germany and Japan* (New York: Farrar, Straus and Giroux, 1994). On Japan, see John W. Dower, *Embracing Defeat: Japan in the Wake of World War II* (New York: W. W. Norton, 1999). More broadly, see Christoph Cornelissen, Lutz Klinkhammer, and Wolfgang Schwentker, eds., *Erinnerungskulturen: Deutschland, Italien und Japan seit 1945* (Frankfurt: Fischer Verlag, 2003), and Elazar Barkan, *The Guilt of Nations: Restitution and Negotiations for Historical Injustices* (New York: Norton, 2000).

Nazis in prominent public positions (e.g., Wolfgang Fränkel, Hans Globke, and Theodor Oberländer).[80] In this regard, the efforts of the East German government to win propaganda points by highlighting the failure of the Federal Republic to deal adequately with the Nazi past played a particularly important role.[81] After the decision was taken to stabilize the GDR through the building of the Berlin Wall in 1961, the East German government had two priorities in its relations with the Federal Republic.[82] The first was to legitimize its own domestic authority by further articulating the longstanding myth of the GDR as the only truly "anti-fascist" German state.[83] The second was to try to secure a legitimate place in the international community by overcoming the West German Hallstein Doctrine denying diplomatic recognition to both the GDR and any state that had diplomatic relations with it. An aggressive propaganda campaign against the alleged fascist restoration in West Germany was a useful tool for both. It simultaneously highlighted the GDR's anti-fascist credentials and put pressure on the West German government to deal with East Block governments in the pursuit of evidence against Nazi criminals.[84]

Equally important for the breakdown of the strategy of democratization via integration in the late 1950s was the fact that in 1958 a series of dramatic new trials confronted the West German public for the first time since Nuremberg with both the full horror of Nazi crimes and the extent to which

---

[80] Oberländer, minister for refugee affairs (*Vertriebenenminister*), had been a population expert for the army during the war. He was forced to resign in 1960 under the pressure of a mock trial staged by the East Germans. Globke, Adenauer's State Secretary, had been one of the leading legal commentators on the Nuremberg race laws of 1935. He remained in office, despite enormous pressure, until the end of the Adenauer administration. Fränkel, named attorney general (Generalbundesanwalt) in March 1961, was forced to resign shortly thereafter. He had been a prosecutor with the German Supreme Court (Reichsgericht) under the Nazis and, in that capacity, had been involved in numerous dubious death sentences. On Oberländer, see Phillip-Christian Wachs, *Der Fall Theodor Oberländer (1905–1998): Ein Lehrstück deutscher Geschichte* (Frankfurt: Campus Verlag, 2000). On Globke, see Klaus Gotto, ed., *Der Staatssekretär Adenauers: Persönlichkeit und politisches Wirken Hans Globkes* (Stuttgart: Klett-Cotta, 1980), and Norbert Jacobs, "Der Streit um Dr. Hans Globke in der öffentlichen Meinung der Bundesrepublik Deutschland, 1949–1973: Ein Beitrag zur politischen Kultur in Deutschland," Ph.D. diss., University of Bonn, 1992. On Fränkel, see von Miquel, *Ahnden oder amnestieren*, pp. 99–122.

[81] Michael Lemke, "Kampagnen gegen Bonn: Die Systemkrise der DDR und die West-Propaganda der DDR, 1960–1963," *Vierteljahrshefte für Zeitgeschichte* 41 (1993): 153–74.

[82] Michael Lemke, "Der Lange Weg zum 'geregelten Nebeneinander': Die Deutschlandpolitik der DDR Mitte der fünfziger bis Mitte der siebziger Jahre," in Christoph Kleßmann, Hans Misselwitz, and Günther Wichert, eds., *Deutsche Vergangenheiten – eine gemeinsame Herausforderung: Der schwierige Umgang mit der doppelten Nachkriegsgeschichte* (Berlin: C. Links, 1999), pp. 61–86.

[83] Herf, *Divided Memory*, p. 163.

[84] Annette Weinke, *Die Verfolgung von NS-Tätern im geteilten Deutschland. Vergangenheitsbewältigung 1949–1969 oder: Eine deutsch-deutsche Beziehungsgeschichte im Kalten Krieg* (Paderborn: F. Schöningh, 2002).

these had been neglected by the judicial authorities. The Arnsberg trial of six former Wehrmacht officers for the murder of foreign workers near Warstein in March 1945 and the trial of SS General Simon and five of his subordinates for death sentences passed against German civilians in April 1945 produced some of the earliest public criticism of the extraordinarily mild treatment accorded Nazi criminals in West German courts.[85] More striking still was the trial of Walter Martin Sommer, the "Beast of Buchenwald," which used dramatic eyewitness testimony to highlight to a much greater extent than previously the incredible brutality of the Nazi concentration camps.[86] Even more controversial was the fact that one of the witnesses in the trial, Dr. Hans Eisele, turned out to be even more deeply incriminated than Sommer himself. Although condemned to death by Allied courts, Eisele had been released from prison in 1952. Exonerated in his subsequent Denazification trial, Eisele had been able to return to his successful medical practice in Munich. At risk of further prosecution after the revelations in the Sommer trial, Eisele fled to Egypt where he successfully fought extradition proceedings and made himself infamous by blaming his tribulations on a Jewish conspiracy.[87]

If this was not evidence enough of the lackadaisical nature of Nazi prosecutions in the Federal Republic, the so-called Ulm Einsatzkommando Trial that same summer further emphasized the lack of any serious or systematic effort to find and prosecute even the most egregious Nazi perpetrators. The lead defendant in the trial, Bernhard Fischer-Schweder, the former police chief in Tilsit on the Lithuanian border, had helped direct the mass executions of Jews and communists in the region in 1941 and 1942. Through a series of utterly absurd coincidences, during which Fischer-Schweder continually pushed his luck by publicly insisting on his right to reintegration in German society, his case finally came to the attention of the Ulm authorities.[88] Along with several of his colleagues, he was eventually tried in Ulm and, in August 1958, sentenced to ten years' imprisonment as an accomplice to murder.[89] As one historian has noted, "[f]or the first time since the Allied trials of the 1940s, the media reports [on the Ulm Trial] brought back to the consciousness of a broad public the kinds of crimes that had been perpetrated, above all in Eastern Europe."[90] Even more importantly, the Ulm Trial, together

---

[85] All of the defendants in the Simon trial were acquitted, while the three convictions in the Arnsberg trial were overturned on appeal. See the verdicts in Rüter et al., eds., *Justiz und NS-Verbrechen*, vol. 14, pp. 563–625 and 699–727.

[86] On the Sommer trial and the ensuing Eisele controversy, see von Miquel, *Ahnden oder amnestieren*, pp. 146–48.

[87] Ibid., p. 148.

[88] On the Ulm Trial, see von Miquel, *Ahnden oder amnestieren*, pp. 151–59.

[89] Rüter et al., eds., *Justiz und NS-Verbrechen*, vol. 15, pp. 41–43.

[90] Lore Marie Peschel-Gutzeit, *Zur rechtlichen Auseinandersetzung mit der NS-Gewaltherrschaft und dem SED-Regime* (Berlin: Walter de Gruyter, 1995), pp. 12–13.

with the Eisele affair, made it clear to both prosecutors and political leaders
at the state level that something had to be done to systematize Nazi prosecutions or such embarrassing scandals were likely to continue. As Ernst
Müller-Meiningen, Jr., noted disapprovingly in the *Süddeutsche Zeitung*,
"up to now, nothing systematic has actually been undertaken against criminals from those days."[91]

Such criticisms generated a surprisingly prompt official reaction. At their
annual conference at Bad Harzburg on October 3, 1958, the State Justice
Ministers from throughout the Federal Republic and West Berlin decided to
establish a central investigative bureau for Nazi crimes, the so-called Central
Office of the State Justice Ministries for the Investigation of National Socialist
Crimes of Violence at Ludwigsburg.[92] A month later, on November 6, 1958,
a ministerial treaty was signed regulating the status of the Central Office as
a common institution of the state justice ministries, staffed and financed by
the Federal States.[93] The Central Office was not a prosecutorial agency but
merely an investigative one. It was charged with collecting evidence on Nazi
crimes and identifying and locating potential defendants, whereupon it was
to turn this evidence over to the relevant local prosecutor's office, usually
the one with jurisdiction over the alleged perpetrator's place of residence. In
political terms, the surprising resolution of the state justice ministers can be
explained, as Marc von Miquel has shown, by their desire to demonstrate
their determination in Nazi prosecutions in order to avoid further scandals, without, it should be added, having to undertake the politically more
difficult task of dealing with former Nazis within their own offices or the
judiciary.[94]

With the founding of the Central Office, a new phase in the history of
West German Nazi trials can be said to have begun. While there was no
immediate increase in the number of convictions, there was a rapid and dramatic increase in the number of official preliminary investigations.[95] Already
in 1959, some 400 preliminary investigations were under way at the Central

---

[91] Ernst Müller-Meiningen, Jr., "Gespenstische Vergangenheit vor Gericht zitiert," SZ, August
30/31, 1958.

[92] Claudia Fröhlich, "Die Gründung der 'Zentralen Stelle' in Ludwigsburg – Alibi oder Beginn
einer systematischen justitiellen Aufarbeitung der NS-Vergangenheit?" in Gerhard Pauli and
Thomas Vormbaum, eds., *Justiz und Nationalsozialismus – Kontinuität und Diskontinuität*
(Berlin: Berliner Wissenschafts-Verlag, 2003), pp. 213–50; Eberhard Rondholz, "Die Lud-
wigsburger Zentrale Stelle zur Aufklärung nationalsozialistischer Verbrechen," *Kritische
Justiz* 20, no. 2 (1987): 207–13; Michael Greve, *Umgang*, pp. 43–55; and von Miquel,
Ahnden oder amnestieren, pp. 162–85.

[93] Rückerl, *NS-Verbrechen*, p. 142.

[94] Von Miquel, *Ahnden oder amnestieren*, p. 172.

[95] Rückerl, *NS-Verbrechen*, p. 329. For the seven years from 1951 through 1957, there were
704 convictions in German courts, whereas for the seven years from 1959 through 1965,
there were 193. It has to be kept in mind, however, that *Totschlag* (manslaughter) fell under
the statute of limitations in 1960, reducing the number of potential cases considerably.

Office, while in 1965–66, there were 6,372 ongoing investigations.[96] From 1958 until roughly the late 1970s, when the broadcast of the American television miniseries *Holocaust* again transformed the politics of the past in the Federal Republic, it would not be going too far to speak of a juridification of the Nazi legacy in West Germany. Trials became not the only but certainly the dominant forum for dealing with the Nazi past. While Heiner Lichtenstein's claim that "Nazi trials were only rarely in the spotlight" may be true in the aggregate, the significance of the exceptions to this rule should not be discounted.[97] This was a period dominated by several large, very public trials, which came to shape much of the public image of Nazism and the Holocaust: the Auschwitz Trial first and foremost but also the Ulm Trial, the trial of two of Eichmann's lieutenants (Hermann Krumey and Otto Hunsche), and, somewhat later, the Majdanek trial – not to mention the Eichmann Trial in Israel.

Therefore, the Auschwitz Trial has to be viewed as indicative of an era. Although originating prior to the founding of the Central Office and thus itself the product of a series of coincidences, the Auschwitz Trial is more representative of the 1960s than the 1950s. The early 1960s in particular was a period of transition between the early years of the Federal Republic, when the Nazi past was treated with great circumspection and former Nazi criminals were actively rehabilitated, and the later 1960s and, '70s, when a younger generation reacted to the Nazi past, the Holocaust in particular, with a great deal more emotionalism, often coupling this with a demand for radical social and political change.[98] The Auschwitz Trial was an important bridge between these two periods. If the 1960s were a period that "on the one hand, still stood in the shadows of the [Nazi] *Volksgemeinschaft* but also, on the other hand, sought to escape these shadows," then the Auschwitz Trial has to be understood as one of the most important aspects of this attempt to escape the burdens of the past.[99]

Particularly important, in this regard, is the fact that, since the legacy of the Nazi past was largely juridified in this period, it was transferred to the

---

[96] Ibid., p. 330.

[97] Heiner Lichtenstein, "NS-Prozesse und Öffentlichkeit," in *Nationalsozialismus und Justiz: Die Aufarbeitung von Gewaltverbrechen damals und heute* (Münster: agenda Verlag, 1993), p. 74. Cf. Ulrich. Kröger, "Die Ahndung von NS-Verbrechen vor Westdeutschen Gerichte und ihre Rezeption in der deutschen Öffentlichkeit 1958 bis 1965 unter besonderer Berücksichtigung von 'Spiegel,' 'Stern,' 'Zeit,' 'SZ,' 'FAZ,' 'Welt,' 'Bild,' 'Hamburger Abendblatt,' 'NZ' und 'Neuem Deutschland,' Ph.D. diss., University of Hamburg, 1973.

[98] Bude, *Bilanz*, pp. 86–91; Jeremy Varon, *Bringing the War Home: The Weather Underground, the Red Army Faction, and Revolutionary Violence in the Sixties and Seventies* (Berkeley: University of California Press, 2004), pp. 276–84; and more generally, Axel Schildt, Detlev Siegfried, and Karl Christian Lammers, eds., *Dynamische Zeiten: Die 60er Jahre in den beiden deutschen Gesellschaften* (Hamburg: Christians, 2000).

[99] Von Miquel, *Ahnden oder amnestieren*, p. 145.

realm of law. Given this, one must keep in mind the ways that the juridical form of law itself, its formal character as a system of rules for adjudicating conflicts, set the ground rules for the Auschwitz Trial.[100] It channeled the actions of the various participants in determinant ways. It dictated what kinds of things could be said and by whom and, above all, how evidence was to be evaluated and guilt determined. At the same time, however, this should not be taken to mean that the macro-structure of German law precluded independent action or contingency in the trial. Rather, the juridical structures of the trial established *boundary conditions*, within which individual trial actors operated, and which they tried to mobilize or manipulate for their own ends.

At the same time, the law does not exhaust itself in juridical formalism. All trials are also representational. If nothing else, they always re-present the state's legitimate authority *to judge* and *to coerce*.[101] Law is not just a set of self-contained, self-referential rules for regulating conduct and adjudicating conflicts, its juridical dimension; it is also a mode for articulating and justifying these adjudicative procedures and decisions to society at large, its representational dimension.[102] But because representations are inherently "slippery," their meanings never completely fixed or determined, trials are also always open to the possibility of hermeneutic contestation, for the creative reinterpretation of the crimes being re-presented. Trials are thus not only juridical struggles over guilt, but also representational struggles to decipher the contested meaning of guilt.

Four contexts thus emerge as particularly important for the history of the Auschwitz Trial. At the most general level, there are the constraints of the law itself in both its juridical and representational dimensions. At a slightly less general level, there is the context of German law in particular, especially the categories of the law of homicide as applied in Nazi cases. Then there

---

[100] H. L. A. Hart, *The Concept of Law*, 2nd ed. (Oxford: Oxford University Press, 1994), pp. 79–99. In this respect, it also parallels what Judith Shklar has called "legalism." See Judith N. Shklar, *Legalism: Law, Morals and Political Trials* (Cambridge: Harvard University Press, 1964). I use the term "juridical," rather than merely "formal," to allude to certain imperialistic aspects of the law, its tendency to "colonize" (in Jürgen Habermas's phrase) other dimensions of human existence and to subsume them under general rules, a process that Habermas refers to as juridification. See Jürgen Habermas, *The Theory of Communicative Action*, vol. 2 (Boston: Beacon, 1987), pp. 356–73.

[101] This notion refers to but is not identical with Foucault's analysis of spectacular punishment. Foucault notes that with the decline of torture and public execution, the law's representational function does not disappear; it is merely transformed. "Now the scandal and the light are to be distributed differently; it is the conviction itself that marks the offender with the unequivocally negative sign; the publicity has shifted to the trial...." Michel Foucault, *Discipline and Punish: The Birth of the Prison* (New York: Vintage, 1977), p. 9.

[102] Robert Cover, "Nomos and Narrative," in *Narrative, Violence and the Law: The Essays of Robert Cover*, ed. Martha Minow, Michael Ryan, and Austin Sarat (Ann Arbor: University of Michigan Press, 1995), pp. 95–96.

is the international political context of the Cold War and the inter-German struggle for international legitimacy. Finally, there are the politics of the past in the Federal Republic itself, the way the Auschwitz Trial both played off of and shaped existing and newly emerging sensibilities about the meaning of the Nazi past and the need for justice for Nazi crimes. It is only in the confluence of these four contexts that the Auschwitz Trial can be properly understood.

I

Prelude

It was a matter of some luck that the Frankfurt Auschwitz Trial ever took place at all.[1] As with almost all German Nazi trials in the first postwar decades, it was a private allegation, rather than any systematic investigation, that initially brought the case to the attention of authorities. In the spring of 1958, a convicted con man named Adolf Rögner wrote to the Stuttgart prosecutor's office, claiming that one Wilhelm Boger, formerly of the Auschwitz Political Section (Politische Abteilung, or PA), the camp Gestapo, lived in the vicinity and that he had committed murder and other crimes while at Auschwitz. Initially, the investigation was handled from Stuttgart but was transferred to Frankfurt in 1959. Boger subsequently became one of the "star" defendants in the Auschwitz Trial. Less typical perhaps was the enthusiasm with which the Frankfurt authorities, under the guidance of the Hessian attorney general Fritz Bauer, pursued the case. Yet here, too, there was a considerable element of luck involved. In the closing days of World War II, an Auschwitz survivor salvaged a number of Auschwitz documents from a burning building in Breslau. When these were turned over to the Hessian Attorney General's Office in the early 1960s, they formed the legal basis for centralizing all Auschwitz-related prosecutions in Frankfurt. These two fortuitous events – the self-serving but true allegations of a known criminal and the happenstance rescue from the wreckage of war of a snippet of the Nazis' own self-incriminating papers – form the essential backdrop to the Auschwitz Trial.

Above all, what the trial's pre-history reveals is that the success of the investigation depended crucially on the efforts both of the investigating

---

[1] See Werner Renz, "Der I. Frankfurter Auschwitz-Prozess: Zwei Vorgeschichten," *1999: Zeitschrift für Geschichtswissenschaft* 50 (2002): 622–41, and Rebecca Elisabeth Wittmann, "The Wheels of Justice Turn Slowly: The Pretrial Investigation of the Frankfurt Auschwitz Trial 1963–1965," *Central European History* 35 (2002): 345–78.

authorities and of nongovernmental actors. The efforts of Hermann Lang-bein, then Secretary of the International Auschwitz Committee (IAC), proved to be particularly important both pragmatically, as a guide to wit-nesses, and politically, as a tenacious, if not always welcome, prod to more vigorous action by the authorities. Despite the sometimes quite close coop-eration between the investigating authorities and nongovernmental actors, the particular requirements of the juridical setting itself, together with the political pressures of the Cold War, meant that the relationship was often quite tendentious. Both felt they were pursuing justice, yet both understood that term quite differently.

For the prosecutors conducting the preliminary investigations, one of the principle concerns was always to respect the procedural boundaries of the rule of law. This can be viewed as partially a tactical response to a system of legal checks and balances, where prosecutorial practice was subject to judicial review and an excessively aggressive investigation risked becoming counterproductive if the case were thrown out for procedural improprieties. But the prosecutorial respect for the rule of law went beyond such tactical considerations. For the prosecutors involved in the Auschwitz investigation, the law was an end in itself. The whole point of the investigation was to fulfill their legal obligation to pursue criminal prosecutions. Yet Auschwitz survivors, whose testimony necessarily provided the bulk of the evidence, often had little sympathy for the legal niceties of prosecutorial procedure. For them, law was the means for pursuing justice, not its embodiment. They found it both incomprehensible and insulting that the law could be as much an obstacle as an avenue to that justice.

Just as it was shaped by its legal context, so too was the Auschwitz inves-tigation shaped by its political context; in this case, that means the Cold War. Because many Holocaust survivors were, for obvious reasons, from "the East," the West German authorities were forced, in the course of their investigations, into a level of contact with East Block citizens and real or imagined Communist fellow-travelers that was uncommon in the late 1950s. What is perhaps more surprising, though, given the context, is the degree to which West German prosecutors, particularly those in Frankfurt, were able to overcome whatever concerns they may have had in this regard and pursue an investigation that was eventually to lead, in its small way, to a loosen-ing of the Hallstein Doctrine and to help pave the way for Willy Brandt's *Ostpolitik* a decade later.

The Boy Who (Almost) Cried Wolf

The opening salvo of the trial was fired from a very dubious quarter when, on March 1, 1958, Adolf Rögner, a career criminal then serving time for fraud, wrote a letter to the Stuttgart prosecutor's office (Staatsanwaltschaft).[2] Rögner alleged that one Wilhelm Boger, a resident of the Stuttgart suburbs, had committed the most serious crimes while serving in the Political Section at Auschwitz.[3] The letter refers to the so-called Boger Swing (*Boger Schaukel*), a device whereby inmates were hung upside down from a metal rod, so that their exposed buttocks and genitals could be beaten with a whip or club. Rögner stated: "Boger is severely incriminated for his crimes against humanity committed in Auschwitz (mass murder, selections, manslaughter (*Totschlag*), coercing confessions with and without making use of the swing, etc.)."[4] As a result of these allegations, the prosecutor's office ordered the police to begin an investigation of Boger.[5] On April 10, the Stuttgart police reported that Boger had indeed been an Oberscharführer (staff sergeant) in Auschwitz and recommended that the case be turned over to the local police for further investigation.[6]

Despite this prompt action, the Stuttgart prosecutors were initially quite skeptical of Rögner's accusations. In particular, they noted that Rögner had a history of making false accusations regarding Nazi crimes. On May 13, the Stuttgart prosecutor's office ordered the police to take a personal deposition from Rögner. Prosecutor Horst Weber, in charge of the case, felt this was necessary "because, on the one hand, the man making these allegations is, according to the clear indications from his previous accusations, a vengeful psychopath; on the other hand, his information against Boger cannot be dismissed out of hand due to the seriousness of the charges. Rather, it must be carefully investigated."[7]

The police report on Rögner's deposition evinces a similar skepticism. The report noted that Rögner's knowledge of events and places in Auschwitz was striking, although he was less certain about dates and times. "His comprehensive and detailed knowledge regarding events in Auschwitz might be explained by the fact that – according to the warden – he is in possession of considerable [historical] materials with which he has occupied himself

---

[2] Rögner's arrest record stretched back to the 1920s. See Ldst. Bruchsal to OStA Munich (April 9, 1958), Frankfurt Staatsanwaltschaft, Ermittlungssache gegen Beyer (a.k.a. Baer) u.a. [subsequently "gegen Mulka"] (hereafter FFStA) 4 Ks 2/63, Bd. 1, Bl. 24–26.

[3] Adolf Rögner to Stuttgart StA (March 1, 1958), FFStA 4 Ks 2/63, Bd. 1, Bl. 1–2. Also cited in Hermann Langbein, *Der Auschwitz-Prozeß: Eine Dokumentation*, vol. 1 (Frankfurt: Verlag Neue Kritik, 1995 [1965]), pp. 21–22. For Rögner's arrest record, see Landeskriminalamt Baden-Württemberg to Stuttgart StA (August 20, 1958), FFStA 4 Ks 2/63, Bd. 1, Bl. 48–51.

[4] Rögner to Stuttgart StA (March 1, 1958), FFStA 4 Ks 2/63, Bd. 1, Bl. 1; Langbein, *Auschwitz-Prozeß*, p. 21.

[5] Stuttgart StA to Kriminalpolizei (March 17, 1958), FFStA 4 Ks 2/63, Bd. 1, Bl. 3.

[6] Stuttgart Polizeipräsidium to Stuttgart StA (April 10, 1958), FFStA 4 Ks 2/63, Bd. 1, Bl. 4. Boger lived not in Stuttgart proper but rather in the suburb of Hemmingen, Kreis Leonberg, which is why the Stuttgart police recommended that the investigation be turned over to the proper jurisdiction.

[7] Vermerk, Weber (May 13, 1958), FFStA 4 Ks 2/63, Bd. 1, Bl. 7.

throughout his time in prison."[8] The warden had further noted that Rögner's books on war crimes were finally taken away from him "because he makes so many accusations against former members of the SS that it had to be assumed that Rögner was drawing his knowledge from his reading and then presenting it to the authorities as his own information." The interrogating officer concluded that "[o]n the basis of Rögner's demeanor, the undersigned has the impression that all his thoughts and desires are oriented towards occupying the criminal authorities with his purported or actual information." In particular, the officer was disturbed that Rögner seemed proud of his activities as an anti-Nazi witness and his work for the Americans after the war identifying alleged Nazi criminals. "'You can believe me,'" the report quotes Rögner as saying, "'that more than a few (*schon mancher*) Nazis have already been executed on the basis of my testimony.'"

Nor was Rögner's case helped by his often-petulant interactions with the West German authorities. In a letter to the Munich Prosecutor's Office, the warden at Rögner's prison noted that Rögner was constantly complaining about his treatment and that he often wrote to various higher authorities, trying to get information from them about ongoing Nazi investigations and bragging about his role as a prosecution witness in Nazi cases.[9] "What is more, this very querulous man, who is constantly making the most hateful, ungrounded attacks against the West German judiciary and against his treatment in correctional facilities, has repeatedly made ungrounded criminal accusations against correctional officials and police officers." The warden cited a letter from Rögner to the Baden-Würtemberg FDP (December 2, 1957), obviously read by prison officials, wherein Rögner claimed, "I am 100% oriented toward the East and, as soon as I am released, I am going immediately to Krakow, where I will reside permanently." In the charged political atmosphere of the Cold War, such claims were hardly likely to win Rögner much sympathy among West German officials.

Under these circumstances, the official skepticism regarding Rögner's allegations is hardly surprising, especially given that he was indeed convicted of perjury in a different Nazi case shortly thereafter.[10] In light of this, it is difficult to say whether the investigation of Wilhelm Boger would ever have amounted to much had it not been for the subsequent intervention of the International Auschwitz Committee (IAC) and its then Secretary, Hermann

---

[8] Bericht über Vernehmung von Adolf Rögner (signed Wasserlos) (June 6, 1958), FFStA 4 Ks 2/63, Bd. 1, Bl. 8–9.

[9] Ldst. Bruchsal to OStA Munich (April 9, 1958), FFStA 4 Ks 2/63, Bd. 1, Bl. 24–26.

[10] Rögner was convicted in a Munich court of "false witness and perjury" on July 15, 1958. He was sentenced to three years, six months, in prison and permanently deprived of his right to testify under oath. This explains why he did not testify in the Auschwitz Trial, assuming the prosecution would have wanted him to in the first place, which is far from certain. See Stuttgart StA to Justizministerium Baden-Württemberg (August 14, 1958), FFStA 4 Ks 2/636, Bd. 1, Bl. 39.

Langbein. According to Langbein, Rögner had also written to the IAC at about the same time he sent his initial letter to Stuttgart.[11] Subsequently, on May 9, Langbein wrote to the Stuttgart authorities, inquiring as to the status of the presumably ongoing investigation against Boger and offering to provide further evidence if needed.[12] Langbein later noted, "I consciously did not make reference to the accusations of A.R. [Rögner]. As it turned out, however, the judiciary nonetheless still did not work any faster. A sluggish correspondence ensued, leading to no concrete results; as a consequence, I intervened, initially with the Stuttgart prosecutor [in charge of the case] and – when this discussion produced thoroughly unsatisfactory results – with his superior."[13]

As it happens, Langbein's impression of the lackadaisical attitude of the Stuttgart prosecutor's office is at best only partially accurate. In fact, although the prosecutor's office was indeed reluctant to order Boger's arrest, as Langbein repeatedly urged, they nonetheless continued to investigate the case throughout that summer and fall. The Central Office was not yet active, and consequently, the Stuttgart prosecutors were compelled to rely on their own limited resources, which were not well suited to the investigation of Nazi crimes. In particular, the prosecutors were hard pressed to find sources of evidence other than Rögner. In this context, the evidentiary resources of the IAC proved crucial to the investigation, particularly their ability to find more reliable witnesses to Boger's crimes. At the same time, the record indicates that Langbein's persistent hectoring of the Stuttgart authorities was equally crucial in overcoming their perhaps Cold War–inspired hesitancy in the case.

On May 21, the Stuttgart prosecutor's office wrote to the IAC, requesting any further information that might be relevant to the ongoing investigation of Boger.[14] Langbein promptly replied, stating that he would be happy to share further information, including the names of potential witnesses, once Boger was under arrest; until then, Langbein said, there was too great a risk that Boger would get wind of the investigation and take flight to make any open appeals for witnesses among members of the IAC.[15] This was especially true, given that Boger had already evaded prosecution once. Shortly after the end of the war, Boger had escaped from the train taking him to stand trial in Poland and gone into hiding. Langbein did, however, append a formal one-page personal deposition, leveling further charges against Boger. He indicated that he had personally seen Boger severely beat a Polish inmate for writing

---

[11] Langbein, *Auschwitz-Prozeß*, p. 22.
[12] Langbein to Stuttgart StA (May 9, 1958), FFStA 4 Ks 2/63, Bl. 22a; Langbein, *Auschwitz-Prozeß*, pp. 22–23.
[13] Langbein, *Auschwitz-Prozeß*, p. 23.
[14] Stuttgart StA to IAC (May 21, 1958), FFStA 4 Ks 2/63, Bd. 1, Bl. 27.
[15] Langbein to Stuttgart StA (May 29, 1958), FFStA 4 Ks 2/63, Bd. 1, Bl. 31.

letters; the Pole was subsequently shot, although Langbein did not indicate whether Boger had actually shot him personally.[16]

Throughout July, there was an exchange of letters between Langbein and the Stuttgart prosecutor's office, in which Langbein repeatedly urged the authorities to arrest Boger and the prosecutors persistently asked Langbein to first gather more evidence, "to see if, after an examination of the evidence, there is sufficient cause to issue a warrant for Boger's arrest."[17] This greatly irritated Langbein, who responded that the IAC found this position to be "extremely alienating."[18] "Is it not enough to point out that, after the liberation of Europe from the domination of German National Socialism, Boger was sought and arrested as a criminal precisely for his crimes in Auschwitz and that he could only evade extradition to Poland through flight?" Langbein did, however, enclose a photo of Boger per the prosecutors' request.

The following week, the Stuttgart prosecutor's office ordered the police to take another deposition from Rögner. In particular, they wanted to know whether he would be able to identify Boger from the photo provided by Langbein, as well as whether there was further evidence of Boger's crimes in the documents Rögner had in his possession.[19] On August 18, the prosecutor's office requested information regarding Boger from a variety of other organizations (including the Stuttgart Standesamt, the Zentralrat der Juden in Deutschland, and the Kriminalhauptstelle).[20] It is possible, though the documentary record provides no specific evidence for this, that in addition to seeking further evidence in their investigation, the prosecutor's office was hoping to reduce its dependence on the IAC and the prickly Langbein. In the event, none of these other organizations had any useful information.[21] So the prosecutors remained reliant on the IAC.

On August 20, the police reported to the prosecutor's office on Rögner's most recent deposition.[22] The report noted that Rögner was able to identify Boger immediately on being shown photos of five different men and that he was, in principle, willing to share information from his files but would not surrender them. He did not want the courts to keep them, since he intended to take them to the East with him after he got out of prison. In this context,

---

[16] Langbein Statement (May 29, 1958), FFStA 4 Ks 2/63, Bd. 1, Bl. 32.
[17] Stuttgart StA to Langbein (July 15, 1958), FFStA 4 Ks 2/63, Bd. 1, Bl. 35. See also Langbein to Stuttgart StA (July 9, 1958), FFStA 4 Ks 2/63, Bd. 1, Bl. 34.
[18] Langbein to Stuttgart StA (July 27, 1958), FFStA 4 Ks 2/63, Bd. 1, Bl. 36–37.
[19] Stuttgart StA to Landeskriminalamt Stuttgart (August 2, 1958), FFStA 4 Ks 2/63, Bd. 1, Bl. 37–38.
[20] Stuttgart StA to Standesamt, Zentralrat der Juden in Deutschland, and Kriminalhauptstelle (August 18, 1958), FFStA 4 Ks 2/63, Bd. 1, Bl. 40–45.
[21] See, e.g., Zentralrat der Juden in Deutschland to Stuttgart StA (August 25, 1958), FFStA 4 Ks 2/63, Bd. 1, Bl. 46. The Zentralrat said that they had no information regarding Boger.
[22] Landeskriminalamt Baden-Württemberg to Stuttgart StA (August 20, 1958), FFStA 4 Ks 2/63, Bd. 1, Bl. 48–51.

Rögner was also able to name numerous other SS men involved in crimes at Auschwitz, including several who were later to become defendants in the Auschwitz Trial (Hans Stark, Klaus Dylewski, and Josef Klehr). Nonetheless, the police remained generally skeptical of Rögner's reliability as a witness. "Even though it may be assumed that Rögner, as a Kapo, had the opportunity to observe events in the KZ [*Konzentrationslager*, or concentration camp] that an ordinary KZ inmate could not have seen, it still seems unlikely that he personally witnessed all of the events he describes. Rather, it is far more likely that he is drawing his knowledge largely from the trials that he has seen, sometimes as a witness. It should also be assumed that the purported materials he has gathered for use against the persons he named come from the same source."[23]

According to the police, then, the fact that Rögner had previously testified against Nazis made him an unreliable witness against Nazis because he might have been influenced by those trials; this, despite the fact that German criminal procedure does not prohibit the use of hearsay evidence, especially during preliminary investigations.[24] Still, the report concluded, it would be worth examining Rögner's materials, if only to see whether any of the people he had incriminated had already been tried.

At the end of August, Langbein sent further information to the Stuttgart prosecutor's office.[25] He included a translated copy of a report dated September 16, 1944, that had been smuggled out of Auschwitz by the camp resistance. The report names some of the worst offenders (*Hauptschuldigen*) and accuses Boger of torture and mass executions. Langbein also enclosed a copy of the so-called *Bunkerbuch*, which lists the fates of inmates consigned to the infamous Block 11, the Gestapo bunker in Auschwitz where Boger worked.[26] Langbein also expanded his own previous statement, "in response to a comment in a letter from the Justice Ministry of Baden-Würtemberg from 7 August 1958," indicating that "Boger was very active in choosing those who were to be executed and that he took part in every such selection."[27] Finally, Langbein reiterated that he was unwilling to make a general appeal for witnesses until such time as Boger had been arrested, again citing the flight risk,

---

[23] Ibid., Bl. 51.

[24] It is true that German law stipulates a preference for direct evidence over indirect and that indirect evidence cannot substitute for direct evidence in a trial but does not prohibit hearsay testimony in the manner of American law. See Karl Peters, *Strafprozeß: Ein Lehrbuch*, 4th rev. ed. (Heidelberg: C. F. Müller Juristischer Verlag, 1985), pp. 317, 344. For the American prohibition of hearsay evidence and exceptions, see Rules 802–803, *Federal Rules of Evidence Handbook* (Cincinnati: Anderson, 2001).

[25] Langbein to Stuttgart StA (August 30, 1958), FFStA 4 Ks 2/63, Bd. 1, Bl. 59–65.

[26] This was originally published in the first issue of *Zeszyty Osiecimskie* (in German, *Auschwitz Hefte*, the official documentary publications of the Auschwitz Museum). See *Hefte von Auschwitz* 1 (1959), pp. 45–85.

[27] Langbein to Stuttgart StA (August 30, 1958), FFStA 4 Ks 2/63, Bd. 1, Bl. 62.

but that he was nonetheless enclosing a short list of five potential witnesses (including several who would later testify in the Auschwitz Trial itself).[28]

In early September, Langbein sent a further witness statement to the Stuttgart prosecutor's office, as well as the name of a further potential witness.[29] An additional witness statement in Czech, forwarded by Langbein, prompted a very revealing reaction within the prosecutor's office. A prosecutor working in the political department, one Dr. Bech, wrote to his superior complaining that "[t]his letter was given to us by the main customs office in Stuttgart, together with a series of other postal materials containing printed matter from the Soviet Zone [which is] dangerous to the state. Since the printed matter is in a foreign language, I am unable to ascertain whether it is merely a description of National Socialist crimes or whether it also contains communist propaganda."[30] Bech asked for further instructions but also pointed out that according to regulations, it would be appropriate to open a criminal investigation against Langbein. In a handwritten note at the bottom of the page, he added that he was only passing on this matter to point out the importance of the work done by the "political department . . . in preventing the unforeseeable consequences of mishandling [such documents]."

Beginning in September, the Stuttgart prosecutor's office ordered the police to take depositions from all of Langbein's witnesses currently residing in Germany.[31] Prosecutor Weber met with Langbein at Langbein's request. This was the meeting that Langbein later described as "thoroughly unsatisfactory."[32] For his part, Weber seems to have been equally dissatisfied with the meeting, noting that "Langbein indulged in subjective criticisms of the investigative measures undertaken, which I rejected in the proper manner. Apparently, he subsequently protested to the [Justice] Ministry."[33] Nonetheless, despite his clear irritation with Langbein, Weber sent out a series of letters that same day to various police precincts throughout Germany requesting that they take depositions from potential witnesses against Boger.[34]

On the following day, September 12, Weber met with Rögner and confiscated his documents pertaining to Nazi crimes.[35] These were to be officially

[28] Ibid., Bl. 60. The three witnesses who would subsequently testify in the trial were Henryk Bartosziewicz, Stanislaw Kaminski, and Ludwig Wörl.
[29] Langbein to Stuttgart StA (September 3, 1958), FFStA 4 Ks 2/63, Bd. 1, Bl. 69–70.
[30] Bech to OStA (September 4, 1958), FFStA 4 Ks 2/63, Bd. 1, Bl. 71.
[31] Stuttgart StA to Munich Kriminalpolizei (September 5, 1958), FFStA 4 Ks 2/63, Bd. 1, Bl. 73; Stuttgart StA to Kiel Kriminalpolizei (September 5, 1958), FFStA 4 Ks 2/63, Bd. 1, Bl. 74.
[32] Langbein, *Auschwitz-Prozeß*, p. 23.
[33] Vermerk, Weber (September 11, 1958), FFStA 4 Ks 2/63, Bd. 1, Bl. 76.
[34] Stuttgart StA to Kriminalpolizei in Esslingen/Neckar, Frankfurt, Hanover and Munich (September 11, 1958), FFStA 4 Ks 2/63, Bd. 1, Bl. 79–82.
[35] Weber, Beschlagnahme der Unterlagen Rögner (September 12, 1959), FFStA 4 Ks 2/63, Bd. 1, Bl. 85.

evaluated. Weber evinced the same distaste for Rögner apparent in the police reports. "Rögner protested my statements in an excited tone. . . . I indicated to Rögner that he was here to be questioned by me and that I would not be questioned by him." Rögner's documents consisted primarily of lists of SS functionaries from Auschwitz, often with their current addresses, lists of former Auschwitz inmates, also often with current addresses, and copies of his correspondence with numerous prosecutor's offices throughout Germany and with the IAC in Vienna.[36] Throughout his correspondence, Rögner repeatedly asserted his intention to take up residence in the East on his release from prison and that, therefore, the authorities ought to make use of his knowledge while they still could.[37]

Throughout September, the process of taking witness depositions against Boger continued.[38] Finally, on October 1, 1958, the Stuttgart prosecutor's office requested and was issued a warrant for Boger's arrest, "in that he [Boger], as an SS-Oberscharführer, shot an inmate with a pistol during the course of an execution. He did so on the basis of blood lust and in recognition that the orders for the execution were illegal."[39] On October 8, 1958, Boger was arrested. At his initial judicial deposition, on October 9, Boger claimed, "I can only explain the charges against me in that former criminal inmates, who served as Kapos in the camp, have made [these] accusations against me because they are hoping to get reparations [*Haftentschädigung*] to which they are not otherwise entitled."[40] Given the authorities' prior skepticism vis-à-vis Rögner, this statement may indicate that Boger was given some information about the source of the charges against him, but this remains speculation.[41]

---

[36] Auswertung der Unterlagen Rögner (September 23, 1958), FFStA 4 Ks 2/63, Bd. 1, Bl. 87–101.

[37] See, e.g., Rögner's letter to the StA Ansbach (n.d.), claiming, "'I intend shortly to give all this material to the East Zone but I am willing to go over it with you personally, insofar as you are interested; the evaluation would take several days." In ibid., Bl. 92.

[38] See, e.g., statement by Paul Leo Scheidel (September 24, 1958), FFStA 4 Ks 2/63, Bd. 1, Bl. 111–115. Scheidel had been named as a potential witness by Langbein in his meeting with Weber. Scheidel was able to testify to having been tortured by Boger on the swing, as well as to having personally witnessed an execution in which Boger killed at least one inmate. This was the decisive testimony that led to Boger's arrest.

[39] Haftbefehlsantrag and Haftbefehl for Boger (October 1, 1958), FFStA 4 Ks 2/63, Bd. 1, Bl. 128–30.

[40] Richterliche Vernehmung des Beschuldigten Boger (October 9, 1958), FFStA 4 Ks 2/63, Bd. 1, Bl. 135–36.

[41] Under German law, a defendant is to be informed immediately upon arrest of the charges against him. He is also to be informed of the "essential circumstances" of the allegations against him. See *Strafprozßordnung, Gerichtsverfassungsgesetz, Nebengesetze und ergänzende Bestimmungen*, Beck'sche Kurzkommentare, vol. 6, commented by Otto Schwarz and Theodor Kleinknecht (Munich: C. H. Beck'sche Verlagsbuchhandlung, 1963), §114 StPO, p. 181. Cf. Peters, *Strafprozeß*, p. 420. Since the warrant was issued based on testimony by Scheidel, not Rögner, there is no reason per se why he would have been informed of Rögner's allegations or character.

As for the charges against him, Boger requested that the authorities examine his Denazification files, which he claimed would prove him innocent. When interrogated by the police immediately following his arrest, he specifically denied any participation in selections or executions at the Black Wall, the courtyard wall outside Block 11 where inmates were executed. He did admit to having been present at such executions, however.[42] With regard to his methods of interrogation, he reminded the police, obviously trying to win their collegial sympathy, that he too had been a police officer. "I was trained by the Würtemberg criminal police as a detective. I believed that I could get by using the methods typical there and I had great success with these in all my subsequent postings – in Auschwitz as well."[43] When pressed, Boger did admit that his direct superior in the Political Section, Maximilian Grabner, had ordered so-called intensive interrogations and that, under direct orders, he had hit inmates with a club in the course of these. He denied, however, that the inmates had suffered any physical injury in the process. He also admitted to being present at interrogations using the so-called Boger Swing, but claimed that he had heard the appellation *Boger* Swing for the first time during the present interrogation. He repeatedly emphasized that all intensive interrogations were conducted under direct, superior orders, establishing a theme that was to prove central to the defense strategy in the Auschwitz Trial. Boger concluded his police interrogation by noting how "odd" he found it that such allegations were only now being made, fourteen years after the war.

In the meantime, on October 1, Langbein had written once again to the Stuttgart prosecutor's office, this time directly to the chief prosecutor (Oberstaatsanwalt) Robert Schabel, in order to inquire, once again, why Boger had not yet been arrested, as well as to provide a list of eleven Polish witnesses against Boger.[44] Given that the decision to issue a warrant for Boger's arrest must have been take at some point in late September, it is striking that Langbein was not informed of this decision. Clearly, while the prosecutors were willing to use Langbein and the IAC as a resource, they did not view them as partners in the investigative process. In his letter, Langbein further noted that these new witnesses could be found because it was possible to place ads in the Polish press without fear that Boger might hear of this and escape. On October 10, chief prosecutor Schabel replied, informing Langbein that Boger had been arrested on the 8th and asking for further assistance in locating witnesses. He also asked whether it would be possible to get a map of the camp – a striking indication of just how ill equipped West German prosecutors were to handle Nazi cases.[45] Schabel assured Langbein that

---

[42] Festnahme und polizeiliche Vernehmung des Beschuldigten Boger (October 8, 1958), FFStA 4 Ks 2/63, Bd. 1, Bl. 137–43.

[43] Ibid., Bl. 142.

[44] Langbein to Schabel (October 1, 1958), FFStA 4 Ks 2/63, Bd. 1, Bl. 146–47.

[45] Schabel to Langbein (October 10, 1958), FFStA 4 Ks 2/63, Bd. 1, Bl. 148.

"those measures will be taken which are called for by the seriousness of the proceedings."

In the following months, the investigation of Boger continued apace, as did the tendentious relationship between the Stuttgart prosecutor's office and the IAC. On November 5, Langbein met with Stuttgart chief prosecutor Schabel and gave him signed statements against Boger by seven Polish witnesses.[46] At this meeting, Schabel informed Langbein that the difficulties of the case, particularly the large number of foreign witnesses, all of whom would eventually have to be deposed by the German authorities before a trial could be convened, meant that things would probably proceed slowly. He also warned Langbein against giving further information to the press, as this might simply serve as a warning to any potential co-defendants. Above all, Schabel defended his office against charges of foot-dragging, informing Langbein of the various steps that had been taken to date in the investigation.

Nonetheless, the prosecutor's office clearly felt a degree of pressure from Langbein. On November 6, they issued a statement to the press defending their handling of the case.[47] The statement sketched the course of the investigation, as well as relations with the IAC. In particular, it noted that a degree of initial caution in the case was justified, given the dubious source of the initial charges. Furthermore, the IAC's insistence that it would not provide information against Boger until he had been arrested had been a source of difficulty, since such an arrest could not be made legally until concrete and reliable evidence was available against the accused. Only after Langbein provided the prosecutors with the names of further witnesses (on September 11), one of whom was able to incriminate Boger concretely, could an arrest be made. The statement concluded, somewhat captiously, "The prosecutor's office is surprised that Mr. Langbein finds our activities disconcerting. The prosecutor's office had the impression, in the course of a $1\frac{1}{2}$ hour meeting between Mr. Langbein, the chief prosecutor and the head of the responsible prosecutorial section, that he was thoroughly satisfied with the measures already undertaken and those planned for the future. In any case, this is what Mr. Langbein said. The prosecutor's office cannot understand why we are now being accused of handling the Boger case irresolutely."[48]

For his part, Langbein both recognized the prosecutors' need for juridically viable evidence and, at the same time, clearly felt that this requirement was exaggerated given the crimes at issue. On September 27, he had written to Henryk Bartoszewicz of Lodz, Poland, thanking him for his prior written deposition against Boger but asking him whether it would be possible to "be somewhat more precise" in order to ensure the legal value of his

---

[46] Vermerk, Schabel (November 5, 1958), FFStA 4 Ks 2/63, Bd. 2, Bl. 242. The witness statements are included in the files, FFStA 4 Ks 2/63, Bd. 2, Bl. 222–39.

[47] Pressemitteilung der Stuttgart StA (November 6, 1958), FFStA 4 Ks 2/63, Bd. 2, Bl. 244–46.

[48] Ibid.

statement.[49] In particular, Langbein noted, it was necessary to specify Boger's direct personal responsibility for the executions Bartoszewicz had described in his previous statement. "You must excuse me for asking such questions. We both know full well what Boger has on his conscience. However, our Committee has now set itself the task of providing the prosecutor's office in Stuttgart with compelling material, in order to induce them finally to issue a warrant for Boger's arrest." Clearly, Langbein felt that the truth itself did not require such specificity, only the law; this was why he felt it necessary to apologize for even asking. This tension between the story that witnesses wanted to tell and the story that juridical actors wanted and needed them to tell would resurface with considerable vigor in the trial itself.

So far, we can see four key themes emerging in the Boger investigation: (1) the importance of local initiative in the trial, (2) the tension between prosecutors and Auschwitz survivors, (3) the large role played by Cold War politics in the investigation, and (4) the attempt by defendants to exploit the question of perpetrator motivation to their tactical advantage. First, as already indicated, the charges came about due to private initiative, rather than as a result of any systematic investigation. In this respect, the earliest origins of the Auschwitz trial correspond with Fritz Bauer's characterization of Nazi investigations in the first postwar decades as "accidental and improvised."[50] The Central Office was not founded until after Boger's arrest, though it did then briefly take over the case from Stuttgart. However, when Frankfurt assumed responsibility for the case in 1959 as part of their consolidation of all Auschwitz investigations under their mandate, the Central Office was left with nothing more than a minor consultative role in the investigation.[51] Thus the Auschwitz Trial was from its earliest moments the product of local rather than federal efforts. In this, it was far more typical of the 1950s than of the 1960s or 1970s.

Second, the ambivalent interactions between the IAC (represented by Langbein) and the Stuttgart prosecutors reveal the complex relationship of mutual dependency and animosity that existed between prosecutors and

---

[49] Langbein to Henryk Bartoszewicz (September 27, 1958), FFStA 4 Ks 2/63, Bd. 2, Bl. 221g.

[50] Fritz Bauer, "Im Namen des Volkes: Die strafrechtliche Bewältigung der Vergangenheit," in *Die Humanität der Rechtsordnung: Ausgewählte Schriften*, ed. Joachim Perels and Irmtrud Wojak (Frankfurt: Campus Verlag, 1998), p. 81.

[51] Thus, e.g., Frankfurt Chief Prosecutor Großmann met with representatives of the Central Office on May 22, 1959, to discuss the Auschwitz investigation, but Frankfurt declined to turn over the investigation to the Central Office. See Vermerk, Großmann (May 23, 1959), Frankfurt Staatsanwaltschaft, Handakten zu der Strafsachen gegen Mulka u.a. (hereafter FFStA HA) 4 Ks 2/63, Bd. 1, Bl. 18–20. The central office did occasionally provide support services for the investigation as when, for example, they wrote to the East German Attorney General on behalf of Frankfurt to request information on the prison term served by the suspect Oswald Kaduk. See OStA Schüle to OStA Frankfurt and OStA Schüle to GStA DDR (October 19, 1959), FFStA HA 4 Ks 2/63, Bd. 1, Bl. 113–14.

survivor organizations in Nazi cases. On the one hand, without the aid of
survivor groups, prosecutors could not possibly hope to build a case, particularly in this period prior to the effective functioning of the Central Office.
As Langbein later noted, "[i]f it were necessary to prove that the judiciary
needed support from among the former victims in preparing such extensive proceedings, then the beginning of the Auschwitz case provides that
evidence."[52] Not only did groups such as the IAC hold the key to finding potential witnesses, but, as the repeated requests for documentation
and even maps reveal, they also had access to essential historical sources
which prosecutors were either too busy or too ill-trained in history to find on
their own.

However, from the point of view of German prosecutors, survivors were
all too inclined to make "unreasonable" or at least juridically infeasible
requests, such as Langbein's insistence on Boger's early arrest. They were also
likely to be quite prickly for psychological reasons as well. For example, the
witness Ludwig Wörl, whose name was given to the Stuttgart prosecutors
by Langbein on August 30,[53] refused to be deposed by the police, whom
he apparently distrusted, and insisted on a judicial deposition instead. This
resulted in a nearly two-month delay in taking his deposition.[54] To the prosecutors, this must have seemed like an unnecessary waste of time and effort.
To survivors, many of whom were, for understandable reasons, deeply suspicious of *German* authorities, such demands would have been fundamentally
reasonable and necessary.

On the other hand, so long as survivors wanted to see justice done in
Nazi cases, which they emphatically did, they were forced to rely on prosecutors and judges whom they often viewed as unreliable, as Langbein's correspondence indicates. Indeed, even a full decade later, Langbein remained
highly critical of a legal process that he saw as excessively benefiting defendants in Nazi cases.[55] Survivors often felt little sympathy for what they perceived as legal nitpicking or worse. The manifest injustice of Nazi atrocities,
and their all too direct personal experience of it, made survivors inclined

---

[52] Langbein, *Auschwitz-Prozeß*, p. 29.
[53] Langbein to Stuttgart StA (August 30, 1958), FFStA 4 Ks 2/63, Bd. 1 Bl. 59–60.
[54] Prosecutor Weber asked the police in Munich, where Wörl resided, to take his deposition
    in early September. See Stuttgart StA (Weber) to Munich Kriminalpolizei (September 5, 58),
    FFStA 4 Ks 2/63, Bd. 1, Bl. 73. Wörl, however, refused. See Munich Kriminalpolizei, Vermerk
    (September 19, 1958), FFStA 4 Ks 2/63, Bd. 1, Bl. 84. In November, Weber asked the Munich
    judiciary if they would take Wörl's deposition. Weber to Amtsgericht München btr. Ludwig
    Wörl. (November 3, 1958), FFStA 4 Ks 2/63, Bd. 2, Bl. 202. Wörl did not finally give
    his deposition until November 25. Vernehmung des Zeugen Wörl, Amtsgericht München
    (November 25, 1958), FFStA 4 Ks 2/63, Bd. 2, Bl. 316–18.
[55] Hermann Langbein, "NS-Prozesse in den siebziger Jahren," in Redaktion Kritische Justiz,
    ed., *Der Unrechts-Staat: Recht und Justiz im Nationalsozialismus* (Baden-Baden: Nomos
    Verlagsgesellschaft, 1983), pp. 158–63.

to privilege the claims of a higher justice over the rule of law rigorously construed.

In the Boger case, this mutual ambivalence was complicated by Rögner's dubious personal character, which very nearly created a "boy-cries-wolf" scenario, in that his truthful accusations were almost ignored amid the flood of his bogus allegations. This was why Langbein deliberately tried to avoid having to rely on Rögner's testimony, to the point of not mentioning him at all in his correspondence with prosecutors. Indeed, in 1960, the IAC was forced to reprimand Rögner in writing for his unremitting and counterproductive hostility toward the prosecuting authorities. Tadeusz Holuj, Langbein's replacement as IAC general secretary, wrote, "I must insist on the goodwill of the prosecutors who are preparing this case. . . . There are no intrigues against you here."[56] The IAC, both under Langbein and later, was determined not to let a loose cannons such as Rögner ruin what they clearly perceived to be a major opportunity to see justice done.

Nor was the IAC simply overreacting in this case, either. Not only were prosecutors and police justifiably suspicious of Rögner, there was the very real possibility that Rögner's efforts to exploit his status as a victim of Nazism for personal gain could derail the investigation altogether. In June of 1962, Rögner, now out of prison, very nearly wound up being arrested again for trying to extort money from one of the defendants.[57] If there had been too many such incidents, the Auschwitz investigation would have ground to a halt.

Furthermore, as an official organization of Auschwitz survivors, the IAC represented a constituency whose sole source of unity lay in a shared history of suffering. As the Auschwitz Trial was to reveal, this was often insufficient to overcome past and present political divisions among the survivors, making it difficult for the IAC or any other organization to speak as *the* voice of Auschwitz survivors. National differences were the first major source of tension among survivors.

For example, the head of the German Auschwitz Committee, Ludwig Wörl, the witness who was so reluctant to be deposed by the German police, was at times openly anti-Polish in his attitudes.[58] In late 1959, he wrote to Rögner, alleging that "that fool" Langbein was terrified that the investigation would expand to include crimes committed by Auschwitz inmates. This

---

56 Holuj to Rögner (November 8, 1960), FFStA HA 4 Ks 2/63, Bd. 4, Bl. 588.
57 Rögner had written to the defendant Viktor Capesius demanding money in exchange for finding defense witnesses on his behalf. Capesius's defense attorney informed the prosecutors. Prosecutor Kügler spoke to Rögner by phone and warned him that if he did not desist, he would be arrested again. Vermerk, Kügler (June 27, 1962), FFStA HA 4Ks 2/63 Bd. 8, Bl. 1547.
58 For Wörl's affiliation with the German Auschwitz Committee (*Deutsches Auschwitz Komitee*), see Wörl to Vogel (February 25, 1961), FFStA HA 4 Ks 2/63, Bd. 5, Bl. 786–786R.

would threaten to "take the bread right out of his [Langbein's] mouth."[59] In general, such inmate-on-inmate crimes were committed by so-called *Funktionshäftlinge* (functionary inmates), especially Kapos, most of whom were career criminals, often from Germany. This did not prevent Wörl from blaming these crimes exclusively on Polish inmates. "Without even noticing it, the German Greens [criminal inmates] were caught in the web of the Polish criminals who used them quite cleverly in the course of so-called dirty work, i.e. murder. Our hooligans were for the most part too stupid to see what kind of game was being played." It is easy to see how this kind of animosity among survivors could get out of hand and make a successful prosecution difficult.[60] Indeed, during the trial, the defense tried to exploit such divisions among the survivors, both to shift blame away from their clients and to sow seeds of doubt concerning the reliability of survivor testimony; while they largely failed in the former project, the latter effort was often all too successful.[61]

Despite the efforts by both sides to maintain a working relationship in the face of these threats, the very testiness of the correspondence between Stuttgart and Vienna, the reciprocal recriminations of indifference to Nazi crimes, on the one hand, and ignorance of the law, on the other, reveal a deeper tension. Indeed, the mutual distrust between prosecutors and the IAC continued even after the proceedings had been transferred to the much more sympathetic environs of Frankfurt. In 1959, at a Frankfurt press conference called to discuss the impending trial, Langbein read – with obvious distaste – a letter he had recently received from Frankfurt chief prosecutor Horst Wolf. Wolf wrote:

You will have noticed during your repeated visits to Frankfurt how seriously we take the obligation to master this particularly horrible period in our past thoroughly and quickly. But please understand the constraints within which we must work. We are neither permitted to nor will we interfere with the principles of the rule of law as embodied in our constitution and the corresponding laws. These impose strict standards – in terms of the prerequisites for arresting someone and for ascertaining guilt, the necessity for judicial hearings and an unimpeded defense, to name but a few – even at the risk that the legal benefits of our free, democratic social order may be granted to some who do not deserve them.[62]

---

[59] Wörl to Rögner (December 8, 1959), FFSTA HA 4 Ks 2/63, Bd. 1, Bl. 164–65.

[60] Wörl himself was aware of this risk but thought it unavoidable. He correctly surmised that the defense would bring up inmate crimes in an attempt to shift blame from the SS to inmates. "This division between criminals in SS uniforms and in inmate clothes is a uniquely idiotic delusion of Langbein's and is purely a product of his fear of an expansion of the case." Ibid.

[61] On the defense use of political and national divisions among survivor witnesses, see chapter 7 below.

[62] Wolf to Langbein (December 12, 1959), FFStA HA 4 Ks 2/63, Bd. 1, Bl. 162–63. Quoted verbatim in "Der Auschwitz-Prozeß wird weiter vorbereitet," *Frankfurter Neue Presse* (FNP), December 15, 1959.

Wolf also reiterated Schabel's earlier warning that, in this context, any premature or incautious public statements regarding what was an ongoing investigation were inappropriate and served only to jeopardize the investigation, "thereby aiding the accused."[63]

After reading this letter, Langbein stated that, with this in mind, he would in the future abstain from providing the press with information regarding the status of the ongoing investigation. But he also pointed out that one of the most severely incriminated defendants (Boger), though now under arrest, had lived freely under his own name for years. From his perspective and that of other survivors, Langbein concluded, the actions of many prosecutors were difficult to understand. "It is incomprehensible to former concentration camp inmates when people who played a leading role in the deportations today claim that they could not have known what, for example, 'Special Treatment' meant and, as a consequence, are set free."[64]

After another Langbein press conference in the spring of 1960, things got so bad that the Frankfurt prosecutor's office decided to break off relations with him and the IAC.[65] While the Frankfurt prosecutor's office ultimately relented and maintained some contact with Langbein, calling him as one of their lead witnesses in the trial and also continuing to give him at least the same limited information regarding the ongoing investigation they gave many organizations as a matter of courtesy, they remained cautious in their dealings with him.[66] Thus, in December, chief prosecutor Wolf wrote to Langbein, in response to a request for an update on the status of the investigation. Wolf explained, "As you know, I do not give out information concerning the state of the Auschwitz investigation unless there is some special reason to."[67] Despite Wolf's phrasing, this marked a departure from Frankfurt's earlier practice of keeping Langbein well informed on the course of the investigation.

This mutual incomprehension between lawyers (both prosecutors and, as it turned out, especially defense counsel) and survivors was to form a central point of tension in the trial. Whether sincerely or, in the case of at least some

---

[63] Ibid.

[64] Ibid. This statement is a summary of Langbein's comments, not a direct quote.

[65] Vermerk, Kügler (June 28, 1960), FFStA HA 4 Ks 2/63, Bd. 3, Bl. 422–23.

[66] In February, as part of a routine update to various organizations (e.g., the Institute of Documentation in Israel for the Investigation of Nazi War Crimes in Haifa and the Auschwitz museum in Poland), they sent Langbein a list of suspects confirmed dead. FFStA to Langbein (February 24, 1961), FFStA HA 4 Ks 2/63, Bd. 5, Bl. 794. A week later, Langbein replied, suggesting that not everyone on the list might actually be dead. Langbein to Kügler and Vogel (March 2, 1961), FFStA HA 4 Ks 2/63, Bd. 5, Bl. 804–804R. Frankfurt replied with a polite but curt letter, reiterating the carefulness of their investigation and insisting that their list was accurate. Vogel to Langbein (March 10, 1961), FFStA HA 4 Ks 2/63, Bd. 5, Bl. 805.

[67] Langbein to Wolf (December 14, 1960), FFStA HA 4 Ks 2/63, Bd. 5, Bl. 830–31 and Wolf to Langbein FFStA HA 4 Ks 2/63 Bd. 5, Bl. 832–33.

defense attorneys, cynically, the lawyers continually stressed the importance of respecting the rule of law in the strictest terms. As did Langbein, many of the survivors involved in the trial clearly found this bewildering, if not insulting. One Auschwitz survivor, Norbert Wolheim, for instance, referred to the court's rejection of his testimony in an earlier Auschwitz related trial for "imprecision" as "an insult to the memory of our murdered relatives and comrades" and threatened that survivors would be reluctant to continue testifying if such verdicts continued.[68] In a similar vein, Wörl warned prosecutor Vogel that witnesses would have to be better treated than in previous trials, if they "were to be convinced of the importance of their testimony."[69] For survivors such as Wörl and Wolheim, Nazi trials were an opportunity both to bear witness, to speak the truth of their suffering and that of the multitudes incapable of ever speaking again, and to see justice done, a justice that they felt went beyond the "mere" rule of law. In this sense, the Auschwitz Trial proved to be a battleground, if a decidedly biased one, between distinct visions of justice: one, the justice *of* law, the other, a justice *beyond* law.

The Cold War further complicated relations both between prosecutors and survivor groups, the IAC in particular, and among survivors. This is the third major theme to emerge in the course of the Boger investigation. Admittedly, the prosecutorial distrust of Rögner was to an extent based on a not unjustified skepticism regarding his reliability as a witness. At the same time, however, this was also clearly exacerbated by Rögner's political baiting of the West German authorities by repeatedly emphasizing his communist sympathies (surely a dubious strategy on his part). The dismayed reaction of the prosecutor's office at receiving materials written in Czech indicates the irrational extent to which these concerns could be taken. Even though, as far as the documentary record reveals, no formal investigation was ever opened against Langbein for forwarding such material, the mere suggestion that such an investigation would have been appropriate betrays a marked degree of paranoia. After all, if the documents were in a foreign language that even the prosecutor charged with censoring them could not understand, how much damage could they have done, even had they contained "communist propaganda"? Subsequently, allegations that the IAC was itself a communist fellow-traveler organization were to become a significant factor in the investigation and the trial itself, as defense attorneys leveled charges of witness tampering against both the IAC and East Block governments.[70]

[68] Wolheim to Vogel (December 28, 1959), FFStA HA 4 Ks 2/63, Bd. 2, Bl. 177–79.
[69] Wörl to Vogel (November 10, 1961), FFStA HA 4 Ks 2/63. Bd. 8, Bl. 1366–70.
[70] The exact extent to which the IAC was in fact a communist organization remains unclear. It is true that in his youth, Langbein had been a communist, fighting in Spain on the Republican side and was deported to Auschwitz from a French internment camp as a communist party activist. In 1958, however, Langbein broke with the communist party. (See the brief

This was further exacerbated by a simmering distrust of the IAC among various Jewish organizations. The World Jewish Congress (WJC) in New York, for instance, repeatedly expressed concern over press accounts of the close cooperation between the IAC and the Frankfurt prosecutor's office. In January 1960, Nehemiah Robinson of the WJC wrote to Ober-staatsanwalt Wolf in Frankfurt, saying that he had received a letter from Langbein asking him to update Frankfurt on the WJC's efforts on behalf of the Auschwitz investigation. "As is to be expected," Robinson said, Lang-bein had complained about the lack of prosecutorial zeal.[71] "Personally," Robinson continued, "I am not thrilled at too great an activity by the IAC. People do not think much of communist (or communist-front) organizations in the Federal Republic. A stronger identification of the committee with the investigation could therefore be very damaging, however much useful infor-mation the committee might be able to provide." In a rough draft reply that was never sent, lead prosecutor Hanns Großmann gave vent to some of his frustration with Langbein, accusing him of claiming unwarranted credit for initiating the investigation and of trying to unduly influence its course, in particular by trying to prevent the prosecutor's office from contacting other survivor organizations.[72]

In the final draft, though, Großmann, having evidently regained his com-posure, took a more diplomatic tack. Admitting that the Auschwitz Com-mittee had been helpful for the investigation, he added that it had been under way before the committee got involved. "The investigation – with all due consideration of its many unique features – will naturally be conducted in full accordance with prevailing legal procedures." It was possible that Lang-bein misunderstood some of these legal technicalities. "Legal procedures stipulate the content and extent of the cooperation of third parties, includ-ing the Auschwitz Committee. Any sort of 'identification' of the Auschwitz Committee with the investigation is thereby excluded."[73]

Robinson continued to worry about the IAC's ongoing efforts to paint itself as the driving force behind the Auschwitz investigation, however. Later

---

biographical sketch at http://gfpa.uibk.ac.at/per/lahe.htm, accessed on August 17, 2002). In 1961 Langbein left the IAC and became general secretary for a competing organization, the Comité International des Camps based in Brussels. It is unclear whether he left voluntarily or was forced out and how much of this had to do with the politics of the IAC. His replacement as general secretary, the previous president of the IAC, Tadeusz Holuj, was Polish and clearly had a close working relationship with organizations, such as the Auschwitz Museum, that had close ties to the Polish government. See, e.g., the letter from Kazimierz Smoleń of the Auschwitz Museum to Holuj (November 8, 1960), FFStA HA 4 Ks 2/63, Bd. 4, Bl. 587–88. Whether this means that in fact the IAC was working at the behest of the Polish government or communist party remains to be established.

[71] Robinson to Wolf (January 13, 1960), FFStA HA 4 Ks 2/63, Bd. 2, Bl. 193–94.
[72] Unsent draft, Großmann to Robinson (February 1, 1960), FFStA HA 4 Ks 2/63, Bd. 2, Bl. 195–97.
[73] Großmann to Robinson (February 1, 1960), FFStA HA 4 Ks 2/63, Bd. 2, Bl. 198–99.

that year, he wrote to the Central Office, again inquiring about the extent of the IAC's influence on the Auschwitz investigation.[74] As the Central Office was not directly involved in the Auschwitz case, they sent the letter on to Frankfurt. In early July, prosecutor Georg Friedrich Vogel tried again to assuage Robinson's fears. "It would be incomprehensible and regrettable if the current investigation or any assistance rendered to it were to be mobilized for propaganda purposes. The investigation is being conducted exclusively according to the prevailing legal procedures. . . . Any considerations or interests on the part of Mr. Langbein or the IAC that deviate from this must and will be disregarded."[75]

The mere fact that a large percentage of prosecution witnesses understandably came from the East was often taken to be inherently suspicious. Similar concerns were raised regarding documents provided by East Block governments. Such anti-Communist fears not only gave the nationalist right a trump card to play in its efforts to discredit the Auschwitz Trial, but also plagued efforts to use the trial for pedagogical purposes. It is important to note that, unlike Stuttgart, the Frankfurt prosecutor's office itself never seemed to share these concerns. This may be due to the influence of Fritz Bauer, a longtime supporter of the Sozialdemokratische Partei Deutschlands (SPD) and an old friend of both Kurt Schumacher and Willy Brandt.[76] Thus, while Frankfurt responded to Robinson's fears regarding the IAC, it was only to assert that such fears were unwarranted. From the prosecution's point of view, the problem with Langbein was his ignorance of the law and an unfortunate tendency to air grievances in the press, not his politics, whatever those may have been. As we shall see, the Frankfurt prosecutor's office evinced an admirable readiness to work with East Block authorities whenever this appeared called for by their case, often even in the face of considerable skepticism from the federal authorities in Bonn.

Finally, and perhaps most importantly for the conduct of the Auschwitz Trial itself, Boger's reaction to the charges against him is highly revealing. Although it does not appear that Boger had a chance to consult an attorney prior to his initial depositions, he nonetheless began to lay the groundwork, whether consciously or not, for what was to become one of the central defense tactics in the trial.[77] In his third deposition, taken by prosecutor Weber, Boger not only denied any criminal wrongdoing, but also repeatedly

[74] Robinson to Schüle (June 6, 1960), FFStA HA 4 Ks 2/63, Bd. 3, Bl. 427.
[75] Vogel to Robinson (July 4, 1960), FFStA HA 4 Ks 2/63, Bd. 3, Bl. 428–29.
[76] Matthias Meusch, *Von der Diktatur zur Demokratie: Fritz Bauer und die Aufarbeitung der NS-Verbrechen in Hessen (1956–1968)* (Wiesbaden: Historische Kommission für Nassau, 2001).
[77] The first reference to an attorney for Boger comes with his power of attorney granted to Rudolf Aschenauer of November 11, 1959. Vollmacht, Boger (November 11, 1959), FFStA 4 Ks 2/63, Bd. 3, Bl. 475.

insisted that he had personally disapproved of his orders.[78] "I again energetically deny that any of the intensive interrogations conducted by me led to
any long-term damage to an inmate's health, much less to someone's death.
It has also perhaps not been made sufficiently clear in the previous protocols that I found these intensive interrogations repugnant from the very
start." He further insisted, "I was not committed body and soul to what
went on in Auschwitz. This is indicated by the fact that I had three nervous breakdowns in $1\frac{1}{2}$ years. I was given permission to bring my family
there, which I did, because the atmosphere in the camp made me extremely
uneasy."

Although probably made not on the basis of legal advice, but merely
instinct, these were tactically savvy claims. Under German law the distinction
between a perpetrator and an accomplice hinges on the extent to which it can
be demonstrated that a defendant made the criminal act "his own," in the
sense of subjectively affirming the criminal motives behind it. By claiming
to have been morally and emotionally opposed to the crimes of Auschwitz,
Boger was laying the groundwork for an argument that he was at worst
an accomplice rather than a perpetrator. As we shall see, this had distinct
practical advantages, given that accomplices generally received much milder
sentences than perpetrators. Although it is impossible to reconstruct, on the
basis of the documentary record, the extent to which Boger may have been
doing this consciously, the possibility cannot be dismissed out of hand. On
the one hand, it is certainly true that Boger was neither the most intelligent
nor well educated of defendants. On the other hand, he had been trained
as a police detective, if in the context of the political police, and the law of
homicide as applied to his case was largely identical to that in force at the
time he received his training.[79] Furthermore, at the time of his arrest, Boger
told the police that he had been expecting something like this to happen but
that he had not been worried because he had a clear conscience.[80] To the
extent that Boger was aware of the possibility that he might be charged with
Nazi crimes, it is at least possible that he had worked out a defensive strategy
in advance. In any event, this general approach of denying criminal motives
when it proved impossible to deny criminal actions proved to be one of the
most frequent defense tactics in the Auschwitz Trial itself.

Furthermore, regardless of Boger's tactical motivation (or lack thereof),
the fact that, from the very beginning, he himself chose to emphasize his

[78] Staatsanwaltschaftliche Vernehmung des Beschuldigten Boger (October 13 and 14, 1958),
FFStA 4 Ks 2/63, Bd. 2, Bl. 163–84.
[79] It is true that §211 StGB pertaining to homicide was changed in 1942, shifting the emphasis
from intentionality to subjective disposition. However, the law of perpetration, which is
what is most relevant here, had not changed substantially from the time Boger received his
police training.
[80] Festnahme und polizeiliche Vernehmung des Beschuldigten Boger (October 8, 1958), FFStA
4 Ks 2/63, Bd. 1, Bl. 137–43.

subjective motives is highly revealing. The fact is that even this most obviously and undeniably sadistic of Nazi perpetrators personally believed, or at
least claimed to believe, that his motives in Auschwitz had been, if not noble,
at least not criminal. How much of this was part of a secondary rationaliza-
tion process on his part and how much of it reflects his actual attitudes while
at Auschwitz is impossible to reconstruct after the fact. But the possibility
that Boger was sincere in these claims certainly cannot be dismissed out of
hand.[81]

In either case, what Boger never denied was that people were beaten and
killed in Auschwitz. He denied having killed people personally. He denied
the severity of the beatings. He insisted that, to the extent he "intensively
interrogated" (i.e., tortured) prisoners, he was directly ordered to do so. He
claimed not to have supported these acts morally or emotionally. But Boger,
like the other defendants in the Auschwitz Trial, never denied that crimes
were committed at Auschwitz, only that he himself bore responsibility for
those crimes. He was, nonetheless, at times quite proud of his efficiency. In
particular, he noted with distinct pleasure during the trial that, while he was
in charge of the "escape department," Auschwitz had the lowest escape rate
of any concentration camp.[82]

By focusing on the presumed innocence of his motives, as well as his
functional efficiency, Boger revealed a fundamental disconnect in his perception of the relationship between means and ends, which is typical of the
defendants' mentality in the Auschwitz Trial. In the course of the trial, it
rapidly became apparent that, in the face of massive eyewitness testimony
to the contrary, many of the defendants would not be able to plausibly deny
any criminal wrongdoing whatsoever. The mass of evidence fatally undermined the initial defense policy of total denial. Even though many of the
defendants, including Boger, maintained a rule of total denial well past the
point of plausibility, they also all maintained throughout the trial that they
had been personally opposed to the atrocities at Auschwitz, that they had
sabotaged them to the limited extent of their abilities, and that they themselves had suffered horribly under the strain of having to work in such a
terrible and terrifying environment. Indeed, while most of the defendants
eventually admitted to having participated, however reluctantly (according
to them), in the efficient functioning of the camp – in the form of interrogations, selections, injections, executions, and gassings – none of them
ever admitted to having embraced these activities as a good or necessary

---

[81] The notion that they were pursuing anti-Jewish and other racist policies not out of personal
animosity but out of a sense of historical and political obligation was not uncommon among
higher-ranking SS officials. See Ulrich Herbert, *Best: Biographische Studien über Radikalismus, Weltanschauung und Vernunft*, 2nd ed. (Bonn: Dietz, 1996), pp. 203–8.

[82] Bernd Naumann, *Auschwitz: A Report on the Proceedings against Mulka and Others before
the Court at Frankfurt*, trans. Jean Steinberg (New York: Frederick A. Praeger, 1966), p. 13.

thing. What the defendants never acknowledged – and Boger here provides us with an early example of this mentality – was that the efficient functioning of Auschwitz meant murder. According to their mindset, efficiency was separated, affectively and even causally, from the murderous ends achieved by that efficiency. So it was possible for the defendants, sincerely or cynically as the case may be, to claim to have opposed the ends of Auschwitz while admitting to having aided in the implementation of its means.

Echoes from the Wreckage

The question remains as to how the Boger investigation ended up in Frankfurt in the first place and how what started out as the investigation of one defendant became a large-scale, systematic investigation of the entirety of what in German legal terms came to be known as *Tatkomplex-Auschwitz* (criminal complex Auschwitz). In early 1959, the new Central Office took over the Boger investigation from the Stuttgart prosecutor's office, with the express intention of conducting a more comprehensive investigation of *all* crimes committed at Auschwitz, not just Boger's.[83] According to Langbein, at this point, the investigation took on "a new tone, a new spirit."[84] Certainly, the Central Office, not surprisingly perhaps, given its mandate, showed greater interest not only in cooperating with the IAC, but also in expanding the investigation into a systematic inquiry into any Auschwitz crimes whose perpetrators might still be found. The director, Erwin Schüle, who had served as chief prosecutor in the Ulm Einsatzkommando Trial, wrote to Langbein on February 3, asking him to expand on and gather evidence against a list of suspects.[85] In this spirit of active cooperation, we see the salutary effect that the Central Office had on the investigation of Nazi crimes in the Federal Republic. Also, because the Central Office dealt exclusively with preliminary investigations of Nazi cases, they not only had an obviously greater intensity of focus but tended to be less juridically fastidious in their dealings with survivor groups than ordinary prosecutors. As it turned out, however, the Central Office was not to be in charge of the Auschwitz investigation for long.

On December 18, 1958, several assessors in the Wiesbaden Reparations Office celebrated the holidays by singing anti-Semitic songs. "They sang so loudly that a few days later, the *Frankfurter Rundschau* published a series of articles looking behind the curtains at the bizarre reparations practices

---

[83] See, e.g., the letter from the director of the Central Office to Langbein (January 19, 1959), in Langbein, *Auschwitz-Prozeß*, p. 28.
[84] Ibid.
[85] Schüle to Langbein (February 3, 1959), in ibid., p. 29.

in Wiesbaden."[86] As a result, one Emil Wulkan (a.k.a. Vulkan), a former Auschwitz inmate who was having no luck with his own reparations application, turned to the *Frankfurter Rundschau* for help. In the course of an interview with reporter Thomas Gnielka (on January 1, 1959), either Wulkan mentioned in passing that he had in his possession documents from Auschwitz or Gnielka happened upon them while in Wulkan's apartment, depending on which version of the story one follows.[87] These documents comprised a correspondence between the headquarters at Auschwitz and SS and Police Court XV in Breslau from 1942.[88] They included lists of Auschwitz inmates "shot while trying to escape" and gave the names of the guards involved in the shootings.

Wulkan had acquired these documents during the siege of Breslau in early May 1945, when a friend of his, a *Volkstum* officer who was staying at Wulkan's apartment during lulls in the fighting, happened to mention that he had seen large numbers of papers "concerning Jews and their interrogation" amid the burning rubble of an office building.[89] Wulkan asked his friend to fetch the papers for him, although only a small percentage could actually be rescued from the fires engulfing the wrecked building. Wulkan held onto these documents after the war, although he said that he had periodically allowed "organizations concerned with the fate of concentration camp inmates to examine them."[90] At the conclusion of their interview, Gnielka asked Wulkan whether he could keep these documents in order to pass them on to the proper authorities for use in Nazi trials. Wulkan agreed gladly.

On January 15, 1959, Gnielka passed the documents along to the Hessian Attorney General, Fritz Bauer.[91] These documents gave the Frankfurt prosecutors the opportunity to claim jurisdiction over all crimes committed in Auschwitz. As Bauer said in a subsequent radio interview, "with these KZ papers, we had a little corner [*Zipfel*] of Auschwitz in Frankfurt."[92] Frankfurt submitted these documents to the Bundesgerichtshof (BGH) in Karlsruhe and requested jurisdiction.[93] In April 1959 Frankfurt was granted

[86] Horst Wolf, "Auschwitz–Fabrik des Todes," *Frankfurter Rundschau* (FR), December 17, 1963.
[87] The *FR* reported that Wulkan mentioned the documents. See ibid. Wulkan himself, in his deposition to the police, said that Gnielka came across the documents. See Langbein, *Auschwitz-Prozeß*, p. 30. Cf. Thomas Gnielka, "Die Henker von Auschwitz: Ein Prozeß und seine Vorgeschichte," in *Metall* 16 (1961).
[88] See Werner Renz, "Der erste Frankfurter Auschwitz-Prozeß: Völkermord als Strafsache," *Zeitschrift für Sozialgeschichte des 20. und 21. Jahrhunderts* 15 (September 2000): 14.
[89] Wulkan, Vernehmung, in Langbein, *Auschwitz-Prozeß*, p. 30.
[90] Ibid.
[91] See Gnielka to Bauer (January 15, 1959), FFStA 4 Ks 2/63, Bd. AB 1a, Bl. 72.
[92] *FR*, December 17, 1963.
[93] See Bauer to Central Office (February 15, 1959), FFStA 4 Ks 2/63, Bd. 1a, Bl. 70 and Verfügung, Bauer (February 15, 1959), FFStA 4 Ks 2/63, Bd. 1a, Bl. 10–11.

jurisdiction over all Auschwitz-related crimes by the BGH.[94] The initial suspect list comprised 94 former Auschwitz guards and staff. As a result, the Central Office transferred its Auschwitz files to Frankfurt on June 19, 1959. From that point on the investigation was conducted in Frankfurt. Bauer asked two young prosecutors, Joachim Kügler and Georg Friedrich Vogel, to work on the case, under lead prosecutor Hanns Großmann.[95] Together with another junior prosecutor, Gerhard Wiese, they formed the prosecution team for the trial as well.

Despite the tensions with the IAC outlined above, the Frankfurt prosecutors worked with considerable efficiency and zeal on their investigation of Auschwitz-related crimes. From the very beginning, the plan was to stage a large-scale trial against multiple defendants that would depict the entirety of *Tatkomplex-Auschwitz*, rather than hold a number of smaller trials against individual defendants. Bauer in particular was highly critical of the practice of dividing Nazi cases into discrete individual trials. "The courts tried to divide the total event, e.g. the mass murder of millions in the extermination camps, into episodes, for instance the murder of A by X, of B by Y or C by Z. They wanted to prove in detail the individual actions of individual defendants. But this approach was a rape of what had happened, which was not a sum of individual events."[96] He was determined to avoid such an outcome in Frankfurt and in his initial request for jurisdiction over the case, made it clear that the investigation was to cover multiple suspects.

From the time they began their investigation until early 1961, the Frankfurt prosecutor's office managed to investigate allegations against at least 290 potential suspects.[97] Suspects were divided into two groups, those against whom concrete accusations had been made in the course of witness depositions (at least 120) and those against whom no specific allegations had been made but whom there was reason to suspect they might have committed crimes (e.g., because their names appeared on Allied lists of suspected war criminals). These two groups were then each further subdivided into three sub-groups, those whose identity and place of residence were known, those whose identity was known but whose whereabouts could not (yet) be determined, and those about whom nothing specific was known.[98] As of April 1961, thirteen suspects were under arrest and a further seven had been

---

[94] BGH (April 17, 1959), FFStA, Ks 2/63, Bd. 1a, Bl. 15–19.
[95] Langbein, *Auschwitz-Prozeß*, p. 31. See also "Boger in Frankfurt vor Gericht," *Frankfurter Allgemeine Zeitung* (FAZ), June 29, 1959. Kügler and Vogel were both assigned to the case by Fritz Bauer personally. See Renz, "Der erste Frankfurter Auschwitz-Prozeß," p. 15.
[96] Bauer, "Im Namen des Volkes: Die strafrechtliche Bewältigung der Vergangenheit," in Perels and Wojak, eds., *Die Humanität der Rechtsordnung*, p. 83.
[97] See Vermerk, Großmann (February 1, 1961), FFStA HA 4 Ks 2/63, Bd. 5, Bl. 748–49. The numbers given here are incomplete; 290 thus represents a minimum number.
[98] See ibid. See also Vfg., Großmann (January 2, 1961), FFStA HA 4 Ks 2/63, Bd. 5, Bl. 690.

arrested but had been released on bail or for health reasons. Fifteen arrest warrants were outstanding.[99]

During the course of their investigation, literally hundreds of witness depositions were taken, and these formed the evidentiary basis of all of the cases that proceeded to a formal indictment. In addition to witnesses provided by the IAC, Frankfurt was able to find additional witnesses with the help of various other organizations, such as the WJC and the Institute of Documentation in Israel for the Investigation of Nazi War Crimes. Since both of these organizations were located abroad, Frankfurt prepared a questionnaire for use in the preliminary screening of witnesses, which allowed them to determine which witnesses would be useful to depose formally.[100] Relevant witnesses were then asked to give formal depositions to the authorities in their home countries.

At the end of 1960, the prosecution's efforts paid off spectacularly and Frankfurt was able to announce that, after a nationwide manhunt, they had been able to locate and arrest Richard Baer, the last commandant at Auschwitz.[101] Baer had been working under the assumed name of Karl Neumann as a forester on the estate of Otto von Bismarck (the great-grandson of *the* Bismarck).[102] He had been recognized by a coworker when his picture was published in the *Bild-Zeitung*, incidentally contradicting the prosecution's earlier claims to Langbein that publicity could only harm their investigation. On a snowy December evening, prosecutor Kügler drove to the small town of Dassendorf, near the Bismarck estate. After a small car accident in the driving snowstorm, he met with the local police. Together they drove to the home of the coworker who had recognized Baer initially. Due to the late hour (10:00 P.M.), the coworker had to be rousted from his bed but he confirmed that he had immediately recognized Baer from his photo. "Chin, nose and mouth, as well as the deep-set eyes matched in his opinion. Neumann had claimed, however, that he had been a cook for Hermann Göring. He was an intelligent bloke and it was surprising that he worked as a forester. He lived a reserved life, though he did receive female visits occasionally."[103]

[99] FFStA to Hessischen Minister der Justiz (April 21, 1961), FFStA HA 4 Ks 2/63, Bd. 5, Bl. 859–63.

[100] Fragebogen, FFStA HA 4 Ks 2/63, Bd. 1, Bl. 151–52. The idea for such a questionnaire came initially from Robinson at the WJC. See Vermerk, Vogel (November 5, 1959), FFStA HA 4 Ks 2/63, Bd. 1, Bl. 129.

[101] See "KZ-Kommandant Bär gefaßt," FAZ, December 21, 1960; "'Ich war Offizier, bitte, behandeln Sie mich entsprechend!'" FAZ, December 22, 1960; "Letzter Kommandant des KZ Auschwitz gefaßt," *Abendpost*, December 21, 1960.

[102] The following account is based on Vermerk, Kügler (December 21, 1960), FFStA HA 4 Ks 2/63, Bd. 4, Bl. 659–63. Much of this information appears in newspaper accounts of Baer's arrest as well, indicating that the Frankfurt prosecutor's office was more than happy to share information with the press when it was to their benefit.

[103] Ibid., Bl. 659.

Unable to find Neumann's boss to get a writing sample for comparison (to confirm his identity), Kügler and the others spent the night nearby.
The next morning, they set off into the forest searching for Baer. Along the
way, they met another worker, who said that Neumann/Baer was cutting
trees a few kilometers deeper in the woods. He led them through the snow
and slush to the place where Baer was working. Spying him in the distance
through the fog, the police drew their weapons and ran toward him. Kügler
shouted at him to put his hands up and he surrendered. As they got closer,
Kügler recognized the man as Baer. Handcuffing him, the police demanded
to know his name, which he insisted repeatedly was Neumann. "As we were
taking him back to the car, he asked urgently if we could stop, as he had
soiled himself. We allowed him this and determined that he was covered
in excrement. Observing all security precautions, he was allowed to clean
himself off."[104]
They drove back to Baer's house, where they were met by a woman at
the door. "'Papi, what's going on?'" she asked. Baer held out his handcuffed
hands. "In response to my question who she was, the woman responded,
'Frau Baer.'" Kügler allowed Baer to change and wash up. The two repeatedly referred to one another has "my husband" and "my wife," though Baer
insisted that this did not mean anything. While Baer was cleaning up, Kügler
took Mrs. Baer aside and asked her whether the suspect was her husband,
to which she replied, "Please allow me to believe that he is not my husband." But then Baer asked her, "Tell me, what should I do? I don't want
to mess anything up." "For me," she replied, "you are Karl Neumann."
Kügler explained to Baer that there was sufficient evidence to determine his
real identity, whereupon Baer "pulled himself together and said, 'Good, I
am Richard Baer. Please, treat me accordingly.'"[105] Baer later told one of the
police officers that, when the photos first appeared in *Bild*, he had thought
about turning himself in but was talked out of it by an acquaintance. "He
also thought it would be foolish to turn himself in, after all he had not been
found in the preceding fifteen years."[106]
The arrest of Baer represented a considerable coup for the Frankfurt prosecutors, as it allowed them put on trial the highest-ranking member of the
Auschwitz hierarchy still alive, the first two camp commanders having been
executed in Poland after the war. It also allowed them to show the kind of
concrete progress in the investigation that Langbein had been demanding.
Unfortunately, that triumph proved to be short-lived. Baer died in jail on June
17, 1963, two months after the indictment was issued. Baer's death represented more than simply a loss of publicity for the Frankfurt prosecution;
it also meant that the plan to hold a trial of the entire Auschwitz hierarchy would have to proceed without the head of that hierarchy. In the trial,

[104] Ibid., Bl. 661.
[105] Ibid., Bl. 662.
[106] Ibid.

Baer's absence also facilitated the defense's strategy in the trial of obfuscating the chain of command in Auschwitz and denying the independent decision-making authority of subordinate officers.

After Baer's death, the prosecutors had to make due with Robert Mulka, former adjutant to the first camp commandant, Rudolf Höss, as their lead defendant. [107] This meant that all of the defendants could claim, with at least some degree of plausibility, to have been acting only under direct superior orders while at Auschwitz, a claim that was to prove central to the defense tactics in the trial. Without the commanding officer on trial, it was always possible to shift responsibility to a higher level in the bureaucracy.

In the spring of 1961, the prosecutors began preparations for convening an official judicial preliminary investigation (*Voruntersuchung*).[108] In keeping with Bauer's desire for a large, systematic trial, the plan was to convene an investigation against roughly twenty-five persons, including the thirteen then under arrest and the seven out on bail, plus approximately five others yet to be determined, hopefully from among the camp's medical personnel.[109] By late June, a draft of the motion to convene was completed.[110] After internal review, the prosecution made their motion to convene a judicial preliminary investigation on July 12, 1961.[111] The motion covered twenty-four suspects, seventeen of whom eventually became defendants in the Auschwitz Trial. Of the seven who did not become defendants in the trial, some, like Baer, died, and others had the charges against them dropped in the course of the preliminary investigation due to lack of sufficient evidence. By the time the trial convened in December 1963, an additional five defendants were added to the list of defendants, making for a total of twenty-two defendants at the start of the trial.

Shortly thereafter, Judge Heinz Düx took over the investigation.[112] Judge Düx conducted the investigation with considerable vigor and a level of personal engagement hardly typical of the German judiciary in the early 1960s. Düx questioned more than 1,500 witnesses in the course of his investigation.[113] When he was denied permission for an official visit to Auschwitz to

---

[107] Mulka was arrested in November 1960, shortly before Baer. See FFStA 4 Ks 2/63, Bl. 6979.

[108] Langbein, *Auschwitz-Prozeß*, p. 32. Prior to the reform of the penal code in 1974, German law divided the preliminary investigation of a case into two portions, an investigation conducted by the prosecutor's office and an official judicial investigation conducted under the authority of a judge.

[109] Vermerk, Großmann (May 18, 1961), FFStA HA 4 Ks 2/63, Bd. 6, Bl. 915–20.

[110] See, e.g., the editorial comments by Großmann. Vermerk, Großmann (June 19, 1961), FFStA 4 Ks 2/63, Bd. 6, Bl. 950–950R.

[111] Voruntersuchungsantrag, FFStA 4 Ks 2/63, Bd. 52, Bl. 9379–547.

[112] Heinz Düx, "Der Auschwitz-Prozess: Ein unerwünschtes Strafverfahren in den Zeiten der Verbrechensleugnung und des Kalten Krieges," in Irmtrud Wojak and Susanne Meinl, eds., *Im Labyrinth der Schuld: Täter-Opfer-Ankläger* (Frankfurt: Campus Verlag, 2003), pp. 267–84.

[113] Christa Piotrowski, "Die Unfähigkeit zur Sühne: Vor 25 Jahren Urteilsverkündung im 'Auschwitz-Prozeß' in Frankfurt," *Weltspiegel*, August 19, 1990.

examine the scene of the crime personally, he requested permission to under-take the visit at his own expense as a private citizen. This request was also denied. Düx later recalled that he was told "not to give into any 'temptations'; in slightly coded language, it was threateningly implied that the Polish state or some organization might be paying the travel expenses."[114] Only after repeated requests was Düx finally given permission to visit Auschwitz as a private citizen. The level of Düx's engagement is further revealed by the fact that he was one of the few German judges involved in Nazi trials who main-tained his interest in Nazi crimes after the proceedings were over, writing numerous commentaries over the years on Nazi crimes and Nazi trials.[115] His diligence was crucial in making the Auschwitz Trial a comprehensive and thorough affair.

As with Langbein's earlier interventions in the investigatory process, Düx's engagement reveals the importance that individual actors could have for the unfolding of the Auschwitz Trial, though here too the juridical constraints never ceased to operate. In particular, the fact that Düx did not, could not, undertake his visit to Auschwitz, even as a private citizen, until he received official permission to do so, reveals the extent to which he was constrained by his official role as an investigating judge.

Finally, on April 16, 1963, a formal indictment was brought against "Mulka and others" for crimes committed at Auschwitz.[116] With this, the preliminary investigation came to an official close and the Auschwitz Trial proper can be said to have begun, although the main proceedings themselves did not convene until December 20.

The centrality of the Breslau documents in bringing the case to Frankfurt reveals the fundamental importance of good luck in Nazi cases. Although Wulkan's documents were not to prove decisive in the final instance for the Auschwitz Trial itself (they are hardly mentioned in the final verdict), they were crucial in bringing the case to Frankfurt, where there was consider-ably more prosecutorial zeal for the proceedings than had been the case in Stuttgart. Nazi investigations, Düx later noted, "can be conducted in a delib-erately protracted manner that takes years, so that in the end, the mucking-up [*Versandung*] of the proceedings is preordained."[117] According to Düx, the only reason this did not happen in the Auschwitz case was because Fritz Bauer was in charge of the investigation. "He emphatically dedicated himself to the Auschwitz investigation, undeterred by the hatred and malice of those people who wanted to cover Nazi crimes with the veil of forgetfulness."[118]

---

[114] Heinz Düx, "Der Ungewohlte Prozeß," *Die Tageszeitung*, August 21, 1995.

[115] See, e.g., Heinz Düx, "Warum die Mörder noch immer unter uns sind: Das unbewältigte Problem der NS-Verbrechen," *Die Tat*, March 13, 1978; idem., "Richter und Zivilcourage," *Die Tat*, September 22, 1978; and the interview, "Was der Auschwitz-Prozeß bewirkt hat," *Blick nach Rechts* 12, no. 19 (1995): 4–5.

[116] On the indictment, see chapter 4 below.

[117] Düx, "Ungewohlte Prozeß."

[118] Ibid.

This in itself further reveals the significance of individual interest in such cases. While the details of Fritz Bauer's specific role in preparing and conducting the Auschwitz Trial remains unclear, he clearly played a significant role in determining that the Auschwitz Trial would be a "big," historically important trial.[119] Again, according to Düx, "The Auschwitz Trial...was something new in German legal history. Previously, there were no such trials; no one wanted them either. It is thanks to the then Hessian Attorney General, Fritz Bauer, that this trial took place after all."[120]

As a former émigré and Nazi victim himself, Bauer felt that not only did Nazi crimes require vigorous prosecution, but also that they could serve a vital pedagogical purpose in instructing his fellow citizens in their own responsibility for these crimes.[121] In a 1960 Good Friday address dedicating a memorial to 300 victims of Gestapo reprisals at Bittermark, Bauer noted: "In the face of all the ghastly and appalling things that the Eichmann Trial has once again revealed to us and to the entire world, everyone asks, we ask ourselves – how these things were possible after ten thousand years of the human pursuit of civilization [*Gesittung*] and culture. We ask in order to learn and in order to prevent a new disaster."[122] For Bauer, the purpose of such trials was ultimately pedagogical, to teach the Germans the necessity of resisting tyranny in all its forms, even at the risk of one's own life.[123] It seems likely, then, that Bauer was looking for an opportunity to conduct his own Eichmann Trial, a trial of such magnitude and importance that its lessons could not be evaded or denied. That the Auschwitz Trial ultimately failed in this task does nothing to diminish the significance of Bauer's efforts in bringing this trial to fruition.

---

[119] Perels and Wojak, "Einleitung," p. 17. See also Gerhard Werle and Thomas Wandres, *Auschwitz vor Gericht: Völkermord und bundesdeutsche Strafjustiz* (Munich: Verlag C. H. Beck, 1995), pp. 47–50.

[120] Düx, "Was der Auschwitz-Prozeß bewirkt hat," p. 4.

[121] Bauer had himself been in a concentration camp prior to his emigration to Denmark and, following the German invasion, to Sweden, where he spent the remainder of the war. For a brief biographical overview of Bauer's life, see Ilsa Staff, "Fritz Bauer (1903–1968): 'Im Kampf um des Menschen Rechte,'" in Redaktion Kritische Justiz, eds., *Streitbare Juristen: Eine andere Tradition* (Baden-Baden: Nomos Verlag, 1988), pp. 440–50.

[122] Fritz Bauer, *Wir aber wollen Male richten euch zum Gedächtnis* (Dortmund: Schul- und Kulturamt der Stadt Dortmund, 1960), p. 9.

[123] Bauer, "Zu den Naziverbrecher-Prozessen," in Perels and Wojak, eds., *Die Humanität der Rechtsordnung*, p. 114.

2

The Antinomies of German Law

Motivation, Action, and Guilt

As the preliminary investigation for the Auschwitz Trial demonstrates, German criminal law itself formed one of the crucial structures of action for the participants.[1] This becomes even truer once one turns one's attention to the trial proper. Consequently, an understanding of the central features of German criminal law is indispensable for an understanding of the Auschwitz Trial. The single most important thing to remember about German Nazi trials is that they took place under existing statutory law (*Strafgesetzbuch*, or StGB). This means that, to a much greater extent than trials conducted under either international law (e.g., the Nuremberg trial) or under the charge of "crimes against humanity" (e.g., the Barbie trial in France), German Nazi trials, including the Auschwitz Trial, were profoundly dependent on "ordinary" criminal procedure and legal categories.

This led to several serious jurisprudential problems when it came to prosecuting Nazi genocide. In these legal technicalities, we see the ways in which German criminal law was, quite simply, not well equipped – conceptually or procedurally – to deal with genocide, the ways in which it fundamentally lacked the theoretical apparatus to grasp and render judgment on systematic, bureaucratically organized, state-sponsored mass murder. In this chapter, I consider three specific jurisprudential difficulties, each of which had a tremendous impact not only on the concrete legal practices involved in Nazi trials, but also on the way the Holocaust itself could be conceptualized and interpreted in a legal setting.

I argue that German law was particularly subjectivist in orientation and that, due to this subjectivism, German courts could not adequately represent many of the most significant elements of the complex historical process of exterminating European Jewry. In other words, while this chapter itself is

---

[1] On German criminal law generally, see John H. Langbein, *Comparative Criminal Procedure: Germany* (St. Paul: West Publishing, 1977), and Gerhard Robbers, *An Introduction to German Law*, trans. Michael Jewell (Baden-Baden: Nomos Verlag, 1998), pp. 141–92.

primarily concerned with a series of complicated and occasionally opaque
debates among German legal scholars, the goal is to outline the conceptual vocabulary of the German law, which both defined the way that the
Auschwitz trial unfolded and the tactical options open to its participants,
and became, de facto, a central part of the vocabulary of remembrance in
West German Holocaust trials.

Whether any form of criminal prosecution is truly capable of grasping the
historical character of the Holocaust adequately must remain in this context
an open question; however, given the kinds of stinging critiques that have
been leveled at other types of Nazi prosecutions, by Hannah Arendt, Karl
Jaspers, or Alain Finkielkraut, among others, one can certainly say that no
legal form is unproblematic when confronting the Holocaust.[2] What I am
concerned with here is the specific character of the *German* efforts to deal
with the legacy of the Holocaust in a juridical setting.

The subjectivism of German law became problematic for the prosecution of Nazi genocide at even the most basic level, that of the definition of
murder itself, which is defined as the killing of another human being on the
basis of a statutorily defined set of motives. The specificity of German criminal law becomes particularly clear if one contrasts it with the common law
tradition, which conceptualizes many key categories quite differently. Certainly, it is safe to say that the German law of homicide is strikingly different
from Anglo-American law in the way it treats the question of motivation
and individual responsibility. In particular, the key element in the American
law of homicide is intention, that "malice aforethought" that Blackstone
called the "grand criterion" for establishing murder.[3] Malice aforethought
is constituted, in one way or another, by intent.[4] Furthermore, "[n]early all

[2] See Hannah Arendt, *Eichmann in Jerusalem: A Report on the Banality of Evil* (New York:
Penguin, 1963); Karl Jaspers, *Wohin treibt die Bundesrepublik? Tatsachen, Gefahren, Chan-
cen* (Munich: Piper, 1966); and Alain Finkielkraut, *Remembering in Vain: The Klaus Barbie
Trial and Crimes against Humanity*, trans. Roxanne Lapidus with Sima Godfry (New York:
Columbia University Press, 1992). However, for a strong defense of criminal prosecutions, see
Alan S. Rosenbaum, *Prosecuting Nazi War Criminals* (Boulder: Westview, 1993), and Mark
Osiel, *Mass Atrocity, Collective Memory and the Law* (New Brunswick: Transaction, 1997).

[3] William Blackstone, *Commentaries on the Laws of England*, vol. 4 (Chicago: University of
Chicago Press, 1979 [1769]), p. 198. Cf. Joshua Dressler, *Understanding Criminal Law*, 2nd
ed. (New York: Matthew Bender, 1995), p. 467. On intention and the Anglo-American law
of homicide more generally, see H. L. A. Hart, "Intention and Punishment," in *Punishment
and Responsibility* (Oxford: Oxford University Press, 1968), pp. 113–35; Anthony Kenny,
"Intention and *Mens Rea* in Murder," in P. M. S. Hacker and J. Raz, eds., *Law, Morality,
and Society: Essays in Honour of H. L. A. Hart* (Oxford: Clarendon, 1977), pp. 161–74. On
England specifically, see R. A. Duff, *Intention, Agency and Criminal Liability: Philosophy
of Action and the Criminal Law* (Oxford: Basil Blackwell, 1990). On the category of malice
aforethought more generally, as well as the problems it poses in the western legal tradition, see
Leo Katz, *Bad Acts and Guilty Minds: Conundrums of the Criminal Law* (Chicago: University
of Chicago Press, 1982).

[4] Dressler, *Understanding Criminal Law*, p. 468. The felony murder rule as it exists in some
states is an exception to this identification of malice aforethought with intent.

states that grade murder by degrees provide that a 'willful, deliberate, pre-meditated' killing," that is one characterized by a "specific intent to kill," is murder in the first degree.[5] Murders lacking such characteristics are deemed second-degree murder. Other than having murder in mind, then, the specific content of the perpetrator's motives for killing is not relevant to the legal definition of murder under American law. Similarly, under American law, an accomplice is likewise defined by his or her intent. "S is an accomplice of P in the commission of an offense if he intentionally assists P to engage in the conduct that constituted the crime."[6]

In determining whether a given homicide constitutes murder, it is largely a matter of indifference to American law *why* a murderer intended to com-mit his or her crime, only that he or she committed it deliberately.[7] "The psychological makeup and personal peculiarities of the suspect do not enter into this assessment."[8] Furthermore, intent is generally demonstrated under American law according to the so-called natural-and-probable consequences rule, which holds that a person intended the results of his or her actions (in this case, the death of another human being) if these consequences were natural and probable and could thus have been foreseen by any ordinary person. Any action that could reasonably be expected to result in the death of another human being will be considered intentional, and hence murder under American law. In other words, intent is an imputed and objective fea-ture of the human condition, not a subjective state of mind. Not so with German law, where murder is defined largely in relation to a specific set of statutorily defined motives.

The second aspect of German criminal law that has proved troublesome during Nazi trials is the distinction between a perpetrator (*Täter*) and an accomplice (*Gehilfe*). Again, unlike American law, where intent remains the defining attribute of an accomplice, this distinction is made in German law largely on the basis of the defendant's specific motives for acting as he or she did. In practical terms, the main significance of this distinction is that, at the time of the Auschwitz Trial, judges were allowed to take mitigat-ing circumstances into account in sentencing accomplices but not perpe-trators, which tended to have a tremendous impact on the severity of the punishment imposed.[9] In this too, German law differs from American law,

---

[5] Ibid., pp. 472, 474.

[6] Ibid., p. 428.

[7] The specific intentions of the accused are, however, often considered during the sentencing phase in American murder cases.

[8] George P. Fletcher, *Basic Concepts of Criminal Law* (Oxford: Oxford University Press, 1998), p. 76.

[9] The law of homicide was changed on October 1, 1968, to mandate a sentence reduction for accomplices. This had disastrous consequences for the planned trials against members of the Reichssicherheitshauptamt, who would have been prosecutable only as accomplices, but whose crimes now fell under the statute of limitations and had to be called off. See Jörg Friedrich, *Die kalte Amnestie: NS-Täter in der Bundesrepublik*, rev. ed. (Munich:

which generally treats accomplices as severely as perpetrators.[10] This distinction, even more than the definition of murder, also proved crucial in shaping the Auschwitz Trial.

Finally, I examine the German legal understanding of guilt, arguing that it too rests on subjectivist foundations. Specifically, guilt in German law assumes a direct causal link between free, subjective, individual decisions and behavioral outcomes in the world; motives, in this sense, are held to cause results. This assumption of a direct causal link between individual motives and social outcomes profoundly shaped (and distorted) the interpretation of genocide in the Auschwitz trial, making it extremely difficult to grasp the systematic nature of the Holocaust as an undertaking where the specific motives of the perpetrators in fact varied considerably and can hardly be seen at the individual level as decisive for the extermination process.

Types of Killing: *Mord* and *Totschlag*

The first, and from a pragmatic legal point of view, most significant jurisprudential problem confronting the participants in Nazi trials was the distinction between *Mord* (murder) and *Totschlag* (manslaughter). §211 StGB defines *Mord* as follows: "A murderer is anyone who kills a human being out of blood lust, in order to satisfy their sexual desire, out of greed or other base motives, maliciously [*grausam*] or treacherously [*heimtückisch*] or by means dangerous to the public at large or in order to enable or conceal another crime." §212 StGB defines *Totschlag* more simply as anyone who kills another person without being a murderer under the above definition. *Totschlag* is thus a broader category than manslaughter is in American law, and encompasses crimes that would be considered second-degree murder in the United States.

The relevance of this distinction is twofold. First, *Totschlag* fell under the statute of limitations in 1960. Thereafter, it became necessary for prosecutors to demonstrate that any given Nazi crime met the specific criteria for *Mord* in order to bring an indictment. This made it considerably more difficult to indict Nazi criminals after 1960, since it was no longer enough simply to demonstrate that they had killed another human being or even that they had killed thousands; the prosecutor also had to prove that it was a specific kind of killing. While it is impossible to give the exact the number of potential Nazi

Piper, 1994 [1984]), pp. 434–38; Marc von Miquel, *Ahnden oder amnestieren? Westdeutsche Justiz und Vergangenheitspolitik in den sechziger Jahren* (Göttingen: Wallstein Verlag, 2004), pp. 327–43; Ulrich Herbert, *Best: Biographische Studien über Radikalismus, Weltanschauung und Vernunft, 1903–1989*, 2nd ed. (Bonn: Dietz Verlag, 1996), pp. 507–10; and Michael Greve, *Der justitielle und rechtspolitischen Umgang mit den NS-Gewaltverbrechen in den sechziger Jahren* (Frankfurt: Peter Lang, 2001), pp. 352–85.
[10] Fletcher, *Basic Concepts*, p. 189.

killers who could not be brought to trial as a consequence of this distinction, the former director of the Central Office, Adalbert Rückerl, estimates that it was "considerable."[11]

Second, it is important to note the precise definition of *Mord* under §211.[12] There are three different sets of factors that can make the act of killing *Mord*: (1) the motives of the perpetrator (blood lust, sexual desire, or other "base motives"), (2) the means used in the killing (malicious or treacherous), and (3) the purpose of the killing (to enable or conceal another crime). In the case of Nazi crimes, by far the most significant of these factors was the first set: the motives of the perpetrator. Of the various motives listed in §211, only two have really come into question for Nazi crimes: "blood lust" and other "base motives."[13] Blood lust is defined by the German High Court of Appeals, the Bundesgerichtshof (BGH), as an act done "on the basis of an unnatural joy at the destruction of human life."[14] The other relevant motive for *Mord* is the statutorily unspecified category of "base motives." These are judged, again according to German legal practice, as those "'which according to healthy sensibilities are ethically particularly despicable.'"[15] In other words, *Mord* is in these cases based on motives that are, from the perspective of some presumed but unspecified norm, unnatural and reprehensible, that is, not shared by the majority of (right thinking) persons. As a rule, German courts have held that, in point of fact, blood lust and other base motives need not be characterized by foresight or intent, but can take the form of affective outbursts, which disable cognitive foresight.[16] It is important to note, however, that the use of the term "healthy"

---

[11] Rückerl, *NS-Verbrechen vor Gericht*, p. 155.

[12] It should be noted that the German murder statute was changed on September 4, 1941, and that the emphasis on subjective motivation was greatly increased in the new version; the prior version was much closer to its Anglo-American counterpart, with a strong emphasis on premeditation. However, this earlier formulation has not found any application in West German Nazi trials, because according to the German legal interpretation of the principle of *in dubio pro reo* (doubt favors the defendant), any homicide committed prior to September 4, 1941, and brought to trial only after the war, would have to meet both definitions of *Mord* in order to be tried. See ibid., p. 126.

[13] Kerstin Freudiger, *Die juristische Aufarbeitung von NS-Verbrechen* (Tübingen: Mohr Siebeck, 2002), pp. 138–42.

[14] BGH Urteil from July 7, 1953, in *Neue Juristische Wochenschrift* 6 (1953): 1440. Hereafter, NJW.

[15] *Entscheidungen des Bundesgerichtshofs in Strafsachen*, vol. 3 (Berlin: Carl Heymanns Verlag, 1957), p. 133. Hereafter, BGHSt. Cf. Adolf Schönke and Horst Schröder, *Strafgesetzbuch: Kommentar*, 11th ed. (Munich: C. H. Beck'sche Verlagsbuchhandlung, 1963), p. 873 (§211 1.d.).

[16] "That the defendant was not driven to his act by either an emotional impulse or by cognitive reflection alone, but rather that both an emotional impulse and cognitive reflection played a role does not, in itself, constitute a contradiction. Rather, this is far more in agreement with the general experience that human action cannot, in many cases, be traced to a single solitary motive but must be derived from an entire bundle of motives." OGHBrZ, Cologne

means that more is at stake than mere normative consensus. Although what exactly constitutes a healthy sensibility remains unclear, the vocabulary suggests an implicit, disenchanted natural law perspective that presumes a fair degree of normative transparency in law. Presumably, it would not be possible for a majority to declare euthanasia to be legal under this standard, for example.

In terms of Nazi crimes, it has mainly been possible to demonstrate blood lust for perpetrators from the lower ranks, those who did "the actual killing" (to borrow a phrase from Tolstoy), while base motives have tended to be easier to demonstrate across the board.[17] Although racism has been held to constitute, prima facie, a base motive, political ideology per se does not, unless exacerbated by other factors.[18] For example, in 1950 the Oberste Gerichtshof (Appeals Court) in Cologne upheld a lower court conviction of a Nazi concentration camp guard for *Mord*. The appeals court stated that

the decisive idea for the attitude of the defendant at the time was that the life of a political opponent was to be viewed as absolutely valueless. In this respect, he did not act as, say, a perpetrator of conviction who believed that the political beliefs of his opponents were false and unhealthy [*unheilvoll*] and that his own values were the only valid ones, that is as a perpetrator who decided on his action, in order to aid the victory of his convictions. Rather, his actions came far more from his need for revenge [*Geltungsbedürfnis*]. He expected to be recognized and rewarded for his actions. The Schwurgericht properly saw in this base motives in the sense of §211, Abs. 2 StGB.[19]

The most striking thing about both of these motivational determinants of *Mord* is that, since they concern internal states of affairs, they can usually be demonstrated only on the basis of indirect evidence (e.g., laughing while killing someone or acting in excess of one's orders), except in those rare cases where direct statements made by the perpetrators at the time of the crime are available.[20] Ex post facto statements regarding the perpetrator's motives are held to be tainted and/or irrelevant and, hence, inadmissible. In other words, at least with respect to Nazi trials, German courts have tended to place less emphasis on explicit psychologizing than on presumptive inferences drawn from the objective circumstances of the crime. It is true that

(January 31, 1950). Cited in NJW, vol. 3 no. 9 (1950): 357. In this, German law moves in exactly the opposite direction from American law.

[17] Leo Tolstoy, "The Raid," in *The Raid and Other Stories*, trans. Louise Maude and Aylmer Maude (Oxford: Oxford University Press, 1982), p. 1. Jürgen Baumann, "Die strafrechtliche Problematik der nationalsozialistischen Gewaltverbrechen," in Reinhard Henkys, *Die nationalsozialistischen Gewaltverbrechen: Geschichte und Gericht* (Stuttgart: Kreuz Verlag, 1964), pp. 290–91. See also Freudiger, *NS-Verbrechen*, pp. 138–42, 267–70.
[18] Rückerl, *NS-Verbrechen*, p. 126.
[19] OGHBrZ, Cologne (March 7, 1950). Cited in NJW 3 (1950): 434–35.
[20] Baumann, "Die strafrechtliche Problematik," pp. 290–91.

psychiatric testimony was taken during the Auschwitz Trial, but its role was restricted to determining whether the two defendants who were under the age of maturity for some portion of their time in Auschwitz should be sentenced under juvenile law.[21] As one psychiatrist pointed out in his testimony, no contemporary expert was in a position to say for certain what the psychological situation was for a given defendant twenty years previously.[22] Consequently, the Frankfurt court was understandably cautious in making use of psychiatric testimony in reaching its decisions.

In this respect, it should be remembered that one of the central characteristics of the continental legal system is that it is inquisitorial rather than adversarial. Thus the central duty of the German court is, in principle, to find the truth of the matter at hand, not to adjudicate between agonistic parties. That means that instead of depending on outside experts to advise on a defendant's state of mind, German courts, in their truth-finding capacity, have sought to find "objective" indices of "subjective" dispositions. This adds a curious dimension to the subjectivism of German law in actual practice. In essence, there are two components to the "facts" of any case (*Tatbestand*): objective factors and subjective factors (*Tatbezogene* and *Täterbezogene*). The subjective factors consist primarily in the court's findings concerning the defendants' motives at the time of the crime. The function of the objective factors, on the other hand, is twofold. First, they establish what the defendant in fact did or did not do. Obviously, this is the first and most essential task in any trial. Acquittals in Nazi cases have generally but not always been the result of the failure to prove that the defendant committed a crime. However, the objective factors in a trial play a second and, for our purposes, more interesting role, in that they also serve to indicate the character of the subjective factors constituting a particular *Tatbestand*.

For example, the defendant Johann Schoberth was acquitted in the Auschwitz Trial on all three counts against him. On two counts, he was acquitted due to insufficient evidence that he had even participated in the crimes in question (selecting Jews for gassing and supervising the gassing operations). In the third case, however, the court found that Schoberth had indeed participated in an illegal execution of inmates in the Small Crematorium. It nonetheless acquitted him on this count as well, because it felt that it had not been proven that Schoberth *knew* this execution to be illegal.[23] "The possibility that he was told that the civilians had been

---

[21] Vogel, *Plädoyer* for Stark, FBI SAP: FAP1/StA 2, p. 64. The defendant Hans Stark was sentenced under juvenile law, largely on the basis of the psychiatric testimony. In the other case, that of Johann Schoberth, the question became moot when he was acquitted on all counts.

[22] Ibid., p. 64.

[23] Contrary to the assertion of Freudiger, *NS-Verbrechen*, pp. 328–32.

judicially condemned and therefore had to be shot cannot be ruled out. For the defendant Schoberth, there was no opportunity to check if a given death sentence was legal or not."[24] The lack of evidence here pertained not to Schoberth's actions but to his state of mind.

As for the second category of factors that define *Mord*, the manner in which the killing is done (maliciously or treacherously), while it would seem, on the face of it, that these are objective descriptors that could apply to almost all Nazi killings, this has not generally been held to be the case. As the jurist Jürgen Baumann puts it: "It is interesting that, although malice seems to be an objective characteristic pertaining to the way in which a crime is carried out, it is almost universally agreed that only the addition of a 'merciless, cold-blooded attitude' qualifies as *Mord*."[25] Or as Schönke and Schröder define it in their commentary on the StGB: "A killing is malicious, when it imposes particularly severe bodily or mental suffering via either the severity, the duration, or the repetition of the pain inflicted and when it *furthermore* comes from a cold-blooded and merciless sensibility."[26] Thus, in addition to the objective infliction of severe pain, it is necessary that the perpetrator do so on the basis of certain internal dispositions.

For example, a particularly brutal killing may not qualify as *Mord*, if the perpetrator is not in a position to prevent this brutality and it could thus not be ascertained that his attitude was necessarily cold-blooded and merciless. This means that, although most Nazi killings were in some meaningful sense "malicious," this alone has not always legally qualified them as *Mord*. Here again what counts is the cold-bloodedness of the act; that is to say, *Mord* is still determined by the internal psychological disposition of the perpetrator. Furthermore, the definition of "treacherous" likewise emphasizes a specific subjective aspect. As the BGH puts it: "The concept of 'treacherousness' has as its essential content, according to common usage, the notion of a hostile orientation of will by the perpetrator against the victim. This hostile attitude by the perpetrator toward the victim reveals itself in that the former abuses the latter's guilelessness and defenselessness for the purpose of killing him."[27] In this instance, the manner of the killing, the element of deception it entails, is seen essentially as an indicator of an internal disposition, namely, hostility.[28] Furthermore, the courts have specified that it is necessary

[24] C. F. Rüter, *Justiz und NS-Verbrechen: Sammlung Deutscher Strafurteile wegen nationalsozialistischer Tötungsverbrechen, 1945–1966*, vol. 21 (Amsterdam: University Press Amsterdam, 1979), p. 747.

[25] Baumann, "Die strafrechtliche Problematik," p. 292.

[26] Adolf Schönke and Horst Schröder, *Strafgesetzbuch: Kommentar*, 10th ed. (Munich: C. H. Beck'sche Verlagsbuchhandlung, 1961), §211, Anm. V 2 b. Emphasis added.

[27] NJW 10 (1957): 70–71.

[28] But, on the other hand, the court also said: "Treacherous killing is not excluded by the fact that the perpetrator acted on the basis of not particularly reprehensible, perhaps even humanly comprehensible, motives." BGH Urteil, September 30, 1952, NJW 5 (1952): 1385.

to abuse *both* the "guilelessness and defenselessness of the victim."[29] One must both deceive and exploit one's victim, in order for a killing to be "treacherous."

German courts have largely held that the third category that qualifies a killing as *Mord* – to enable or conceal another crime – hardly ever applies to Nazi crimes.[30] So, while it was, for example, policy in Auschwitz periodically to liquidate the largely Jewish *Sonderkommandos*, whose gruesome job it was to empty the gas chambers after an execution and cremate the corpses, the Frankfurt court chose not to emphasize that the purpose of such killings was to eliminate potential witnesses.[31] The reasons for this neglect remain unclear. However, given that these killings were fully integrated into the larger genocidal apparatus at Auschwitz, it seems plausible to suppose that their function as a means of covering up the extermination process was secondary to the fact that their victims were Jewish and, hence, slated to die anyway. In any event, for whatever reason, German courts have almost never applied this criterion to Nazi crimes, further restricting the scope of *Mord* to the subjective dispositions of the perpetrators. Therefore, at this very foundational jurisprudential level – who could be indicted and what would have to be proven in a court of law in order to secure a conviction – Nazi trials were bounded by the subjective categories laid out in §211 StGB. Furthermore, those elements in the definition of *Mord* that seem most objective and, in many ways, most characteristic of Nazi genocide (malice, treachery, covering up further crimes) have either been legally defined in equally subjective terms or dismissed as inapplicable to Nazi crimes. Under German law, then, it is not simply a question of whether the defendants killed but why they did so as well.

Types of Killers: Perpetrators and Accomplices

This subjective emphasis pervades the second major legal distinction crucial to Nazi trials as well: that between perpetrators and accomplices. This distinction is in many ways far more complex than that between *Mord* and *Totschlag*, since it involves distinguishing among various participants in one and the same general act. It is also more important, pragmatically and discursively, to the actual conduct of trials since it is a distinction made among defendants already on the docket. Indeed, during the course of the Auschwitz

---

[29] BGH Urteil, June 9, 1964, cited in NJW 17 (1964): 1578–79.
[30] Rückerl, *NS-Verbrechen*, p. 126.
[31] The court, for instance, convicted Wilhelm Boger of *Mord* in at least 100 instances for shooting inmates from the *Sonderkommando* but not because such shootings were designed to eliminate witnesses but because they were retribution for a failed uprising by the inmates. Whether they would still have constituted *Mord* if the executions had been part of the "ordinary" liquidation process is by no means clear. Rüter, *Justiz und NS-Verbrechen*, vol. 21, pp. 475–76.

Trial, this issue proved to be one of the central points of contention between the prosecution and the defense. This distinction is crucial from a practical legal point of view because in cases of *Mord*, the sentencing guidelines under §211 StGB mandate life in prison for a convicted perpetrator. At the time of the Auschwitz Trial, however, §§44, 49 StGB stipulated that an accomplice could be given a milder sentence, if the court felt this was warranted by mitigating circumstances. In Nazi trials, including the Auschwitz Trial, judges almost always took this opportunity to reduce sentences.[32]

The most salient jurisprudential feature of the distinction between a perpetrator and an accomplice is that this determination is ultimately made, once again, largely on the basis of the subjective orientation of the accused toward the crime.[33] The law itself is relatively vague on this point. §49 StGB simply defines an accomplice as "anyone who, through action or advice, knowingly aids a perpetrator in the commission of any action punishable as a crime or misdemeanor [*Vergehen*]." The crucial distinction between aiding in the commission of a crime and committing one remains largely unspecified by the statute itself. This void is filled, somewhat, by a voluminous legal commentary, as well as by a substantial body of case law.

The category of *Täterschaft* (literally, perpetratorship) has been extremely controversial in the legal literature.[34] In particular, the dominant subjective theory of perpetratorship has been challenged from both an objective theoretical perspective and, especially in the postwar period, a synthetic stance associated with Claus Roxin commonly referred to as the *Tatherrschaft* (mastery over the act) theory.[35] Yet in the end, a modified version of the subjective theory has governed judicial practice in West Germany.

[32] See Freudiger, *NS-Verbrechen*, pp. 264–67. For sentencing statistics, see Falko Kruse, "NS-Prozesse und Restauration: Zur justitiellen Verfolgung von NS-Gewaltverbrechen in der Bundesrepublik," in Redaktion Kritische Justiz, ed., *Der Unrechts-Staat: Recht und Justiz im Nationalsozialismus*, vol. 1 (Baden-Baden: Nomos Verlagsgesellschaft, 1983), pp. 164–89. See also Presse- und Informationsamt der Bundesregierung, *Die Verfolgung nationalsozialistischer Straftaten in der Bundesrepublik* (Flensburg: Christian Wolff, 1963), and Albrecht Götz, *Bilanz der Verfolgung von NS-Straftaten* (Cologne: Bundesanzeiger Verlag, 1986).

[33] See Rückerl, *NS-Verbrechen*, pp. 274–81.

[34] Greve, *Umgang*, pp. 145–09.

[35] For the relevant debates, see, among others, Claus Roxin, *Täterschaft und Tatherrschaft*, 6th ed. (Berlin: Walter de Gruyter 1994 [1963]); Claus Roxin, "Straftaten im Rahmen organisatorischer Machtapparate," in Heinrich Grüntzer, ed., *Goltdammer's Archiv für Strafrecht* (Hamburg: R. v. Decker's Verlag, 1963); Werner Hardwig, "Über den Begriff der Täterschaft: Zugleich eine Besprechung der Hablitationschrift von Claus Roxin 'Täterschaft und Tatherrschaft,'" in *Juristen Zeitung*, no. 21 (1965): 667–71; Schönke and Schröder, *Strafgesetzbuch*, 10th ed., p. 245; Jürgen Baumann, "Beihilfe bei eigenhändiger voller Tatbestandserfüllung," NJW 16 (1963): 561–65; Hans-Joachim Korn, "Täterschaft oder Teilnahme bei staatlich organisierten Verbrechen," NJW 18 (1965): 1206–10; Hans Welzel, *Das deutsche Strafrecht: Eine systematische Darstellung* (Berlin: Walter de Gruyter, 1965), pp. 57–58; Hans Welzel, *Um die finale Handlungslehre: Eine Auseinandersetzung mit ihren Kritikern* (Tübingen: Verlag J. C. B. Mohr, 1949).

The subjective theory, of which there are two main variants, emphasizes the inner disposition of the accused. "What the subjective theories share is the fact that, in distinguishing perpetration from participation, they do not look for objective, external factors but only for internal, psychic criteria like the will, intention, motives and attitudes of the participants."[36] What distinguishes the two subjective theories is which particular internal criteria they choose to emphasize.

The so-called *dolus* theory (*dolus* meaning malice aforethought in Latin) focuses on the supposedly divergent will of the perpetrator versus the accomplice. The "classic formulation" (Roxin) of the *dolus* theory is found in a Reichsgericht decision from 1881.[37] The court held: "If the co-perpetrator desires [*willen*] to complete his own act, and the accomplice, by contrast, only wants to support a foreign act, that of the perpetrator, the only possible meaning of this fact is that the accomplice's will is dependent on the perpetrator's, that he subordinates his will to the perpetrator's, that he leaves it up to the perpetrator to decide whether the act is completed or not."[38] A perpetrator, on the other hand, recognizes no will as "superordinate to his own," and if there are multiple perpetrators, the will of each is "of the same quality" as all the others, and all wills are equally causal for the crime in question.

One could hardly ask for a clearer formulation of the subjective emphasis of German legal thinking. This decision clearly draws on Kant's distinction between autonomy and heteronomy, where the former is the independent obedience to an internal moral law, and the latter is any act done in accordance with "external" pressures, including those of one's own desires. Willing is, on this account, antecedent to action and heteronomy is as much an act of will as autonomy, though only in the sense that one willfully surrenders one's autonomy to external compulsions.[39] The Reichsgericht, however, followed a path slightly different from that of Kant himself. They held any will acting criminally, that is, according to a bad maxim (*dolus*), to be *autonomous*, in the sense that it was causally superordinate to a heteronomous will merely abetting such a criminal act. For the court, in the

[36] Roxin, *Täterschaft und Tatherrschaft*, p. 51.
[37] Ibid., p. 53.
[38] *Entscheidungen des Reichsgerichts in Strafsachen*, vol. 3 (Leipzig: Verlag von Beit und Comp, 1881), p. 181. Hereafter, RGSt.
[39] For Kant, the capacity for autonomous action raises the dilemma of what he calls "radical evil," the empirical fact that human beings *choose* not to follow the law, to act heteronomously according to evil maxims, and do so universally. Kant writes: "Hence we can call this a natural propensity to evil, and as we must, after all, ever hold man himself responsible for it, we can further call it a *radical* innate *evil* in human nature (yet none the less brought upon us by ourselves)." Immanuel Kant, *Religion within the Limits of Reason Alone*, trans. Theodore M. Greene and Hoyt H. Hudson (New York: Harper Torchbooks, 1960 [1793]), p. 28.

case of a criminal will, Kant's "radical evil" is operative, in the sense that an evil maxim is freely chosen; in the case of the accomplice, on the other hand, some apparently more mundane evil is at work, a kind of radical heteronomy, so to speak, where choice is merely abrogated as such.[40] The central assumption is that an evil result is the consequence of an evil aim, that will is causal. The various and sundry *means* of achieving this evil result, on the other hand, including the aid of others, are subordinate to the willing of it.

The second of the subjective theories of *Täterschaft* is the so-called interest theory. According to this theory, the perpetrator is the person who has an "interest" in the success of the criminal act. This theory was most clearly articulated in 1940 by the Reichsgericht in the infamous *Badewannenfall* (bathroom case).[41] In this case, the mother of a small child convinced her sister to drown the child for her. The court convicted the mother as the perpetrator and the sister, who actually physically drowned the child, as an accomplice, provoking considerable public outcry.[42] The court wrote: "Whether an act can be considered a person's own can be determined primarily, if not exclusively, by the degree of interest he or she has in its success."[43] Since it was in the mother's interest for the child to die, the sister who *merely* killed the child was not actually considered the perpetrator of the murder. Like the *dolus* theory, the interest theory focused squarely on the subjective dispositions of the participants to a crime. Unlike the *dolus* theory, however, it concentrated on the vaguely defined "interests" of the accused. This approach, while it by no means conceptualizes interest in strictly materialist terms, certainly presumed a radically autonomous actor capable of acting deliberately in pursuit of a clearly perceived (self) interest. Again, the aim of an act is considered more important that the means used to carry it out, though a neo-Kantian "radical evil" is here supplanted by the more mundane category of interest.

Although the category of perpetratorship was hotly contested in the legal scholarship of the postwar period, there was actually something like a consensus on the topic in judicial practice – though this was not unambiguous. In the 1950s and '60s, Germany's highest criminal court of appeals, the BGH, was relatively consistent in applying the subjective theory of perpetratorship in its rulings. In this, the high court was simply continuing a tradition that stretched back to the nineteenth century. In the course of the twentieth

---

[40] Kant would have viewed this idea of radical heteronomy, or the abrogation of choice as such, as an impossibility. He would have viewed the accomplice's *choice* to abrogate choice as equally symptomatic of man's radical evil. However, given the clearly hierarchical nature of the courts' characterization of perpetrators and accomplices, it would hardly have seemed appropriate to classify them as equivalent examples of some more general moral phenomenon.

[41] RGSt, vol. 74 (1940): 84–85.

[42] Baumann, "Die strafrechtliche Problematik," p. 307.

[43] RGSt, vol. 74, p. 85.

century, despite the growing chorus of dissent among legal scholars, such as Claus Roxin and Hans Welzel, the German high court remained generally faithful to its subjectivist definition of perpetration.[44] That having been said, however, the BGH was not totally immune to the influence of competing theories and did occasionally venture to incorporate objective elements into its decisions, producing more confusion than clarity in the process.[45]

In the early 1950s, for instance, the court handed down a ruling on the question of whether a wife who neglects to prevent her husband's suicide could be punished as a perpetrator, since accomplices to suicide were not subject to criminal sanctions. The court ruled that a person with a legal obligation to preserve the life of another (e.g., a spouse) could in fact be punished for failing to act to prevent that death. Essentially, the court argued that such an obligation has an objective character. "As a rule, the person with an obligation to provide aid has total, or at least a considerable, mastery over the situation and can, through his intervention, decisively shape the course of events."[46] A person who violates this objective obligation, according to the court, cannot be an accomplice, regardless of his or her intentions vis-à-vis the criminal outcome, but must be considered a perpetrator. "It is not a question of whatever arbitrary meaning the person with the obligation subjectively attaches to his inactivity but of what significance this inactivity in fact has for the course of events. Therefore, in a case such as this, the intentionality of a perpetrator can be taken as given."[47] In this case, then, the court modified the subjective theory to say that the perpetrator's subjective disposition toward the act is relevant only in its objective dimension. However, the court added significantly, "Whether this constitutes a general legal principle for separating perpetrators from accomplices is a question that can be left aside."[48] The court thus left open the possibility that this was a unique case, where the specific legal obligations of one spouse to another constituted an objective category superimposed on the otherwise subjective question of perpetratorship.

In two influential cases from the mid-1950s, the court further accentuated certain objective elements in its definition of perpetratorship, without thereby substantially abandoning its adherence to the subjective theory in general. In the first case (June 15, 1954) an employee had helped his employer

---

[44] Whether any of this can be attributed to the high degree of personnel continuity between the Reichsgericht and the Bundesgerichtshof is unclear. See Gerhard Pauli, *Die Rechtsprechung des Reichsgerichts in Strafsachen zwischen 1933 und 1945 und ihre Fortwirkung in der Rechtsprechung des Bundesgerichtshofs* (Berlin: W. de Gruyter, 1992).

[45] For a general consideration of BGH decisions regarding the perpetrator/accomplice distinction, including among others those discussed here, see Roxin, *Tatherrschaft*, pp. 90–106 and 557–624.

[46] BGHSt, vol. 2 (1952): 156.

[47] Ibid.

[48] Ibid.

to steal cattle. The court had to decide whether he acted as a co-perpetrator
of the theft or merely as an accomplice. The court held that, in defining a perpetrator, "formalistic phrases, such as 'the accused made the act his own . . .'
are insufficient."[49] While the "inner orientation of will" remained the decisive indicator of perpetratorship, this inner orientation generally could be
discerned only through external, objective indicators, such as having control
over the course of events. "Only a person with such a strong inner relationship to the sequence of events, as well as their successful criminal outcome,
such that both are substantially dependent on his will, can be considered
a co-perpetrator."[50] Thus, in this case, the court said that the determining
factor was whether the employee left all significant decisions as to the time
and manner of the theft to his boss, which he had, making him an accomplice. In other words, the employee's subjective orientation toward the crime
was ascertained on the basis of the (limited) degree of objective control he
exercised over it.

In the second case (May 17, 1955), the court developed this line of argumentation further, claiming that the objective character of a given participant's activities was not per se relevant in distinguishing perpetrators from
accomplices. The court again emphasized the centrality of the subjective orientation of the participants. In particular, though, in cases where there were
multiple participants, this disposition had an objective component, since
each perpetrator could complete his actions only by means of the actions
of others. "His inner disposition toward the total event must, therefore, be
such that it allows his contribution to the crime to be seen not simply as
supporting a foreign activity but as one part of the general activity of all
participants and, correspondingly, that posits the actions of the others as
an extension of his own activity."[51] The only way to determine whether a
given participant had such a disposition was by means of objective indices:
"The common phrase, a co-perpetrator is anyone who desires the act as 'his
own' can be easily misunderstood. This orientation of will is not an inner
factum, which the judge can authoritatively discern. It is far more a matter
of normative [*wertende*] judgment. The extent to which a given participant
helps to control the course of events, so that the circumstances and success
of the act depend to a considerable extent on his will, provides an essential
indication of whether he posses such a disposition."[52]

In both these cases, the high court felt it necessary to supplement its
focus on the subjective with additional objective factors. The court explicitly
maintained that the defining element in perpetratorship is the relationship
between a given participant's will and the criminal act, that is, a perpetrator

[49] Monatsschrift für Deutsches Recht 8 (1954): pp. 529. Hereafter MDR.
[50] Ibid.
[51] *Juristische Rundschau* 8 (August 1955): 305.
[52] Ibid.

was someone who made the criminal act "his or her own" in the sense of incorporating it into his or her will. However, the court further held that this relationship could not be ascertained on a purely subjective level. Often, the only indication of an actor's orientation toward his or her act would lie in the character of that act itself. However, it is extremely important to note that in neither case do the objective features of the act take on any particular significance in and of themselves. "In distinguishing between a co-perpetrator and an accomplice, it is not a matter of the character of the external act itself but of the inner orientation of the will."[53] The act is merely *indicative* of the will.[54]

Half a year later (January 10, 1956), the court again took up the issue of perpetratorship. In this case, a man was convicted as a *perpetrator* of murder for killing his mistress's husband, despite her having goaded him into the act; that is, he undertook the act in her interest and was still considered a perpetrator. The court declared: "Whoever kills another human being with his own hands is fundamentally a perpetrator, even when he does so under the influence and in the presence of another."[55] The court thus deliberately and explicitly abandoned the interest theory that the Reichsgericht had first articulated in 1940 in the *Badewannenfall*, establishing in the process what looked to be a fundamental legal principle, namely, that single-handedly killing another person constituted perpetratorship, regardless of the role of others in instigating the crime.[56] As it turned out, however, this principle proved to be quite limited in its scope.

At the same time, the court also explicitly declined to render judgment on the validity of more objective theories of perpetratorship in general, saying that such a finding was not necessary in this case. Instead, the court built on the precedents of the two preceding cases, holding that the subjective theory, properly understood, reached the appropriate verdict. The court reiterated the centrality of the participant's orientation of will to deciding issues of perpetratorship but added that "this orientation of will is not a simple internal matter."[57] Rather, the court again emphasized that this subjective orientation was a matter of normative judgment for the court, based on an evaluation of "all the circumstances" surrounding the crime, including particularly the degree of control that the accused exercised over the course

---

[53] MDR (1954): 529.

[54] Unsurprisingly, Roxin was highly critical of the synthetic nature of these decisions, applauding their "objective" turn while condemning their inconsistency. Roxin, *Tatherrschaft*, p. 95.

[55] BGHSt, vol. 8 (1956): 393.

[56] In November 1950, in its very first decision to touch on the issue of perpetratorship, the court had left open the question of whether someone who single-handedly kills another might merely be an accomplice, rather than a perpetrator or co-perpetrator. See NJW 4 (1951): 120.

[57] BGHSt, vol. 8 (1956): 396.

of events.[58] In this case, the court found the accused to be the perpetrator, despite his having an "obedient character" and being "subordinate" to his mistress, because "all the circumstances," that is, the conduct of the murder, pointed to his will being oriented toward the success of the crime. In particular, "without him, it [the crime] could not have happened in the way it was planned."[59] Once again, then, the court found that objective indicators were crucial for determining what it still considered to be the subjective determinant of perpetratorship: the accused's subjective disposition toward the act. In this case, actually killing someone was held to be a strong indicator of having wanted to kill him, of making the crime "one's own."

However, it is extremely important to note that the court was at great pains to limit explicitly the applicability of this decision to Nazi trials. In evaluating precedents, the court discussed three prior decisions regarding perpetratorship in Nazi crimes.[60] In the first two cases, soldiers who shot civilians under orders were found to be accomplices, while in the last case, the accused was convicted as a perpetrator because he had shown particular "enthusiasm" during the executions. These precedents, the court said, did not in any way conflict with the current ruling that actually killing someone generally constituted perpetratorship. The situation of "soldiers" (all of the accused in the three precedent cases were in fact SS men) was declared to be unlike that of civilian defendants in murder cases: "The strict military hierarchy, the training of soldiers to follow orders without contradiction, and the general lack of education about the limits of this duty could lead to a situation where a commanding officer committed a criminal act by using his subordinates like tools. In this case, the orientation of these subordinates to the crime could not be adjudged to constitute a 'perpetrator's will' in the above sense."[61] In other words, the court declared that the current decision would not apply in Nazi cases, where different standards were to apply in keeping with the court's emphasis on "all the circumstances" of the crime.

Roxin criticized this restriction, arguing that the court itself was unaware of the full significance of its decision. He claimed that, even more clearly than in the preceding two decisions, this case committed the court to a quasi-objective theory of perpetratorship, presumably his *Tatherrschaft* theory. Roxin claimed that in two significant respects, this decision went beyond previous efforts to incorporate objective indices into a broadly subjective theory of perpetratorship. First of all, the court abandoned its prior emphasis on subordination to the will of another (as in, e.g., its decision of

[58] Ibid.
[59] Ibid.: 398.
[60] BGHSt, vol. 2 (1950): 251; NJW 4 (1951): 323; and unpublished decision, July 5, 1951, 3 StR 333/51.
[61] BGHSt, vol. 8 (1956): 397.

June 16, 1954), since in the current case, such subordination was present without affecting perpetratorship. Abandoning the notion of subordination of will, however, "practically means abandoning the subjective theory altogether."[62] Second, Roxin argued that the court considerably expanded the significance of the defendant's actual external contribution to a crime in this decision. In the previous cases, the court had said explicitly (if nonsensically, from Roxin's point of view) that the external contribution of the accused was not per se relevant to his status as perpetrator. In this case, however, with its emphasis on "all the circumstances" of the crime, such external indices were all that remained to indicate perpetration. In particular, the court declared the defendant to be a perpetrator, despite his subordination to the victim's wife, because he had personally undertaken to hit the victim over the head with an ax. According to Roxin, therefore, in this ruling, "perpetratorship is derived from the particular significance of the defendant's contribution to the crime, which the court had previously declared to be unimportant."[63] Thus, according to Roxin, the court had significantly expanded the significance of the objective determinants of perpetratorship without, however, fully realizing it. Indeed, the court maintained that it was still operating within the boundaries of the subjective theory, a situation likely to produce more confusion than clarity in further legal practice.[64]

On the other hand, Jürgen Baumann defended the apparent confusion of this decision, saying that in fact, the court was simply extending its consistent – and appropriate – application of the subjective theory. He noted that the court subsequently clarified this ruling (March 10, 1961), to indicate that "mastery over the act is merely one indicator of whether the defendant is a co-perpetrator, and the absence of (total?) [sic] mastery over the act at the time of commission is held to be legally irrelevant."[65] Baumann highlighted the fact (so self-contradictory in Roxin's view) that the court explicitly declared itself in agreement with previous, subjectively oriented decisions. He argued that the January 10, 1956, decision was simply intended to correct the "overstatement" of the interest theory in the *Badewannenfall*, in order to make it clear "that having an interest in the success of a criminal endeavor is only one of many possible indices [for perpetratorship]."[66] This decision was not, on Baumann's view, in any sense an incorporation of objective elements into the theory of perpetratorship in any role save as indicators of the

---

[62] Roxin, *Tatherrschaft*, p. 97.
[63] Ibid., p. 98.
[64] "The dichotomy between the substantive content and the theoretical justification manifest in this decision, makes it difficult to assess the impact this judgment might have on future judicial practice." Ibid., p. 98.
[65] Jürgen Baumann, "Tatherrschaft in der Rechtsprechung des BGH," NJW 15 (1962): 375.
[66] Ibid., p. 376.

(actually relevant) subjective orientation of will. That Baumann's assessment of the court's intentions was essentially correct, however accurate Roxin's critique of its confusions may have been, became manifest in the next major BGH decision regarding perpetratorship.

While there were several BGH decisions pertaining to perpetratorship in the interim, the court's next truly substantial decision came in 1962.[67] This was the infamous Staschynskij ruling. In this case, a KGB agent single-handedly murdered two Ukrainian émigrés in Germany. He was captured and convicted as an accomplice to murder. On appeal the BGH upheld his conviction as an accomplice, rather than as a perpetrator. The BGH stated: "In cases of murder, as with other crimes, an accomplice is anyone who does not commit the act as his own but merely participates, as a tool or assistant, in a foreign deed."[68] The court explicitly considered and rejected the so-called material-objective theory as "too schematic and narrow" because it ignored "certain special motives . . . which are very powerful yet are not encompassed in general criminology."[69] The court argued further that crimes committed under Nazism, for instance, would specifically fall outside such general criminological categories. It claimed that the criminal motives in this case were not necessarily those of the person actually carrying out the state's orders. "These dangerous criminal motives do not originate with the subordinate who carries out a given order but with the holders of state power who crassly misuse it."[70]

Thus, the BGH held that in the case of state-organized murder, in particular, the actual executioner may well not be the perpetrator, despite its earlier claim that directly killing someone *generally* constituted a prima facie indication of perpetratorship. However, it should be noted that the court did not entirely rule out the possibility that a subordinate acting on state orders *could* be a perpetrator. It held that "whosoever willingly yields to murderous political agitation, silences his conscience and incorporates alien criminal goals into the foundation of his own convictions and actions . . . is, as a rule, a perpetrator."[71] The court held that it was possible for a subordinate to be a perpetrator but only if it could be demonstrated that he had internalized the criminal motives of his superiors. In the case of Nazi trials, this meant effectively that prosecutors had to demonstrate that any given defendant had internalized the motives of the so-called main perpetrators (*Haupttäter*): Hitler, Himmler, and Heydrich.[72] The most obvious and widely criticized consequence of this way of interpreting the

---

[67] See the discussion in Roxin, *Tatherrschaft*, pp. 98–106.
[68] BGHSt, vol. 18 (1963): 89.
[69] Ibid., pp. 95 and 93.
[70] Ibid., pp. 93–94.
[71] Ibid., p. 94.
[72] On the doctrine of three main perpetrators, see Friedrich, *Die kalte Amnestie*, pp. 227–37.

subjective theory of perpetratorship was that it made it far more difficult to convict low-ranking Nazi offenders as perpetrators, rather than accomplices, with all of the sentencing advantages for the defendants that that implied.[73]

The Staschynskij decision clearly indicates that, whatever counter-tendencies may have been present in the court's previous rulings, it had no intention of abandoning the subjective theory in differentiating perpetrators from accomplices. In this respect, Baumann's interpretation of the court's direction proved to be more accurate than Roxin's. As can be imagined, Roxin was highly critical of the Staschynskij decision. He claimed that the only boundary remaining between a perpetrator and an accomplice after this ruling was whether a given participant was eager or reluctant to participate in the crime: "This, however, provides no usable marker of the distinction. The way that conviction and disapproval, agreement and weakness mix in the soul of a free actor is inaccessible to judicial inquiry, which often only takes place long after the fact."[74]

The German high court, however, seems to have remained unmoved by such arguments against the subjective theory. Indeed, while not generally deigning to address such criticisms directly, the court clearly rejected the logic of Roxin's *Tatherrschaft* theory as well as of any other variant of the objective theory, except insofar as pragmatic considerations compelled the court to allow objective indices to be considered in ascertaining the subjective disposition of defendants. As we shall see, in the Auschwitz Trial, this subjective distinction between a perpetrator and an accomplice was to become the source of considerable conflict and was the decisive factor in the way that the defense conducted its case.

Guilt and Agency

There is a third crucial category in German criminal law where subjectivism reigns supreme: guilt. Guilt is in many respects *the* foundational concept of criminal law. This is because whatever else it does, criminal law *punishes*, that is, it inflicts violence on people. This fact is brought out even more clearly in the German term *Strafrecht*, which literally translated means "punishment law." Although German law no longer recognizes the death penalty, these punishments are often quite serious, including life in prison and the permanent loss of citizenship rights for perpetrators of *Mord*. "Therefore," as one introductory textbook on German law puts it, "we are confronted with the most important problem for criminal law: What gives the state the right to

---

[73] See, e.g., ibid., pp. 350–59, and Ralph Giordano, *Die zweite Schuld oder Von der Last Deutscher zu sein* (Hamburg: Rasch und Röhring Verlag, 1987), pp. 130–31.

[74] Roxin, *Tatherrschaft*, p. 564.

subject its citizens to such far-reaching sanctions?"[75] If the state's sanction, that is, the violence that the state does to its citizens in the name of law, is not to be purely arbitrary, it must be justified on some basis. Indeed, it has been argued (by Max Weber, among others) that one of the defining characteristics of law is that it is *legitimate* violence.[76] But on what basis is this violence to be considered legitimate? The mere fact that there is a perceived need to justify the punitive function of law does not mean that this preordains the specific character of that justification, which tends to develop according to a logic of its own. The punitive character of law becomes, on this reading, at least partially a *hermeneutic* problem. In other words, law is both an act of violence and an act of interpretation, or as Robert Cover has put it: "Neither legal interpretation nor the violence which it occasions may be properly understood apart from one another."[77] In the western legal tradition, guilt has tended to serve as a category of both violence and interpretation, making it the legitimating category *par excellence* for criminal law.

It is true that there have been efforts to justify the law's penal sanctions without reference to guilt. In particular, instrumental theories have generally avoided making reference to the concept of guilt, at least as a normative category, preferring to focus on the instrumental goal that punishment is intended to pursue, namely, the prevention of crime. Punishment is simply a means to obtain some end and is justified on the basis of its efficiency in this regard. Such instrumental theories come in two forms: the theories of special and general prevention.

The theory of special prevention holds that it is the task of criminal law to deter a given individual perpetrator from committing any further crimes. It seeks to rehabilitate the criminal or to quarantine him, to make him once again into a citizen or to isolate him from the rest of society. In Germany, such an approach has been broadly therapeutic in orientation. According to this theory, society "is oriented toward healing rather than retribution."[78] This means that the legal order need not worry about finding some "transjuridical" justification for its sanctions "since it is not a matter of forcing acknowledgment of the law but only of reorienting anyone who deviates from the norm so that he becomes like every one else."[79] Such theories of

---

[75] Claus Roxin, Gunther Arzt, and Klaus Tiedemann, *Einführung in das Strafrecht, und Strafprozeßrecht*, 3rd rev. ed. (Heidelberg: C. F. Müller Juristischer Verlag, 1994), p. 2.

[76] Max Weber, *Economy and Society: An Outline of Interpretive Sociology*, vol. 1 (Berkeley: University of California Press, 1978), pp. 212–16.

[77] Robert Cover, "Violence and the Word," in *Narrative, Violence and the Law: The Essays of Robert Cover*, ed. Martha Minow et al. (Ann Arbor: University of Michigan Press, 1993), p. 203.

[78] Paul Bockelmann, *Schuld und Sühne*, 2nd ed. (Göttingen: Vandenhoeck & Ruprecht, 1958), p. 16.

[79] Ibid.

punishment are perforce highly critical of the concept of guilt. As Fritz Bauer, the Hessian Attorney General in charge of the Auschwitz Trial put it, "The concepts of guilt and atonement are the fool's gold of Pharisees who are, from a humane perspective, hardly encouraging and who make it difficult for the perpetrator to reintegrate into the social organism."[80]

The theory of general prevention, on the other hand, argues that the purpose of criminal sanction is to deter *potential* criminals, that is, "to motivate the general populace to obey the law."[81] It is not so much therapeutic as prophylactic, aiming to deter rather than amend. For theories of general prevention, punishment of individual perpetrators is justified because of the example it sets for other (potential) perpetrators. Like the theory of special prevention, though, the theory of general prevention needs no transjuridical justification; the justification of punishment is compliance with the law.

However important such deterrent theories are in legal and legislative practice, they ultimately fail as justifications for punishment.[82] The most basic criticism of both approaches is that they cannot specify the proper balance between means and ends, between punishment and deterrence. For instance, there is no reason, in principle, why the most draconian punishments could not be imposed for trivial crimes according to the theory of general prevention, based on the assumption that such extreme sentences would have considerable deterrent effect, no matter how tyrannical their general political consequences. On the other hand, the therapeutic inclination of the theory of special prevention tends actually to limit sharply the potential for punishment of any sort in favor of other forms of resocialization (e.g., medical treatment). Indeed, when there is little or no chance of the offender repeating the offense (as with Nazi crimes), it is hard to see how special prevention justifies any punishment whatsoever.[83] As for the theory of general prevention, since it treats the punishment of any given perpetrator as simply an example for the rest of the population, it is a matter of indifference what impact the sentence has on his own chances for resocialization or criminal recidivism. The individual perpetrator recedes to the status of a token, standing in for "punishment" as such. Why individuals selected at random could not serve equally well as such tokens cannot be explained by such a theory. Certainly, it has been a general consensus among German legal

---

[80] Fritz Bauer, *Das Verbrechen und die Gesellschaft* (Munich: Ernst Reinhardt Verlag, 1957), p. 173.

[81] Roxin et al., *Strafrecht*, p. 8.

[82] Ibid., pp. 7–8.

[83] Indeed, this represents an unresolved antinomy in the thought of Fritz Bauer, who was a strong advocate of the resocialization of criminals yet also, obviously, a key proponent of trying and punishing Nazi perpetrators. To the extent that he was aware of this paradox, he resolved it by stressing the pedagogical function of Nazi trials as a form of social therapy. See, e.g., Bauer, "Im Namen des Volkes," in Perels and Wojak, eds., *Die Humanität der Rechtsordnung*, p. 90.

scholars since World War II that such instrumental theories of punishment are inadequate.

Günther Jakobs sums up the dilemma that has caused German jurists largely to eschew purely instrumental theories of punishment and to embrace guilt as a foundational concept for criminal jurisprudence.[84] He argues that the concept of guilt (or some equivalent) must be used to legitimate punishment, lest the law violate Kant's categorical imperative and treat people as objects, rather than as subjects. Yet Kantian retributive justice likewise encounters problems that make it untenable as a viable alternative to instrumental theories of justice.[85] According to Jakobs, in modern societies, punishment must also serve some purpose, that is, must also be instrumental in orientation, or it likewise becomes illegitimate because it is literally purposeless.[86] Purely retributive justice lacks this instrumental dimension. The problem, according to Jakobs, is to justify punishment normatively without allowing that justification to interfere with the special and/or general preventative function of the law. Guilt can serve such a purpose if it is conceptualized in such a way that balances the retributive and instrumental aspects of punishment.

In practice, for German criminal law, this balance has been struck in the legal notion of "reproachability." This concept was first articulated in Reinhard Frank's seminal 1907 essay *On the Structure of Guilt as a Concept*, arguably the most significant German text on legal guilt since the time of Kant.[87] In a deliberate attempt to overcome what he perceived as the inadequacies of nineteenth-century legal thought, Frank proposed what was to become the working theory of guilt and punishment for the German legal system throughout most of the twentieth-century. Frank's essay began with a critique of the then dominant theories of guilt in the classical and modern schools of legal thought. He wrote: "As diversely as guilt is conceptualized in modern jurisprudence, there is nonetheless nearly unanimous agreement that the essence of guilt lies in a psychic relationship to a certain something

---

[84] Günther Jakobs, *Das Schuldprinzip* (Opladen: Westdeutscher Verlag, 1993), p. 8.

[85] For Kant, "only the law of retribution [*ius talionis*] – it being understood, of course, that this is applied by a court (not by your private judgment) – can specify definitely the quality and the quantity of punishment; all other principles are fluctuating and unsuited for a sentence of pure and strict justice because extraneous considerations are mixed into them." Immanuel Kant, *The Metaphysics of Morals*, trans. Mary Gregor (Cambridge: Cambridge University Press, 1996), pp. 105–6.

[86] "[I]f the principle of guilt substantially restricts the deployment of instrumental means, then punishment threatens to become unsuited to achieving it ends and *therefore* to become illegitimate." Jakobs, *Schuldbegriff*, p. 8.

[87] Reinhard Frank, *Über den Aufbau des Schuldbegriffs* (Giessen: Alfred Töpelmann, 1907). On Kant's influence, see Wolfgang Naucke, "Über den Einfluß Kants auf Theorie und Praxis des Strafrechts im 19. Jahrhundert," in J. Blühdorn and J. Ritter, eds., *Philosophie und Rechtswissenschaft: Zum Problem ihrer Beziehung im 19. Jahrhundert* (Frankfurt: Vittorio Klosterman, 1969); and also Gerd-Walter Küsters, *Kants Rechtsphilosophie* (Darmstadt: Wissenschaftliche Buchgesellschaft, 1988).

or the possibility of such a relationship."[88] This "something" was always seen to lie in the external world. It was not important, he argued, whether this "something" was a legal or factual category or whether the relationship itself was one of will or intent.[89] "The main point is the restriction of the concept of guilt to the internal side [of human beings]."[90] In effect what this internalist doctrine of guilt meant was that guilt was equated with intention or negligence and nothing else. Most significantly, according to Frank, what this approach to guilt neglected was the "accompanying circumstances" of the crime.[91]

However, he continued, if one turned to actual legal practice (or to the mundane linguistic usage of the term "guilt"), one saw immediately that such circumstances were highly relevant to the meaning of guilt. For instance, the courts regularly took the circumstances of a crime into account as mitigating the degree of the defendant's guilt. If circumstances could mitigate guilt, surely they could eliminate it altogether as well. (The classic example of such circumstances is duress, where the defendant acts under external compulsion.)[92] Therefore, Frank maintained, it was necessary to expand the concept of guilt to include external circumstances, as well as the internal factors of intention or negligence.

In fact, Frank claimed, the dominant theories of guilt missed two of the three elements of guilt. These were (1) the defendant's fitness to be tried (*Zurechnungsfähigkeit*), (2) his or her intention or negligence, and (3) the accompanying circumstances of the crime.[93] The existing theories could capture only the second element. Perhaps more significant, though, was the reason that the dominant theories missed these other elements of guilt. They treated the relation of guilt to intention/negligence as one of genus to species, that is to say, hierarchically, with guilt being seen as a superordinate category to intention/negligence. In reality, said Frank, guilt was a "composite concept" comprised of all three elements. What was needed, then, was a vocabulary that highlighted the equal significance of all three elements of guilt without privileging any one of them. Frank wrote: "In searching for a brief catch phrase which contains all the above named elements of guilt, I can

---

[88] Frank, *Schuldbegriff*, p. 3.
[89] There was a heated debate in the late nineteenth-century between Karl Binding and Franz von Liszt's protégé, Hugo Heinemann, over whether the essence of guilt lay in an abstractly denoted intention/will or in the psychological facticity of individual criminals. See, e.g., Karl Binding, *Die Normen und Ihre Übertretung: Eine Untersuchung über die rechtsmässige Handlung und die Arten des Delikts*, 2nd ed., 4 vols. (Leipzig: Felix Meiner, 1914 [1877]), and Hugo Heinemann, "Die Binding'sche Schuldlehre: Ein Beitrag zu ihrer Widerlegung," in Franz von Liszt, ed., *Abhandlungen des kriminalistischen Seminars zu Marburg* (Freiburg: J. C. B. Mohr, 1889).
[90] Frank, *Schuldbegriff*, p. 3.
[91] Ibid., p. 4.
[92] Ibid., p. 7.
[93] Ibid., p. 10.

find no term save reproachability [*Vorwerfbarkeit*]. Guilt is reproachability. The term is not elegant but I know no better."[94]

This term had several advantages, according to Frank. First, it could be derived both synthetically (as above) and analytically. Analytically, one could deduce the elements of guilt from the concept of guilt as follows: In order to reproach someone for his or her act, he or she must be fit to be reproached (capable of understanding his or her act) and have acted intentionally or negligently, and the circumstances of his or her act must be "normal," in the sense that they did not preclude guilt in some way. Second, the term was pragmatically useful in legal practice because it offered a unified explanation of both ordinary punishment and the omission of punishment in extraordinary situations (such as when the defendant acted under duress). Indeed, Frank argued, the Supreme Court (Reichsgericht) already took accompanying circumstances into account regularly. The current theories could explain this practice only in extremely convoluted ways, by expanding and contracting the meaning of intention as necessary. His theory offered a more elegant and logical foundation for existing legal practice.[95]

Indeed, German courts, especially in the post–World War II era, took up Frank's suggestions with vigor, but not only, and probably not even mainly, because of their logical elegance. Rather, the appeal was that Frank's theory offered a way to retain the moral rigor of Kantian retributivism while opening up a space for instrumental action within law; Frank's theory was seen as squaring the circle of retributive and instrumental punishment. Like retributive theories, it treats the perpetrator as an autonomous subject, yet in encompassing all the circumstances of the crime, it makes room for instrumental considerations as well.

Despite its insistence on the significance of accompanying circumstances, Frank's theory of guilt contains a profound emphasis on individual agency, a notion that individuals choose autonomously to act contra the law, and that it is this choice that grounds their legal reproof. Social results are viewed as being the consequence of free individual choices. The "accompanying circumstances" of a person's life are little more than the stage where such individual moral dramas play out; in the end, our lives are what we make of them, and in a very real sense, we *deserve* the results – for good or for ill. It is particularly significant that accompanying circumstances matter for Frank only when they are abnormal and that they can only ever preclude guilt, not cause it. Under ordinary circumstances, people choose their guilt. Under abnormal circumstances, their choices may be so circumscribed as to mitigate that guilt. But under any circumstances, guilt itself remains the result of free choice.

[94] Ibid., p. 11.
[95] Ibid., p. 15.

This was particularly important in the postwar era when the sterile legal positivism of the nineteenth-century tradition was often blamed for the all too eager cooperation of the German judiciary with the Nazi regime. In the aftermath of World War II, German courts sought a way to ground punishment in a moral category, without binding themselves to abstract categories too inflexible to combat the political intolerance and blind obedience they saw as the roots of Nazism. The courts seized on reproachability as just such a category. In 1952, the BGH declared (in a seminal ruling): "Punishment presupposes guilt. Guilt is reproachability. With the censuring verdict of guilt, the perpetrator is reproached that he did not behave in accordance with the law, that he could have decided in favor of the law. The internal foundation of the reproach of guilt resides in the fact that human beings are endowed with the capacity for free, responsible, ethical self-determination and, therefore, are capable of deciding for law and against illegality. . . . "[96]

The appeal of the concept of reproachability emerges quite plainly here; it lies in the decisionistic moment of reproach. The perpetrator is punished for his decision, for which he is responsible because he could have decided (and could in future decide) differently. Punishment therefore is a retribution for free action. At the same time, though, the threat of punishment can (and is expected to) be incorporated instrumentally into the decision-making process of perpetrators, both actual and potential – thus satisfying the demands of preventative theorists. This is the so-called unified theory of punishment.[97]

Frank himself foresaw this facet of his work (though without fully articulating its practical implications) when he argued that his approach overcame the apparent contradiction between what he called will-oriented and foresight-oriented theories of guilt. While will-oriented theories argued that guilt lay in willing a given criminal result, the foresight theories argued that what mattered was the perpetrator's specific notion about what would result from his action. In reality, these amounted to the same thing, Frank argued. Guilt arises from the willed activity undertaken in full (or partial) awareness of the consequences. "*Dolus* is the knowledge of the legal definition of a crime or the circumstances which ground the punishment of some act, when such knowledge accompanies a willed action."[98] In short, guilt is viewed as both will and foresight, a subjective capacity for orienting action according to external factors.

In this way, will as a faculty of practical reason, and foresight as an empirical factum, are simultaneously incorporated into the definition of guilt. In other words, based on an assumption of free will, the German legal system

---

[96] BGHSt, vol. 2 (1950): 200.
[97] In German: the *Vereinigungstheorie*. On this, see Roxin et al., *Einführung in das Strafrecht*, pp. 9 and 45–47.
[98] Frank, *Schuldbegriff*, p. 25.

assumes a specific kind of causal nexus between motivation and action, which renders human behavior susceptible to moral, and hence legal, judgment. In harmony with this assumption, the remaining categories of German criminal law have likewise focused on the subjective aspect of criminal behavior. If criminal law is, fundamentally, a law of guilt and if, in turn, guilt is fundamentally a matter of ill will enacted in a specific context, then what precisely a given defendant *willed* and the *relationship* between this will and the accompanying circumstances are matters of utmost consequence in the law. Hence the subjective distinctions between *Mord* and *Totschlag* and between a perpetrator and an accomplice derive from the foundational assumption that legal punishment is a legitimate reproach to the perpetrator for the crime that his will caused.

It was precisely this assumption of a causal nexus between motivation (will) and behavior that was to prove so troublesome during the Auschwitz Trial, however. The guilt of the defendants and their status as either perpetrators or accomplices depended heavily on how the court evaluated their subjective dispositions in Auschwitz. This determined to a degree not only what kind of evidence was sought and presented in the trial, but also how that evidence was evaluated and interpreted. Yet this strong focus on the will of the individual defendants as the central category in determining their guilt made it extremely difficult for the trial to understand adequately or to render judgment on Auschwitz.

Auschwitz, after all, was not just a site of murder; it was an apparatus of extermination. It was the lethal apex of a vast bureaucratic system, involving literally hundreds of thousands of perpetrators, all designed to annihilate not just individuals qua individuals – though the camp certainly did that as well – but entire racially defined groups, Jews in particular. This points to two aspects of Nazi genocide that German criminal law was particularly ill suited to grasping. First, as Max Weber pointed out, one of the central reasons for the superior efficiency of bureaucracies over other forms of social coordination is that they render the subjective motives of their individual members structurally irrelevant to coordinated social outcomes.[99] In other words, the fact that the court found that the defendants in the Auschwitz Trial participated in genocide and other atrocities for a wide variety of motives made an enormous difference legally, even though those subjective differences in orientation had been functionally irrelevant in Auschwitz. Second, the driving force behind Auschwitz – but not necessarily behind every individual perpetrator – had been a violent anti-Semitic ideology. It is true that recent empirical studies have challenged somewhat Hannah Arendt's thesis that bureaucrats in the Holocaust represented a banal evil, an evil without passion, an evil of "thoughtlessness" as she called it, a technocratic, rather than

[99] Weber, *Economy and Society*, pp. 956–1005.

an ideological evil.[100] Nonetheless, the court found, plausibly enough, that the defendants had acted on the basis of a wide range of individual motives. Consequently, the driving force of anti-Semitic passion as itself one of the central *causes* of Auschwitz, irregardless of whether any given perpetrator happened to share personally that anti-Semitism, became difficult to discern, save as a matter of Hitler's own subjective will. That anti-Semitism could become structurally causal in ways that extended beyond the subjective orientation of individuals, including Hitler, was something the court could not grasp adequately given the legal understanding of guilt.

In this context, the accompanying circumstances of any individual action must be viewed as at least potentially causal, not merely mitigating. Guilt as reproachability, in this context, makes it exceedingly difficult to assess the social causation of the Holocaust.[101] Consequently, one of the German law's most basic assumptions – that individual actions are the sole result of individual decisions – is challenged by the very character of the most significant set of crimes any legal system has ever had to confront.

[100] Hannah Arendt, *The Life of the Mind* (New York: Harcourt, Brace, Jovanovich, 1978), pp. 3–4. For empirical challenges to Arendt's thesis, see, among others, Michael Thad Allen, *The Business of Genocide: The SS, Slave Labor, and the Concentration Camps* (Chapel Hill: University of North Carolina Press, 2002); Yaacov Lozowick, *Hitler's Bureaucrats: The Nazi Security Police and the Banality of Evil*, trans. Haim Watzman (London: Continuum, 2000); and Michael Wildt, *Generation des Unbedingten: Das Führungskorps des Reichssicherheitshauptamtes* (Hamburg: Hamburger Edition, 2002).

[101] Generally, H. L. A. Hart and A. M. Honoré, *Causation in the Law*, 2nd ed. (Oxford: Clarendon, 1985).

3

The Trial Actors

As an aspect of social dramas, trials obviously have actors, and this in a dual sense. The participants in a trial are actors in the sociological sense of being agents, that is, those who enact and, in a significant sense, "cause" the events that unfold. But trial participants are also actors in the theatrical sense that they have prescribed roles to play. The script in a trial is of course much looser and more improvisational than in most plays, but it is no less a script for that. Who the trial actors are, which roles they play, the kinds of things they can and cannot say, and their scope for effective action are all largely prescribed by the structure of law and the code of criminal procedure. Agency in a trial thus consists in improvisational variations on legally established themes.[1]

In this sense, one can usefully compare the relationship between law and legal actors to that between strategy and tactics in the sense developed by the French social theorist, Michel de Certeau. For de Certeau, strategies are "force-relationships" exercised autonomously on an exterior environment by a "subject of will and power," whether an individual or, more typically, an institution. Tactics, by contrast, are a calculus of force relationships exercised by those without such an autonomous social location.[2] If strategies, according to de Certeau, are the sovereign imposition of a "political, economic and scientific rationality" on an exterior domain (everyday life), "a tactic insinuates itself into the other's place, fragmentarily, without taking it over in its entirety, without being able to keep it at a distance."[3] Thus,

---

[1] Cf. William H. Sewell's claim that social structures "are constituted by mutually sustaining cultural schemas and sets of resources that empower and constrain social action and tend to be reproduced by that action." William H. Sewell, Jr., "A Theory of Structure: Duality, Agency, and Transformation," *American Journal of Sociology* 86 (July 1992): 27. Law, however, has a more rigid, formal dimension to it, what I am calling the juridical, than most social structures not based on specific written codes.

[2] Michel de Certeau, *The Practice of Everyday Life*, trans. Steven Rendall (Berkeley: University of California Press, 1984), p. xix.

[3] Ibid.

according to de Certeau, strategy constitutes autonomy, a sign of power. Tactics are grafted onto the strategies of others and, as such, constitute the "weapons of the weak."[4] Tactical autonomy consists only in the clever manipulation of existing strategic sites or structures. But as manipulations, tactics do open the possibility of autonomy, of agency. They create "ways of operating," "styles" that "intervene in a field which regulates them at a first level... but they introduce into it a way of turning it to their advantage that obeys other rules and constitutes something like a second level interwoven into the first."[5] In this sense, then, the law itself can be said to constitute the strategic field on which legal actors, including even such seemingly sovereign agents as judges and prosecutors, tactically improvise their activities; the law constrains and channels but does not determine in detail the actions of individuals.

In this chapter, I analyze the roles played by the major categories of actors in the Frankfurt Auschwitz Trial. I am here concerned with these roles in their "typical," strategic instantiations, that is, what would *ordinarily* be expected of the various categories of trial actors in a German courtroom. Clearly, not all actors in the Auschwitz Trial conformed exactly to these expectations. They pursued their own tactics. But in the main, the obligations and opportunities for action stipulated by German law channeled the conduct of the Auschwitz Trial participants in discernable ways. It is particularly important to note that the actors in German trials, while superficially occupying positions similar to those of their American or British counterparts, in fact operated under often substantially different ground rules. Of course the tactical improvisations by German trial actors were also determined by their individual personalities and their extra-legal cultural, political, and moral values as well; legal actors do not cease to be human beings on entering the courtroom. Bauer, Düx, and Langbein all provide examples of how important individual values and experiences could be for the course of events. However, as the prehistory of the Auschwitz Trial demonstrates, even the most capable and resourceful individuals were forced to act within the established context of law. This becomes even truer when the scene of action shifts to the courtroom itself.

Furthermore, the unfortunate fact is that very little biographical information is available regarding many of the participants in the Auschwitz Trial. This makes it often difficult to ascertain the degree to which individual personalities and histories shaped behavior. Often, the best one can hope for is to be able to extrapolate subjective contributions to the trial from the deviations in behavior from the legally stipulated norm. For example, the

---

[4] "The weak must continually turn to their own ends forces alien to them." Ibid. Cf. James C. Scott, *Weapons of the Weak: Everyday Forms of Peasant Resistance* (New Haven: Yale University Press, 1985).

[5] Ibid., pp. 29–30.

GDR civil counsel Friedrich Kaul's persistent endeavors to turn the trial into a platform for East German propaganda clearly owed more to his political obligations to the Politburo than they did to the West German code of criminal procedure. Only if one understands the precise nature of the role assigned by law to the various actors can one hope to ascertain where the official script ended and their improvisations began.

German Courts

The composition of German courts and the authority granted to various actors are dictated under German law by the StPO (Strafprozeßordnung, Criminal Procedure Act) and the GVG (Gerichtsverfassungsgesetz, Constitution of Courts Act), both enacted in 1877.[6] In the 1960s, major criminal cases were tried before so-called *Schwurgerichte*, which were state courts (*Landgerichte*) designated to try serious criminal offenses per §§79–80 GVG. Trials before such courts had seven main groups of actors: judges, jurors, prosecuting attorneys, counsel for the civil plaintiffs (*Nebenkläger*), defense counsel, defendants, and witnesses. Each of these groups of actors had a distinct relationship to the law and to the state. Broadly speaking, one could divide these groups into those who represented the state in one way or another (judges, jurors, prosecutors) and those who represented private citizens, either in confrontation with the state (defendants, defense counsel) or as adjuncts to the state (civil plaintiffs, witnesses). One could further categorize these groups according to whether they were charged with applying the law (judges, jurors, attorneys), were on trial under the law (defendants), or were to serve as aides to the law (witnesses). In other words, some actors were structurally the subjects of law in the trial, others were its direct objects, and still others were the indirect objects of law. These distinct relations to the law and to the state helped to determine the kinds of tactical improvisations available to the various trial actors within the context of the strategic field of law itself.

Under German law, judges and jurors can be said to comprise the court proper. *Schwurgerichte,* like the Auschwitz court, were comprised of three sitting judges and six regular jurors (§81 GVG). In addition, because the trial was expected to take a long time to complete, the Auschwitz court had two alternate judges and three alternate jurors. Two of the alternate jurors eventually served as regular jurors.[7] In principle, there is little division of

---

[6] *Strafprozeßordnung, Gerichtsverfassungsgesetz, Nebengesetze und ergänzende Bestimmungen,* Beck'sche Kurzkommentare, vol. 6, commented by Otto Schwarz and Theodor Kleinknecht (Munich: C. H. Beck'sche Verlagsbuchhandlung, 1963). Hereafter StPO or GVG, depending on whether the Criminal Procedure Act or the Constitution of Courts Act is being cited. The commentary itself will be cited as Schwarz and Kleinknecht, *Kurzkommentar.*

[7] Hermann Langbein, *Der Auschwitz-Prozeß: Eine Dokumentation,* vol. 2 (Frankfurt Verlag Neue Kritik, 1995), p. 934.

labor between judges and jurors in German trials. Both decide matters of both fact and law, and both decide together the final verdicts and the sentences to be imposed. They both have equal authority in the course of the trial (§84 GVG), and both groups are given an equal voice in deciding the final verdict (§82 GVG).

At the time of the Auschwitz Trial, German courts for serious criminal offenses were so-called mixed courts, an amalgam of a judicial and a jury court. Despite their formal equality, however, jurors are, in practice, much less proactive during a trial than German judges are. Because the German criminal system is, like most continental legal systems, inquisitorial, rather than, as in the Anglo-American system, antagonistic, the role of the judge during a trial is both more active and more decisive.[8] German judges do not merely regulate the conflict between two antagonistic parties, leaving it to the jury to decide the ultimate outcome; nor are they restricted to deciding matter of law, leaving determinations of fact to the jury. Rather, German judges combine the disparate functions of cross-examining witnesses, deciding on legal motions, and passing sentence on the accused; they are quite literally judge, jury, and examining attorney all in one.

It is the judges, the presiding judge (*Gerichtsvorsitzender*), above all, who do the lion's share of the questioning in a trial, not the competing attorneys. It is the judges who articulate – both orally, at the trial's conclusion, and in written form, as the basis for future appeals and precedents – the evidentiary and legal bases for the final verdict(s). German judges are under a strict obligation to evaluate the case in terms of the statutory penal code. "The task of the judge is to decide or regulate events that are presented to him in accordance with the legal order. Judicial activity consists in the application of law."[9] In this sense, although judges (and jurors) are free to evaluate evidence according to their individual consciences, they are strictly bound to written, positive law.

Fundamentally, therefore, the German judge is an inquisitor, rather than a referee. One must be careful not to confuse an inquisitor with a prosecutor, however. The German judge, in principle, represents neither the prosecution nor the defense but rather stands under an obligation "to investigate the truth by virtue of his or her office."[10] The judge is expected to be strictly nonpartisan. As an inquisitor, it is his obligation and right to evaluate any and all evidence relevant to the final verdict according to his free conscience, the so-called principle of "free evidentiary evaluation" (*freie*

---

[8] On the differences between inquisitorial and antagonistic legal systems, see René David and John E. C. Brierley, *Major Legal Systems in the World Today: An Introduction to the Comparative Study of Law*, 2nd ed. (New York: Free Press, 1978 [1968]).

[9] Karl Peters, *Strafprozeß: Ein Lehrbuch*, 4th ed. (Heidelberg: C. F. Müller Juristischer Verlag, 1985), p. 106.

[10] StPO, §244.

Beweiswürdigung).[11] This stands in contrast both to pre-nineteenth-century German legal practice and Anglo-American criminal procedure, where the rules of evidence were and are often much stricter.[12]

It is this obligation to evaluate freely any and all evidence that grounds the judicial interrogation of witnesses under German law. However, this questioning is done, again in contrast to the Anglo-American legal system, on the basis of an extensive written indictment. In other words, the judge is presented with a complete case, with all the relevant testimony and evidence, prior to the official convening of the trial. Because this indictment represents the prosecution's case, however, and not a judicial verdict, it does not obviate the need to conduct a formal, public trial. Nor is a judge constrained only to investigate the evidence presented by the prosecution or the defense (though he or she is obligated to accept motions to introduce evidence, insofar as these are deemed relevant to the proceedings).[13]

In the Auschwitz Trial, the presiding judge was Hans Hofmeyer.[14] Born in 1905, he studied law at Frankfurt, Munich, and Gießen.[15] He completed the first state exam in 1928 and the second in 1931. In 1936, Hofmeyer was appointed a municipal judge (*Amtsgerichtsrat*). During the war, he served as a military judge, although despite the best efforts of the East German press to imply otherwise, he apparently did not engage in any overtly objectionable activities during this time.[16] In this respect, Hofmeyer's career was typical of many of the judges who presided over German Nazi trials. Because only relatively senior judges were allowed to preside over serious criminal cases, the presiding judges in Nazi cases had for the most part come of age professionally during the Third Reich. The pragmatic (and perhaps ideological) decision not to pursue an overly vigorous Denazification policy within the judiciary meant that more often than not the judges being asked to try Nazi cases had themselves been more or less active judicial participants in the Nazi regime.[17] Unsurprisingly, many survivors, as well as the entirety of the East German press, found this system to be perverse.

[11] StPO, §261.
[12] E.g., German courts allow hearsay evidence under certain circumstances, unlike American courts. See Claus Roxin, Gunther Arzt, and Klaus Tiedemann, *Einführung in das Strafrecht und Strafprozeßrecht*, 3rd rev. ed. (Heidelberg: C. F. Müller Juristischer Verlag, 1994), pp. 129–30.
[13] §244 StPO.
[14] The adjunct judges were Walter Hotz and Josef Perseke. Werner Hummerich and Günter Seiboldt served as alternate judges. Perseke also served as *Berichterstatter*, which is to say that he took the court's official notes and was responsible for drafting the final written verdict.
[15] The following information comes from Gerhard Ziegler, "Fanatiker der Sachlichkeit: Hans Hofmeyer – der Vorsitzende im Auschwitz-Prozeß," *Die Zeit*, August 27, 1965.
[16] See, e.g., "Prozeß gegen SS-Henker von Auschwitz," *Neues Deutschland*, December 21, 1963.
[17] Ingo Müller, *Furchtbare Juristen: Die unbewältigte Vergangenheit unserer Justiz* (Munich: Knauer, 1989), pp. 210–21.

After the war, Hofmeyer returned to Frankfurt where he resumed his judicial activities, initially as a judge in the criminal courts, and then throughout the mid- to late 1950s in the civil courts, before returning to the criminal courts shortly prior to the start of the Auschwitz Trial. Initially, Hofmeyer had been intended to serve not as the presiding judge in the Auschwitz case but as an associate judge. However, the initial presiding judge, Hans Forester, was removed from the case in the fall of 1963 due to a possible conflict of interest, as he had relatives who had been persecuted by the Nazis.[18] In general Hofmeyer's career can be summed up as follows: "Hofmeyer had neither a 'meteoric career' nor was he well known to the public through spectacular trials. His career proceeded in a thoroughly 'normal' manner. It was the dead straight path of an outstanding jurist and a seasoned trial leader, who was fully capable of handling every stage of a trial."[19]

Judge Hofmeyer's case reveals the complex interaction between individual biography and stipulated role in legal trials. On the one hand, little in Hofmeyer's background indicated that he was likely to be up to the task of managing a trial of such magnitude, much less balancing the competing demands of law, morality, history, and politics that emerged in the Auschwitz Trial. And yet he clearly grew into his role during this trial. As *Die Welt* put it: "The presiding judge in the Auschwitz Trial is a sober man given to intellectual pleasures, disdainful of judicial fireworks. If there is any such thing as a healthy human understanding, then he possesses it. He often poses one or two questions more than another judge would because he cannot understand what cannot be understood."[20] In particular, his tone of skeptical irony when confronted with blatant falsehoods on the part of the defendants or some particularly egregious lawyerly chicanery on the part of the defense attorneys set the tone for the trial as a whole. Hofmeyer never let the profound moral seriousness of the proceedings drop from sight. Clearly, he himself was deeply moved by the trial in ways that a "good," that is, nonpartisan, German judge ordinarily would not admit. Hofmeyer concluded his oral verdict by noting with evident emotion that he would never again be able to look into the eyes of a child without seeing the "hollow and uncomprehending eyes" of the children who died at Auschwitz.[21] Writing in the *Sonntagsblatt*, Hans Schüler commented, "This judge, as little adept at rhetorical eloquence as the majority of his professional colleagues, found words at the end of the trial to indicate that he and the court he led for twenty months

---

[18] See Beschluß, 3. Strafkammer, FFM, "Entbindung Senatspräsident Forester wegen Besorgnis der Befangenheit" (October 14, 1963), FFStA 4 Ks 2/63, Bd. 88, Bl. 17212. Cf. "Vorsitzender für den Auschwitz-Prozeß gesucht," *FNP*, October 22, 1963, and "Beginn des Auschwitz-Prozesses wieder fraglich," *FAZ*, October 22, 1963.

[19] Ziegler, "Fanatiker der Sachlichkeit."

[20] "Vorsitzender: Sie können uns doch nicht einseitig informieren," *Die Welt*, March 21, 1964.

[21] Tape recording (hereafter TR), August 20, 1963, 183rd Session, FBI SAP, CD AP365, T66–67.

represented a justice that can only be inadequately symbolized by a blind goddess."[22]

And yet this same judge, capable of articulating such a powerful personal vision of the moral consequences of Auschwitz, remained very much bound to his assigned role. "It is certain," he declared early in his judgment, "that this is a normal criminal trial, whatever its background. The court could only pass judgment according to the laws it has sworn to uphold. And these laws demand, on both the subjective and objective sides, an exact determination of the concrete guilt of the defendants."[23] This was not, he insisted, "an Auschwitz Trial... but rather a trial against Mulka and others."[24] After the trial was over, Hofmeyer even tried to persuade his colleagues that such large-scale, systematic trials were unworkable and violated the legal rights of the accused. As a consequence, he argued, they should be discontinued in favor of multiple, smaller trials custom-tailored to individual defendants.[25] In other words, whatever personal impact the Auschwitz Trial may have had on Hans Hofmeyer the man, however much his inability to ever look into the eyes of children again without thinking of Auschwitz may have marked a biographical rupture for him, Hans Hofmeyer the judge remained bound and committed to his judicial role in the strictest possible sense. For him, law prescribed the character of justice, not the other way around. Not even Auschwitz could change this.

Of course, Hofmeyer did not determine the Auschwitz verdict alone. Not only were the other judges actively involved; so too were the jurors. German jurors play both a more active and less decisive role than do their Anglo-American counterparts. Unlike Anglo-American jurors, German jurors decide matters of law as well as matters of fact. According to §§30, 82 GVG, jurors "exercise the judicial office to the full extent and with the same right to vote as professional judges."[26] German jurors are excluded only from making decisions over whether to admit evidence, witnesses, or counsel to the proceedings.[27] Otherwise, they fully participate in all legal decisions during the trial, such as whether to allow a given defendant to be taken into investigative custody (*Untersuchungshaft*).[28] However, because the professional judges participate in the final determination of guilt and in the

[22] Hans Schüler, "Das Urteil: Nach dem Auschwitz-Prozeß," *Sonntagsblatt*, August 29, 1965.
[23] TR, August 19, 1963, 182nd Session, FBI SAP, CD AP357, T39.
[24] Ibid., T13.
[25] Hans Hofmeyer, "Prozessrechtliche Probleme und praktische Schwierigkeiten bei der Durchführung der Prozesse," in Ständigen Deputation des deutschen Juristentages, ed., *Probleme der Verfolgung und Ahndung von nationalsozialistischen Gewaltverbrechen: Sonderveranstaltung des 46. Deutschen Juristentages in Essen*, vol. 2 (Munich: C. H. Beck'sche Verlagsbuchhandlung, 1967).
[26] §82 GVG. See also §30 GVG.
[27] §§27, 31 StPO.
[28] Schwarz and Kleinknecht, *Kurzkommentar*, p. 661.

sentencing process, German jurors do not have the exclusive right to determine the fate of the accused accorded their Anglo-American counterparts.

Thus, in German mixed courts the question of the deliberative process itself is decisive in determining the influence of jurors on trial verdicts. Under German law, the presiding judge directs the deliberations and counts the final vote(s).[29] The vote itself is determined by absolute majority.[30] Jurors vote by age, starting with the youngest. They vote before the professional judges, who vote by seniority.[31] Given that there were six jurors and only three judges in the Auschwitz Trial, the jurors in principle were decisive in deciding the verdicts. The fact that the jurors vote before the judges during deliberations is clearly intended to protect their decision-making autonomy. In practice, however, it is difficult to imagine that the professional judges did not dominate the determinations of both law and fact. This cannot be demonstrated on the basis of the documentary record, since the court's deliberations were kept strictly secret and no notes were entered into the record. However, Hofmeyer, as the presiding judge, led the deliberations and was thus largely in a position to dictate the framework for the discussions and to establish the specific issues to be considered. Indeed, German law even dictates the general content and the specific sequence of the deliberations.[32] In particular, given the complexities surrounding the question of perpetratorship and mitigating circumstances under German law, it seems especially likely that in the Auschwitz Trial, the professional judges would have dominated the discussion of this particularly important issue.[33]

Legal commentators have noted that, in the postwar period, the jury system has become fully integrated into German criminal legal procedure. However, "particularly in big trials that last months or even years, it can be doubted whether the participation of judicial lay persons has any demonstrable value. The jury court, a cornerstone of Anglo-American criminal proceedings, plays for us rather a symbolic role oriented toward democratic representation."[34] Given the class and gender composition of the Auschwitz trial jury, it seems particularly likely that it functioned in such a symbolic role. Four of the six jurors were women. Three of these were housewives and one was a secretary. The two men were both workers. Similarly, two of the three alternate jurors were housewives and the third was a (male) clerk.[35] This preponderance of women on the Auschwitz jury who did not have paid

[29] §194 GVG.

[30] §196 GVG.

[31] §197 GVG. There are partial exceptions to these rules, in that the *Berichterstatter* always votes first and the presiding judge always votes last.

[32] Schwarz and Kleinknecht, *Kurzkommentar*, p. 716.

[33] On mitigating circumstances, see BGHSt 4 (1954), pp. 8–11.

[34] Roxin et al., *Strafrecht*, p. 143.

[35] See Langbein, *Auschwitz-Prozeß*, vol. 2, p. 934. Two of the initial six regular jurors were forced to withdraw due to illness during the trial and were replaced by alternates.

employment can be accounted for by the fact that it was all but impossible for anyone else to dedicate over a year and a half to the task of being a juror in this case.[36]

Given that no biographical information beyond their names and occupations is available for the Auschwitz Trial jurors, it is impossible to draw any but the most speculative conclusions regarding their likely interaction with the professional judges on the court.[37] Nonetheless, it seems likely that the Auschwitz jurors remained largely passive spectators in the trial, their deliberations and decisions strongly shaped by the professional judges. In a society as hierarchical and deferential as Germany's still was in the early 1960s, it is difficult to imagine a housewife or an industrial worker openly contradicting the opinion of an academically certified professional judge on matters of law. In particular, legal decisions in German trials are matters of "subsumption," that is, of evaluating the established facts of a case in terms of their specific "fit" with the relevant legal statutes. Under these circumstances, a fairly refined technical understanding of the specific content of the law becomes imperative to the decision-making process, particularly if the decision is to survive the appeals process. And it is precisely in this arena that professional judges would have had a decisive advantage over lay jurors. It seems plausible therefore to suppose that the deliberations in the Auschwitz Trial were in fact dominated by the professional judges and that the jurors played at best a minor role in deciding both the final verdict and any legal motions brought before the court during the trial.[38]

Unlike the court proper, the prosecution in German criminal cases is not completely independent in a formal sense. Prosecutors are civil servants and, as such, are legally subordinate to their bureaucratic superiors.[39] At the same time, however, prosecutors also stand under an explicit obligation to aid in determining the legal "truth" in a given case. As Karl Peters puts it in his analysis of German criminal procedure, "the law is not a boundary condition for prosecutorial activity but rather its goal."[40] In other words, unlike their Anglo-American counterparts, German prosecutors are not strictly partisan actors in a trial whose exclusive goal is to present their case in the best light

---

[36] A number of potential jurors asked to be excused for work-related reasons, while others pled health concerns or other excuses. See FFStA 4 Ks 2/63, Bd. 126, Bl. 20458, Bl. 20543–44, Bl. 20461–63, Bl. 20467, Bl. 20473–80.

[37] The jurors rejected a request from the *Frankfurter Rundschau* to interview them during the trial for a newspaper profile. See Hofmeyer to *Frankfurter Rundschau* (March 24, 1964), FFStA 4 Ks 2/63, Bd. 91, Bl. 17854.

[38] Defense attorney Hans Laternser expressed his own, admittedly tactically motivated, skepticism concerning the ability of the jurors to reach an independent conclusion in such a complex case. See Hans Laternser, *Die andere Seite im Auschwitz-Prozeß, 1963–1965: Reden eines Verteidigers* (Stuttgart: Seewald Verlag, 1966), pp. 54–55.

[39] §146 GVG.

[40] Peters, *Strafprozeß*, pp. 161–62.

possible. Rather, they are civil servants under a dual obligation to the state and to the law.[41] In principle, they function as a "bridge" between the executive and the judiciary.[42] "The prosecutor is obligated to aid the judge in his struggle to find the actual facts of the case and to properly apply the law."[43] Given that the state generally has an undeniable interest in securing a conviction, this places prosecutors in a somewhat ambivalent position. They must seek to present a compelling case but are not allowed, under the law, to resort to the kind of one-sided maneuvers possible in American courts.[44]

Under the so-called legality principle, German prosecutors have both the exclusive right to bring criminal charges and also, if there is sufficient evidence that a crime has been committed, a formal obligation in fact to do so.[45] Naturally, this obligation carries with it an obligation to investigate all suspected crimes as well. It does not matter whether the victims of the crime have made a private complaint.[46] This obligation to investigate under the legality principle explains the fact that, despite manifest reluctance, the Stuttgart prosecutor's office immediately began an investigation against Boger on receipt of Rögner's allegations.[47]

There are two ways in which the prosecutor's office can initiate formal judicial proceedings in a case.[48] In complex cases, the office can move to open a formal preliminary investigation (*Voruntersuchung*) under the supervision of an investigating magistrate prior to drafting an indictment; in simple cases, it can simply issue an indictment immediately. Because the Auschwitz case was enormously complex, the prosecution requested a judicial investigation prior to drafting a formal indictment. In this sense, one could say that the prosecutor's office formally initiated the Auschwitz Trial twice, once by requesting a judicial investigation and once by submitting a formal indictment. In practice, these two moments actually flowed rather seamlessly into one another, since the written indictment was heavily based on the results of the preliminary judicial investigation.

Because, under German law, it is the judges rather than the attorneys who dominate the interrogation of witnesses and defendants during the course

---

[41] It should be noted that the prosecution's juridical obligation is to the law, not to the courts. Prosecutors are explicitly viewed as independent of the courts. §150 GVG.

[42] Schwarz and Kleinknecht, *Kurzkommentar*, p. 680.

[43] Ibid., p. 681.

[44] German prosecutors have a legal obligation, for instance, to present any exculpatory evidence to the court. Ibid., p. 680.

[45] Peters, *Strafprozeß*, pp. 167–71. See also §152 StPO. There are limited exceptions to this rule under the so-called opportunity principle and with private charges, neither of which applied in the Auschwitz case. See §153 StPO and §374 StPO.

[46] Roxin, Arzt and Tiedemann, *Strafrecht*, p. 151.

[47] See chapter 1.

[48] §170 StPO.

of the trial itself, prosecutors (and defense attorneys) play a much more limited role during a trial than do their Anglo-American counterparts. Like the defense, prosecutors have the right to cross-examine witnesses, but in a more supplementary than leading role.[49] Therefore, one could say that the single most important contribution that German prosecutors make to a trial is the drafting of the formal written indictment at the conclusion of the preliminary investigation. This formal indictment recommends the charges to be brought against the defendant(s), though these are not formally finalized until a court passes the so-called order to convene (*Eröffnungsbeschluß*). For instance, as we see below, the Auschwitz indictment recommended that all of the defendants be charged as perpetrators of *Mord*, but the order to convene reduced the charges against more than half of the defendants to accessory to *Mord*. The formal indictment also presents what the prosecutors take to be the relevant evidence in the case as determined by the results of the preliminary investigation. "The prosecutor's office must consider how to structure the indictment, how to portray the essential results of the investigation and what evidence to present in order to thus influence the course of the main proceedings. The proper selection of evidence, i.e., that evidence which best serves the truth, secures the proper trial result."[50] In effect, the prosecution prepares and presents its entire case *before* the trial; their task during the trial is to make sure the points made in the indictment are sufficiently considered. During the course of the main proceedings, the judges will conduct their interrogations largely on the basis of this indictment. Thus, it is indirectly, by means of the indictment, that the prosecution shapes and directs the course of the trial.

The prosecution's second moment in the sun, so to speak, comes at the end of the main proceedings, when they present their *Plädoyers*, or closing arguments. German *Plädoyers* are somewhat different from Anglo-American closing arguments, in that they contain specific sentencing recommendations as well as general arguments about relevant matters of fact and law. They are, quite literally, *pleas*. In German trials, the prosecution makes its closing arguments before those of the civil counsel or the defense. The prosecution thus presents the court with its first synthetic overview of how the trial ought to be interpreted.

There were four prosecutors in the Auschwitz Trial.[51] The lead prosecutor was Hanns [*sic*] Großmann, who was promoted to *Oberstaatsanwalt* during the course of the trial.[52] Großmann was not particularly active during the trial, though as we have seen, he did participate actively in the preliminary

49 Peter, *Strafprozeß*, p. 178.
50 Ibid., pp. 546–47.
51 See Langbein, *Auschwitz-Prozeß*, vol. 2, p. 934.
52 Großmann's name is spelled "Hans" in Langbein and other sources, but in the files, he himself signed it Hanns.

investigation. Most of the day-to-day work was left to his three subordinates: Joachim Kügler, Georg Friedrich Vogel, and Gerhard Wiese. They served as *Sachbearbeiter*, that is, they were charged with the detail work on the case, the evaluation of the evidence, the drafting of the indictment, the cross-examination of the witnesses, and, in their closing arguments, making the case against the individual defendants.

Unlike either the court or the prosecution, the remaining participants in a German trial are private actors with no immediate relation to the state. This does not mean, however, that their field of action is not legally regulated. On the contrary, the code of criminal procedure stipulates in some detail the obligations and powers of these private actors as well. They remain, in this sense, tactical agents operating within the strategic boundaries of law. From an Anglo-American perspective, perhaps the most unusual private actors in German trials are the civil plaintiffs, so-called *Nebenkläger*. These are victims or their immediate family who join the prosecution in accusing the defendants.[53] Literally translated, the term means "associate accusers," and as the term implies, the counsel for the *Nebenkläger* function as adjunct prosecutors. Unlike the official state prosecutors, the civil counsel play no official role in the investigative stage of the trial or in the preparation of the written indictment, though the prosecution may informally keep them abreast of developments.[54] Their primary role is to represent the interests of the victims during the actual trial.

The civil counsel have most of the same rights in a trial as prosecutors do.[55] They can call and cross-examine witnesses. They can make motions to present evidence. They are allowed to make a closing argument, which need not correspond with the pleas entered by the prosecution. Since civil counsel do not participate in the drafting of the indictment, it is largely in their closing arguments that they are able to *interpret* the evidence, to provide a coherent factual and legal account of the crime and the culpability of the defendants.

In the Auschwitz Trial, there were two groups of *Nebenkläger*. In the first instance, there were fifteen relatives of Auschwitz victims from twelve different countries, who were represented by two attorneys, Henry Ormond and his associate Christian Raabe.[56] Ormond had served as a prosecutor and judge in the Weimar Republic. Arrested by the Gestapo and sent to

---

[53] In addition to relatives of victims, other categories of persons are eligible to serve as civil plaintiffs as well, though none did so in the Auschwitz Trial. See §395 StPO.

[54] Thus, the Frankfurt prosecutor's office corresponded periodically with civil counsel Henry Ormond, informing him of the important developments in the investiation. See, e.g., Vogel to Ormond (December 29, 1961), FFStA HA 4 Ks 2/63, Bd. 8, Bl. 1405, informing him that Mulka had been released from investigative detention.

[55] §397 StPO.

[56] See the list enclosed in Ormond to FFStA (November 4, 1963), FFStA 4 Ks 2/63, Bd. 88, Bl. 17299–300.

Dachau, he was released after five months and spent the war in exile in England.[57] After the war, he returned to Germany and served on the British Control Commission for press affairs and was one of the co-founders of the news magazine *Der Spiegel*. From 1950 on, he worked as a private attorney based in Frankfurt.[58] Ormond took considerable interest in Nazi cases, having helped sue I. G. Farben in 1950 on behalf of former concentration camp inmates, and even provided some documents to the prosecutor's office during the preliminary investigation.[59] Perhaps his most important contribution to the Auschwitz Trial, however, was his motion to have the court visit Auschwitz itself to conduct a so-called *Tatortsbesichtigung*, an official examination of the scene of the crime. This proved to be one of the most dramatic and, in the context of the Cold War, politically significant moments in the trial.

The second group of *Nebenkläger* consisted of relatives of Auschwitz victims resident in the GDR. Friedrich Karl Kaul, the "star attorney" for the Sozialistische Einheitspartei (SED), represented them.[60] Kaul was particularly well suited for this role.[61] Born in 1906, Kaul studied law in the waning years of the Weimar Republic and, in 1932, joined the "Rote Hilfe" (Red Aid) organization, which provided legal assistance to political prisoners. In 1933, Kaul was disbarred on racial grounds and was arrested by the Gestapo in 1935 for political reasons. Released from Dachau in 1937, Kaul emigrated to Colombia and, eventually, to the United Sates, where he was again interned for the duration of the war. In 1946, Kaul returned to East Berlin, joined the SED, and resumed his legal career. Admitted to the bar in Berlin in 1948, prior to the formal division of the Berlin judiciary, Kaul was one of the few East German attorneys licensed to practice in the Federal Republic. He made a name for himself defending communists in the political trails of the 1950s and defended the Communist Party before the constitutional court when it was banned. In 1961, the BGH barred Kaul

---

[57] Benjamin B. Ferencz, *Less Than Slaves: Jewish Forced Labor and the Quest for Compensation* (Bloomington: Indiana University Press, 2002), p. 5.

[58] See the brief biographical note in Henry Ormond, "Gedanken zum Problem der Schreibtischmörder," *Tribüne* 4, no. 14 (1965): 1511–17. No biographical information is available for Raabe.

[59] See, e.g., Ormond to Vogel (July 21, 1960), FFStA HA 4 Ks 2/63, Bd. 3, Bl. 453, and Ormond to Vogel and Kügler (January 8, 1962), FFStA HA 4 Ks 2/63, Bd. 8, Bl. 1426. On Ormond and I. G. Farben, see Ferencz, *Less Than Slaves*, p. 35.

[60] See, e.g., "Auschwitz-Prozeß: SED-Staranwalt kam umsonst," *Abendpost*, December 21, 1963; "SED-Anwalt als Nebenkläger," *Abendpost*, January 7, 1964; and Bernd Naumann, "Der Ost-Berliner Anwalt Kaul im Auschwitz-Prozeß als Nebenkläger," FAZ, January 7, 1964.

[61] For biographical information on Kaul, see Annette Rosskopf, "Anwalt antifaschistischer Offensiven: Der DDR-Nebenklagevertreter Friedrich Karl Kaul," in Irmtrud Wojak, ed., *"Gerichtstag halten über uns selbst...": Geschichte und Wirkung des ersten Frankfurter Auschwitz-Prozesses* (Frankfurt: Campus Verlag, 2001), pp. 142–44.

from practicing as a *defense* attorney in the Federal Republic.[62] According to the court, Kaul had voluntarily subordinated himself to the SED and, therefore, could not operate with the requisite juridical independence. As a result, "Kaul began to look for other areas of activity in the West."[63] His first thought was to act as civil counsel in the Eichmann Trial, but this was thwarted when the Israelis eliminated civil counsel from their code of criminal procedure shortly before the trial started. The plan, however, was easily transferred to West German Nazi trials, and Kaul was to become one of the most significant players in the Auschwitz Trial.[64]

Kaul's principle adversary in the Auschwitz Trial was defense counsel Hans Laternser.[65] As did Kaul, Laternser completed his legal training just as the Nazis were seizing power in Germany. In 1934, he opened a law office in Frankfurt, specializing mainly in tax law. During the Third Reich, Laternser managed to avoid joining the Nazi party and, on occasion, had minor trouble with the regime.[66] He even defended a staff member of a Catholic nursing home who was under attack by the regime for the Church's opposition to its euthanasia program.[67] It is ironic, then, that Laternser, who on account of his lack of Nazi party membership was one of the first German lawyers allowed to resume practice immediately after the war, began his postwar legal career defending clients accused of murder in euthanasia cases. Laternser's big break, however, the one that would largely determine the future course of his legal career as a specialist in Nazi cases, came when Robert M. W. Kempner, assistant trial counsel for the American prosecution at Nuremberg, asked Laternser to take on the defense of the Oberkommando der Wehrmacht (OKW).[68] After the end of the case against the OKW, Laternser undertook the defense of various individual defendants in the successor trials under American military courts at Nuremberg.[69] In the wake of

---

[62] Beschluß des BGH (March 2, 1961), NJW 17 (1961): 614.

[63] Rosskopf, "Anwalt," p. 144.

[64] See chapter 5.

[65] For biographical information on Laternser, see Christian Dirks, "Selekteure als Lebensretter: Die Verteidigungsstrategie des Rechtsanwalts Dr. Hans Laternser," in Wojak, ed., *"Gerichtstag halten,"* pp. 163–67.

[66] Laternser cleverly managed to have his cake and eat it too in this regard. While he applied to join the Nazi party, a necessity for a practicing attorney, he neglected to send the requisite ID photos and was thus never formally admitted. Ibid., p. 165.

[67] Ibid., p. 165.

[68] Ibid., p. 167. One of the innovations in the Nuremberg trial was that various organizations were formally charged as criminal organizations. See Eugene Davidson, *The Trial of the Germans: An Account of the Twenty-two Defendants before the International Military Tribunal at Nuremberg* (New York: Collier, 1966), pp. 553–79, and Bradley F. Smith, *Reaching Judgment at Nuremberg* (New York: Basic, 1977), pp. 143–70.

[69] Dirks, "Selekteure als Lebensretter," p. 168. See also Hans Laternser, *Verteidigung deutscher Soldaten: Plädoyers vor alliierten Gerichten* (Bonn: Rolf Bohnemeier, 1950). On the successor trials more generally, see Telford Taylor, *Final Report to the Secretary of the Army on the*

the Nuremberg trials, Laternser made a career for himself defending Wehrmacht officers. Laternser was therefore a natural candidate to serve as a
defense attorney in the Auschwitz Trial. At the request of their relatives, he
and his associate Fritz Steinacker took on the cases of several of the medical
personnel (Laternser) and members of the Political Section (Steinacker).[70]

Not only was Laternser one of the most tenacious of the defense attorneys
in the trial, he was also one of the most politically engaged. He constantly
tried to mobilize political themes for his defense, questioning the reliability of
witnesses from East Block countries, vehemently objecting to Kaul's admission as civil counsel, and generally calling into question the court's right to
hold such trials in the first place. In the years since the Nuremberg trials,
Laternser had developed close ties to the German nationalist right, including a close friendship with his longtime client Gerhard Frey, publisher of the
far-right *Deutsche National- und Soldaten-Zeitung.*[71] Fritz Bauer became so
exasperated with Laternser's tactics that he later told his friend Kempner, "I
will never forgive you for what you did to me there."[72]

It is tempting, when considering the role of defense attorneys in the
Auschwitz Trial, to take Hans Laternser as typical. Laternser was already
well known for his earlier role in Nazi trials, and from press accounts of
the trial, one could easily get the impression that he was practically the only
defense attorney in the trial. And yet it would be an error to identify all of
the no less than twenty-one different defense attorneys who participated in
the trial at one point or another with Laternser.[73] Like Kaul, Laternser was a
consummate political animal, and in this both can be viewed as attempting
to evade the juridical constraints of the trial in favor of the more tactically
open terrain of the political. But also like Kaul, Laternser was something
an anomaly in the trial, which is precisely why both tended to attract so
much attention in the press. Laternser's colleagues on the defense were, by
contrast, less Promethean figures. Although, based on the kinds of legal
arguments they advanced in their closing arguments, many of them appear
to have been equally committed to the nationalist right in their politics, they
were generally less flamboyant and aggressive in their tactics.[74] By and large,
they accepted the restrictions of their juridical role with far more grace than

Nurnberg [sic] *War Crimes Trials under Control Council Law No. 10* (Buffalo: William
S. Hein, 1997 [1949]), and for both U.S. and German doubts about these trials, see Frank
M. Buscher, *The U.S. War Crimes Trial Program in Germany, 1945–1949* (New York: Green-
wood, 1989), pp. 31–34, 98–99.

[70] Laternser represented Capesius, Frank, and Schatz. Steinacker represented Dylewski and
Broad. Dirks, "Selekteure als Lebensretter," p. 170. See also Laternser, *Die andere Seite,*
pp. 389–91.

[71] Ibid., p. 185.

[72] Robert M. W. Kempner, *Ankläger einer Epoche: Lebenserinnerungen* (Frankfurt: Ullstein,
1983), p. 234.

[73] See the list in Langbein, *Auschwitz-Prozeß,* vol. 2, pp. 935–36.

[74] However, it should be noted that at least one defense attorney, Hermann Stolting II, was
accused during the course of the Auschwitz trial for his role in passing illegal death sentences

the iconoclastic and ideologically motivated Laternser. Whether this reflected a deeper moral understanding of the precariousness of their position as the defenders of men charged with one of the greatest crimes in human history or whether it merely reflected a different tactical sense of the best way to represent their clients is impossible to say. Either way, it is precisely Laternser's dramatic persona that makes it misleading to view him as typical of the defense attorneys in the trial.

Under German law, every defendant is entitled to representation by an attorney.[75] German defendants may choose their own representation, or if they are unwilling or unable to do so, for financial or other reasons, the court may appoint an attorney on their behalf. It is also possible for the defendants to request that the court defray the expenses of an attorney of their choosing.[76] Unlike in the American judicial system, there is no public defender's office; rather, court-appointed private attorneys serve this function.

Unlike the court or the prosecution, defense counsel are partisan actors in a German criminal trial, obliged to act "in the best interests of their client."[77] At the same time, defense counsel, like all German trial participants with the partial exception of the defendants, have a formal legal obligation to the truth. They may not lie. These dual obligations, to serve the best interests of the client and to tell the truth, place defense attorneys in a somewhat ambiguous situation. This ambiguity is resolved in practice in the following way: "What an attorney says must be true but the attorney need not say everything that is true."[78] In this sense, a defense attorney's obligation to his client takes precedence over his obligation to the truth, which is the exact opposite of the situation of the prosecutor, where his obligation to the truth outweighs his obligation to the state. As Laternser put it: "I do not think much of defense attorneys who seek at every stage of the trial to distance themselves from their clients simply in order to avoid the possibility that people who do not understand such judicial matters will misunderstand the situation. Defense attorneys who distance themselves from their clients would do better to avoid such cases because such distancing not only does not help their clients but rather, at times, does them only considerable harm."[79]

In many respects, given that the inquisitorial character of German criminal procedure restricts the active role that defense attorneys can play during a

as a prosecutor before the Sondergericht in Bromberg during the war. See Valeska von Roques, "Namen, die keiner mehr nennt," *Vorwärts*, June 10, 1964.

[75] §137 StPO. In many cases, particularly those of a serious or complex nature, a defendant may be required to have legal representation by the court. See §140 StPO.

[76] §141 StPO. Freely selected defense attorneys are called *Wahlverteidiger*, ones appointed by the court, *Pflichtverteidiger*. An attorney appointed by the court may decline only for "important reasons." Schwarz and Kleinknecht, *Kurzkommentare*, p. 221.

[77] Justus R. G. Warburg, *Die anwaltliche Praxis in Strafsachen* (Stuttgart: Verlag W. Kohlhammer, 1985), p. 6.

[78] Ibid., p. 5.

[79] Laternser, *Die andere Seite*, p. 14.

trial, they are confined to the role of "priests," who listen to and counsel their clients through the difficult process of being tried.[80] As Justus Warburg puts it: "The defense attorney's task is to stand by his client. That means: the defense attorney must *listen* to his client, to *understand* him, insofar as this is possible, to *protect* him against an often biased public and to *represent* his interests to the prosecuting agencies. In concrete terms, this as a rule means that he guards and, as circumstances warrant, actively intervenes in the trial to ensure that it proceeds in a formally and materially correct manner."[81] Therefore, a German defense attorney ought in principle be less concerned with "presenting a case" than with ensuring the fairness of the proceedings. Since German criminal trials are principally concerned with finding the truth, it is assumed that a fair trial will lead to a fair outcome. Consequently, German defense attorneys will call witnesses or present evidence primarily as a means of balancing the incriminating evidence presented by the prosecution in the formal indictment, rather than as a means of constructing a coherent counter-narrative of the events in question. In questioning hostile witnesses, they seek, as a rule, to draw out ambiguities or uncertainties that undermine the witness's credibility as a source of "truth."

As with the civil counsel, the exception to this generally *corrective* function of German defense attorneys comes in their closing arguments. Once again, it is in these closing statements that the defense counsel present their interpretation of the trial, of the evidence gathered, and of the legal questions raised. As do both the prosecution and the civil counsel, defense attorneys make sentencing recommendations in their closing arguments. Not surprisingly, they will usually recommend that their clients be acquitted, but not always. In cases where there is an overwhelming preponderance of incriminating evidence, defense counsel will sometimes choose to recommend criminal sanctions, though, needless to say, these will invariably be milder than those suggested by the prosecution.

The men whom these attorneys defended in the Auschwitz Trial played perhaps the most unusual, certainly the most portentous role in the entire trial. By definition, it is the defendants who have the most at stake in a trial. Although Germany abolished the death penalty after World War II, many of the Auschwitz defendants were facing life in prison and the permanent loss of their citizenship rights. Equally important, the trial had the potential to challenge their entire self-understanding, the retrospective self-justifications these men had constructed over twenty years to explain to themselves what they had done in that hellish corner of Poland all those years ago.[82] A conviction

[80] Warburg, *Die anwaltliche Praxis*, p. 7.
[81] Ibid.
[82] On the central importance of ex post facto self-justification for many Holocaust perpetrators in the years after the war, see Ulrich Herbert, *Best: Biographische Studien über Radikalismus, Weltanschauung und Vernunft, 1903–1989*, 2nd ed. (Bonn: Dietz Verlag, 1996), pp. 477–90.

not only meant the loss of personal freedom, but also posed the threat of a loss of subjective psychological coherence as well.[83] In this sense, the tactics adopted by the defendants and their attorneys can be viewed as responding to a dual challenge: a juridical threat to their freedom and a representational threat to their self-perception. Particularly in cases where the mass of evidence made acquittal unlikely, the efforts by the defendants to shape the trial, to present a counter-narrative of obedience, legality, and duress, can be viewed as an attempt to reclaim tactically in the representational arena what appeared to be lost in the juridical: a sense of moral self-worth.

The defendants' status as legal actors was equally unusual. One of the most important functions of the code of criminal procedure is to protect the rights of the accused. The fundamental principle, *in dubio pro reo*, the presumption of innocence that underlies much of the modern western legal tradition, is intended to protect citizens from the arbitrary exercise of the state's coercive authority. Particularly in the aftermath of the Third Reich, for which such legal niceties were irrelevant obstructions to the enactment of the leader's will, both the German legal code and the judiciary took defendants' rights very seriously. Not only were the defendants granted the first and last word in any criminal trial but, in a gesture that can only seem odd from an Anglo-American perspective, are even allowed, de facto, to lie in their own defense.[84] Technically, defendants do not have a *right* to lie and are obligated to tell the truth if they choose to speak in their own defense. But this obligation has an *ethical,* rather than a legal character.[85] Lies by a defendant are considered a "non-prohibited means of defense" and, in order to protect the defendant's right to legal self-defense, "may not be punished."[86] Therefore, no additional sanctions are attached to perjury by defendants in German criminal trials. The point of this is to protect defendants from potential coercion, even if used to elicit true statements. Such perjury on the part of a defendant may, however, be held against him during the sentencing phase of a trial as being indicative of his generally criminal character.[87]

A trial is, in the most direct sense, *about* the defendants, but they also participate *in* the trial as well. The defendant thus plays a dual role. He is both a passive and an active participant in the trial, its object and its subject, an actor and a source of evidence. "In the first instance, [the defendant] is

---

[83] See the post-trial interviews with two of the Auschwitz defendants, where they continued to maintain their innocence, even though there was no juridical reason to do so. Ebbo Demant, ed., *Auschwitz – "Direkt von der Rampe weg..." Kaduk, Erber, Klehr: Drei Täter geben zu Protokoll* (Reinbeck: Rowohlt Taschenbuch Verlag, 1979).

[84] Roxin et al., *Strafrecht*, p. 134. See also Peters, *Strafprozeß*, pp. 207–8.

[85] Peters, *Strafprozeß*, p. 207.

[86] Hans-Jürgen Bruns, *Strafzumessungsrecht: Gesamtdarstellung*, 2nd ed. (Cologne: Carl Heymans Verlag, 1974), p. 601.

[87] Peters, *Strafprozeß*, pp. 207–8, and Bruns, *Strafzumessungsrecht*, p. 601.

what the proceedings are about [*auf den hin gehandelt wird*]. He is sub-ordinated to the proceedings. He is compelled to appear before the court. Coercive measures are applied to him. But however much he is exposed to the proceedings, he also retains the opportunity to take part in the proceedings as well. He can meaningfully influence both the form of the proceedings as well as the ascertainment of the actual facts [of the case]."[88] In the context of these multiple roles, a German defendant has a number of specific rights under the law, including the right to be present, the right to a defense, the right to be heard, and the right to appeal.[89] Because the defendant will often be unfamiliar with the law, judges are obligated as objective, nonpartisan actors to protect all of the defendant's rights in order to ensure a fair trial. In this sense, the juridical is somewhat unusual as a strategic field, in that it deliberately and formally creates a space for tactical counter-maneuvers on the part of its most direct objects.

In the Auschwitz Trial, twenty-four defendants were indicted; twenty-two remained in the dock at the trial's opening and twenty at its conclusion.[90] They ranged in rank from major to private and represented every major administrative sub-unit of the camp with the exceptions of the camp's economic administration. The defendants can be divided into five groups (see Table 1) according to their camp function.[91] Group 1 comprised the camp's administrative executive and was represented in the trial by the two surviving camp adjutants. Functionally, this group had been responsible for the day-to-day administration of the camp, for the procuring of supplies, for liaising with higher authorities in the chain of command, for supervising and evaluating the camp personnel, and so on.

The second group represented the so-called Schutzhaftlagerführung, those responsible for the protective custody camps that made up Auschwitz (Auschwitz I, Auschwitz II/Birkenau, and Monowitz). These men served as camp leaders (Lagerführer) who were directly in charge of the protective custody camps, report leaders (Rapportführer) who assisted the camp leaders and were particularly responsible for the roll-call, and block leaders (Blockführer) who were each responsible for an individual barracks. These were the men who bore the most direct responsibility for the daily lives of

---

[88] Peters, *Strafprozeß*, p. 203.

[89] There are seven specific rights, which are enumerated in ibid., pp. 204–10.

[90] Richard Baer died on June 17, 1963, in investigative detention. Hans Nierzwicki had his case separated from the proceedings shortly prior to the opening of the trial for health reasons. Two other defendants had their cases severed during the trial, also for health reasons. Heinrich Bischoff (case severed on March 13, 1964) died on October 26, 1964. Gerhard Neubert (case severed on July 23, 1964) later served as a defendant in the so-called Second Auschwitz Trial.

[91] For a general overview of the SS at Auschwitz, see Aleksander Lasik, "Historical-Sociological Profile of the Auschwitz SS," in Yisrael Gutman and Michael Berenbaum, eds., *Anatomy of the Auschwitz Death Camp* (Bloomington: Indiana University Press, 1994), pp. 271–87.

TABLE I. *Defendants by category and rank.*

Group	Name	Highest rank while at Auschwitz
1. Executive Administration	Robert Mulka	Hauptsturmführer (captain)
	Karl Höcker	Obersturmführer (First Lieutenant)
2. Protective Custody Leadership	Franz Hofmann	Hauptsturmführer
	Oswald Kaduk[a]	Unterscharführer (corporal)
	Stefan Baretzki	Sturmmann (private)
3. Political Section	Wilhelm Boger	Oberscharführer (Staff Sergeant)
	Hans Stark	Oberscharführer
	Klaus Dylewski	Oberscharführer
	Perry Broad	Rottenführer (Private First Class)
	Bruno Schlage	Unterscharführer
	Johann Schoberth	Unterscharführer
4. Medical Service	Dr. Franz Lucas	Obersturmführer
	Dr. Viktor Capesius	Sturmbannführer (Major)
	Dr. Willi Frank	Hauptsturmführer
	Dr. Willi Schatz	Untersturmführer (Second Lieutenant)
	Josef Klehr	Oberscharführer
	Herbert Scherpe	Oberscharführer
	Emil Hantl	Rottenführer
	Arthur Breitwieser	Rottenführer
5. Inmate Kapos	Emil Bednarek	–

[a] Kaduk denied having been promoted to Oberscharführer (Staff Sergeant), claiming to have remained an Unterscharführer his whole time in Auschwitz.

the inmates at Auschwitz. They were, according to Rudolph Höß, the "real masters of the prisoner's whole life" in the camp.[92]

The third group was the camp Gestapo, or Political Section. They were responsible for breaches of "discipline" in the camp, everything from petty theft to acts of resistance, attempts at escape, or just plain bad luck. Inmates suspected of breaches of discipline were taken to the infamous Block 11, where they were interrogated, usually under torture. Few survived. The Political Section was also responsible for the quasi-judicial executions of members of the Polish intelligentsia and resistance, usually conducted in the courtyard outside Block 11, at the Black Wall. Finally, the Political Section was responsible for registering inmates admitted to the camp in the central card catalogue.

[92] Rudolf Höß, *Commandant of Auschwitz*, trans. Constantine FitzGibbon (London: Weidenfeld and Nicolson, 1959), p. 108. In German: Rudolf Höß, *Kommandant von Auschwitz: Autobiographische Aufzeichnungen* (Stuttgart: Deutsche Verlags-Anstalt, 1958).

The fourth group represented the camp medical service. They were variously occupied in the SS or inmate infirmaries as physicians, dentists, pharmacists, or medics. As medical "experts," the officers were in charge of the "ramp selections," where Jews arriving on deportation trains were separated into those capable of work and the old, ill, unskilled, or unlucky, who were gassed immediately.[93] The enlisted medics helped with the numerous selections conducted in the inmate infirmary, where the weak and ill were either sent to the gas chambers or killed on site. In this context, they were responsible for the so-called injections, whereby sick inmates, including children, were killed with a phenol injection directly into the heart.

The fifth and final group was represented by a lone defendant, Emil Bednarek. He had been a Kapo, an inmate who assisted the SS in running the camp and who was responsible for order and efficiency, both inside the camp and on work details. In this capacity, Kapos were often more feared than the SS. They had more to lose and often reacted to the slightest provocation with enormous brutality. Of course, given the many complexities of what Primo Levi called the "gray zone," one cannot but notice a certain irony in putting an Auschwitz *inmate* on trial, whatever his crimes.[94]

The final group of actors in a German trial, the witnesses, is in many ways the most important. Particularly in a trial that relies primarily on witnesses for evidence, as the Auschwitz Trial did, it is their testimony that largely determines the outcome of the proceedings. At the same time, at least in the Auschwitz Trial, the witnesses were also the least cohesive group. In general, witnesses can be divided into two main groups: eyewitnesses (*Zeugen*), who are called on to report facts based on their own direct perceptions, and expert witnesses (*Sachverständiger*), who are to aid the court in evaluating the fact of the case on the basis of their professional expertise.

Under German law, witnesses are obliged to appear when summoned and to testify under "solemn oath" unless excused as relatives of the defendants or because of professional confidentiality.[95] Under German law, however, a witness is not sworn until after he or she has testified, and the court may forgo this oath if the testimony was unhelpful or if it feels the witness may have committed perjury.[96] Witnesses also have certain rights, including, in particular, the right to be heard. This means that the witness may not be interrupted or cut off, so long as his or her testimony is relevant to the

---

[93] As a rule, non-Jews were formally registered in the camp and were not subject to the selection process or the subsequent gassings. There were occasional exceptions to this, however, for Poles, Gypsies, and Soviet POWs. See Franciszek Piper, "The Number of Victims," in Gutman and Berenbaum, eds., *Anatomy of the Auschwitz Death Camp*, pp. 68–70, and Robert Jan van Pelt, *The Case for Auschwitz: Evidence from the Irving Trial* (Bloomington: Indiana University Press, 2002), p. 116.

[94] Primo Levi, *The Drowned and the Saved* (New York: Vintage, 1988), pp. 36–69.

[95] See Peters, *Strafprozeß*, pp. 346–58. See also §§48, 51–53, 59, 66c StPO.

[96] §61 StPO.

TABLE 2. *Witness testimony in the Auschwitz Trial*

Witness category	Testified in person	Testimony read
Former inmate	211	37
Former SS man	85	6
Other	63	7

Source: Herman Langbein, *Der Auschwitz-Prozeß*, vol. 1, p. 44.

proceedings. In addition, a witness is allowed to testify as long as he or she sees fit. "Long-windedness and awkwardness, however unfortunate they may be, are to be tolerated."[97] Witnesses also have a right to be treated with respect. "Disparaging remarks by the court, the prosecution or the defense, are beneath their office."[98] Under German law, only the court may call witnesses during a trial, though the prosecution, defense, and civil plaintiffs all have the right to move to call witnesses. In keeping with the court's obligation to the truth, such motions may be declined only if the witness cannot be reached or if his or her testimony is likely to be irrelevant.[99]

In the Auschwitz Trial, 359 eyewitnesses testified, thirteen of them on more than one occasion.[100] In addition, forty-eight written depositions were read into the record during the trial in cases where the witness had either died or could not attend the trial (usually due to ill health). For obvious reasons, the vast majority of these eyewitnesses were camp survivors (see Table 2). However, a surprisingly large number of former SS men testified as well. Even more surprising is the fact that most of them were called by the prosecution, a move Hermann Langbein called "ill advised."[101]

Among the survivor witnesses, political prisoners (mostly Poles) formed the largest single category, though Jewish survivors comprised a sizable group as well (see Table 3). Many of these survivor witnesses had been so-called *Funktionshäftlinge* (inmate functionaries). There are two reasons for this. First, this group had the best chances of surviving the camp, since they generally worked under better conditions than did ordinary inmates working at hard labor. They also often had better chances of "organizing" extra rations or medical treatment for themselves. Second, such inmate functionaries also tended to make better witnesses, in the juridical sense, because their duties often allowed them to observe more of the camp and to get a better sense of how it functioned than ordinary inmates could.

[97] Peters, *Strafprozeß*, p. 359.
[98] Ibid.
[99] §244 StPO.
[100] Langbein, *Auschwitz-Prozeß*, p. 43.
[101] Ibid., p. 44.

TABLE 3. *Auschwitz Trial Survivor Testimony by Category*

Reason in Auschwitz	Testified in person	Testimony read
Jewish	90	6
Gypsy	4	2
Political prisoner	104	28
Criminal prisoner	13	1

Source: Hermann Langbein, Der Auschwitz-Prozeß, vol. 1, p. 44.

The enormous diversity of the witnesses in the Auschwitz Trial makes any sweeping generalizations about their role and experiences in the trial risky. Nonetheless, the survivor witnesses in particular found themselves in an awkward position during the trial. On the one hand, in accordance with their right to be heard, they had the opportunity to *bear witness*, to tell their unique, individual stories of suffering and loss, to commemorate in some real sense those who had died. In other words, testifying provided many witnesses with the opportunity to make tactical use of the trial to tell the stories they felt were important. On the other hand, this effort was in constant tension with the court's juridical need, repeatedly emphasized by the defense for tactical reasons, for exact, precise testimony regarding the specific activity of individual defendants on specific occasions against identifiable victims. This tension was to form one of the leitmotifs during the evidentiary phase of the Auschwitz Trial.

In addition to these 359 eyewitnesses, ten different experts testified during the trial. Five of these were historians, three from the Institute for Contemporary History in Munich (Hans Buchheim, Martin Broszat, and Helmut Krausnick), one from Bonn University (Hans-Adolf Jacobsen), and one from the East Berlin German Academy of Sciences (Jürgen Kuczynski). In addition, the court consulted several nonhistorians. The handwriting expert Johannes Mülhaus was consulted on three separate occasions to confirm the authenticity of written documents or signatures. Kurt Hinrichsen, an attorney with the Central Office, gave testimony regarding the defense by higher orders. Two physicians (Dr. Helmut Lechler and Dr. Karl Luff) testified regarding the potential applicability of juvenile law to the defendants Stark and Schoberth, who had both been underage for part of their time at Auschwitz. Finally, Dr. Günther Vetter testified regarding an operation he performed on the defendant Schlage in 1943.

In the final analysis, one could say that only the law itself exercised strategy in de Certeau's sense in the Auschwitz Trial. In other words, the law set the agenda for other actors in the trial, it determined the parameters within which they exercised their own tactical, responsive agency. The law channeled without precisely determining their actions. Since the law in question, the German law of homicide, had been enacted in 1871 for entirely different purposes and with entirely different kinds of crimes in mind, this fact helps to explain why none of the actors in the trial proved able to grasp completely the moral and historical complexity of Auschwitz. The limitations of the law in the face of genocide created structural blinders that prevented any of the actors from seeing fully the historical reality of the case before them.

4

Indictment and Order to Convene, April–July 1963

The trial, which opened on December 20, 1963, was to be the payoff for all the years of hard work by prosecutors, judges, and representatives of the IAC. The trial was to be monumental in every sense, a thorough encapsulation of both the crimes of Auschwitz *and* the Federal Republic's efforts to master them. And monumental it was, lasting 183 sessions, until August 20, 1965. Hundreds of witnesses were called, thousands of hours of testimony taken, countless legal maneuvers attempted, sometimes successfully, sometimes not, and, at the end, a judgment, an authoritative judicial proclamation of fact and law, a verdict of guilt or innocence bearing penal sanctions for unimaginable horrors.

And yet all of this did not unfold arbitrarily. Even more than the preliminary investigation, the trial was a regulated event, divided into legally stipulated stages and conducted by actors with limited room for maneuver. On the most basic level, the actual course of the Auschwitz Trial was largely dictated by the German code of criminal procedure, which stipulates the stages in any criminal trial. There are three formal stages in any criminal case: a preliminary investigation, a so-called in-between phase (*Zwischenverfahren*), and the trial proper, termed the main proceedings (*Hauptverhandlung*). The preliminary investigation is conducted by the responsible prosecutor's office, in cooperation with the police, and may result in a preliminary judicial investigation as well. It terminates either with the case being dropped or with the drafting of a formal written indictment. In the latter case, the proceedings then move to the in-between phase, where a court considers the prosecution's indictment. The convening court can both amend the charges (§207 II StPO) and, if they feel the evidence presented is insufficient, even dismiss the case altogether (§204 I StPO).[1] The in-between phase

---

[1] Karl Peters, *Strafprozeß: Ein Lehrbuch*, 4th rev. ed. (Heidelberg: C. F. Müller Juristischer Verlag, 1985), pp. 465–66. The convening court thus plays a role somewhat similar to that of a grand jury under American law.

terminates with the official order to convene, the *Eröffnungsbeschluß*. This lists the final, official charges against the defendants and "forms the foundation of the further proceedings. This alone enables and bounds the main proceeding and the verdict."[2] In other words, the order to convene, not the indictment, forms the legal basis for the trial itself. The indictment remains, in effect, the prosecution's *case*, not the actual charges considered by the trial court.

The main proceedings themselves are further divided into four stages. First, the defendants are questioned regarding their biographies (*Vernehmung zur Person*), informed of the charges against them through a reading of the official order to convene, and subsequently questioned again regarding these charges (*Vernehmung zur Sache*). This is followed by the evidentiary phase of the trial (*Beweisaufnahme*), where witnesses testify and the court examines any physical, documentary, or other evidence. This generally constitutes the bulk of any trial. In the Auschwitz Trial, the evidentiary phase consumed 141 of the 183 total trial sessions. Following the evidentiary phase, the prosecution, civil counsel, and defense make their closing arguments and are given the opportunity to make rebuttals. The defendants themselves are given the final word. Finally, the trial concludes with the reading of the final judgment (*Urteil*), which gives the verdict against each defendant, the sentence to be imposed, and a preliminary account of the evidentiary and legal grounds for these decisions. The final judgment is subsequently elaborated in written form, which is used as the basis for any appeals. Once the appeals process has been terminated, the verdicts and sentences are considered legally valid (*Rechtskräftig*).

By the time the Auschwitz Trial officially convened, it had already had a five-year prehistory. Under the strictures of German law, the prosecution had already made perhaps its most important contribution to the trial before it even started. In drafting the formal indictment, the prosecution laid out the playing field on which the trial would take place. The order to convene further specified and narrowed this field of action. Together, the indictment and the order to convene defined the specific charges against the defendants. Although the German courts are free to examine evidence as they see fit, if new crimes come to light during a trial, the court may consider them only based on a subsidiary indictment (*Nachtragsanklage*) brought by the prosecution.[3] If no such subsidiary indictment is made, these new crimes may not be considered in the final verdict.[4]

---

[2] Ibid., p. 465.
[3] "The scope of the main proceedings is determined by the indictments admitted by the order to convene. The court may not expand its investigation beyond the thus designated acts or persons." Ibid., pp. 550–51.
[4] §266 StPO.

Indictment

The Auschwitz indictment is a dual document, both historiographic and juridical in character. These two aspects reflect the challenge faced by the prosecution in trying to subsume Nazi genocide under ordinary law, and thus form distinct sections in the indictment. Part one, covering 195 of the indictment's 698 pages, provides a narrative history of Auschwitz in the general context of the historical development of the SS, the concentration camp system, and Nazi policy toward Poland and the Jews. Part two outlines the specific charges against the individual defendants and the evidence supporting these charges. In principle, the indictment's dual character was meant to acknowledge and deal with the fact that the defendant's crimes at Auschwitz were part of a broad, systematic, bureaucratically organized socio-historical context. In practice, however, the two parts of the indictment remained oddly disconnected, as if they belonged in two different documents.

The historical portion of the indictment is particularly interesting, as it provided in many respects a much more systematic and coherent account of Auschwitz than emerged in the trial itself. Clearly, the prosecution felt that this trial had an important historical dimension that went well beyond typical criminal trials. "This is a question not of revenge, but rather of an attempt to master a particularly painful chapter of our historical past by means of criminal law. It is a matter for Germans to punish crimes in their own country."[5] For the prosecution, the juridical question of punishment was inseparable from the representational question of mastering Germany's past.

At the same time, even here the indictment retained its character as a legal document, concerned with providing only such historical information as needed to indict specific defendants. It was not a general history, nor was it ever intended to be made public.[6] This internal, juridical character is revealed in numerous ways, small and large. For instance, quotes were often not cited, unless they came from witnesses questioned during the preliminary investigation. More importantly, the narrative restricted itself to those aspects of German history from 1933 to 1945 that were held to bear directly on the alleged crimes of the accused, meaning specifically the history of the SS, the concentration camp system in general, and Auschwitz in particular. There were no detours through broader social, political, economic, legal, or foreign policy questions posed by Nazism, World War II, or the Holocaust. Whether the history of the SS, the concentration camps, and Auschwitz can

---

[5] FFStA to Max Faas (January 2, 1961), FFStA HA 4 Ks 2/63, Bd. 5, Bl. 689. Faas had written to the prosecutor's office the week before complaining about the arrest of Baer after such a long time and arguing that, since the Allies had not punished their war criminals, there was no reason for the Germans to hold such trials. See Faas to FFStA (December 29, 1960), FFStA HA 4 Ks 2/63, Bd. 5, Bl. 688–88R.

[6] To this day, the indictment is available only in archives.

be properly understood without reference to the broader history of the Third Reich as a whole is a question that was never even broached in the indictment. This narrow focus in turn structured the character of the historical narrative in the indictment and the types of truth claims it made, the most important being a marked tendency to refer exclusively to Nazi or National Socialist (rather than *German*) crimes and a strong emphasis on the role of Adolf Hitler.

The historical section of the indictment opened by noting not only that World War II killed millions on the field of battle or through military action against civilian targets, but also that millions more were killed "in the course of a systematic policy of extermination [*Ausrottungspolitik*] on the part of the National Socialist powers."[7] The gas chambers of Auschwitz were seen as a symbol for this. According to the indictment, there were two main groups of victims in the context of this genocidal policy: Jews and inmates no longer capable of work. Most Jews were killed as part of the so-called Final Solution and were exterminated immediately on their arrival at Auschwitz. Those few who were deemed useful as laborers were admitted to the camp, where they shared the fate of the various other prisoners (Polish civilians, Gypsies, Soviet POWs, political opponents of the regime, members of the resistance, etc.).

Once those admitted to the camp were no longer capable of work, which generally happened quickly as a result of the terrible living conditions, they too were systematically exterminated by various means, including regular executions, in-camp selections where inmates were sent to the gas chambers, and so-called injections, whereby inmates in the camp infirmary with little prospect for a rapid recovery were injected with phenol in the heart. "In this way, countless people died because of their descent or because, due to illness, they could no longer 'positively contribute' to the realization of Hitler's war. The unimaginable extent and character of the crimes committed in this camp mark it as the largest extermination camp of all time."[8]

This part of the indictment then led into a brief history of the SS and the concentration camp system, which served as a prelude to the internal history of Auschwitz that formed the bulk of the indictment's historical section. Of the two preliminary elements leading up to the discussion of Auschwitz, the SS was considered more briefly. Noting that Himmler had transformed the SS from a bodyguard into the "party's ideological fighting unit," the indictment argued that the crucial development for the SS occurred when Himmler gained control over the police as well, effectively uniting the two organizations.[9] Of particular importance was the indictment's consideration of the military SS, which was divided into two elements: *Verfügungstruppen*

---

[7] "Anklageschrift," FFStA 4 Ks 2/63, Bd. 78–80, p. 115. Pagination is internal to the *Anklageschrift*.
[8] Ibid., p. 116.
[9] Ibid., pp. 117–18.

(Special Service Troops) and *Totenkopfverbände* (Death's Head Units). After 1940, units in combat were designated Waffen SS (Armed SS), but this actually included troops from both categories and so was not a fully autonomous organizational entity. According to the indictment, the *Totenkopfverbände* were intended from the start to serve as "domestic political fighting troops," and provided the "permanent staff" for the concentration camps.[10] From 1939 on, these troops were responsible for the internal administration and supervision of the camps. Meanwhile, according to the indictment, the Waffen SS in the camps was distinct from this permanent staff and "merely provided the guards for the guard towers and for work details."[11]

However, it is difficult to reconcile this portrait of a relatively clear division of labor between the Death's Head and Waffen SS with the status of the defendants in the Auschwitz Trial, most of whom in fact held ranks in the Waffen SS and none of whom were "merely" guards.[12] Indeed, one of the striking things that emerges from the SS careers of the Auschwitz Trial defendants is the porousness of the boundary between the camp and fighting SS. Johann Schoberth, for example, joined the Waffen SS in 1941 and was twice wounded on the Eastern Front before being transferred to duty in Auschwitz in early 1943.[13] The defendant Hans Stark, on the other hand, initially joined the Death's Head SS in 1937 and served in various concentration camps, including Auschwitz, before serving at the front in 1943.[14] So, based on the indictment's own account, it is clear that members of both the Death's Head and Waffen SS moved back and forth between frontline and camp duty. The indictment here did not fully confront its own evidence. Rather, it fell victim to the widespread myth that the Waffen SS had been ordinary soldiers and that only the Death's Head units had been directly involved in genocidal operations. This would not be the only time that the Auschwitz Trial failed to acknowledge fully the significance its own evidence.

While the indictment's treatment of the history of the concentration camp system was similarly instrumental, in that the primary point of interest was the direct path to Auschwitz, it was nonetheless also more systematic and historically grounded than the treatment of the SS. The indictment indicated that political violence was integral to Nazi rule from the very start and that this terror had a legal basis, listing the various statutes

---

[10] On the history of the Death's Head SS, see especially Charles W. Sydnor, Jr., *Soldiers of Destruction: The SS Death's Head Division, 1933–1945* (Princeton: Princeton University Press, 1977).

[11] "Anklageschrift," pp. 128–29.

[12] Cf. Karin Orth, *Die Konzentrationslager-SS: Sozialstrukturelle Analysen und biographische Studien* (Göttingen: Wallstein, 2000), pp. 156–57, and Miroslav Kárný, "Waffen-SS und Konzentrationslager," *Jahrbuch für Geschichte* 33 (1986): 231–61.

[13] "Anklageschrift," pp. 482–83.

[14] Ibid., pp. 433–35.

enacted by the Nazis in 1933 authorizing the "destruction" of their ene-mies.[15] Such an open acknowledgment that the Nazi terror in fact relied on legal foundations posed potentially very tricky problems for the indict-ment, given that German Nazi prosecutions rested on the legal presump-tion that Nazi crimes were always already crimes, that they had been illegal under German law at the time of their commission.[16] Therefore, the indict-ment once again had to evade the full complexity of its own findings.[17] The indictment simply contended that the stereotypical and abstract reasons given for protective custody arrests (*Schutzhaft*) made them illegal, with-out delving into the full complexity of executive measures under the Nazi dictatorship.[18]

According to the indictment, the key moment in the historical develop-ment of the concentration camp system was 1936, when Himmler's SS took over control of the camps from Göring's Interior Ministry, thus laying the foundation for the SS's control over Auschwitz. From the very start, the indictment argued, the camps had a dual function. On the one hand, they were an instrument of social control through terror.[19] At the same time, the camps were also to provide slave labor for the Reich. The use of slave labor was subsequently instrumentalized even further as part of the Nazi's broader genocidal project, in the form of "extermination through work."[20] In other words, on the indictment's account, political terror, racial genocide, and the economic exploitation of slave labor all merged seamlessly together in the concentration camps. In the context of this dual function – control and exploitation – four distinct groups were held by the SS to "belong" in the camps: political opponents, criminals (including homosexuals), asocials, and racial undesirables (primarily Jews and Gypsies).[21]

The indictment further provided a detailed organizational typology of the camps, making two points that were to prove crucial in the Auschwitz Trial. First, it noted that functional tasks in the camps were strictly regu-lated according to *Lagerordnungen* (camp regulations), such that one could ascertain a person's duties according to his place in the camp organization. Second, the indictment indicated that "tasks that initially seem harmless were

---

[15] Ibid., p. 132.
[16] Devin O. Pendas, "Truth and Its Consequences: Reflections on Political, Historical and Legal 'Truth' in West German Holocaust Trials," *traverse: Zeitschrift für Geschichte* 11 (2004): 25–38. In fact, the legality of Nazi law was much more complex than the prosecution assumed. See Michael Stolleis, *The Law under the Swastika: Studies on Legal History in Nazi Germany* (Chicago: University of Chicago Press, 1998), pp. 167–84.
[17] Gerhard Werle and Thomas Wandres, *Auschwitz vor Gericht: Völkermord und bundes-deutscher Strafjustiz* (Munich: C. H. Beck, 1995), pp. 33–40.
[18] "Anklageschrift," p. 134.
[19] Ibid., p. 141.
[20] Ibid., pp. 156–47.
[21] Ibid., pp. 147–50.

often criminal in the context of running an extermination camp."[22] Thus, for example, the director of the motor pool in Auschwitz was in charge of arranging transportation from the ramp where inmates arrived to the gas chambers where they were murdered. The indictment here sketched the basic features of the prosecution's case against those defendants charged primarily with organizing and supervising genocide in Auschwitz. They were indicted, and would be convicted if everything went according the prosecution's plan, on the basis of their functional role in the camp's division of labor, as determined by a "reading" of the camp bureaucracy. Bureaucratic procedure would here provide the "proof" of individual culpability.

The bulk (148 pages) of the indictment's historical excurses was taken up by the history of Auschwitz itself. Like the concentration camp system in general, Auschwitz too served a dual function, determined, on the one hand, by Nazi policy in Poland and, on the other, by Nazi anti-Jewish policy. In the first instance, the indictment contended, Auschwitz stood at the center of Nazi occupation policy in Poland. This was, in turn, unique among the occupied territories both because of the long duration of the German occupation and because it formed "a point of application and field for the exercise of radical, *völkish*, nationalist ideological theories and policies."[23] Auschwitz's first function was thus to "protect" Germans by subordinating and exploiting Poles according to a racialist population politics.[24]

It was for this purpose that Auschwitz was initially built on the site of a former Polish army barracks in June 1940. By the time it acquired its second, even more murderous function as one of the central killing sites in the so-called Final Solution of the Jewish Question in early 1942, most of the camp's physical and organizational structure was already in place. The indictment outlined both in considerable detail. Auschwitz was divided into three principle camps (in addition to numerous, smaller satellite camps): Auschwitz I, Auschwitz II/Birkenau, and Monowitz.[25]

Even before Auschwitz became an official extermination center for Jews in 1942, living conditions inside the camp were extraordinarily murderous.

---

[22] Ibid., p. 155.

[23] Ibid., p. 162.

[24] Ibid., p. 172. The implicit link that the indictment draws between Nazi population policy in general and the extermination of the Jews in particular prefigures the later ideas of Götz Aly. See Götz Aly and Susanne Heim, *Vordenker der Vernichtung: Auschwitz und die deutschen Pläne für eine neue europäische Ordnung* (Frankfurt: Fischer Verlag, 1997), and Götz Aly, *"Final Solution": Nazi Population Policy and the Murder of the European Jews* (London: Arnold, 1999).

[25] Auschwitz I was the original camp located in the former Polish barracks. Consequently, it had better living conditions than Birkenau, which consisted of wooden barracks based on the German army's design for horse stables. Monowitz was located near the factory I. G. Farben was building for the production of synthetic rubber (the *Bunawerks*). Cf. Yisrael Gutman, "Auschwitz – An Overview," in Yisrael Gutman and Michael Berenbaum, eds., *Anatomy of the Auschwitz Death Camp* (Bloomington: Indiana University Press, 1994), pp. 5–33.

The indictment listed the many various ways an inmate could die in the camp, ranging from starvation and illness to suicide and the often-fatal disciplinary measures employed in the camp.[26] Of the 400,000 inmates officially registered at Auschwitz, that is, not counting those gassed immediately on arrival, 360,000 died, according to the indictment's calculation.[27] In effect, the indictment contended that Auschwitz was an extermination camp well before it became a site for the deliberate genocide of the Jews.

And yet for all its prior brutality, Auschwitz became an even more terrible and terrifying place in September 1941 with the experimental gassing of 600 Soviet POWs in the basement of Block 11. This was the precursor to the subsequent decision to turn Auschwitz into one of the main killing centers in the Holocaust. Starting in early 1942, improvised gas chambers were constructed from existing buildings near the camp (Krematorium I and Bunkers I and II). In early 1943, these were replaced by more efficient, purpose-built facilities combining gas chambers and crematoria under one roof (Krematoria III–V), although Bunkers I and II were kept for "overflow."[28] The principle purpose of these killing facilities was the extermination of European Jewry.

The indictment's interpretation of the Holocaust, in line with the existing historiography of the time, could today be described as "intentionalist."[29] It stressed the role of Hitler and Nazi anti-Semitism and claimed that "Hitler, Himmler, Göring and Heydrich planned the 'Final Solution of the Jewish Question,' namely the physical annihilation of all European Jews, for a long time."[30] This intentionalism, however, reflects not only the state of historiographic knowledge at the time, but also the juridical constraints within which the prosecution was drafting its history of Auschwitz. After all, German courts had long declared Hitler, Himmler, and Heydrich to be the "main perpetrators" of the Holocaust and all others to have been either their co-perpetrators or their accomplices.[31] Even had alternate, "functionalist"

---

[26] Ibid., pp. 185–236.

[27] Ibid., p. 185. The most recent scholarly accounts give much lower mortality figures for registered inmates. Both Piper and Van Pelt conclude that around 200,000 registered inmates died at Auschwitz. See Piper, "Number of Victims," p. 71, and van Pelt, *Case*, p. 116.

[28] "Anklageschrift," p. 260.

[29] The prosecution indicated their debt to Gerald Reitlinger's book as the only general history of the Holocaust available at the time. "Voruntersuchungsantrag," FFStA 4 Ks 2/63, Bd. 52, Bl. 9380. See Gerald Reitlinger, *Die Endlösung: Hitlers Versuch der Ausrottung der Juden Europas, 1939–1945* (Berlin: Colloquium Verlag, 1956). In English: Gerald Reitlinger, *The Final Solution: The Attempt to Exterminate the Jews of Europe, 1939–1945* (New York: A. S. Barnes, 1953). On intentionalism more generally, see Ian Kershaw, *The Nazi Dictatorship: Problems and Perspectives of Interpretation*, 4th ed. (London: Arnold, 2000), pp. 95–98.

[30] "Anklageschrift," p. 243.

[31] On the legal thesis that there were three main perpetrators of the Holocaust, see Jörg Friedrich, *Die kalte Amnestie: NS-Täter in der Bundesrepublik*, rev. ed. (Munich: Piper, 1994), pp. 227–37.

interpretations of the Holocaust been available to the prosecution, it is unlikely that they would have been legally useful.[32]

Nevertheless, the indictment itself pointed to the systematic character of the Holocaust in ways that belied any straightforward interpretation of Hitler, Himmler, Heydrich, and here Göring as the sole main perpetrators of the genocide, merely assisted by their subordinates. The indictment, for instance, outlined the sophisticated process of deporting victims to Auschwitz, which the Reichssicherheitshauptamt, or Reich Security Main Office (RSHA) arranged in cooperation with the German *Reichsbahn*.[33] Clearly, the social cooperation involved in such a process was enormous and actively involved major segments of both the Nazi party and the government bureaucracy.[34] Yet for the indictment, this remained entirely an expression of Hitler's will. Even if the indictment indicated the bureaucratic precision with which the camp functioned and used evidence that pointed to the integration of Auschwitz into a larger apparatus of political terror and genocide, its concern was, as it had to be in the legal context, the crimes committed at Auschwitz, not their connection with a more extensive criminal regime. For all that the prosecution recognized the importance of historical background for their case, their primary focus remained, as it had to, the guilt of the defendants being indicted. In this, we see one of the most fundamental mechanisms through which the juridical structure of the trial sharply delimited the extent to which it could mobilize and give voice to extra-legal representational concerns, that is, to provide the kind of history lesson Bauer and others hoped it could.

The prosecution also took great care to stress the terrible cruelty of the gassing operations in Auschwitz, as evinced by the following statement from former SS-Unterscharführer Richard Böck: "I simply cannot describe how these people screamed. That lasted about eight or ten minutes and then everything was quiet. A short while later, some inmates opened the door and you could still see a blue fog hanging over the giant tangle of corpses. The corpses were cramped together in such a way that you could not tell to whom the individual appendages and body parts belonged. For example, I noticed that one of the victims had stuck his index finger several centimeters into the eye-sockets of another. This gives you a sense of how indescribably terrible the death throes of this person must have been. I felt so ill that I

---

[32] Functionalism was not developed until the 1970s and 1980s. See Kershaw, *Nazi Dictatorship*, pp. 98–102. In any event, the intentionalism/functionalism debate now seems to be winding down. See, e.g., George C. Browder, "Perpetrator Character and Motivation: An Emerging Consensus?" *Holocaust and Genocide Studies* 17 (Winter 2003): 480–97.

[33] "Anklageschrift," pp. 262–75.

[34] These themes subsequently developed by Raul Hilberg. See Hilberg, *The Destruction of the Jews*, rev. ed. (New York: Holmes and Meier, 1985), 3 vols. On the railroads specifically, see Raul Hilberg, *Sonderzüge nach Auschwitz* (Frankfurt: Ullstein, 1987).

almost vomited."[35] The visceral physicality of this description is immediately striking. These victims are no mere statistics; they suffered terribly in acute, bodily ways. This description makes it plain that killing people with gas was not, at its point of application, a bureaucratic operation conducted with cold detachment but an excruciatingly brutal form of murder.

The prosecution was trying to make it clear to both the judges in the *Zwischenverfahren* and the eventual trial judges that, based on the brutality of the gassing operations, not only were these crimes *Mord* per §211 StGB but only a perpetrator, not an accomplice, could kill people in such a terrible way. It seems likely that the prosecution feared – not without justification as it turned out – that the judges would be inclined to view the actual genocidal operations at Auschwitz as lacking sufficient objective brutality and independent scope for action to be considered perpetrator crimes. Because the killers in these operations were more clearly part of a largely bureaucratic apparatus than those who individually tortured their victims to death, the prosecution worried that the judges would be inclined to view them, as they in fact ultimately did in most cases, as mere accomplices. By driving home the brutality of the gassing procedure, the prosecution hoped to head off such an interpretation and demonstrate that gassing was no less brutal than torture and that it consequently had all of the objective features of an "excessive act," one that demonstrated the "perpetrator's will" of those who committed it.[36] Here one can see the interaction of juridical, tactical, and historiographical imperatives in the Auschwitz Trial. The prosecution was trying, on the one hand, to demonstrate historically "how the extermination machinery in Auschwitz operated."[37] On the other hand, the prosecution was also trying to mobilize this historical interpretation for the tactical purposes of securing a conviction of the defendants. The presentation of historical evidence was here being driven as much by the desire to win a conviction in the Auschwitz case as by any internal historiographical logic.

This combination of juridical, tactical, and historiographical imperatives can be seen even more clearly in what was undoubtedly the more juridically significant portion of the indictment, the charges against the individual

---

[35] "Anklageschrift," pp. 273–74. Böck gave a watered-down version of this testimony in the trial on August 3, 1964. See Langbein, *Auschwitz*, vol. 1, p. 74.

[36] The category of excessive acts has generally been held, in German Nazi crimes, to pertain to those carried out arbitrarily, without superior orders. To the extent that the prosecution was trying implicitly to characterize gassing as likewise an excessive act, this would represent something of a legal innovation on their part. See Herbert Jäger, *Verbrechen unter totalitärer Herrschaft: Studien zur nationalsozialistischer Gewaltkriminalität* (Frankfurt: Suhrkamp, 1982), pp. 22–43.

[37] This was, according to prosecutor Kügler, the "point of the trial". See Joachim Kügler, "Es hat das Leben verändert," in Irmtrud Wojak and Susanne Meinl, eds., *Im Labyrinth der Schuld: Täter-Opfer-Ankläger* (Frankfurt: Campus Verlag, 2003), p. 308.

defendants. It should be self-evident, given that the function of this document was to present a legal case against these defendants, that juridical and tactical considerations would play a decisive role. It is perhaps somewhat less obvious that issues of historical interpretation would be crucial outside the context of the explicitly historiographic sections of the document. Yet given the character of these crimes as historical events that took place in a complex political and organizational context some twenty years before they were investigated as crimes, it was inevitable that they would have to be considered historically as well as legally.

The defendants were all charged as perpetrators of *Mord*. These charges can be divided into two broad categories: first, generalized murders, often with no specifically identifiable individual victims or dates, in which the defendants participated along with others, and, second, specific murders of identifiable individual victims, in which the defendants could be demonstrated to have participated directly in the actual killing themselves. The paradigmatic instance of generalized murder was the genocidal operation of the camp itself (ramp selections and gassings), for which the two adjutants Mulka and Höcker and the higher-ranking camp medical personnel were charged.[38] All of the other defendants were charged with at least some specific murders, which can be subdivided into several categories: executions at the Black Wall, usually under direct orders; "intensive interrogations" (torture) by members of the Political Section; selections inside the camp, in the arrest block, and in the inmate hospital; the murder by phenol injection of patients from the inmate hospital; and various individual atrocities committed on the independent initiative of the defendants.[39]

Because the defendants could be charged only with crimes that could be directly attributed to them personally, it was very important, juridically and tactically, to specify these charges in as much detail as possible. Whenever possible, the indictment listed specific instances of the alleged crimes, including exact dates and the names of the victims. This was obviously much easier with specific murders than it was for more generalized ones. For instance, the indictment charged that "on a number of occasions in early 1943, at times while drunk, [the defendant Kaduk] beat inmates in Block 8 and then strangled them to death by laying a walking stick over their throats and standing on it; in this way he killed, among others, the diamond dealer Moritz Polakewitz, the former secretary of the Antwerp Jewish Council, as well as other inmates from Block 8a whose names are not known."[40]

---

[38] The sole exception to this rule is that Viktor Capesius, the camp pharmacist, was charged with participating in lethal medical experiments, in addition to his involvement in the genocidal killing process. "Anklageschrift," pp. 46–48.

[39] Ibid., pp. 18–58.

[40] Ibid., p. 35.

In cases where such precise information was unavailable, the indictment tried to at least indicate the approximate time frame for the alleged criminal activity and as many identifying details regarding the victims as possible. The indictment alleged, for example, that Franz Hofmann "forced approximately ten or twelve enfeebled Soviet POWs to stand naked outside during the winter of 1942 or 1943, so that they froze to death as a result of the great cold." It also charged that "in January of 1944, [Hofmann], together with the defendant Kaduk and the then Rapportführer (Wilhelm) Clausen, selected approximately 600 inmates, including children, in the old laundry between Blocks 1 and 2 and sent them to the gas chambers."[41]

When it came to generalized murders as part of the extermination process, the bureaucratic division of labor at Auschwitz often posed considerable challenges to this drive for specificity, since the concrete actions of any given defendant could often not be demonstrated with any precision. In such cases, the indictment was forced to fall back on that very bureaucratic organization, in order to reconstruct what the defendants *must have done*, given their role in the camp hierarchy. Thus, the indictment charged the camp adjutant, Robert Mulka, with *Mord* in an unknown number of cases, specifically for aiding the efficient functioning of the camp's extermination program. Mulka was accused of aiding the "realization of the National Socialist extermination program" by carrying out his duties as adjutant.[42]

Since the prosecution could not rely on eyewitness testimony to make their case here as they could for specific murders, they relied instead on an indirect "reading" of the camp's organization and the functional division of labor within that organization. The case against Mulka is typical. "Even during his period as company commander of a guard unit, the accused gave or transmitted orders that related to both the function of the concentration camp as an extermination camp as well as to its function as a site of mass murder. These were directed toward the killing of inmates."[43] The duties of a company commander included, according to the indictment, assigning both execution details for the illegal killing of persons designated by the Gestapo and guard details for arriving transports, whose tasks included "securing the selections and transporting [victims] to the gas chambers in such a way that persons designated for execution by Zyklon B were deprived of any opportunity for escape or resistance from the moment of their arrival to the moment they entered the gas chambers."[44]

Once Mulka became camp adjutant, his role in the extermination process expanded accordingly. "In the context of Auschwitz's function as a site of mass extermination, the camp headquarters (i.e. after camp commandant

---

41 Ibid., pp. 32–33.
42 Ibid., p. 18.
43 Ibid., p. 342.
44 Ibid., p. 343.

Höß, principally Mulka) was exclusively responsible for the preparation and execution of the extermination measures."[45] As adjutant, Mulka's duties included transmitting the duty roster to the various camp personnel assigned to serve during selections or gassing operations, as well as arranging transport from the motor pool to take the victims from the train depot to the gas chambers; the indictment lists twenty-two witnesses who testified to this effect.[46]

Significantly, with the exception of the witness testimony regarding Mulka's duties procuring motor transport to take the victims to the gas chambers, the indictment did not provide any concrete examples of Mulka's actually carrying out such functions. Instead, the claims remained at the rather abstract level of what his functional duties *must have been*, not what he could be shown to have actually done. Among Mulka's duties, the indictment asserted, was the direct supervision of selections and the transportation of victims to the gas chambers; his job was to ensure that this "'proceeded in an orderly manner.'"[47] To support this claim the indictment cited testimony from Heinrich Hykes (a former SS man) and the defendants Kaduk and Hofmann. Hofmann's testimony is particularly revealing of the kind of evidence the indictment was able to produce against Mulka. Hofmann stated: "Everyone in Auschwitz had to do duty on the ramp, whether they belonged to the headquarters, the administration, guard company leadership, or the Political Section. When I am told that the defendant Mulka claims to have never been present for the arrival of a transport, I can only laugh. Members of the headquarters staff were assigned to ramp duty just like members of the protective custody camp staff. Mulka's statement that he was never there should be treated just as if I were to claim never to have been there."[48]

Note that Hofmann did not provide an account of any specific instance where he personally saw Mulka on the ramp; he merely asserted that "everyone" had to do ramp duty. This is typical of the kind of evidence available to support the general charges against many of the defendants. It represents a clever tactical effort by the prosecution to exploit the very bureaucratic division of labor that in some ways made their task so difficult. Often, it was impossible to assign definitive responsibility for a given action to any single individual, since numerous individuals in various camp departments were involved. At the same time, however, this division of labor allowed the prosecution to infer plausibly what many of the defendants must have done, given their place in the camp hierarchy. In other words, the regularized assignment of tasks in the camp allowed the prosecution to make a circumstantial case against some of the defendants on this basis, even in the absence

45 Ibid., p. 350.
46 Ibid., p. 352.
47 Ibid., p. 354.
48 Ibid., pp. 354–55.

of more persuasive eyewitness testimony. This mode of presentation shifted the tactical burden onto the defendants, who now had to demonstrate that they had been, for some reason, an exception to the rules that governed the division of labor in the camp.

Even at this preliminary stage, the defense objected strenuously to these sorts of general allegations. Mulka's attorney at the time, Herbert Ernst Müller, protested that "if one strips the indictment...bare of all of its general, sometimes polemical, comments and looks for a single action for which the defendant could be held responsible, it turns out that there is not one single concrete action which the evidence proves against him."[49] Instead, Müller protested, the prosecution substituted generalities, claiming that an adjutant in Auschwitz must have participated in criminal activities, simply by virtue of his function in the camp. Yet, Müller objected, German law did not possess categories such as "functional suspicion" or "functional culpability."[50] "Functionaries in responsible positions cannot necessarily be suspected of murder, simply because the system within which they exercise their functions, itself has general criminal tendencies."[51] The prosecution was well aware that this might pose a problem for their case, but given the paucity of direct evidence, it had little choice but to fall back on circumstantial evidence.[52]

As effective as such circumstantial evidence could be for the prosecution, they clearly preferred whenever possible to be able to indict defendants on very specific charges derived from explicit eyewitness testimony; the more concrete and specific the evidence, the better. The following examples may be taken as typical. The indictment charged the defendant Wilhelm Boger with participating in executions at the Black Wall. To the extent possible, the indictment attempted to specify exactly when Boger participated in such executions and how many victims were shot on each occasion. The witness Herbert Kurz, for example, described the execution process on one occasion.[53] An inmate named Jakob Kozelczuk (sometimes referred to as Bunker-Jakob), the trustee in Block 11 (the so-called Arrest Block), led two inmates from the Bunker out into the courtyard and stood them facing the Black Wall, one on each side of him. Jakob was a particularly large man, thought by inmates to have been the one-time sparring partner for Max Schmelling,

---

49 Stellungnahme des RA Dr. Müller, FFStA 4 Ks 2/63, Bd. 88, Bl. 17,189.
50 Ibid.
51 Ibid., Bl. 17,190.
52 The prosecution, in a letter to Langbein explaining the dismissal of charges against one of the preliminary suspects, Kurt Uhlenbroock, noted, "Decisive for this decision was the fact that German law does not recognize either guilt by function [*Funktionshaftung*] or punishment based on suspicion alone. Rather, concrete evidence must be provided for every accused that he personally participated in criminal activities." Vogel to Langbein (September 3, 1963), FFStA HA 4 Ks 2/63, Bd. 16, Bl. 2444.
53 "Anklageschrift," pp. 394–98.

and used his size and strength to keep the victims in line during executions.[54] Boger then took a small caliber rifle that, according to inmates, he had had made especially for this purpose, and approached the victims from behind. He stood approximately five or six steps behind them, at a spot marked on the ground for this purpose. He shot the two inmates in the back of the neck (the so-called *Genickschuß*), first the one on the left, then the one on the right. As soon as they fell to the ground, Jakob would drag the bodies aside before going back inside Block 11 and leading two more inmates into the courtyard, whereupon the whole procedure was repeated. On this occasion, according to Kurz, Boger shot at least fifty or sixty inmates. From the prosecution's point of view, this was nearly perfect testimony.

This kind of precise testimony also raised a further issue, which the prosecution was always at great pains to address: namely, how and why the witness was in a position to observe these events and how he could recognize the defendant(s) involved. In this particular case, the indictment pointed out that "the witness already knew the defendant Boger personally at this time (February 1943) because he had previously had to deliver one of his fellow inmates to him [Boger]. The witness had resolved, together with several fellow inmates, to observe the executions from the attic of Block 21. The windows in this block facing the courtyard between Block 10 and 11 were painted over but previous observers had already scratched off some of the paint."[55] What the prosecution tried to do here was to defend the credibility of the witness *avant-la-lettre*, before it could even be called into question. In the trial, it would not prove so easy to defend this credibility against the sharp attacks by the defense.

In addition to the obvious task of demonstrating criminal activity by the defendants, the prosecution also faced the legally more difficult challenge of demonstrating their subjective motivations, a task rendered all the more significant by their decision to charge all of the defendants as perpetrators. Yet, somewhat surprisingly, the prosecution chose not to take on the issue of perpetratorship directly in the indictment.[56] It is possible that the prosecution felt that the evidence against the defendants was so strong and the crimes so serious that the judges reviewing the indictment during the *Zwischenverfahren* would feel compelled to treat all of the defendants as perpetrators. It is also possible that the prosecution was simply trying to evade a particularly difficult issue for tactical reasons. In either case, the prosecution seriously misjudged the situation, given that the review court reduced the charges against roughly half of the defendants from perpetrator to accessory.

[54] In fact, according the prosecution, Kozelczuk had never been Schmelling's sparring partner but inmates believed this on account of his large size. See Vogel to Eytan Liff (August 20, 1963), FFStA HA 4 Ks 2/63, Bd. 16, Bl. 3431–32.
[55] "Anklageschrift," p. 394.
[56] There is no statutory reason for this decision. See §200 StPO.

Still, the prosecution did attempt to deal with the issue of defendant motivation indirectly, by addressing in particular their awareness of the illegality of the actions at the time. In the first instance, where a murder had been committed under orders, the indictment asserted that the defendants had been perfectly aware that these orders were illegal. For instance, in accusing Bruno Schlage of participating in executions at the Black Wall, the indictment stressed that "he knew that the executions were carried out without a proper trial and were illegal."[57] Such claims are important because, since the SS was held after the war to fall under military as well as civilian law, a defendant could be convicted per §47 *Militärstrafgesetzbuch* (MStGB) for carrying out a criminal order only if he knew that order to be illegal; otherwise, sole responsibility fell on the shoulders of the commanding officer.

In the case against Mulka, the indictment went further, asserting that he was aware of "at least the external circumstances that accompanied the extermination system in the concentration camp Auschwitz" even before he was promoted to adjutant.[58] Consequently, "his promotion to adjutant cannot be understood as a one-sided act on the part of the camp commandant" but demonstrated both a degree of trust between Mulka and Höß, as well as the "necessary acquiescence" on Mulka's part.[59] The key point here is that Mulka was an active and *willing* participant in these murders, that he voluntarily acquiesced in their criminal character, and hence internalized the criminal motives animating the Nazi genocide. On this reading, Mulka was a perpetrator, not an accomplice. Similar claims were made regarding the attitudes of the camp medical personnel regarding their role in selecting inmates for the gas chambers, where Dr. Lucas's consultation with his hometown bishop regarding the obligation to follow "immoral orders" was presented as proof of his awareness of the illegality of his actions.[60]

Order to Convene

Under German criminal procedure, the prosecution's indictment does not represent the final word in bringing charges against the defendants. That right is reserved for the courts. The indictment is, in this sense, a recommendation. It is presented to the convening court, which then decides whether and in what form a trial is warranted. In the Auschwitz case, the decisive question for the convening court proved to be the issue of perpetration.

The Third Criminal Division of the *Landgericht* at Frankfurt, which drafted the order to convene, was not convinced by the prosecution's claim that all of the defendants should be charged as perpetrators of *Mord*, and they

---

[57] "Anklageschrift," p. 31.
[58] Ibid., p. 343.
[59] Ibid., p. 344.
[60] Ibid., p. 608.

reduced the charges against half of them to accessory (*Beihilfe*).[61] Clearly, the judges on the panel were not persuaded by either the indictment's tacit argument that the brutal character of the actual genocidal measures at Auschwitz constituted prima facie evidence of a perpetrator's disposition on the part of the defendants or that the defendants' purported awareness of the illegality of their actions provided an indication of their subjective affirmation of those crimes.[62] Still, the *Eröffnungsbeschluß* did charge eleven defendants as perpetrators of *Mord*.[63] In all eleven cases, however, the evidence indicated that the defendants had directly and personally killed their victims. Here, the court followed the BGH's ruling that "[w]hoever kills another human being with his own hands is fundamentally a perpetrator, even when he does so under the influence and in the presence of another."[64] In all but three cases where the court charged the defendants as perpetrators (Bednarek, Capesius, Hofmann), at least some of the victims could be identified by name. The convening judges were evidently willing to consider someone a perpetrator only if his actions very closely resembled those of an "ordinary" murderer as envisioned by the penal code.

Those defendants whose crimes at Auschwitz did not extend beyond the conscientious fulfillment of their duties, however murderous, were considered only accomplices. In contrast to the defendants charged as perpetrators, who were alleged to have precisely met the full definition of *Mord* per §211 StGB on the basis of their own independent actions, those charged as accomplices were alleged only to have indirectly participated in the killing of inmates in the course of selections or gassing operations. In other words, those who did not kill with their own hands were not considered perpetrators. However, even some defendants who had personally killed their victims were likewise charged as accomplices.

The key difference in these cases seems to have been the degree of private initiative exercised by the defendant. For instance, the defendant Klehr was charged as a perpetrator. The main allegations against him were that he had participated in selections in the inmate infirmary and had also killed inmates with phenol injections in the heart, a frequent method of "clearing out" the inmate hospital when it became overcrowded. The defendants

---

[61] The charges against Breitwieser, Frank, Hantl, Höcker, Lucas, Mulka, Schatz, Scherpe, Schlage, Schoberth, and Stark were reduced to accessory to *Mord*. In addition, Dylewski and Broad were charged with both *Mord* and accessory to *Mord*. "Eröffnungsbeschluß," FFStA 4 Ks 2/63, Bd. 88, Bl. 17074.

[62] In this, the court was simply following typical judicial practice in concentration camp trials. See Kerstin Freudiger, *Die Juristische Aufarbeitung von NS-Verbrechen* (Tübingen: Mohr Siebeck, 2002), p. 151.

[63] Boger, Dylewski, Broad, Hofmann, Kaduk, Baretzki, Bischoff, Dr. Capesius, Klehr, Nierzwicki (dropped from the proceedings prior to the trial for health reasons), and Bednarek.

[64] BGHSt, vol. 8 (1956), p. 393.

Scherpe and Hantl were similarly alleged to have participated in hospital selections and to have injected inmates with phenol. And yet they were charged only as accomplices. The key difference was that whereas Scherpe and Hantl always worked in cooperation with an SS physician, who was both their superior officer and who formally oversaw the process of selecting inmates for injection, Klehr was accused of both having independently selected hospital patients and of having committed individual atrocities.[65] Because Klehr operated on his own, outside the bureaucratically defined division of labor in the camp, the *Eröffnungsbeschluß* considered him to be a perpetrator, whereas defendants such as Scherpe or Hantl, who were charged with many of the same crimes, were charged as accomplices because they had merely fulfilled their officially designated duties, however murderous these may have been. Here we see an early indication of that bifurcation of defendants into two groups that would become so apparent in the final verdict: those who had killed with their own hands and those who had "merely" participated in genocide.

[65] "Eröffnungsbeschluß," FFStA 4 Ks 2/63, Bd. 88, Bl. 17096–99, 17100–101.

5

Opening Moves

December 20, 1963, to February 6, 1964

On a cold, crisp December morning in 1963, judges and lawyers in their traditional robes with white collars, defendants in conservative suits accompanied by uniformed police guards, spectators bundled up against the weather, and over a hundred journalists from around the world gathered in the central meeting hall of Frankfurt's medieval city hall for the opening of the Auschwitz Trial. A handwritten sign on the door announced the "proceedings against Mulka and others."[1] At the front of the room stood a series of poster-sized maps of Auschwitz, while the entryway was bedecked with flowers for the city council's Christmas party.[2] For twenty minutes before the start of the proceedings, television crews and photojournalists were allowed to take pictures in the improvised courtroom. They focused their attention on the defendants escorted into the room from investigative detention. "Some of the accused shy away from this kind of publicity. They hide their faces behind notebooks and file folders or they sink their heads deep in their hands. They wait nervously under the scrutiny of the cameras for the trial to begin. The 'free' defendants, those not in investigative detention, remain almost unnoticed."[3]

This fascination with the defendants, at least those photogenic ones in police custody, is of course a staple of photojournalism. In this case, however, it is also an entirely apt metaphor for the start of a German trial, which begins by interrogating the defendants regarding both their biographies and the facts of the cases against them. Trials are always in some significant sense *about* the defendants, but that does not necessarily mean that the defendants themselves are always the central actors in the proceedings. Often their attorneys speak on their behalf, prosecutors and witnesses make allegations against them, and judges and jurors deliberate their fate;

---

[1] "Verhandlung gegen Mulka und andere," *FAZ*, December 21, 1963.
[2] Ibid.
[3] Hans-Jürgen Hoyer, "'Ich wußte nicht, was Auschwitz ist,'" *FR*, December 21, 1963.

the defendants themselves can often remain an enigma in a trial. However, German criminal procedure quite deliberately places them center-stage at the start of a trial; it is their opportunity to tell, in their own words, their side of the story. And yet the Auschwitz Trial was no ordinary criminal trial; it was suffused with politics, the politics of memory and the politics of the Cold War. This too formed part of the trial's drama.

The Cold War Enters the Courtroom

Like all German criminal trials, the Auschwitz Trial was supposed to open with the spotlight firmly on the defendants. Yet before the court could even begin questioning the defendants, it was spectacularly confronted with the fact that this was not, and could not be, an ordinary criminal trial no matter how hard Judge Hofmeyer tried to keep the proceedings within narrow juridical bounds. Friedrich Karl Kaul, with a flare for the dramatic matched only by his great adversary Laternser, arrived in the courtroom to demand a seat as a civil counsel, much to the delight of the media. "The 120 domestic and foreign journalists sense what is in the air this morning, as they crowd into the Frankfurt city council chambers in the venerable 'Römer' for the opening of the trial, intending to rip aside the 'veil of the past.' It is a short, thickset man who stands in the concentrated fire of the flash bulbs long before the court convenes. The first target of the cameramen was not the large posters showing maps of the camp or the model of the crematoria. Instead they concentrated on this little man. His name? Professor Dr. F. K. Kaul, star attorney for the East Zone."[4]

Kaul had convinced the Central Committee of the SED that by serving as civil counsel in Nazi trials, he could turn these into a forum for East German propaganda.[5] In making his case for such efforts to Walter Ulbricht, Kaul argued that since the West Germans were trying to "intimidate" the East German government by threatening to bring murder charges against border guards for "their dutiful actions against criminals" (i.e., shooting people trying to cross the Berlin Wall), it was imperative to strike back. "A whole series of counter-measures are possible on the so-called 'juridi- cal' [*justiziel*] level that will soon rob the class enemy of their interest in

---

[4] Max Karl Feiden, "Einer der 21 Angeklagten im Auschwitz Trial ist noch Stolz auf seine niedrige SS-Nummer," *Ruhr-Nachrichten*, December 21, 1963.

[5] Kaul to ZK SED (June 21, 1961), Bundesarchiv, Berlin-Lichterfelde (BAB), Stiftung Archiv der Parteien und Massenorganizationen der DDR (SAPMO), DY 30/IV 2/2.028/57, Bl. 205. For Kaul's role in East German propaganda efforts in West German Nazi trials, cf. Annette Rosskopf, "Anwalt antifaschistischer Offensive: Der DDR-Nebenklagevertreter Friedrich Karl Kaul," in Irmtrud Wojak, ed., *"Gerichtstag halten über uns selbst...": Geschichte und Wirkung des ersten Frankfurter Auschwitz-Prozesses* (Frankfurt: Campus Verlag, 2001), pp. 141–61, and Annette Weinke, "Strafverfolgung nationalsozialistischer Verbrechen in den frühen Sechzigern: Eine Replik," *Mittelweg 36* 3 (2001): 45–48.

these terroristic measures."[6] Indeed, Kaul argued that such judicial counter-
measures were particularly appropriate in West Germany because Bonn hid
its "imperialist-fascistic core values [*Grundkonzeption*]" behind an "almost
inflationarily exaggerated judicial and legal [i.e., juridical] authoritarian
practice ('*Rechtsstaat*')."[7] According to Kaul, "our strategic goal should be
to convince people of the universally valid point that the GDR is the only
legitimate representative of the German nation, since only under the social
order realized there can the Nazi past be overcome and any type of regression
to that past be prevented."[8]

At the suggestion of Albert Norden, who had since 1960 been in charge of
the GDR's propaganda offensive against the "renazified Federal Republic,"
the Politburo of the Central Committee of the SED decided to use Kaul to
try to turn the Auschwitz Trial to its own purposes.[9] "The large Auschwitz
Trial starting on December 20 in West Germany will be turned into a tribunal
against IG Farben by the GDR. Well-known personalities from the GDR, like
comrades Minister (Erich) Markowtisch, Bruno Baum, Stefan Heymann and
other former Auschwitz inmates will testify or serve as civil plaintiffs in this
trial and will bring to light new allegations against IG Farben."[10] Within
two weeks, Kaul had begun assembling the necessary paperwork for his
application to serve as civil counsel.[11]

In finding appropriate clients to serve as civil plaintiffs, Kaul confronted
two distinct problems. First, as he informed the Central Committee, it was
not enough that he find GDR citizens whose relatives had died in Auschwitz.
Rather, West German law required that "they have been killed by one of the
twenty-four [*sic*] defendants. So far, we are lacking any evidence for this."[12]
At the same time, because the point of Kaul's participation in the Auschwitz
Trial was primarily political, and since, furthermore, the civil plaintiffs might
have to testify in the trial, it was imperative that the persons in question
be politically "100% reliable."[13] To resolve both these problems simultaneously, Kaul cooperated closely with the East German Attorney General's
Office, though he himself seemed to feel that the problem of finding plaintiffs

---

[6] Kaul to Ulbricht (September 4, 1961), BAB, SAPMO DY 30/IV 2/2.028/57, Bl. 215.

[7] Friedrich Karl Kaul, "Überlegungen bettfd. Notwendigkeit eines Ausschusses für justizielle
    Fragen von gesamtdeutscher Bedeutung" (n.d. [probably late 1961]), BAB, SAPMO, DY
    30/IV 2/2.028/57, Bl. 237.

[8] Ibid., Bl. 237–38.

[9] Michael Lemke, "Kampagnen gegen Bonn: Die Systemkrise der DDR und die West-
    Propaganda der DDR, 1960–1963," *Vierteljahrshefte für Zeitgeschichte* 41 (1993): 153–74.

[10] Beschluß des Politbüros (November 19, 1963), BAB, SAPMO, DY 30/J IV 2/2 A-999.

[11] Vollmachten, Entwurf I/Sk (December 5, 1963), BAB, Nachlaß Kaul, N 2503, Bd. 195.

[12] Kaul to Arne Rehahn, ZK SED (December 4, 1963), BAB, Nachlaß Kaul, N 2503, Bd. 195.

[13] Kaul to ZK SED (n.d.), BAB, Nachlaß Kaul, N 2503, Bd. 199. Kaul did note that in some
    cases, the civil plaintiffs could be excused from testifying for health reasons but that some at
    least would have to go to Frankfurt. See also Rosskopf, "Anwalt antifaschistischer Offen-
    siven," pp. 147–48.

who would pass legal muster in the West German courts was more pressing than their political reliability.[14] This was all the more true since Kaul felt it imperative that he be able to serve as civil counsel right from the very start of the trial, if he was to deal competently with the "'pinnacle' of the West German Nazi defenders," such as Laternser and defense attorney Stolting.[15]

On December 5, 1963, Kaul sent the Frankfurt court his formal application to serve as counsel for nine GDR citizens in the cases against sixteen of the accused.[16] The prosecutor's office advised the court to reject the application, not as a matter of principle but simply because, as Kaul had feared, it was "ungrounded."[17] And indeed, there was very little in Kaul's application to connect his clients to the accused or even to prove that they were in fact related to the victims in question. Rather, Kaul simply asserted that relatives of his clients died in Auschwitz and that, therefore, the accused must have been connected. Based on the prosecution's advice, Hofmeyer sent a letter to Kaul on December 9, informing him that in its present form, his application to serve as civil counsel in the trial was unlikely to be approved but that if he could provide better documentation, the court would be glad to consider his application.[18] Kaul evidently never received the letter, however.

Kaul arrived in Frankfurt on December 19, 1963, the day before the trial began, armed with sworn affidavits from his clients attesting that their relatives had been killed in Auschwitz, though at this point, the linkages to the defendants remained vague and speculative.[19] When Kaul showed up at Frankfurt's central court building, the secretary informed him of Hofmeyer's letter from the preceding week. Nonetheless, Kaul, having already spoken of this matter with presiding judge of the Third Criminal Chamber, responsible for ruling on his application, remained optimistic that the affidavits he had brought with him would suffice.[20] However, Kaul's optimism soon proved to be misplaced.

The secretary told him that the Third Criminal Chamber no longer met on Thursdays and that he would have to present his affidavits directly

---

[14] See, e.g., Kaul to Oberste StA der DDR (December 5, 1963), BAB, Nachlaß Kaul, N 2503, Bd. 195.

[15] Kaul to Rehahn (December 4, 1963), BAB, Nachlaß Kaul, N 2503, Bd. 195.

[16] Kaul, Antrag (December 5, 1963), FFStA 4 Ks 2/63, Bd. 89, Bl. 17,478.

[17] FFStA to Hofmeyer (December 9, 1963), FFStA 4 Ks 2/630, Bd. 89, Bl. 17, 460.

[18] Hofmeyer to Kaul (December 9, 1963), FFStA 4 Ks 2/63, Bd. 89, Bl. 17, 459.

[19] See Addendum I/Kr (December 18, 1963) to Vollmachten of December 5, 1963, BAB, Nachlaß Kaul, N 2503, Bd. 196.

[20] Friedrich Karl Kaul, "Bericht über den Auschwitz-Prozeß: Donnerstag 19 Dezember und Freitag 20 Dezember 1963" (December 21, 1963), BAB, Nachlaß Kaul, N 2503, p. 1. [Pagination internal.] This report, like all of Kaul's reports on the trial, was sent to the *Komitee der Antifaschistichen Widerstandskämpfer in der DDR* (Committee of Anti-Fascist Resistance Fighters in the GDR), the East German Attorney General's Office, and the Central Committee of the SED.

to the presiding trial judge. Chasing Hofmeyer back and forth between the courthouse and the city council chambers, Kaul was finally told that Hofmeyer was too busy to meet and that he should leave his affidavits with the secretary. "This refusal to see me was the first sign that my admission as civil counsel was in jeopardy."[21] In a worried conversation with Großmann, the lead prosecutor, Kaul was told that there was no doubt he would be admitted and that, indeed, the prosecution had already reserved a seat in the courtroom for him. But once he heard that Hofmeyer had refused to see Kaul, Großmann immediately back-pedaled, saying that, of course, "he could not say for sure."[22]

The next morning, when he arrived in the improvised courtroom in the city council chambers, Kaul found out from his friend, the East German legal reporter Rudolf Hirsch, that at a press conference the preceding day, Hofmeyer had declared the status of Kaul's application to be "doubtful."[23] Fearing that he might not even be admitted to the courtroom, Kaul had arrived already wearing his lawyer's robes in order to avoid being stopped by the tight security checks surrounding the trial. In the meantime, waiting for the trial to begin, Kaul relished the media attention he was receiving. "With routinized composure, well aware of his rare worth, he allows the storm of attention to roll over him, visibly enjoying it. He knows the stage and his role."[24] When the trial opened at 8:30 A.M., Kaul found out to his great surprise that he was not the only civil counsel but that Ormond had been admitted "already in July 1963!"[25] According to Kaul, Ormond avoided him. "Obviously," Kaul added with noticeable venom, "we are dealing here with members of the *other* Auschwitz Committee."[26]

After rapidly acknowledging Ormond's formal admission as civil counsel, Hofmeyer turned to Kaul and asked for an additional copy of his application, since the original was still with the *Beschlußkammer*. He then explained that client statements alone did not constitute proof that they were related to Auschwitz victims. Kaul responded that he had documentary evidence (e.g., marriage licenses and birth certificates) for three of his clients. But before he could even hand them over to the court, Laternser rose in protest. He objected that Kaul should not even be allowed to speak, since until he was formally admitted as civil counsel, he was "not even a participant in this

---

[21] Ibid., p. 2.

[22] Ibid.

[23] Ibid. On Hirsch, see Rudolf Hirsch, *Um die Endlösung: Prozeßberichte über den Lischka-Prozeß in Köln und den Auschwitz-Prozeß in Frankfurt/M.* (Rudolstadt: Greifenverlag, 1982).

[24] Hoyer, "'Ich wußte nicht, was Auschwitz ist.'"

[25] Kaul, "Bericht 19 and 20 December 1963," p. 3.

[26] Ibid., p. 2. It is not clear exactly what Kaul is referring to here. It could either be Ludwig Wörl's Deutsches Auschwitz-Komitee or the Comité International des Camps, the organization Langbein moved to after he left the IAC.

trial in the legal sense."[27] When Kaul tried to respond, the court refused to recognize him. The prosecution suggested a compromise: that the matter be postponed and that the court hold a special session to consider Kaul's application. Kaul's attempt to respond was again denied by the court.

Laternser, however, objected, this time at great length, saying that it was irrelevant whether Kaul could pass the formal legal hurdles regarding his clients, since he was not, and ought not to be, allowed to take part in West German trials in the first place. Based on his written protest of December 19 (i.e., the day before the trial opened), Laternser's main objection was political; he argued that Kaul was an instrument of the East German government and should not be allowed in a West German courtroom under any circumstances. To support this claim, Laternser cited both the 1962 decision by the three Allied powers governing West Berlin barring Kaul from the city, as well as the BGH decision prohibiting Kaul from practicing as a defense attorney.[28] In both cases, Laternser stressed, the key point was that Kaul did not possess the requisite "independence" to practice law in West Germany.[29] In particular, the BGH had held that an attorney "who does not conduct his defense independently but rather follows directives from uninvolved political parties is legally excluded from serving as a defense attorney."[30] Laternser argued that, by extension, Kaul ought not to be allowed to practice as a civil counsel, either, since the position entailed the same lawyerly responsibilities.

Once again, Kaul was denied permission to respond by the court. Instead, the prosecution was allowed to respond to Laternser's objections. They pointed out that while Kaul was barred from West Berlin, West Berlin was not West Germany and that therefore the ban was irrelevant. They also pointed out, rightly, that the BGH decision was technically valid only for that particular case and did not constitute a general disbarment for Kaul.[31] At this point, despite the animosity Kaul had perceived earlier, Ormond intervened on his behalf. He explained that the court did not have the right to prohibit Kaul from speaking, since by applying to serve as civil counsel, he was already a formal participant in the trial until such time as the court officially rejected the application. "A point I had been trying to make for twenty minutes," Kaul noted in his report.[32]

Yet once again, the court declined to let Kaul speak, instead giving Laternser the opportunity to respond to the prosecution's points. Laternser simply

[27] Ibid., p. 3.
[28] Hans Laternser, *Die andere Seite im Auschwitz-Prozeß, 1963/65* (Stuttgart: Seewald Verlag, 1966), pp. 392–95. See also BGH Beschluß (March 2, 1961), NJW 14 (1961): 614.
[29] Ibid.
[30] BGH Beschluß (March 2, 1961), NJW 14 (1961): 614. Cited in Laternser, *Andere Seite*, p. 392.
[31] Kaul, "Bericht 19 and 20 December 1963," p. 4. Laternser cited, but for obvious reasons chose not to emphasize, this aspect of the BGH decision. Laternser, *Andere Seite*, p. 394.
[32] Kaul, "Bericht 19 and 20 December 1963," p. 4.

reiterated his earlier objections. Finally, after nearly half an hour, Kaul was given permission to respond. In a fit of pique, he nearly brought his response to a close before it even started. He complained that he had not been allowed to respond for so long and pointed out that even if the law did not grant him the right to speak, "it would have been a *nobile officium* – a duty to decency – to have allowed me to respond immediately to Laternser's objections."[33] Hofmeyer, clearly annoyed, interrupted and demanded to know whether Kaul meant this as a criticism of his manner of directing the proceedings. Kaul was in jeopardy of being silenced once more. "I explained to him that since he had finally granted me the right to speak, I did not understand the point of his question."[34]

Kaul then launched, "in a swell of rhetoric, packed with Latin quotes," into his counter-arguments before Hofmeyer could decide whether or not he had indeed been insulted.[35] As far as his ban in West Berlin was concerned, Kaul asserted that this was "above all a product of the Cold War" and that many prominent West Berlin judicial figures, including the president of the court where Kaul was licensed, had objected to this measure.[36] After all, Kaul continued, such measures were contrary to efforts to "normalize relations in Berlin," a claim that provoked considerable unrest in the courtroom.[37] As for the issue of his independence, Kaul asserted that "in this case, one could rest assured that I would act with the utmost independence, that was guaranteed by the very nature of the crimes under debate, by the fact that I am a member of the German Socialist Unity Party, a citizen of the GDR, a member of a Jewish family who had themselves suffered greatly under the Auschwitz murderers and, finally, a concentration camp inmate myself."[38]

After Kaul's performance, the court withdrew to chambers to consider the matter. After a long recess, the court returned and announced a compromise proposal. It formally rejected Kaul's application but did so solely on technical grounds. The court pointed out that Kaul's application did not contain adequate evidence either of a personal connection between his clients and the victims in question or that any of the defendants were implicated in the murder of those victims. From this Kaul concluded rightly that if he could provide that evidence, the court would positively reconsider his application.[39]

Kaul hurried back to East Berlin to gather the necessary evidence. By the start of January, Kaul had found three additional clients (Margarete

[33] Ibid., p. 5.
[34] Ibid.
[35] Ekkhard Häussermann, "Rededuele im Auschwitz-Prozeß," *Kölnische Rundschau,* December 21, 1963.
[36] Kaul, "Bericht 19 and 20 December 1963," p. 5.
[37] Ibid. On the public outcry, see Hoyer, "'Ich wußte nicht, was Auschwitz ist.'"
[38] Ibid., p. 6.
[39] Ibid., pp. 6–7.

Dombrowsky, Käte Jaffe, and Curt Olschowski) whom he felt could provide the requisite concrete evidence.[40] On January 6, 1964, the third trial session, Kaul returned with his new evidence. Laternser nonetheless continued to protest Kaul's admission as civil counsel.[41] He again complained that Kaul was allowed to speak before being formally admitted as civil counsel.[42] Kaul, allowed this time to respond, noted that "in the interests of the legal profession," he felt it necessary to defend his right to speak and pointed out the irony that Laternser, otherwise "so strongly oriented toward formalities," was objecting to his presence, since his application did not pertain to any of Laternser's clients.[43] After conferring in chambers, the court decided per Ormond's argument on the opening day, that Kaul indeed had the right to speak. Despite this defeat, Laternser argued that Kaul's application still ought to be rejected, as it would be impossible for him to be present without permission from the "so-called GDR." "We know the lack of freedom in this system; another interpretation is simply not possible."[44] Therefore, Kaul must be working directly for the East German government. In response, Kaul simply laughed quietly over his notes.[45] "In conclusion, Kaul noted that he regretted that the rights of the civil counsel had been drawn into such turbulent political waters. He stood before this court for purely humane and matter-of-fact reasons."[46]

Of course, as the documentary record demonstrates, Laternser's Cold War paranoia was, at least in this case, by no means misplaced. Kaul was indeed working at the behest of the Politburo and was clearly pursuing goals that were far more political than they were legal. But it would be a mistake to take this to mean that Kaul was not acting "independently." All evidence indicates that Kaul was a true believer in state socialism; his political agenda in the trial stemmed at least as much from his own political convictions as it did from any tactical interests on the part of the GDR government. This may not have been the kind of independence the German legal code had in mind for its attorneys, but it would be a mistake to see Kaul as simply a lackey. The initiative for using the Auschwitz Trial for propaganda purposes was his. The Politburo merely followed his lead in this matter. Kaul and not the East German government was the driving force behind his activities in the Auschwitz Trial. In this respect, Kaul's political agenda in the trial was at least as independent as Laternser's own.

---

[40] Vollmachten (January 2, 1964), BAB, Nachlaß Kaul, N 2503, Bd. 196.
[41] Kaul, "Bericht Nr. 1, Zeitspann 6 Januar 1964 bis 17 Januar 1964," BAB, Nachlaß Kaul, N 2503, Bd. 198, p. 1.
[42] Bernd Naumann, "Der Ost-Berliner Anwalt Kaul im Auschwitz-Prozeß als Nebenkläger," FAZ, January 7, 1964.
[43] Ibid.
[44] Gerhard Mauz, "Friedrich Kaul kommt auf Katzenpfoten," *Die Welt*, January 7, 1964.
[45] Ibid.
[46] Naumann, "Ost-Berliner Anwalt."

On this occasion both the prosecution and civil counsel Ormond supported Kaul's application. Furthermore, the evidence in Kaul's application was, to an extent, more concrete this time. Therefore the court decided to admit Kaul as civil counsel, but at this point, only for two of his three clients against the defendants Neubert and Klehr; in the third case, the court still found the factual basis for the application to be insufficiently grounded. "There are no fundamental objections to Kaul's serving as civil counsel," the court ruled. "He is licensed by the West Berlin *Kammergericht*, this license has not yet been revoked and there are no well-grounded fears or suspicions to indicate that he would violate his legal duties in future."[47] By the end of the month, Kaul was able to gather sufficient additional evidence to expand his activities and was, over Laternser's objections, admitted to the cases versus Broad, Capesius, Dylewski, Frank, and Schatz as well.[48]

The battle over whether to admit Kaul to the trial was only the first example of the impact of the political imperatives of the Cold War on the trial. In this case, the court's insistent adherence to juridical norms enabled it to adjudicate between competing political agendas – Kaul's and Laternser's – without having to take an explicitly political stand itself. As Gerhard Mauz commented in *Die Welt*, "In admitting [Kaul], the *Rechtsstaat* has bowed down beyond all measure to its own order."[49] The apparently apolitical decision-making process of the law was not, then, without political consequences.[50] In this case, it gave Kaul the opportunity to try to demonstrate to his superiors on the Politburo that he had been right to pursue political propaganda on a "juridical level."

Interrogating the Defendants

Once the political and technical legal maneuverings concerning Kaul's application to serve as civil counsel were finally dispensed with, the court could turn to the actual business at hand: the interrogation of the defendants. The first step was to question them regarding their individual biographies, the *Vernehmung zur Person*. This took three days (December 20 and 30, 1963, and January 6, 1964). According to the *Hamburger Abendblatt*, one question

---

[47] Beschluß, Frankfurt Schwurgericht (January 6, 1964), BAB, Nachlaß Kaul, N 2503, Bd. 196.
[48] Beschluß des 3. Strafsenats des Oberlandesgerichts Frankfurt (January 29, 1964), BAB, Nachlaß Kaul, N 2503, Bd. 196. The higher court also decisively rejected Laternser's argument that Kaul's disbarment as a defense attorney had any bearing on his activities as civil counsel.
[49] Gerhard Mauz, "Kaul kommt auf Katzenpfoten."
[50] The West German government itself was quite concerned about Kaul's admission as civil counsel, though it too recognized that under German criminal procedure, there was no legitimate way to exclude him. See Bundesminister für gesamtdeutsche Fragen (BgF) to Bundesministerium der Justiz (BMJ) (January 3, 1964), BAK, B 141/34743, BMJ 4000/6E (661), Bd. 2, Bl. 208, and BMJ to BgF (February 3, 1964), BAK, B 141/34743, BMJ 4000/6E (661), Bd. 2, Bl. 234–35.

above all obsessed the court: How it was that such ordinary Germans came to serve in Auschwitz, "even if it is not always posed in these terms."[51]

All of the defendants tried to emphasize the element of luck involved in both their decisions to join the SS in the first place and, especially, in their being posted to Auschwitz. At least six of the initial twenty-two defendants claimed to have been drafted into the SS (Baretzki, Bischoff, Hantl, Schatz, Schlage, and Schoberth). The defendant Kaduk also claimed to have been drafted, but only after having previously volunteered. Two others (Klehr and Scherpe) were transferred into the Waffen or Death's Head SS after having previously joined the general SS voluntarily.[52] These defendants insisted that they had not necessarily *wanted* to be in the SS and that their membership in that organization certainly said nothing about their ideological convictions. As the defendant Bruno Schlage put it, "I have never been active politically, either before or after 1933 or from 1945 to this day."[53]

Yet even those defendants who had voluntarily joined the SS tried to emphasize that this decision was the result not of an ideological affirmation of Nazi values but of circumstances and happenstance. Perhaps the paradigmatic instance of this is the case of Franz Hofmann, who claimed to have joined the NSDAP and the SS in mid-1932 "for business reasons."[54] He was unemployed at the time and presumably hoped that party membership would help him find a job. He further stressed the fact that his brother already owned an SS uniform he could use. "It meant I didn't have to spend any money; after all, I was unemployed."[55] On Hofmann's account, then, nothing more than a combination of opportunism and desperation brought him into the SS.

Robert Mulka, a World War I veteran, had been discharged from the reserve officer corps because of a criminal conviction stemming from payroll fraud during his time in the Freikorps after the war. When World War II broke out, Mulka, as a good patriot, volunteered for military service, but because of his earlier criminal conviction, he was denied entry into the Wehrmacht officer corps. He could have served as an enlisted man, but he deemed this "dishonorable" and refused.[56] Because he felt guilty about not contributing to the war effort, however, he volunteered for the Waffen SS. Mulka also took the opportunity, "his sonorous voice not sparing in theatricality," to stress his activities rescuing victims of the Allied firebombing of Hamburg.[57]

---

[51] Erik Verg, "Wie konnte ein Deutscher zum Dienst nach Auschwitz kommen?" *Hamburger Abendblatt*, December 21, 1963.

[52] For brief biographies of the defendants, see Naumann, *Auschwitz*, pp. 10–26.

[53] Ibid., p. 17.

[54] Ibid., p. 26.

[55] Ibid.

[56] Langbein, *Der Auschwitz-Prozeß: Eine Dokumentation*, vol. 1 (Frankfurt: Verlag Neue Kritik, 1995), p. 163.

[57] "Verhandlung gegen Mulka und Andere," FAZ, December 21, 1963.

The case of Hans Stark may also be taken as indicative of the kinds of reasons the defendants gave for joining the SS. Stark's father was a police officer and gave his sons a "typically Prussian education" stressing obedience and duty.[58] When Stark failed to meet his father's stringent expectations in school, his father decided that he needed firm guidance. To that end, his father wanted to enroll him in the Labor Service or the Wehrmacht, but Stark was too young for either. The SS, however, accepted sixteen-year-old recruits, and his father gave him written permission to enlist. "At the age of sixteen years and five months, Hans Stark began his service in the 2nd SS Death's Head brigade 'Brandenburg' at Oranienburg; he was the youngest recruit there."[59]

If the defendants were insistent that they had not joined the SS out of ideological conviction, they were, if anything, even more adamant in stressing that they had been posted to Auschwitz without any doing on their part.[60] Lead defendant Robert Mulka famously declared that, at the time of his posting, he "didn't know what Auschwitz was."[61] Gerhard Neubert ended up at Auschwitz as a result of difficulties in wartime transport. "He returned from home leave two days late only to find his company gone, whereupon he was assigned to the guard company at Auschwitz, sometime in February or March 1943. 'I asked: Is this a replacement unit? Am I in the right place? They told me: Here you're always in the right place.'"[62] The defendant Schoberth stressed that he had been transferred to Auschwitz only after being twice wounded, so that he was no longer fit for combat duty.[63] Broad and Scherpe insisted that only their myopia, which rendered them unfit for front-line service, led to their being posted to Auschwitz.[64] Kaduk and Dr. Frank, too, were transferred to Auschwitz only after prolonged bouts of illness.[65]

Many of the defendants also claimed to have repeatedly sought transfer to the front rather than continue to serve at Auschwitz. Dr. Lucas, for instance, stated: "Immediately on my arrival at the Auschwitz train station, I received my first horrible impression as a column of inmates marched past on their way to work. That same day, I was invited to share my first glass of schnapps. I was asked whether I had already heard anything about the gas chambers. After these were explained to me, I said that I was a doctor and my job was

[58] Naumann, *Auschwitz*, p. 14.
[59] Ibid.
[60] Herbert Neumann, "Angeblich wollte keiner als SS-Mann nach Auschwitz," *Weser Kurier,* December 21, 1963.
[61] Hoyer, "'Ich wußte nicht, was Auschwitz ist'"; Werner Wiechmann, "Die Auschwitz-Henker sprechen," *Westfälische Rundschau,* December 21, 1963; and "Die Verbrecher von Auschwitz," *Berliner Morgenpost,* December 21, 1963.
[62] Naumann, *Auschwitz,* p. 25.
[63] Ibid., p. 17.
[64] Ibid., pp. 16, 24.
[65] Ibid., pp. 18, 21.

to save human lives, not exterminate them. I wrote a letter to my former commanding officer, but the answer only said that orders were orders, we were in the fifth year of the war and that my old unit was to be disbanded. I should do everything in order to not stand out."[66] In a similar vein, Neubert claimed that when he was inducted into the SS, rather than the police as he had requested, he had made strenuous efforts to avoid service. "No 'correspondence' testifying to his strenuous efforts can be found. 'No, as recently as yesterday I spoke to some lawyers, but nothing exists any more,' he tells the court."[67]

That the defendants were at least partially successful in portraying themselves as innocent victims of fate can be garnered from the following press account. "Admittedly, these are all claims made by the defendants. But a roughly thirty-year-old journalist said, deeply affected, 'Thank God that I was too young back then.'"[68] This journalist clearly felt, not without some justification, that almost any German male of draft age during the war, including himself had he been a few years older, could have ended up in the defendants' shoes. The main point the defendants were trying to make was that they had joined the SS not as committed Nazi ideologues but as ordinary men caught up in the sweep of events. It was not their doing that they had had to serve at Auschwitz but the result of bureaucratic snafus, poor health, or plain bad luck. These hard-luck stories served two functions. First, they were designed to elicit general sympathy, presumably especially among the jurors, many of whom must have had husbands, brothers, or fathers who served in the war. Second, although many of the defendants probably still hoped to win acquittal at this early stage in the trial, by stressing the accidental character of their being in the SS and at Auschwitz, they were establishing what would become the principle fall-back position of the defense: namely, that the defendants were not perpetrators but at worst accomplices, with all of the practical benefits in terms of sentencing that this entailed. In other words, the defendants' version of how they ended up at Auschwitz, while often no doubt truthful enough, also served as a tactical exploitation of the juridical obsession with perpetrator motivation. As one reporter put it with regard to Mulka, "If all that is true, then even the Frankfurt court will not be able do much with this defendant."[69]

Needless to say, however, the defendants did not entirely control the course of their interrogations. The open-ended questioning brought to light aspects of their biographies that hardly served their tactical interests. Although the court chose not to emphasize this fact, and the defendants for obvious reasons mostly tried actively to *de-emphasize* it, the *Vernehmung zur Person* also

[66] Langbein, *Auschwitz*, p. 600.
[67] Naumann, *Auschwitz*, p. 25.
[68] Verg, "Wie konnte ein Deutscher zum Dienst nach Auschwitz kommen?"
[69] Ibid.

revealed that many of the defendants had been at least nominal Nazis prior
to the war, prior even to the Nazi seizure of power. Bischoff, Boger, Frank,
Hofmann, Lucas, and Schatz all joined the NSDAP prior to the Nazi seizure
of power, and Stark joined the SS in 1937. Boger and Frank, in particular,
were "old fighters." Boger joined the Hitler Youth and the SA in 1929 and the
SS in 1930. During his interrogation, Boger declared that he was still proud
of his low membership number in the Nazi party.[70] Frank's roots in the Nazi
party stretched back even further. He was one of the founding members of the
Regensburg branch of the NSDAP in 1922 and had participated in Hitler's
"Beer Hall Putsch" in 1923. In addition, both Frank and Mulka had been
Freikorps members after World War I. Frank participated in the suppression
of labor unrest in the Ruhr, while Mulka was a member of the right-wing
Baltic Guard, "'to prevent the advance of Bolshevism in the West.'"[71] So,
while the defendants' stress on the accidental character of their arrival at
Auschwitz certainly contains a kernel of truth, it should not be forgotten
that this was also a tactical maneuver on their part, designed to aid in their
defense.

On January 6, 1964, after the conclusion of the *Vernehmungen zur Person,* the *Eröffnungsbeschluß* was read out loud in court, so that the defendants would be officially informed of the specific charges against them. Over
the next twelve trial sessions, the defendants were given the opportunity to
respond to these charges during the *Vernehmungen zur Sache* (interrogations regarding the facts of the case). Unlike the *Vernehmungen zur Person,*
where the defendants were legally obligated to respond, they had the option
of remaining silent during the *Vernehmungen zur Sache.* Two defendants,
Boger and Kaduk, chose to exercise this option and declined to comment.[72]

The remaining defendants, however, all took the opportunity to speak
on their own behalf. The most immediately striking thing about their testimony is their near blanket denial of all the charges. With very few exceptions, they denied having participated in any criminal activities while at
Auschwitz. However implausibly, many of the defendants claimed to know
almost nothing of even the most basic functioning of the camp. Schlage, who
worked in Block 11, adjacent to the Black Wall where systematic executions
were conducted, claimed merely to have heard rumors about these.[73] Mulka
stated, "Personally, I never heard anything about executions in the camp,

---

[70] Max Karl Feiden, "Einer der 21 Angeklagten im Auschwitz-Prozeß ist noch stolz auf seine
niedrige SS-Nummer," *Ruhr-Nachrichten,* December 21, 1963.

[71] Naumann, *Auschwitz,* p. 10.

[72] Although civil counsel Ormond was able briefly to get Kaduk's goat, prompting him to
declare that there was no such thing as "standing cells" at Auschwitz (standing cells were
isolation cells in Block 11, where inmates had no room to sit or lie down; inmates were often
left to starve to death in these), Kaduk pompously declared: "Let us stick to the truth. I said
so to the Soviet Major, and I am saying so here." Ibid., p. 55.

[73] Ibid., p. 47.

never reported anything, never ordered anything. I never heard shots."[74] Even more provocatively, when asked about the gas chambers, he claimed, "I heard about them, but I never saw them myself."[75] Indeed, Mulka even went so far as to claim to have never once set foot inside the camp proper, but only to have observed inmates entering through the gate from his office window.[76]

For his part, the defendant Broad laid claim to an even more sweeping ignorance, all the more surprising given that he had written a thorough and detailed report about the camp for his British captors after the war (the so-called Broad Report).

"Did you know that all these transports were gassed?"
   "I knew nothing about it and saw nothing."
"Did you know that entire barracks were gassed?"
   "I heard nothing about selections inside the camp."
"Did you know that the chief of the Political Section [to which Broad was assigned] was given prisoners for liquidation who were then 'injected'?"
   "I never heard about that."[77]

Wherever the defendants were assigned, the criminal activity seemed to have taken place elsewhere. Whatever their duties, these almost never seemed to have entailed killing anyone. To hear them tell it, one would think that killing in Auschwitz was done by way of rumor.

The precise character of these denials varied, depending on whether the charges against the defendants were general or specific. In the former case, where the charges depended heavily on a reading of the camp's hierarchical division of labor, the defendants claimed either that the court did not properly understand the camp hierarchy or that they had occupied an anomalous position within that hierarchy. Thus Mulka, the former adjutant, at times seemed piqued at the extent of the court's civilian ignorance. "Robert Mulka can obviously not comprehend that there are people who do not know what the duties of a company commander are."[78] The other former adjutant, Karl Höcker, similarly claimed with regard to his duties as company commander that he could not issue orders or assign his men to participate in the extermination process, even had he known about these activities:

His jurisdiction over the company was fictitious; he was a company commander on paper only.
   "I think, Your Honor, you do not understand how things were."
   "No, I don't think I do."

[74] "'Nichts gehört, nichts gemeldet, nichts befohlen,'" *Stuttgarter Zeitung*, January 10, 1964.
[75] Paul Mevissen, "Der Adjutant des Teufels," *Abendpost*, January 10, 1964.
[76] Naumann, *Auschwitz*, p. 30.
[77] Ibid., p. 39.
[78] Gerhard Ziegler, "'... und hier war das Krematorium,'" FR, January 10, 1964.

Höcker explains once more: He had been a company commander but had not held the powers ordinarily held by a company commander.

"It was only a paper collection of members of various sections. They were under me only in so far as personnel matters were concerned, not functionally."[79]

In these cases, where the charges were general, the defendants tried to turn the prosecution's case on its head. Because the prosecution relied on an interpretation of the camp hierarchy, the issue turned on the precise character of that hierarchy. If the defendants could plausibly reinterpret that hierarchy, then the prosecution's case would collapse. Accordingly, one of the central questions during the evidentiary phase of the trial would be whether or not the defendants had behaved in a manner typical of their rank and position. They were aided in their efforts to deny their responsibility by the fact that criminal law and bureaucracy operate on fundamentally different principles. The former assigns unitary responsibility; the latter divides it. German criminal law could punish individuals only for their specific actions, but in a bureaucracy, a given outcome may well be the result not only of the concrete actions of numerous individuals, but also of a series of interlocking decisions taken at various levels within the hierarchy. In a bureaucracy, the whole is frequently greater than the apparent sum of its parts. Consequently, it may well be difficult, if not impossible, to find one individual responsible for a given outcome or to parse collective responsibility into discreet sub-units.

One would presume that in cases where the defendants were charged with specific crimes against identifiable witnesses, usually on the basis of eyewitness testimony, it would have been more difficult for them simply to deny these accusations altogether. And yet that is precisely what most of them did. Thus, the inmate Kapo Bednarek was charged exclusively with specific instances of beating or otherwise abusing inmates to death. His typical response: "Not a word of truth."[80] Franz Hofmann tried to provide creative reinterpretations of the specific charges against him. Alleged to have killed an inmate by throwing a glass bottle at his head, Hofmann recounted a very different version of the story. "Well, some high-ranking people from Berlin were expected. Some oak-leaf-decorated dignitary. As I was running past the kitchen I saw a bottle on the ground. I picked it up, called out to a prisoner and an SS man standing nearby, and threw the bottle over to them. Well, they apparently hadn't heard me; the SS man keeled over; I ran to him and had no time to bother about the visitors. Well, then I called the medical officer and the next day the SS man was brought to the St. Nikolai army hospital. There I visited him and apologized. I also brought him a little something I managed to buy at the time."[81] On Hofmann's account, then, not only had

---

[79] Naumann, *Auschwitz*, p. 35.
[80] "Kein Wort daran ist wahr!" *Allgemeine Wochenzeitung der Juden in Deutschland* (AWJD), February 14, 1964.
[81] Naumann, *Auschwitz*, p. 50.

no one died in the incident but the "victim" was not even an inmate but one of his own comrades. Tragedy is here reconfigured as farce.

In some cases, however, either because the evidence was too overwhelming or because the defendant hoped for clemency if he was honest, the defendants chose to admit to having participated in certain killing operations. The defendants consistently denied, however, that they exercised any causal agency in such killings. Josef Klehr, for instance, admitted to killing inmates by injection but immediately stressed that this was done only on direct orders from an SS doctor. "Your Honor, let me describe the general situation to you. I was in a straitjacket. Who were we to say anything? We were ciphers, just like the prisoners. In his [the medical officer's] eyes a man without a higher education was nothing. We couldn't possibly dare to ask such questions, or else we too would have been put against the Black Wall."[82] Here again we see the issue of duress emerge, and this question – whether in fact the defendants were at risk if they refused to obey criminal orders – would remain a central issue throughout the trial.

The defendants' denial of the charges against them extended to the subjective side of the charges as well. In other words, they denied not only having committed any criminal wrongdoing but also having approved of such activity when committed by others. In this regard, the defendants often claimed to have been outraged at the goings-on in the camp. Mulka at first denied any knowledge about "special treatment." But when pressed, he answered "excitedly: 'It was murder, Herr Vorsitzender. Yes, it was murder and I was deeply incensed.'"[83] Of the torture performed by the Political Section where he worked and in which he was alleged to have participated, Bruno Schlage could say only, "The method used there was despicable. I paid no attention to anything because I was tired of life and did only that which I had to do."[84] Perhaps most perverse of all, Willy Frank, the Nazi "old fighter" who participated in Hitler's Beer Hall Putsch, declared, "Jews have frequently been guests in my parents' house. I even have an adoptive aunt who is Jewish. I can only say I considered what was happening to be monstrous."[85]

The defendants also claimed to have thought that any orders they received were legally valid. The former adjutant Höcker, for instance, claimed:

"We were told that the Führer decided on the life or death of a prisoner," Höcker says, and that "all orders for executions or punishment were secret. I never read them. I merely entered them into the secret journal."

"Did you ever entertain doubts about the legality of these orders?"

"The camp had no doubts about the legality of these orders. Whatever came from the RSHA was a legal order."

[82] Ibid., p. 71.
[83] "Nichts gehört, nichts gemeldet, nichts befohlen," *Stuttgarter Zeitung*, January 10, 1964.
[84] Naumann, *Auschwitz*, p. 49.
[85] Ibid., p. 63.

No, he did not know that illegal orders do not have to be carried out. "I did not have sufficient legal training for that."[86]

The defendant Hans Stark admitted both to shooting Soviet Commissars and to dropping gas into the gas chambers. He claimed to be ashamed of what he had done then, of having thought it necessary and unavoidable.[87] However, Stark insisted, not only had he not considered the legality of these orders, he had not considered much of anything at all while in Auschwitz. "I had no opinions of my own. None of us had our own opinions. We had been robbed of the capacity for thought. Others did the thinking for us. We simply received directives. Period. No comment."[88]

Although the early days of the trial were dedicated to the defendants' sides of the story, their emphatic, implausible denials tried Judge Hofmeyer's patience on more than one occasion. At one point, after Klehr reiterated his claim never to have independently selected inmates for injection, Hofmeyer retorted: "You've said that already. But these claims were not made just by a certain stratum of witnesses. There are professors, doctors, inmates, who all say that you selected independently, that you killed someone by making 'sport' with them, that you threw women into the fire. How does it happen that all these people from different groups accuse you?"[89] Needless to say, Klehr had no idea. With regard to Schlage's denials, Hofmeyer noted wryly: "'No one did anything. . . . The commandant was not there, the officer in charge only happened to be present, the representative of the Political Section only carried lists, and still another one only came with the keys.' "[90] Such ironic, almost sarcastic commentary would become one of Hofmeyer's hallmarks during the trial. It was his way of indicating where he personally stood with respect to the defendants, without violating the doctrine of judicial objectivity and his legal obligation to the truth.

The defendants' tactical approach during both the *Vernehmungen zur Person* and *zur Sache* represented a kind of game of chicken with the witnesses yet to come. The defendants were not going to cede any ground unnecessarily and were, in effect, daring the witnesses to prove them wrong. During the course of the evidentiary phase, a preponderate weight of evidence could sometimes get defendants to change their stories but only at the point where further denial would cost them all credibility. The defendants, possibly on advice from counsel, though this cannot be substantiated, were pursuing a dual tactic. Their initial effort was to win acquittal by denying any criminal wrongdoing whatsoever. At the same time, they were also establishing a fall-back position. In particular, their repeated insistence that they had personally

[86] Ibid., p. 35.
[87] "Stark: Ich schäme mich," *Die Welt*, January 17, 1964.
[88] "Geständnis im Auschwitz-Prozeß," FNP, January 17, 1964.
[89] "'Als ich vorbeiging, wurde schon gelüftet,'" FAZ, February 1, 1964.
[90] Naumann, *Auschwitz*, p. 48.

found the events at Auschwitz to be abhorrent, that they had tried as best they could to get out, and that they had even helped inmates when possible were all part of this approach. So was their claim that, to the extent that they were compelled to participate in criminal activities, they had believed these to be legal and that, furthermore, they had operated under extreme duress. These claims all laid the foundation for a second legal argument: namely, that they were not perpetrators but at worst accomplices. In effect, the defendants were saying, "Even if we did participate in these horrible things (which we did not), it was only because we were ordered to do so. We did not like this or approve of these actions. We did what we did only because we feared for our lives. This ought to be grounds for acquittal. But if the court refuses to believe this, the worst that can be said is that we were unwilling accomplices in a crime we disapproved of and only participated in reluctantly. Our inner disposition was not that of perpetrators, who make the criminal will their own, but of accomplices participating in a foreign deed." Clearly, the defense's primary goal was to win an acquittal on objective grounds – the defendants did not in fact commit any crimes – but, failing that, to secure a lenient sentence on subjective grounds – the defendants were merely accomplices.

6

Taking Evidence, February 7, 1964, to May 6, 1965

The evidentiary phase of the Frankfurt Auschwitz Trial is perhaps the most difficult to characterize as a whole. Its long duration, the large number of witnesses called, their distinct testimony, their disparate degrees of knowledge about the camp and the defendants, and the fact that some were survivors, some were SS men, and some were historical experts all make easy generalizations impossible. In particular, the fact that, with the exception of the historical experts, the witnesses all testified on the basis of their personal experience means that this testimony necessarily tended to be anecdotal and fragmentary. Each eyewitness testified mainly as to his or her experience of Auschwitz. And those experiences were necessarily distinct. This led to a situation where, rather like the proverbial blind men and the elephant, each witness could describe only a partial, delimited "truth" about Auschwitz. The prosecution clearly hoped that, taken together, these partial truths would constitute a whole truth, the truth of Auschwitz; whether this hope was justified is difficult to assess.

On the one hand, the Auschwitz Trial gathered an enormous amount of data concerning Auschwitz, much of it presented for the first time to a broad public.[1] And on a number of occasions, the pain and suffering of the survivors was so palpable in the courtroom as to be almost unbearable for the spectators and journalists observing the trial.[2] This surely is one of the most important truths about Auschwitz. On the other hand, the diversity, if not outright disparity, among witness testimony in the Auschwitz Trial, the relatively random order in which witnesses appeared, and the way that survivor testimony was intermingled with SS testimony and each was officially given equal status all conspired to prevent a comprehensive or coherent

---

[1] This point is strongly emphasized in Rebecca Elisabeth Wittmann, "Telling the Story: Survivor Testimony and the Narration of the Frankfurt Auschwitz-Trial," *Bulletin of the German Historical Institute*, no. 32 (spring 2003): 93–101.

[2] See, e.g., "Zuschauer forderten Lynchjustiz an Kaduk," *Bonner Rundschau*, April 7, 1964.

picture from emerging. It is no accident, therefore, that Hermann Langbein, in recounting the trial for publication, chose to eschew a chronological organization for a typological one. Indeed, the fragmentary character of witness testimony in the Auschwitz Trial has prompted one literary critic to remark that "[l]ittle in this bizarre courtroom drama leads to a unified vision of the place we call Auschwitz."[3]

Nevertheless, despite the difficulties posed by the fragmentary character of witness testimony in the Auschwitz Trial, certain general features do emerge. For one thing, the court did make a limited effort to construct the witness testimony in a coherent manner by opening the evidentiary phase with background testimony from both historians and a few selected eyewitnesses whose privileged positions in the camp allowed them to describe the general conditions there in some detail. After that, while domestic witnesses tended to testify before foreign ones, witnesses were largely called according to scheduling convenience. A more coherent organizational structure, in particular one oriented toward building complete cases against individual defendants in a specific order – along the lines of the indictment – would have been difficult to achieve, given scheduling problems, the fact that many witnesses testified against multiple defendants, and that some turned out to have nothing useful to say at all.

At the same time, the evidentiary phase was marked by a series of ongoing conflicts that reflected the dual struggle at work in the trial to determine both the juridical outcome and its representational meaning. The first conflict concerned the historical account of Auschwitz to be given in the trial. To provide the necessary historical context for the trial, the prosecution asked several historians from the Institute for Contemporary History in Munich to give expert reports on various aspects of the history of the Third Reich as these pertained to Auschwitz. Never one to let an opportunity slip by, Kaul asked Professor Jürgen Kuczynski from the Humboldt University in East Berlin to give a report concerning the involvement of IG Farben in Auschwitz.[4] Kaul hoped thereby to demonstrate not only that German "Big Business" had been the driving force behind the Holocaust, but also that many of the same elites continued to dominate the life of the Federal Republic. Two quite antithetical visions of the Nazi past emerged.

The second major conflict to emerge concerned the unavoidable tension between what survivor witnesses wanted to tell the court (and the world)

[3] Lawrence L. Langer, *Admitting the Holocaust: Collected Essays* (Oxford: Oxford University Press, 1995), p. 89.
[4] For a perhaps over-sympathetic account of Kuczynski's testimony, see Florian Schmaltz, "Das historische Gutachten Jürgen Kuczynskis zur Rolle der IG Farben und des KZ Monowitz im ersten Frankfurter Auschwitz-Prozess," in Irmtrud Wojak, ed., *"Gerichtstag halten über uns selbst...": Geschichte und Wirkung des ersten Frankfurter Auschwitz-Prozesses* (Frankfurt: Campus Verlag), pp. 117–40.

about Auschwitz and what the court needed to hear from them. In particular, there was a clear contrast between the *experiential* truth of Auschwitz as a site of pain and loss and the *legal* truth of Auschwitz as site of minutely specifiable criminal acts. This tension was exacerbated by the incongruity of interspersing SS and survivor testimony.

Finally, the Cold War remained a constant presence in the trial. Both Kaul and the defense tried to make use of it to their advantage, but whereas Kaul's goals were almost purely political, the defense tried to manipulate the fears of the Cold War to their tactical legal advantage, for example, by questioning the court's legitimacy and by casting doubt on the reliability of witnesses from East Block countries. Nowhere did the Cold War become more of an issue than in the debates surrounding the proposal to have the court visit the scene of the crime at Auschwitz. This proposal not only raised tricky legal questions concerning its feasibility; it also, perforce, touched on the central conflict between the two German states at that time: which of them represented the "real" Germany. The court's eventual visit to Auschwitz in December 1964 thus has to be seen not only as an important juridical moment in the trial, as a source of evidence, but also as part of a much broader battle over the meaning of the present division of Germany in relation to the shared Nazi past, as well as the implications of this conflict for the broader East/West confrontation.

Historical Testimony

The evidentiary phase of the trial commenced with *Gutachten* (expert reports) from historians from the Institute for Contemporary History in Munich on the history and organization of the SS, Nazi policy toward the Jews, Nazi occupation policy in Poland, and the history and structure of the concentration camp system.[5] Here there was a clear coincidence of interest between the historians from the institute and Fritz Bauer, in that both

---

[5] Hans Buchheim, "Organisation von SS und Polizei unter nationalsozialistischer Herrschaft" (February 7, 1964); Helmut Krausnick, "Nationalsozialistische Judenpolitik unter besonderer Berücksichtigung der Judenverfolgung" (February 17, 1964); Martin Broszat "Nationalsozialistische Polenpolitik (February 17 and 28, 1964); Martin Broszat, "Aufbau der Konzentrationslager" (February 21, 1964). In addition, Hans-Adolf Jacobsen of Bonn University presented on "Kommissarbefehl und Massenexekutionen sowjetischer Kriegsgefangener," but not until August 14, 1964. The arrangements for Jacobsen's *Gutachten* were made separately in June 1964. See FFStA HA 4 Ks 2/63, Bd. 20, Bl. 4060–61. All of these, with the exception of Broszat's essay on Nazi policy in Poland, were reprinted in Hans Buchheim et al., *Anatomie des SS-States* (Munich: DTV, 1994 [1967]). Broszat's report on Poland was based on his earlier book: Martin Broszat, *Nationalsozialistische Polenpolitik, 1939–1945* (Frankfurt: Fischer, 1961). For a general consideration of the place of the Holocaust in West German historiography, especially in the first postwar decades, see Nicolas Berg, *Der Holocaust und die westdeutschen Historiker: Erforschung und Erinnerung* (Göttingen: Wallstein, 2003).

were hoping to use this historical testimony for broader, public pedagogical purposes.[6]

In the face of mounting concern regarding a perceived revival of right-wing extremism, the Institute for Contemporary History was, in the early 1960s, looking for an opportunity to increase its "public impact" within Germany.[7] Yet while there was an emerging consensus among the institute's members that they needed to take public action to counteract these trends, it was not so clear how they should do so. Government representatives on the institute's academic advisory board were particularly reluctant to have the institute, as a state-funded organization, work too closely with the press.[8] Therefore, if it wanted to reach out to the German public sphere to try to counteract what was perceived as a relatively systematic campaign of disinformation and distortion by the radical right, the institute would have to find some other venue. The best-case scenario would be to find some highly public yet officially sanctioned opportunity to set straight the record of the Third Reich once and for all.

That opportunity came with the Auschwitz Trial. As early as May 1961, the prosecution team had approached Hans Buchheim, then director of the institute, to discuss the possibility of obtaining historical *Gutachten* for use in the trial.[9] In November, Bauer and the prosecution team met with members of the institute to hammer out the details.[10] The Frankfurt authorities had two reasons for seeking expert testimony from historians in Nazi cases. On the one hand, they were juridically concerned to mount an effective prosecution. To do so, they felt it necessary to counter what they perceived to have been a potent defense tactic in earlier Nazi trials. Because the courts could evaluate only the evidence formally presented to them, unless commonly

[6] For general consideration of the role of historians from the Institute for Contemporary History in the Auschwitz Trial, see Norbert Frei, "Der Frankfurter Auschwitz-Prozeß und die deutsche Zeitgeschichtsforschung," in Fritz Bauer Institut, ed., *Auschwitz: Geschichte, Rezeption und Wirkung* (Frankfurt: Campus Verlag, 1996), pp. 123–38; Irmtrud Wojak, "Herrschaft der Sachverständigen? Zum ersten Frankfurter Auschwitz-Prozeß," in *Kritische Justiz* 32 (1999): 605–16; and Devin O. Pendas, "The Historiography of Horror: The Frankfurt Auschwitz Trial and the German Historical Imagination," in Jeffrey Diefendorf, ed., *Lessons and Legacies VI: New Currents in Holocaust Research* (Evanston: Northwestern University Press, 2004).

[7] Institut für Zeitgeschichte, Munich (hereafter IfZ), ED 105: Hausarchiv (July 30, 1962), "Ergebnisprotokoll der konstituierenden Sitzung des Wissenschaftlichen Beirats des Instituts für Zeitgeschichte München," p. 7.

[8] See, e.g., the controversy surrounding the institute's work with the magazine *Stern*. IfZ, ED 105: Hausarchiv (August 2, 1963), "Ergebnisprotokoll der Sitzung des Wissenschaftliche Beirats des Instituts für Zeitgeschichte München," pp. 16–17.

[9] Vermerk, Großmann (May 3, 1961), FFStA HA 4 Ks 2/63 Bd. 5, Bl. 865.

[10] See Vermerk über eine Besprechung der altpolitischen Dezernenten der Staatsanwaltschaft bei dem Oberlandesgericht und der Staatsanwaltschaften Frankfurt (M.) und Wiesbaden am 7. November 1962 bei Herrn Generalstaatsanwalt Dr. Bauer (November 8, 1962), Hessisches Hauptarchiv (hereafter HHA), Abt. 631a, Nr. 1800, Bd. 84, Bl. 85.

known historical facts were entered into the record, the court could not take them into account.[11] To circumvent this difficulty, Bauer and the historians had already agreed in October that it made sense to have experts give background testimony covering the general political and historical events that formed the indispensable context for these crimes.[12]

On the other hand, Bauer and his prosecutors were, like the historians from the institute, also deeply concerned about the general public understanding of the Nazi past. As we have already seen, Bauer felt that one of the major points of such trials was to serve as public history lessons. Therefore, the omission of history from prior Nazi trials was a problem not only for the successful prosecution of Nazi perpetrators, but also for the public pedagogical value of such trials. At a high-level meeting of authorities involved in Nazi prosecutions, Bauer noted that "there is a further problem in that in previous trials, the defense has succeeded in dismembering the proceedings into small pieces, so that neither the jurors, trial observers nor the general public can get a general picture [of the events in question]."[13] Because they were not as strictly bound by the proceduralism of the legal process as prosecutors, in particular because they were not as constrained by the doctrine of legal relevance, expert witnesses could provide precisely the kind of general overview of Nazism and the Holocaust that had hitherto been impossible to present in Nazi trials.

A Nazi trial without an adequate historical dimension, Bauer implied, could succeed neither as a trial nor as a public event. "The meaning and purpose of the *Gutachten* should be to make the true intentions of the Nazi regime accessible to the court and the German public in the form of scholarly presentations."[14] These were to be academic rather than prosecutorial in character, pedagogical rather than evidentiary in the narrow sense. Above all, the reports were seen by Bauer and the Frankfurt prosecutors as a way to compensate for what might be termed the *history deficit* in previous Nazi trials. They were to present the broad political, institutional, and historical context of the specific events on trial in a given case.

The institute was clearly delighted to have such a public forum in which to present the scholarly findings of its members and was quite pleased with the public attention the reports garnered.[15] The reports themselves were

[11] Ibid., Bl. 86.

[12] Ibid., Bl. 87. Bauer also noted that such background testimony could also be very useful in clarifying the subjective dimension of Nazi crimes as well, in particular the issue of demonstrating that the defendants were well aware of the criminal content of the orders they received.

[13] Protokoll der 4. Arbeitstagung der Leiter der Sonderkommissionen zur Bearbeitung von NS-Gewaltverbrechen in der Zeit vom 9. bis 10. Oktober 1963 in Wiesbaden, HHA, Abt. 503, Nr. 1161, Bl. 21. The quote is a paraphrase rather than a verbatim transcription.

[14] Ibid., Bl. 21–22.

[15] IfZ, ED 105: Hausarchiv, "Tätigkeitsbericht für die Zeit vom 1. Juli 1963 bis 30 Juni. 1964," p. 18. The institute appears to have overestimated the degree of press coverage

well-constructed, cogent historical analyses based on extensive documentary evidence and represented the state of the historiographic field at the time. These reports were in the best philological tradition of German historiography, critically engaging with their sources in great detail. Each presented substantial, highly detailed, empirically grounded accounts of their specific topics. Indeed, in the foreword to the published version of these reports, the authors asserted that this empirico-critical detail was in fact the defining scholarly *and* political facet of their work. They noted that a trial "demands a particularly high degree of rationality and sobriety," since these reports were not simply historical essays but also legal documents that would help to determine the fate of the accused.[16] And it was precisely this extra degree of reason and sobriety that the authors hoped would render their reports especially "salutary" for a public sphere often too inclined to try to master the Nazi past in overly emotional terms.

At the same time, this legal framework proved to be as much a disadvantage as an advantage. In particular, it greatly restricted the scope of these reports. At their November meeting, the prosecution had given the institute a list of specific topics they wanted covered, and for obvious reasons, these topics focused exclusively on elements of the Third Reich of direct relevance to Auschwitz. Above all, this meant a focus on the SS because Auschwitz was the SS institution *par excellence.* As the historians put it: "The centerpiece of the testimony concerns an anatomy of the SS state. That means: It is less a question of what the SS *did* in detail but rather a matter of the origin and function of the power apparatus created by the unification of the SS and the Police; in other words: how totalitarian domination was exercised in daily practice."[17] To describe these reports as an *anatomy* is supremely accurate because what they did, above all, was to dissect the structure and to describe the typology of the SS and its concentration camp system.

This character as an anatomy of the SS state, the result of both the legal context and the underlying interpretive schema, meant that the evolution of that state was treated only immanently, on its own terms. It was examined neither in relation to developments in German history prior to the Nazi seizure of power nor comparatively, in relation to other aspects of German

---

of the reports, however. See, e.g., the most extensive summary, which was in fact quite brief, in Günther von Lojewski, "Der Weg bis zur biologischen Vernichtung," FAZ, February 18, 1964.

[16] Buchheim et al., *Anatomie,* p. 11. Unless otherwise noted, all citations are to the German edition and all translations are my own. While adequate for its purposes, the existing English translation seeks to present a fluid, readable text, sometimes at the cost of linguistic accuracy. I have therefore chosen to rely on the German text. For a general consideration of the difficult relationship between emotionalism and objectivity in West German Holocaust historiography, see Berg, *Holocaust,* pp. 616–21.

[17] Ibid., p. 10. For a critique of this historiographic approach, see Nicolas Berg, "Lesarten des Judenmords," in Ulrich Herbert, ed., *Wandlungsprozesse in Westdeutschland: Belastung, Integration, Liberalisierung, 1945–1980* (Göttingen: Wallstein, 2002), pp. 131–32.

society during the period 1933–45 or to other forms of authoritarian governance. Historical developments were treated in very narrow, institutional forms. The focus was on the level of formal political action by government and/or party elites. The subject matter was administrative regulations and institutional arrangements. To the extent that non-Nazi elements in German society were touched on at all, they were treated as at least limited opponents of the Nazis. The result was a disassociation of the SS state both from German history more generally and from German society as a whole. Indeed, the central thesis of Buchheim's report, that the SS as a pure executor of the Führer's will represented the negation of the state, its antithesis, meant that, by implication, the state itself was exempted in some measure from the guilt accruing to the SS.[18] To call this mode of argumentation an anatomy is perhaps more apt than its authors realized because its function is to trace a schema of typological connections internal to the "organism" in question, in this case the SS and the concentration camps. To stretch the metaphor a bit: The evolutionary history of that organism per se is bracketed and left aside.

There was one exception to this purely internalist approach to the Third Reich. In his account of Nazi anti-Jewish policy, Helmut Krausnick ranged quite freely across European history, tracing its antecedents in the emergence of modern, nontheological anti-Semitism in the nineteenth century. Krausnick in particular traced the origins of Nazi anti-Semitism to the doctrine of Social Darwinism as it emerged in the 1890s.[19] He also stressed the significant role played by Hitler's own pathological hatred of the Jews. Krausnick's report thus represented the sole effort to present a comprehensive history of at least one aspect of the Nazi regime and the Final Solution. But because it focused on only one aspect of the Nazi regime, albeit the one most directly pertinent in the given context, Krausnick's report too seemed somewhat detached from the broader history of Nazism and the Holocaust. There is a curious disconnect between Krausnick's report and the others. Anti-Semitism has a history that transcends not only Nazism but even – to an extent – Germany itself.[20] Otherwise, there is only the institutional history of the SS itself. In other words, anti-Semitism, as the ideological foundation of the Final Solution, is raised to the level of a transcendental, pan-European phenomenon, while the Third Reich is reduced to the history of one of its constituent organizations. The only mediating link between the two is Adolf Hitler, who forms both the culmination of the cultural trajectory of anti-Semitism and the operative principle guiding the anti-normative activity of

[18] Buchheim, *Anatomie*, pp. 22–27.
[19] Ibid. pp. 555–64.
[20] To be fair, through, Krausnick does stress the essential Germaness of the history of anti-Semitism that led up to the Nazi genocide of the Jews. Ibid., p. 556.

the SS. Thus, the historical account of the Third Reich provided by the historians from the Institute for Contemporary History not only was in the service of the legal needs of the Auschwitz Trial, it was fully consonant with the German judiciary's own construction of the Nazi past that posited Hitler as practically the only true perpetrator of the Holocaust.

Bauer and the Frankfurt prosecutors were not the only ones concerned with the history deficit in West German Nazi trials. Kaul too, though principally for political reasons, felt it was essential to get at the "true" history of the Third Reich, that is, its history as "fascism," understood as the authoritarian expression of monopoly capitalism in the face of a legitimation crisis and growing proletarian resistance. If Nazism was, as East Germany's official position insisted, an expression of monopoly capitalism and if, further, that same capitalism continued to dominate the Federal Republic, then West Germany was, if not a full-blown fascist regime, at least perpetually at risk of becoming one. The GDR, meanwhile, by virtue of its official anti-fascism, was thereby posited as the only true home of German freedom and "real" democracy.[21]

How to get this point across in a trial that explicitly excluded any consideration of the relationship between Auschwitz and Big Business, specifically, IG Farben's synthetic rubber plant in the satellite camp of Monowitz? One way, of course, would be to propagandize in the press about this very exclusion, which the East German press did relentlessly.[22] Another would be, per the Politburo's decision, to call East German witnesses who had been in Monowitz to testify about that relationship. But these approaches left the historiographic high ground to the West German "class enemy." Their historians would be present, with all the apparatuses of scholarly authority. Therefore, it was necessary to fight fire with fire, to have an East German scholar of suitable stature present what would in effect be a rebuttal of the West German account.[23]

On February 21, shortly after the historians from the Institute for Contemporary History had begun their reports, Kaul made a written motion to call Jürgen Kuczynski, an economic historian at East Berlin's Humboldt University, to give testimony on "The Integration of Security Police and Economic Interests in the Establishment and Operations of the KZ Auschwitz and its

[21] See Jeffrey Herf, *Divided Memory: The Nazi Past in the Two Germanys* (Cambridge: Harvard University Press, 1997), p. 111.

[22] See, e.g., the pamphlet published in East Germany: Arbeitsgruppe der ehemaligen Häftlinge des Konzentrationslagers Auschwitz, ed., *I.G. Farben-Auschwitz-Massenmord: Über die Blutschuld der I.G. Farben* (Berlin: Komitee der Antifaschistischen Widerstandskämpfer in der DDR, 1964). See also chapter 9.

[23] There is no clear indication in either Kaul's or Kuczynski's files as to who made the initial suggestion for an East German historical report. See Schmaltz, "Das historische Gutachten," pp. 120–21.

Sub-Camps."[24] On February 27, Kaul informed the court that Kuczynski would be present the following day to give his testimony. The next morning, Kaul informed Hofmeyer that Kuczynski was present. The court was scheduled to continue questioning Martin Broszat regarding his first report (February 21) on the concentration camp system, before he delivered his second report on Nazi policy in Poland. Kaul urged Hofmeyer to allow Kuczynski to present between these two, since his testimony was thematically related to Broszat's first report.[25]

After questioning Broszat, Hofmeyer suggested a brief recess. Kaul moved to hear Kuczynski immediately, before Broszat's second presentation. A number of defense attorneys protested, although Laternser was not present.[26] They complained particularly that they knew nothing about Kuczynski and his qualifications. Kaul gave a brief presentation of Kuczynski's qualifications, and the court recessed to consider the matter. At this point, Laternser arrived with a lengthy written objection to Kuczynski's proposed testimony, stressing that his membership in the SED gave sufficient cause to suspect "bias."[27] The court returned without having made a decision. Kaul felt it unwise to "force" the matter in court because he neither wanted to influence negatively the court's attitude toward Kuczynski before he even gave his testimony nor wanted to "create the general impression that for us this trial was merely a matter of political debates."[28]

During the court recess, Broszat approached Kaul and said that he understood what Kaul was trying to prove by bringing up IG Farben in relation to Auschwitz. This was "the typical Marxist view that National Socialism was merely the last chance for capitalism. In fact, history had shown this to be false."[29] Kaul's response, in his report to the Central Committee, was to condemn Broszat's own report on Nazi Poland policy as "flat," asserting that it tried to shift all the blame onto a few dead Nazis while exculpating the Nazi judiciary and the Wehrmacht in particular. Here one can see that both sides clearly perceived that Kuczynski's testimony was intended as

[24] Kaul to Hofmeyer (February 21, 1964), Hauptverhandlungsprotokoll (HVP) (February 28, 1964), Anlage 1 FFStA 4 Ks 2/63, Bd. 96, n.p. See also Kaul, "Bericht über den Auschwitz-Prozeß" (February 21, 1964), BAB, Nachlaß Kaul N 2503, Bd. 198, p. 1. For Kuczynski's report, see Jürgen Kuczynski, "Die Verflechtung von sicherheitzpolizeilichen und wirtschaftlichen Interessen bei der Einrichtung und im Betrieb des KZ Auschwitz und seiner Nebenlager," *Dokumentation der Zeit: Informations-Archiv* 16 (1964): 36–42. Reprinted in Ulrich Schneider, ed., *Auschwitz – Ein Prozeß: Geschichte-Fragen-Wirkungen* (Cologne: PapyRosssa Verlag, 1994), pp. 33–59.
[25] Kaul, "Bericht über den Auschwitz-Prozeß" (February 27 and 28, 1964), BAB, Nachlaß Kaul, N 2503, Bd. 198, p. 2.
[26] HVP (February 28, 1964), FFStA 4 Ks 2/63, Bd. 96, Bl. 169.
[27] Ibid.
[28] Kaul, "Bericht über den Auschwitz-Prozeß" (February 27 and 28, 1964), BAB, Nachlaß Kaul, N 2503, Bd. 198, pp. 2–3.
[29] Ibid., p. 3. Kaul paraphrases Broszat.

a direct challenge to the West German historians, a political and historio-graphical shot across the bow, as it were. Indeed, after his report, in response to prosecutor Kügler's question concerning IG Farben's use of Polish prisoners for labor, Broszat took the opportunity, in Kaul's assessment, largely to exculpate the firm.[30]

The session ended at 4:30 without Hofmeyer announcing a decision concerning Kuczynski's testimony. Kaul immediately went up to him and demanded to know when Kuczynski would be allowed to testify. Hofmeyer responded that a decision could not be made then, since the court never met after 5 P.M., and, anyway, Kuczynski would probably not be able to testify before April since witnesses were already scheduled. The court would have to see when it could fit Kuczynski's testimony in.[31] Although Kaul was clearly annoyed, he informed his superiors in East Berlin that there was nothing they could do about this in procedural terms, since the timing of *Gutachten* was up to the presiding judge. Kaul saw two possible responses. On the one hand, they could wait until Kuczynski was allowed to testify by the court, in which case, his report could not be published or it would become inadmissible. "That means we would have to wait with our weapons holstered."[32] On the other hand, they could publicly protest the court's postponement and simply publish Kuczynski's report and accept that it would be inadmissible.

While it is not entirely clear who made the decision to follow the first course of action or when, the attention that Kuczynski's testimony was expected to garner from the western media clearly tipped the scales in favor of waiting to have him give his testimony in the trial.[33] On March 13, Kaul, at least according to his (perhaps self-serving) report to the Central Committee, managed to pressure Hofmeyer into admitting Kuczynski.[34] In the afternoon session, Helmut Bartsch, a police detective and former SS officer, testified that he had been sent to Auschwitz to investigate charges of

---

[30] In fact, IG Farben's role in the Third Reich was extremely complicated. While it would be going too far to claim, as Kuczynski tried to do, that they were the driving force behind Auschwitz, one could also hardly say that they emerged entirely blameless. For a very nuanced and well-documented assessment, see Peter Hayes, *Industry and Ideology: IG Farben in the Nazi Era*, new ed. (Cambridge: Cambridge University Press, 2001). On Monowitz more specifically, see Bernd Christian Wagner, *IG Auschwitz: Zwangsarbeit und Vernichtung von Häftlingen des Lagers Monowitz, 1941–1945* (Munich: K. G. Sauer, 2000).

[31] Kaul, "Bericht über den Auschwitz-Prozeß" (February 27 and 28, 1964), p. 5.

[32] Ibid.

[33] See, e.g., the letter from Kaul's boss Albert Norden to the SED Science Department asking them to delay a proposed lecture tour by Kuczynski in Cuba because of his impending testimony in the Auschwitz Trial. "We feel this matter is very important because, in contrast to other trials, the Auschwitz Trial is provoking an extraordinary international echo in the capitalist daily press as well." Norden to Hörning (March 9, 1964), BAB, SAPMO DY 30/IV 2/2 028/125.

[34] Kaul, "Bericht über den Auschwitz-Prozeß" (March 23, 1964), BAB, Nachlaß Kaul, N 2503, Bd. 198.

corruption in the camp. Initially, he claimed to have seen and heard nothing of interest in the camp but was forced under questioning to admit that he had, in fact, heard about selections, injections, and murders in Block 11. On Kaul's reading, these constituted bald-faced lies. When it came time to swear in the witness at the end of his testimony, Kaul objected per §60 StPO that this would constitute perjury.[35] After consultation, the court rejected Kaul's objection. However, when it actually came time to swear the witness in, Hofmeyer balked. Kaul described the scene thus: "Everyone had already stood, the witness had already raised his hand to take the oath when the presiding judge interrupted and reminded the witness that his testimony could be interpreted in various ways. He then asked the witness again whether he did not want to decline his testimony, since he was putting himself at risk of prosecution. The witness said no and took the oath. The presiding judge then told me in a very obliging private conversation that Kuczynski would be heard on Thursday at 2:00 P.M."[36] It is impossible to say whether or not this clever legal maneuver had placed Hofmeyer in such an awkward position that he felt compelled to do Kaul a favor, as Kaul clearly thought, but in either case, Kaul had won his first victory in the Kuczynski matter. The triumph was to prove short-lived.

On March 19, Kuczynski arrived again in Frankfurt to present his report.[37] Once again, as was to be expected, Laternser protested, arguing that Kuczynski was not an "expert witness in the sense of the law... who must be in a position to render independent judgment."[38] Since Kuczynski's position as a professor in East Germany was dependent on the government, it was dependent on his toeing the party line in his scholarly activities as well. Clearly, Laternser continued, the East German government was using Kaul and now Kuczynski for political agitation. Defense attorney Karlheinz Staiger, representing Stark and Hofmann, joined in Laternser's protest, asserting that the "question of the participation of business in the events of the Third Reich is of no relevance to the question as to whether or not the defendants here are guilty in the sense of the indictment."[39] On the other hand, Boger's attorney Hans Schallock, as well as Ormond and Großmann,

---

[35] Unlike defendants, witnesses are subject to penalties for perjury, but it should be recalled that under German criminal procedure, witnesses are not sworn in until after their testimony, so that they are criminally liable for the veracity of their testimony only if they take the oath at the end.

[36] Kaul, "Bericht über den Auschwitz-Prozeß" (March 23, 1964). As far as the documentary record indicates, Bartsch was never in fact prosecuted for perjury. Cf. "Ein Kommissar als Zeuge," FAZ, March 16, 1964.

[37] Kaul had formally invited Kuczynski on the 16th. See Kaul to Kuczynski (March 16, 1964), BAB, Nachlaß Kaul, N 2503, Bd. 198. See also HVP (March 19, 1964), FFStA 4 Ks 2/63, Bd. 96, Bl. 226.

[38] Ibid., Anlage 3, Laternser and Steinacker to FF Schwurgericht (March 18, 1964).

[39] Cited in Schmaltz, "Das historische Gutachten," p. 122.

spoke in favor of giving Kuczynski the opportunity to speak.[40] Under questioning from alternate judge Werner Hummerich, Kuczynski said that his scholarly models were "Marx, Engels and Lenin, and that he agreed with their thesis that, in the 'final analysis,' human actions are determined by relations of production."[41] He further declared it to be "a historical fact that the wrong defendants were on trial. The monopoly capitalists and their helpers who now put atomic bombs in the place of gas ovens are the truly guilty ones."[42] Despite these verbal pyrotechnics on Kuczynski's part, the court rejected Laternser's motion, and Kuczynski was finally allowed to give his report.

The report itself "went off without a hitch," as Kaul put it.[43] Indeed, Kuczynski's report could be properly understood as a minor classic of vulgar Marxism.[44] In contrast to the West German historians in the trial, Kuczynski began with a proclamation of certain meta-historical presuppositions. First, he asserted that "the state and decisive segments of the economy have been intimately bound together for thousands of years."[45] Second, he maintained that whenever a state collapses, "the dominant economic strata try to disassociate themselves from the prior activities of the state, or even try to portray themselves as the victims [*Leidträger*] of the prior state form."[46] In other words, Kuczynski took it as a "self-evident" given of history that the state was only a "servant" of economic interests and that these interests would try to disown the state whenever things went terribly wrong in order to preserve their real power.[47] That was precisely what had happened in West Germany in 1945, he argued.

Yet this endeavor was bound to fail, according to Kuczynski, because the documentary record too clearly demonstrated the degree of interconnection between the Nazi regime and the leading sectors of Germany's economy.

[40] Ibid., pp. 122–23.
[41] Gunther von Lojewski, "Boger: 'In keinem Fall richtig,'" FAZ, March 20, 1964.
[42] Gerhard Mauz, "Ein Professor aus Ostberlin: Kuczynski als Sachverständiger erst zugelassen, dann abgelehnt," *Die Welt*, March 20, 1964.
[43] Kaul, "Bericht über Auschwitz-Prozeß" (March 19, 1964), BAB, Nachlaß Kaul, N 2503, Bd. 198, p. 1.
[44] "There is a continuum of positions [within Marxism]. The most orthodox provides one-to-one correlations between the socio-economic base and the intellectual superstructure. This is referred to as economism or vulgar Marxism." Robert M. Young, "Marxism and the History of Science," in R. C. Olby et al., eds., *Companion to the History of Modern Science* (London: Routledge, 1996), pp. 77–86. This form of Marxism has been widely critiqued among western Marxists. See, e.g., Raymond Williams, *Marxism and Literature* (Oxford: Oxford University Press, 1977), pp. 75–141, and, especially, Moishe Postone, *Time, Labor, and Social Domination: A Reinterpretation of Marx's Critical Theory* (Cambridge: Cambridge University Press, 1993), pp. 43–83.
[45] Kuczynski, "Verflechtung," in Schneider, *Auschwitz*, p. 35.
[46] Ibid., pp. 35–36.
[47] Ibid.

To demonstrate this connection in general, he cited a number of documents (mainly from the IG Farben trial at Nuremberg) proving the close cooperation between IG Farben and the Nazis on a number of issues (e.g., the expropriation of the French chemical industry and foreign propaganda). "It should again be remarked," he concluded, "that a fusion of economy and state is nothing unusual in history, that it can be observed everywhere in the world today, and that the necessity of proving it is merely a result of the fact that the participants from the time of Fascism today deny it out of cowardness and guilt." The implication, of course, was that this "fusion" of state and economy was true of the two contemporary German states as well, the one socialist and "truly" democratic, the other capitalist and incipiently fascist.

As for the specific role that IG Farben played at Auschwitz, Kuczynski did not rest content with pointing to the incontrovertible fact that it had cooperated readily with the SS at the camp, had made extensive use of slave labor provided from among the inmates, and had helped run Monowitz in a brutal and murderous fashion.[48] Rather, he somewhat dubiously argued that IG Farben decided to build a factory at Auschwitz in the first place primarily because of the availability of slave labor, that is, that their intention had been from the very beginning to use the SS as slave procurers. "In addition, the concentration camp of Auschwitz was by no means a belated and accidental discovery in the eyes of IG's leadership. Its occupants were rather counted on as a labor reserve from the very beginning and this also meant its steady and increasing expansion by the SS."[49]

In keeping with his meta-historical presuppositions, Kuczynski had to argue not that IG Farben had been an all-too-willing accomplice in the crimes of the SS at Auschwitz but that it had in fact been a decisive co-perpetrator.[50] That Kuczynski was here putting the theoretical cart before the archival horse can be seen in the way he interpreted one of his principle pieces of evidence for IG Farben's primary interest in slave labor. In a deposition concerning his inspection tour of the three proposed sites for

---

[48] Ibid., pp. 54–59. Cf. Hayes, *IG Farben*, pp. xii–xvi, 347–68.

[49] Kuczynski, "Verflechtung," p. 47. Hayes concurs with Kuczynski that "the expansion of the Auschwitz camp owed more to Farben's decision to build a huge factory in the vicinity than vice versa," but he concludes that "IG Farben opted for Auschwitz on grounds other than the existence of the concentration camp and before the system of 'slave labor' in private enterprises had taken clear form.... But that is not to say that the firm had any discernable compunction about embarking on a course of using human beings without their consent and without paying them." Hayes, *IG Farben*, pp. xii, xv. For a critique of Hayes's conclusions, see Thomas Sandkühler and Hans-Walter Schmuhl, "Noch Einmal: Die I. G. Farben und Auschwitz," *Geschichte und Gesellschaft* 19 (1993): 259–67.

[50] "For many events, it will not be possible to determine who bears the greater responsibility, IG or the SS – not because there is insufficient evidence but rather because the responsibility was, in principle, a divided one, and the measure of responsibility was at times greater for the one, at other times, greater for the other." Kuczynski, "Verflechtung," p. 59.

the company's Buna factory, Otto Ambrose had said, "The presence of a concentration camp was at that time, when I made my first report to K. Krauch and Fritz ter Meer, of no significance for the choice of sites. At that time, the decision was made on the basis of the location of Auschwitz."[51] Kuczynski called this "indirect evidence" for the crucial importance of the availability of concentration camp labor for IG Farben's decision. "After all, why say explicitly that the concentration camp played no role in his thinking, if this had not in fact actually been the case?"[52] To be fair, Kuczynski also provided direct evidence, principally a deposition by Heinrich Bütefisch, likewise from the IG Farben trial at Nuremberg, in which he recalled that, among other factors, the availability of concentration camp labor had played a role in the firm's decision to locate its factory at Auschwitz.[53] Nonetheless, rather than interpret these as contradictory pieces of evidence, Kuczynski insisted that when IG Farben representatives said what he wanted them to say, they meant it, but that when they said the opposite, this was merely an indirect indication that they were secretly saying what he wanted them to say.

In the end, Kuczynski concluded that in its relations with the SS at Auschwitz, IG Farben had had the upper hand. Indeed, on his interpretation, the SS was "to a certain extent" merely the "disciplinary executive organ of IG."[54] With this, Kuczynski had seemingly accomplished all that Kaul had hoped for. IG Farben had been placed center stage in the trial and the crimes of Auschwitz had been laid squarely at its feet. All that remained was for Kaul to make explicit what Kuczynski had left implicit in his report: namely, that many of the same IG Farben directors who had been co-perpetrators at Auschwitz were today running the West German economy and, by extension, the West German state. Kuczynski's testimony, however, was to prove far less useful for this project than Kaul might have hoped.

On completing his report, the defense was given an opportunity to cross-examine Kuczynski. Here Kaul and his historian had greatly underestimated their opponents. Rudolf Aschenauer, representing Boger and Lucas, had been a defense attorney at the IG Farben trial at Nuremberg and knew Kuczynski's documents intimately, better, it turned out, than Kuczynski himself did.[55] Aschenauer started by reading two documents from a book, *SS im Einsatz*, published by the East German Kongress-Verlag.[56] These stated "expressis verbis that IG Farben originally did not want concentration camp inmates as

---

[51] Ibid., p. 48. Cf. Hayes, *IG Farben*, p. 349.
[52] Ibid.
[53] Ibid., p. 49.
[54] Ibid., p. 52.
[55] See Schmaltz, "Das historische Gutachten," p. 126.
[56] Komitee der Antifaschistischen Widerstandskämpfer der Deutschen Demokratischen Republik, ed., *SS im Einsatz: Eine Dokumentation über die Verbrechen der SS*, 3rd ed. (Berlin: Kongress-Verlag, 1957).

workers."[57] Kuczynski was not familiar with either document. Aschenauer then started asking Kuczynski questions concerning the IG Farben trial, and it turned out that Kuczynski knew neither how many people were indicted and convicted in the trial nor which IG Farben representatives had been indicted.[58] Indeed, as Florian Schmaltz has pointed out, Kuczynski was not even sufficiently familiar with the IG Farben trial to argue by way of rebuttal that the court itself had come to the conclusion that the availability of inmate labor had been at least one factor in the firm's decision to build a factory at Auschwitz.[59] Finally, Aschenauer was able to point out that depositions Kuczynski had cited from the trial were made during the preliminary investigation and that, in point of fact, the defendants had recanted these during the actual trial.[60]

Kuczynski's credibility was destroyed. The defense moved again to have his testimony dismissed as "biased."[61] Kaul tried to defend Kuczynski's testimony, arguing that the "core" (*Schwerkraft*) of his testimony "consisted of the documents cited and their content corresponded fully with the excerpts quoted by Kuczynski."[62] This rather desperate maneuver on Kaul's part was almost bound to fail. As even he could not fail to notice, Hofmeyer was clearly annoyed and felt "duped" by Kuczynski.[63] The court therefore declared Kuczynski's testimony "biased" and rejected it. The court explicitly cited Aschenauer's cross-examination as the basis for its decision and noted that Kuczynski's failure to mention any recantations by IG Farben officials created the false "impression that [the earlier depositions] were the only available statements." This justified the defense's "skepticism" regarding Kuczynski's independence.[64]

Clearly, Kaul's propaganda maneuver had failed. Not only was Kuczynski's report now juridically worthless, the media attention that the East German government had hoped to generate now turned out to be the very opposite of what they had intended. Contrary to Florian Schmaltz's conclusion that Kuczynski's testimony helped to thematize the role of IG Farben in the Third Reich through its "wide media echo in East and West," in fact his testimony found relatively limited resonance in the West German media. Thus, of nine West German newspaper accounts of that day's trial

[57] Kaul, "Bericht" (March 19, 1964), p. 1.
[58] Ibid.
[59] Schmaltz, "Das historische Gutachten," p. 126.
[60] Kaul, "Bericht" (March 19, 1964), p. 2. Kaul actually overstates Aschenauer's effectiveness here. In fact, only one of the depositions cited by Kuczynski, the one concerning the cooperation between the SS and IG Farben in propaganda matters, was recanted. See Schmaltz, "Das historische Gutachten," p. 127.
[61] HVP (March 19, 1964), FFStA 4 Ks 2/63, Bd. 96, Bl. 229.
[62] Kaul, "Bericht" (March 19, 1964), p. 2.
[63] Ibid.
[64] HVP (March 19, 1964), FFStA 4 Ks 2/63, Bd. 96, Bl. 229.

session, only two (the *Frankfurter Allgemeine Zeitung* and the *Frankfurter Neue Presse*) discussed the substantive content of his report at all.[65] The remainder of the West German press was primarily interested in the political controversy surrounding Kuczynski's testimony.[66]

Kuczynski's defeat at the hands of Aschenauer also gave the conservative press in particular an opportunity to gloat over the ideological and "unscientific" nature of East German scholarship. As Gerhard Mauz, writing in the conservative *Die Welt*, put it, "the rabbit Kaul pulled from his hat was not terribly white."[67] Uwe-Jens Petersen, writing in the *Augsburger Allgemeine*, implicitly contrasted Kuczynski's testimony unfavorably with Martin Broszat's: "The Munich historian Dr. Broszat demonstrated in his report that IG Farben and other firms were not exactly thrilled with the [use of] forced labor in their branch camps and that the chairman of the board, Karl Krauch, was even explicitly opposed to it. Today *Neues Deutschland* wants to put him on the docket, '. . . but instead he gets an honorary pension.' For the SED press, the Frankfurt trial is not a piece of contemporary history that should be reported on factually, but rather it is a dialectical storm-troop attack against our social order."[68] While it is true that, unsurprisingly, the East German press gave a good deal more attention to Kuczynski's testimony, even reprinting extensive excerpts, this hardly compensated for the relatively hostile reception it received in the west.[69] Clearly, Kaul's first serious attempt

[65] Kurt Ernenputsch, "Ost-Berliner Gutachter als befangen abgelehnt," FAZ, March 20, 1964, and "Boger: Der Zeuge muß sich täuschen," FNP, March 20, 1964. Schmaltz cites precisely these two articles but does not appear to have consulted any of the non–Frankfurt-based West German press, a crucial limitation in his evidence.

[66] See Gunther von Lojewski, "Boger: 'In keinem Fall richtig,'" FAZ, March 20, 1964; "Kinder von der SS totgeschlagen," FR, March 20, 1964; "Kontroverse um Ostberliner Experten," *Stuttgarter Nachrichten*, March 20, 1964; and "Todesschreie bis in die Nacht: Ehemaliger Lagerältester aus Auschwitz sagte aus," *Westdeutsche Allgemeine*, March 20, 1964. The *Stuttgarter Zeitung* reprinted an article from the March 6 edition of the SZ; see Ursula von Kardoff, "Die Herren mit den grauen Haaren: Ein Tag beim Auschwitz-Prozeß," *Stuttgarter Zeitung*, March 20, 1964. *Die Zeit*, which, as a weekly, obviously did not necessarily report on every day's events in the trial, took this occasion to report on a "good German," Dr. Wilhelm Münch, who was the only person acquitted in the Warsaw Auschwitz trial in 1947. This was the exact opposite of the message Kaul had been hoping to get across. See Hansjakob Stehle, "In Auschwitz: Ein Mensch unter Mördern," *Die Zeit*, March 20, 1964.

[67] Gerhard Mauz, "Ein Professor aus Ostberlin: Kuczynski als Sachverständiger erst zugelassen, dann abgelehnt," *Die Welt*, March 20, 1964. The following day, *Die Welt* was even more explicit in its condemnation of both Kuczynski and Kaul, noting that it was a matter of principle in the FRG to give those who had atoned for their sins a second chance, something that the East Germans forgot. See "Vorsitzender: Sie können uns doch nicht einseitig informieren. Warum der Professor aus Ostberlin abgelehnt wurde," *Die Welt*, March 21, 1964.

[68] Uwe-Jens Petersen, "Der Auschwitz-Prozeß im Spiegel der SED-Presse," *Augsburger Allgemeine*, March 20, 1964.

[69] See Jürgen Kuczynski, "Die IG-Farben und das KZ-Auschwitz," *Neues Deutschland*, March 20, 1964. See also Werner Otto, "Das Verbrechen der IG-Farben von DDR-Gutachter vor aller Welt enthüllt," *Neues Deutschland*, March 20, 1964.

to put IG Farben on trial had failed in both the Frankfurt court and the court of public opinion.

Background Testimony

In addition to the background testimony delivered by professional historians, several "milieu witnesses" were called on to testify at the start of the trial's evidentiary phase, not because they had any specific information regarding the defendants but to provide a general account of life and death in Auschwitz.[70] Three survivor witnesses in particular – Dr. Otto Wolken, Dr. Ella Lingens, and Hermann Langbein – were asked to recall the character of life in Auschwitz from an inmate's perspective.[71] At Laternser's request, Judge Hofmeyer instructed Langbein "that this was a case dealing with murder, complicity in murder, and so forth, and that in this connection the general conditions prevalent in the Auschwitz camp were naturally of interest."[72] As Langbein himself had noted in a letter to the prosecutor's office the week before his testimony, "In all the years during which the Auschwitz Trial was being prepared in Frankfurt am Main, I was never deposed by the prosecutor's office in a comprehensive way, only with respect to individual questions of detail. I would like to point out that – if my testimony is to have any weight in this trial – it can only be as a general depiction of the situation in Auschwitz. I saw and experienced more than most Auschwitz survivors. With respect to individual defendants, I could hardly make any more concrete statements than other witnesses."[73] At the start of her testimony, Dr. Lingens similarly announced that she did not know any of the defendants personally.[74]

Three general themes emerged in this testimony. The first was the terrible living conditions inside the camp for those "fortunate" enough to survive their arrival, if usually only for a little while. The second was the perversity of the bureaucratic logic with which death was organized in the camp. The main point in both themes was that the exterminatory character of Auschwitz extended well beyond the explicitly genocidal operations in the gas chambers

---

[70] This is what Großmann called them. Vermerk, Großmann (January 29, 1964), FFStA HA 4 Ks 2/63, Bd. 18, Bl. 3709.

[71] Wolken and Lingens were both prisoner-doctors in the camp. Langbein had been a clerk, in charge of the daily death register in the camp.

[72] Bernd Naumann, *Auschwitz: A Report on the Proceedings against Robert Karl Ludwig Mulka and Others before the Court at Frankfurt*, trans. Jean Steinberg (New York: Frederick A. Praeger, 1966), p. 100.

[73] Langbein to Großmann (February 28, 1964), FFStA HA 4 Ks 2/64, Bd. 19, Bl. 3764.

[74] Naumann notes somewhat wryly at this point that, "[u]pon hearing this, the twenty-two men and their counsels undoubtedly felt relieved. There does not seem to be any threat from this side, for if the witness did not personally know any of the former SS men, she cannot tell the court anything useful about any specific case." Naumann, *Auschwitz*, p. 91.

to include almost every aspect of "life" inside the camp. Finally, all three of these initial witnesses stressed the degree of independent responsibility possessed by the SS in Auschwitz. This point was particularly important given the way the defendants consistently tried to portray themselves as powerless cogs in a vast machine whose murderous output was determined by others.

As regards the living conditions inside the camp, Dr. Lingens noted that these "'improved a bit as time went by, but only terribly slowly. Prisoners had to live on a maximum of 700 to 800 calories per day. The average prisoner did not survive for more than four months. No prisoner who came to Auschwitz before the summer of 1944 survived unless he held a special job.'"[75] Dr. Wolken pointed to the plague of "bold and impudent" rats in Birkenau, who would steal meager remnants of bread from inmates while they slept and would even begin to devour the dying before they actually died.[76] The point that Wolken made here with frightening clarity was that death in Auschwitz was not clean and antiseptic, that despite its bureaucratic organization, death in the camp remained painful and terrifying for the victims. This was a point that would be reiterated time and again by survivors in the trial.

At the same time, however, these witnesses made apparent the precision of the bureaucratic apparatus of murder in the camp, the perverse cogency with which it operated. This point was particularly salient given that much of the prosecution's case rested on a "reading" of the camp hierarchy and the "normal" functioning of the bureaucracy. Langbein's comments were particularly revealing in this regard, as he had been directly involved in the administrative apparatus of registering inmate deaths. He stressed that, in contrast to his time in Dachau, where he had had the same duties, the workload at Auschwitz was overwhelming. In Dachau, "'a day in which we had ten deaths was considered a very bad day. In Auschwitz, on the other hand, we worked day and night in shifts at seven typewriters making out death reports.'"[77] The time and date of death was registered for each inmate, but no two inmates could be officially registered as dying at the same time, "on paper that is."[78] Bogus causes of death were also entered for each inmate. "There was one rule: No infectious diseases could appear as the cause of death, and the death had to have some relation to age. A twenty-year-old, for example, could not die of a heart condition."[79]

Every new arrival admitted to the camp had a registration card with his or her name on it. As the inmates died, their cards were transferred from the file cabinet for the living to the one for the dead. Those who were

[75] Ibid., p. 92.
[76] Ibid., p. 86.
[77] Ibid., p. 100.
[78] Ibid.
[79] Ibid.

killed immediately on arrival were not even registered. Langbein was even entrusted with the "secret" monthly report detailing deaths in the camp, including those killed during "special treatment."[80] Langbein here helped to outline the "normal" functioning of the camp bureaucracy. This formed the yardstick against which subsequent testimony could be judged. In particular, the court would be interested to establish whether the defendants had acted in accordance with this normal procedure or not.

The final theme to emerge in this background testimony was the degree of latitude that the SS had in Auschwitz in their treatment of prisoners. Dr. Wolken made a highly significant point with regard to the general culpability of the SS in Auschwitz, when he noted: "The atmosphere in the camp changed almost daily. It depended on the camp commandant, the report leader [*Rapportführer*], the block leader [*Blockführer*] and their whims."[81] Wolken tried to emphasize that there was a level of independent volition affecting conditions in the camp, that the camp leadership had some control over not only who died but how many. Dr. Lingens put this even more pointedly. She stressed that some SS men did in fact obviate the living conditions in the camp and save the lives of at least some inmates. "'Do you wish to say that everyone could decide for himself to be either good or evil in Auschwitz?' the judge asks. 'That is exactly what I wish to say.'"[82] Finally, Langbein noted that since there was disagreement within the SS over whether the most important goal was extermination or exploitation, it was possible for "'SS men [to] preserve some remnant of humanity.'"[83]

These survivors argued that because conditions in the camp varied, that because some SS men treated the inmates worse than others, and that because some even managed to save inmates' lives, they could all be held directly and immediately responsible for the murders in the camp. Although they did not cast their testimony in the juridical language of perpetratorship and subjective motivation, they clearly wanted to emphasize the *individual culpability* of their tormenters. As Dr. Lingens put it: "All of them were good one time... but bad 999,000 times. Among the SS men, only 5–10% were sadists, psychotic criminals [*Triebsverbrecher*] in the clinical sense, where one could say the guilty parties were those who placed these men there. The rest were perfectly capable of deciding between good and evil."[84]

And yet their testimony preserved as well the sense that there was much more at work in Auschwitz than the "good" or "evil" character of individual SS men. Langbein, after noting that the SS could preserve some small measure

[80] Ibid., p. 101. Translation modified.
[81] Langbein, *Auschwitz*, p. 67.
[82] Naumann, *Auschwitz*, p. 93.
[83] Ibid., p. 101.
[84] "Kinder wurden lebendig verbrannt: Der Zufall entschied in Auschwitz über Leben und Tod," FNP, March 3, 1964.

of their humanity in Auschwitz, immediately added, "'But in Auschwitz there were many ways of dying.'"[85] Death stalked the inmates at Auschwitz despite, as well as because of, the actions of individual SS men qua individuals. Although Auschwitz would obviously have been impossible without the active cooperation of hundreds of individual SS men, no one of them was in a position to undo its horror, to save all the lives extinguished there. This fundamental ambiguity concerning the actual causal agent of death in Auschwitz, the individual or the total structure, runs throughout the trial. It would emerge with particular perversity in the closing arguments.

SS Witnesses

The structural dimension of death in Auschwitz was a point that most of the former SS men who testified in the trial repeatedly emphasized, for the obvious reason that they felt it cleared them of any particular, individual guilt. The conflicting interpretations of structure and agency articulated by former SS men witnesses and survivor witnesses constitute the first of the three central conflicts that marked the evidentiary phase of the trial. Two things characterize the testimony of former SS men in the Auschwitz Trial. First, like the defendants, the SS witnesses were particularly concerned to avoid self-incrimination. Although they were not themselves officially on trial, they were all too aware that they were confronting legal authorities and that anything they said could potentially be used against them. Consequently, they sought to evade any indications that they bore personal responsibility for crimes in Auschwitz.[86]

When asked by Judge Hofmeyer whether he had any information regarding the defendants, Dr. Joachim Cäsar, an agricultural expert who had directed the SS agricultural plant at Auschwitz, replied, "I would like to stress one thing: the fact that I came to Auschwitz under these circumstances has troubled me for twenty years, particularly the question of whether it would have been possible for us to do something for the prisoners beyond what we were able to do."[87] In a similar vein, the former SS physician Dr. Wilhelm Münch stated, "'One could react like a normal human being in Auschwitz only for the first few hours. Once one had spent some time there it was impossible to react normally. In that setup everyone was sullied. You were caught and had to go along.'"[88] Münch insisted, however, that with

---

[85] Naumann, *Auschwitz*, p. 101.
[86] By the mid-1960s, former SS men had become increasingly nervous in the face of a renewed wave of Nazi prosecutions anyway. See Ulrich Herbert, *Best: Biographische Studien über Radikalismus, Weltanschauung und Vernunft, 1903–1989*, 2nd ed. (Bonn: Dietz Verlag, 1996), p. 497.
[87] Naumann, *Auschwitz*, p. 96.
[88] Ibid., pp. 95–96.

help from well-placed connections, he had been able to avoid participating in selections or gassings.[89]

The former SS judge, Dr. Konrad Morgen, went so far as to say that his investigations of corruption in Auschwitz had at least helped to publicize the facts of mass murder in Auschwitz among the SS authorities "and [had] created a certain degree of unease."[90] Another SS witness, Helmut Bartsch, also sent to investigate corruption in Auschwitz, was likewise careful to avoid incriminating himself. According to the *Frankfurter Rundschau*, he avoided "letting even just one tiny word too many cross his criminologically schooled lips."[91] But in contrast to Dr. Morgen, the report continued, at least he did not try to give the impression that "that he had reacted with loathing to all the horrors he saw."[92] Hofmeyer asked another SS judge sent to investigate Auschwitz, Gerhard Wiebeck, what he thought his task was:

Witness: to fight corruption and offenses that went beyond the general line.
Hofmeyer bores further: What do you mean by the general line?
Wiebeck: The persecution of the Jews. After all, Hitler ordered that.[93]

In other words, not only did the SS witnesses want to avoid incriminating themselves or even the defendants in the trial, they argued that many of the crimes of Auschwitz, horrible as they may have been, were not crimes.[94] This was in perfect keeping with the defense's approach to the

[89] Kurt Ernenputsch, "Teilnahme an Massenmord war eine Charakterfrage," FAZ, March 3, 1964.
[90] Naumann, *Auschwitz*, p. 105.
[91] "Schillernde Gestalten," FR, March 18, 1964.
[92] Ibid.
[93] "SS-Richter ermittelte im KZ Auschwitz," *Kölnische Rundschau*, October 2, 1964.
[94] See Rebecca Wittmann, "Legitimating the Criminal State: Former Nazi Judges and the Distortion of Justice at the Frankfurt Auschwitz Trial, 1963–1965," in Diefendorf, ed., *Lessons and Legacies VI*, pp. 352–72. Wittmann here argues that the testimony of former SS judges, such as Morgan, "shifted the focus in the courtroom away from Nazi genocide to individual acts of cruelty, suggesting that Nazi orders were more acceptable and 'legal' and therefore that those who herded thousands into the gas chambers were not as guilty as those who shot prisoners without a legal death sentence handed down by Nazi desk officials in Berlin." Ibid., p. 353. Wittmann is absolutely right that this is what many SS witnesses, as well as the defense, *argued* in the trial. She is mistaken, however, when she asserts that the defendants who were accused of genocidal crimes, such as Mulka and Höcker, were convicted as accomplices, rather than perpetrators, as a result of this presumed "legality" of their orders. In fact, the court clearly held such orders to have been criminal, otherwise Mulka and Höcker would have been acquitted. Rather, the key issue was the defendants' subjective orientation toward the criminal orders in question. In other words, perpetrators of genocide were treated as being less guilty not because their orders were legal but because they were found not to have internalized the criminal motives behind such orders. This is further demonstrated by the case of Johann Schoberth, who was acquitted for following orders to execute prisoners, not because such orders were legal – the court found them to have been criminal – but because it could not be shown that he had known them to be illegal. See chapter 2.

matter, despite the fact that the prosecution in fact called most of these SS witnesses.[95]

The second thing to note about SS testimony in the trial is that, since it too was given by "witnesses" with the same official juridical position as survivor witnesses, these evasions and denials were particularly damaging to the proceedings.[96] Structurally, their character as eyewitness testimony gave such denials added plausibility. This created a striking incongruity within the evidentiary phase of the trial, as the two sets of witnesses, SS and survivors, told in some ways similar, in many ways radically divergent, stories about Auschwitz. On the one hand, both agreed that Auschwitz had been a terrible place, one characterized by mass atrocity and genocide. In itself, this is not trivial. Given the ongoing problem of Holocaust denial, the fact that none of the SS witnesses in the Auschwitz Trial, indeed none of the defendants, either, ever denied that mass exterminations took place in the camp is significant.[97] It ought to serve as a useful public antidote to those who claim that this never happened. At the same time, however, the SS witnesses, like the defendants, painted a portrait of Auschwitz where almost no one, themselves least of all, ever actually committed any of the crimes everyone agreed had taken place; this immediately undermined the value of this minimal consensus. A crime without perpetrators runs the risk of becoming a natural catastrophe. And whatever Auschwitz was, it was not a *natural* catastrophe.

Bearing Witness and Being a Witness

The glaring incongruity between what the former SS men had to say about Auschwitz and what the survivors recounted brings us to the second and in many respects dominant conflict that characterized the evidentiary phase of the Auschwitz Trial. This is the conflict between bearing witness and being a witness in the juridical sense. The survivor witnesses wanted, indeed in

---

[95] As Ulrich Herbert has shown, there was considerable cooperation among potential and actual defendants in Nazi trials in preparing their defenses. While it cannot be demonstrated that such coordination took place in the Auschwitz Trial, there was clearly a general SS "line" in Nazi trials that was widely known among SS witnesses and defendants. See Herbert, *Best*, pp. 491–98.

[96] As one reporter put it: "Because of the involuntary identification with the inmates of the concentration camp, the reader or listener of reports about the camp almost always experiences the events from the perspective of those who suffered. The effect is that much more peculiar, then, when this perspective is inverted and the camp with its thousands of people is suddenly only an object for orders and tasks." "Auschwitz aus der Perspektive eines SS-Oberführers: Zeugen Aussage des ehemaligen Leiters der landwirtschaftlichen Betriebe," *Stuttgarter Zeitung*, March 6, 1964.

[97] Deborah E. Lipstadt, *Denying the Holocaust: The Growing Assault on Truth and Memory* (New York: Free Press, 1993).

many cases *needed*, to tell *their* stories.[98] And yet as Judge Hofmeyer politely and the defense attorneys rather more rudely reminded them on numerous occasions, that was not why they had been summoned.[99]

One should keep in mind how psychologically and emotionally difficult it must have been for many of the witnesses to testify about such painful memories. For some witnesses, this may have been cathartic, an opportunity literally to "act out" if not necessarily to "work through" their anger and bitterness at what had happened to them.[100] George Preston, of Delaware, a former Jewish inmate in Auschwitz, took the opportunity during his testimony to reenact Bednarek's former treatment of him. "You fat pig!" he cried, walking back and forth in front of Bednarek, his thumbs hooked under his vest. "Bednarek stands quietly and yet as if blows were raining down on him, small, bent, humiliated, wordless."[101]

But for most witnesses, their testimony offered them less an opportunity to act out their anger than the necessity of reliving their fear. Take, for example, the following description of the witness Simon Gotland, a former member of the work detail assigned to help debark the arriving transports and to sort through the luggage. Speaking in a chaotic mix of the broken French he had picked up since his postwar emigration mingled with his childhood Polish and a bit of Yiddish, he struggled to make himself understood.

His hands gripping the arms of his chair, the heavy-set man sits facing the court as if he needs to be ready to jump up and flee at any moment. He looks helplessly from side to side. He obviously does not understand most of the questions put to him in well-chosen words by the numerous men in black robes. He sometimes starts in shock when his own words come back to him magnified three-fold from the loudspeakers. And the more intensely the memories pour forth from him, the less the remaining trial participants can understand him. It is as if he were surrounded by a wall. Simon Gotland's speech seems for a moment to be a symbol for the fate of many Auschwitz inmates. If they survived, they found themselves once again in a foreign, superficially so intact and cultivated world, one in which there was no room any more for the dark days and hardly any possibility of articulating them in language.[102]

---

[98] Indeed, some witnesses in the trial became, in effect, professional witnesses, not just in trials, but also speaking to public gatherings and school groups. See Alice von Plato, "Vom Zeugen zum Zeitzeugen: Die Zeugen der Anklage im ersten Frankfurter Auschwitz-Prozess (1963–1965)," in Wojak, ed., *"Gerichtstag halten,"* pp. 209–10.

[99] The rudeness of the defense attorneys was a constant sore point for many of the witnesses. See, e.g., the complaint voiced by Maria Swiderska-Swieratowa that defense attorney Hermann Stolting II did not even address the witnesses with the customary "Herr." In Valeska von Roques, "Namen, die keiner mehr nennt," *Vorwärts*, June 10, 1964.

[100] On these Freudian concepts as they pertain to the Holocaust, see Dominick LaCapra, *Representing the Holocaust: History, Theory, Trauma* (Ithaca: Cornell University Press, 1994), pp. 205–23.

[101] Bernd Naumann, "'Ja, was meinen Sie? Die hätten mich ja direkt eingespert,'" FAZ, March 5, 1965.

[102] "Die Sprache die niemand versteht," FNP, July 28, 1964.

Simon Gotland's situation may have been extreme, but his difficulty in communicating his experiences in Auschwitz was hardly unusual. Even witnesses who spoke perfect German struggled to find words that could express even a part of the terror and misery they had lived through. By now, the indescribability of the Holocaust is a well-worn motif in the scholarly literature.[103] And yet the "limits of representation" take on a greater urgency and a painful poignancy when dealing with a direct confrontation between victims and perpetrators. The Auschwitz Trial was a paradigmatic instance of such direct confrontation, one in which the immediate presence of murderers and torturers made it both all the more difficult for the survivors to bear witness and all the more urgent to do so successfully.

Certainly, the defendants went out of their way to make the witnesses' task even more difficult, in part no doubt for tactical reasons, in part also as a symptom of their own deep-seated denial and perhaps even their ongoing hatred. The following story, though more extreme than most, gives a sense of how tense the situation could become when the defendants energetically denied charges being made by witnesses. On April 6, 1964, the former political prisoner Ludwig Wörl testified that he had personally seen Kaduk drive twelve children into the gas chambers at gunpoint. Kaduk shouted that this was not true and refused to calm down, even when Hofmeyer threatened to have him removed from the courtroom.[104] "The witness, however, responds matter-of-factly, though vehemently: 'Kaduk, you are no longer facing me with a pistol in your hand.'"[105] This exchange provoked an enormous uproar in the courtroom. "The audience leapt from their seats, and from among them, one heard voices amid the general racket that cried, 'Kill him, kill the swine Kaduk!'"[106] It is to Wörl's great credit that he was able to maintain his composure during this exchange, but one can only imagine the psychological difficulties this must have cost him.

For many witnesses, it must have been an unpleasant shock to have their testimony questioned. They were recounting their direct experiences, horrors they had seen, blows they had felt, family members they had lost. And yet in a court of law, such implicit claims to authenticity were insufficient grounds for proof. Still, the court's offer of justice made such indignities bearable, if only just. Józef Piwko, for instance, testified that he had seen Wilhelm Boger murder children during the "liquidation" of the Gypsy camp by grabbing them by the legs and beating their heads against a wall. Even civil counsel

---

[103] See, e.g., the essays collected in Saul Friedlander, ed., *Probing the Limits of Representation: Nazism and the "Final Solution"* (Cambridge: Harvard University Press, 1992), or Geoffrey H. Hartman, ed., *Holocaust Remembrance: The Shapes of Memory* (Oxford: Blackwell, 1994).

[104] Horst Hachmann, "Schwerer Zusammenstoß beim Auschwitz-Prozeß," FR, April 7, 1964.

[105] Ibid.

[106] "Tumult im Gerichtssaal: 'Schlagt das Schwein Kaduk tot!'" *Abendpost*, April 7, 1964.

Raabe reacted with astonishment: "'That is probably the most terrible thing we have heard here. It is hard to imagine. Did you really see this?'"[107] "'I do not retract my statement,'" responded Piwko. Hofmeyer too reminded the witness that it was imperative to be truthful when making such incriminating statements. Piwko merely replied, "'Where there is guilt, there must be punishment.'"[108]

Nor did the conduct of some of the defense attorneys help the witnesses much. Their efforts to discredit the witnesses were understandable from a tactical point of view, indeed, were to be expected. However, on a number of occasions, the defense attorneys clearly crossed the line into impropriety. Laternser was particularly guilty of this. The witness Erwin Olszówka testified that Boger had beaten him severely. Laternser accused him of being a communist, claiming that his testimony had been tampered with during a conversation with Hermann Langbein.[109] "'Who really beat you?'" Laternser asked. "'Wasn't it Lachmann, if anyone really beat you at all?'"[110] Although Hofmeyer disallowed the question, how terrible and insulting this must all have seemed.

The almost unbearable tension of being confronted face-to-face with their former tormentors was only exacerbated by the court's repeated insistence on a high level of precision and detail in the witness testimony. Given that watches and calendars were unavailable to inmates in Auschwitz and that twenty years intervened between the events and the testimony, one is tempted to label this insistence unreasonable. It was, however, inherent in the juridical character of the proceedings. The court effectively had no choice but to demand more of the witnesses than they could reasonably deliver. During Wolken's testimony, for instance, the court wanted to know whether he had seen Baretzki participate in executions; Wolken could only reply, "Please, it's been twenty years."[111] The following example of an exchange between Hofmeyer and the witness Stefan Boratyński is typical.

Presiding Judge: How many people did Boger shoot on this day, at a minimum?
Boratyński: I cannot give an exact number. The washroom was full.
Judge: Was it at least six?
Boratyński: Certainly a lot more. The washroom was at least three to four and one-half meters big.
Judge: We must ascertain the minimum number. Was it at least six?
Boratyński: Certainly more than six. Also more than ten.

[107] Kurt Ernenputsch, "'Wo Schuld ist, muß Strafe sein,'" FAZ, April 14, 1964.
[108] Ibid.
[109] "Er schleuderte Kinder an die Wand," FNP, April 14, 1964.
[110] Bernd Naumann, "Ohrfeigen für die Sterbenden," FAZ, April 14, 1964. Gerhard Lachmann was another SS man who worked in the Political Section.
[111] Walter Pfuhl, "'Bitte, es sind 20 Jahre her…': Angeklagter wiedererkannt," *Die Welt*, February 28, 1964.

Boger: I never shot anyone in Auschwitz. The witness is mistaken. I have no reason
to say I didn't shoot if I did shoot.[112]

The witnesses also sometimes got into trouble with the court because their
testimony in the trial contradicted their earlier statements in the preliminary
investigation. The witness Charles Corrin, for instance, had stated during the
preliminary investigation that he had seen the defendant Baretzki "select"
inmates by pointing to them with a walking stick. But during his testimony,
he said merely that Baretzki was one of two or three SS men present during
the selection. Hofmeyer pointed out this contradiction to Corrin.

Corrin: During the selections, I tried to make a good, strong impression, in order not
to look like a *Muselmann* (a completely run-down inmate). Therefore, I did not pay
attention to which SS man pointed to the inmates. Baretzki had a walking stick, but
I wasn't asked at the time whether he pointed with the stick or with his finger.
Judge: It's not a matter whether you were asked. I want to know whether you still
maintain this today.
Corrin: I maintain what I said today. Baretzki was there.
Judge: What happened later with the people who were selected?
Corrin: They remained standing. The others returned to the Block.
Judge: What happened to them later?
Corrin: They were gassed. Everyone said so. That was not news. I couldn't see it
myself, however.[113]

What these two examples reveal with acute clarity is the tension between
what the court needed to know in order to reach its verdict in accordance
with the law and what the witnesses were able to recount. In particular, the
court was not intrinsically interested in what might be termed the experiential
truth of Auschwitz, its impact on the collective and individual biographies
of the survivors. If this came to light, as in the following instance, it did so
tangentially, as a complement to the proceedings, not as their central focus.

The witness Dr. Mauritius Berner was an old acquaintance of the defendant Dr. Capesius. When Berner and his family arrived at Auschwitz, he
told his wife and children to stick close to him. But they were almost immediately separated, when the Germans ordered physicians and pharmacists
to step forward. Berner's wife and children were sent to another group.
Although he did not know at the time that this group was to be gassed,
Berner was nonetheless frantic at being separated. "My wife cried, 'Come
kiss us!' But I never had the chance to embrace my family."[114] Berner turned
to Capesius for help. "Herr Hauptmann," he said, "I have twins. They
need greater care. Could you please allow us to stay together."[115] Capesius

[112] "Zählfehler rettete ihm das Leben," FNP, April 10, 1964.
[113] Kurt Ernenputsch, "'Ich war nur ein kleiner SS-Mann': Stefan Baretzki bestreitet die
Mitwirkung bei Selektionen," FAZ, July 28, 1964.
[114] Langbein, *Auschwitz*, p. 660.
[115] Ibid.

called the children over and showed them to Dr. Mengele, who at that time was conducting experiments on twins. Mengele, however, was not interested, since he needed only identical, not fraternal twins. The children were sent back to the group to be gassed. Capesius, however, reassured Berner that he need not worry, that the children were only going to have a bath and would be back shortly. "In that moment, I was grateful to Capesius from the bottom of my heart. I thought he wanted to help me. I only later discovered what it meant when Mengele got ahold of twins for his experiments."[116]

Prosecutor Kügler asked Berner what his family's names were. "My wife was named Ida, my children Susi – she was twelve and a half at the time – and Helga and Nora, who were both nine and a half." The juridical needs of the court immediately reimposed themselves on the scene. Civil counsel Ormond asked, "Can there be any doubt that it was Capesius whom you encountered on the ramp?" Berner replied, "No, there can be no doubt. I was not the only one to recognize Capesius. Several of my colleagues did as well." Finally, when asked by defense attorney Laternser whether he had known at the time the fate that awaited the two different groups, Berner replied, "No. If I had known, I would have gone with my wife and children."[117]

In this moment, we see the capacity of the trial to both elicit a level of emotional truth that is at once astonishing in a public setting and terribly painful to share ("If I had known, I would have gone with my wife and children"), while almost instantaneously bracketing that truth, reducing the issue to one of identifying the defendant. The fact that Kügler asked Berner to name his lost family members may have provided an opportunity for cathartic mourning, but it was also a gesture of juridical precision; victims with names "counted" more than nameless, faceless ones in the eyes of the law; their deaths were somehow more real. The profound emotional truth of Berner's remembrance becomes simply a factual truth claim, one that is as intrinsically open to question as any other factual statement. Capesius responded to Berner's testimony by noting that "[i]n 1945, a number of Auschwitz inmates went to my wife after their return and offered to testify on my behalf. At that time, neither Dr. Berner nor anyone else claimed that Capesius had selected."[118] Whether or not Capesius was telling the truth here – though it seems unlikely that he was – his denials shift the register of the exchange from the level of experiential truth to that of "factual" truth. Only the latter can truly be debated, but in a sense, only the former truly mattered to Auschwitz survivors.

---

[116] Irmtrud Wojak, ed., *Auschwitz-Prozeß 4 Ks 2/63, Frankfurt am Main* (Cologne: Snoeck Verlagsgesellschaft, 2004), p. 357. Cf. Langbein, *Auschwitz*, p. 660.

[117] Langbein, *Auschwitz*, pp. 660–61. Langbein misreports Berner's daughter's name as Elga. Cf. Wojak, ed., *Auschwitz-Prozeß*, p. 356.

[118] Langbein, *Auschwitz*, p. 661.

This distinction between factual and experiential truth emerges quite clearly in a letter that Ella Lingens wrote to Judge Hofmeyer shortly after her testimony. She noted that, during the hearing, she had said both that the defendant Capesius looked like SS Dr. Fritz Klein and that they had very different facial features and hair. In her letter to Hofmeyer, she said that she had recently seen a photograph of Klein and that it was true that he looked nothing like Capesius. She explained this apparent (factual) contradiction thus: "The similarity for me lies in their shared facial expression. It is this half-intelligence combined with a cold brutality that tries to hide itself behind the mask of a petite bourgeois [*Biedermann*]. I encountered this expression in Capesius's eyes as I had experienced it from Klein at the time and still remembered. Mengele, the maskless cynic, or Rohde, the good-natured yet brutal steer were completely different."[119] The factual truth was that Capesius looked nothing like Klein; the experiential truth was that they were the same kind of person. That similarity was stronger in Lingens's memory than the factual differences in their appearance.

It should be added that this imposition of the factual on the experiential most likely served only to heighten the sense of "shame" – a shame that was not quite shame but was experienced as such – that, according to Primo Levi, was felt by many on liberation from Auschwitz.[120] There were many reasons for this shame: the awareness of having been diminished, of having forgotten everything but survival, of having failed the requirements of human solidarity; a feeling of guilt for not having resisted in a situation where resistance was all but impossible, a feeling that you survived when others, more worthy, did not. Levi famously rejected the idea that bearing witness obviated this shame, arguing that survivors were not the "true witnesses," that they constituted only "an anomalous minority: we are those who by their prevarications or abilities or good luck did not touch bottom. Those who did so, those who saw the Gorgon, have not returned to tell about it or have returned mute, but they are the 'Muslims,' the submerged, the complete witnesses, the ones whose deposition would have a general significance. They are the rule, we are the exception."[121]

But even Levi – perhaps especially Levi – conceded that he and other survivors who told their stories also told the stories of those who did not return, the "drowned" of Auschwitz, if only incompletely and at third hand. Communication was, according to Levi, an innate capacity of the human animal, and to fail to communicate was an ambiguous sign, one that prompted anxiety.[122] The silence that the survivors who testified in the Auschwitz Trial broke was sometimes their own, sometimes that of society, but in either

[119] Lingens to Hofmeyer (March 4, 1964), FFStA HA 4 Ks 2/63, Bd. 21, Bl. 4226.
[120] Primo Levi, *The Drowned and the Saved* (New York: Vintage, 1988), p. 73.
[121] Ibid., pp. 83–84.
[122] Ibid., p. 89.

case, it was an ultimate gesture of generosity and solidarity, with the dead but also with the living. Under these circumstances, as the terrible spectacle of Simon Gotland's testimony reminds us, the will to communicate in many ways mattered more than the facts communicated. To imply otherwise, as the court was often forced to do, could only reinforce the paradox that so troubled Levi near the end of his life: that the privilege of surviving so far outweighed the service of bearing witness.[123]

Yet the court remained, of necessity, bound to the juridical understanding of truth as specific, verifiable, legally relevant statements pertaining to individual defendants. On some occasions the court rejected witness testimony outright, when it seemed to be factually contradictory. In the case of the witness Erwin Kühne from the GDR, for example, Hofmeyer warned him that he should carefully consider whether he in fact wanted to swear to the veracity of his testimony. "'When you say, for example, that camp adjutant Mulka removed you from the Bunker at the end of 1943, then I must point out that Mulka had already left Auschwitz at the start of that year.'"[124] Kühne eventually decided not to be sworn in, in order to avoid the risk of prosecution for perjury. But in any number of other, less drastic cases, the veracity of witness testimony could be called into question on similar grounds. The dates did not match. The witness could not have seen what he claimed to have seen from where he claimed to have seen it. The witness could not possibly have recognized individual defendants at such-and-such a distance. The litany of possible complaints was nearly endless.

The Court Visits the Scene of the Crime

Indeed, it was partially in order to address exactly such concerns regarding the factual veracity of witness claims that the court, after much politicized debate, decided to visit Auschwitz itself.[125] The suggestion to visit the camp came not from the court but from civil counsel Ormond, who also took the lead in making the necessary arrangements with both the Polish and West German authorities. As can be imagined, the idea was not initially met with much enthusiasm by the West German authorities. At that time,

---

[123] Ibid., p. 83.

[124] "Zeugenaussagen voller Wiederspruche," FNP, September 18, 1964.

[125] For other treatments of the court's visit to Auschwitz, see Werner Renz, "Auschwitz als Augenscheinobjekt: Anmerkungen zur Erforschung der Wahrheit im ersten Frankfurter-Prozeß," *Mittelweg 36* 1 (2001): 63–72; Werner Renz, "Tatort Auschwitz: Ortstermin im Auschwitz-Prozess," *Tribüne* 40 (2001): 132–44; Sybille Steinbacher, "'Protokoll vor der Schwarzen Wand': Die Ortsbesichtigung des Frankfurter Schwurgerichts in Auschwitz," in Wojak, ed., *"Gerichtstag halten,"* pp. 61–96; and Annette Weinke, "Strafverfolgung nationalsozialistischer Verbrechen in den frühen Sechzigern: Eine Replik," *Mittelweg 36* 3 (2001): 45–48.

the Federal Republic did not have official diplomatic relations with Poland, and the Hallstein Doctrine denying diplomatic recognition to any state that recognized the GDR was still in full force. Once again the Cold War made its presence felt in the trial, but this time much more was at stake. Unlike earlier Cold War encounters (e.g., Kaul's application for admission or the controversy over Kuczynski's testimony), this time the implications extended well beyond the juridical and representational politics of the Auschwitz Trial and implicated the entire "German question" and the structure of political relations between the East and West in an era on the cusp of détente and Ostpolitik but not yet there.

Formally, the debate began when Ormond made a motion to have the court visit Auschwitz to gather evidence on June 8, 1964, but in reality, controversy was already brewing.[126] As early as April 1962, Ormond had contacted Jan Sehn, the director of the Institute for Criminology in Krakow and an investigating magistrate in the Polish trial of Auschwitz commandant Höß.[127] They had discussed the possibility of an official examination of Auschwitz by the court. In February 1964, Ormond again wrote Sehn, asking whether the necessary arrangements could be made for the court to come to Auschwitz.[128] On March 11, 1964, Sehn received a power of attorney (*Vollmacht*) from the Polish government empowering him to inform the court that "the government of the Peoples Republic of Poland fundamentally looks positively on the proposal for such a visit and that it will assess any application by the court for permission to make such a visit favorably."[129] Sehn gave a copy not only to Ormond, but also to Fritz Bauer, who passed it along to the Hessian Ministry of Justice (HMJ) on April 30.[130]

Somehow – perhaps verbally from Bauer, perhaps from Ormond – the HMJ had gotten wind of all this even before Bauer's letter, and the wheels of controversy began to turn within the West German government. On April 22, the HMJ telephoned the Federal Justice Ministry to inform them that a motion for the court to visit Auschwitz was likely and that the Polish government had already said that they would look favorably on the application.[131] The HMJ said that they had instructed the prosecution not to take a stance on the issue if Ormond made his motion and asked the Federal Justice Ministry to consult with the Foreign Ministry. The Foreign Ministry, however, procrastinated, saying it preferred to wait to see whether such a motion was actually made and what the court's position was before itself

[126] Ormond Antrag, Anlage 1, HVP (June 8, 1963), FFStA 4 Ks 2/63, Bd. 99.
[127] Ormond, Aktenvermerk (March 1, 1962), Nachlaß Ormond, FBI SAP, FAP 1/NK-4. Cited in Renz, "Augenscheinobjekt," p. 66.
[128] Ormond to Sehn, Anlage 1, HVP (February 3, 1964), FFStA 4 Ks 2/63, Bd. 99.
[129] Justizministerium der Volksrepublik Poland to Sehn (April 11, 1964) in Ibid.
[130] Bauer to HMJ (April 30, 1964), HHA, HMJ III (IV-1076/59), Bd. 4, Bl. 120.
[131] BMJ Vermerk (May 5, 1964), BAK, B 141/22762, Bl. 1. Unless otherwise noted, all BA quotations are paraphrases, rather than verbatim transcriptions.

taking a position.[132] Such bureaucratic procrastination was to prove a major theme in the ensuing debates. Nonetheless, on June 5, the HMJ noted in an internal memo that, per conversations with the Federal Justice Ministry and the Foreign Ministry, the federal government was likely to reject any request to have the entire court visit Poland.[133] On June 5, the HMJ asked the attorney general (Bauer) to determine the legal usefulness and feasibility of the proposed visit before allowing the prosecution to take a position.[134] By June 9 at the latest, the HMJ had explicitly instructed the prosecution to oppose any motion for a court visit to Auschwitz.[135]

On June 8, Ormond finally made his much anticipated motion. Hofmeyer responded with considerable skepticism, noting that in principle, such an official court visit would constitute a violation of Poland's state sovereignty. As was to be expected, Laternser concurred.[136] In his written objection, Laternser also argued that an examination of the scene of the crime was, after twenty years, "a contradiction in terms."[137] Furthermore, he contended that political conditions made such a journey impossible, especially since it probably meant a journey through the "Soviet Occupied Zone" [SBZ] (i.e., East Germany).[138] Even if the East German government promised safe passage, as Kaul had assured the court they would, "the kind of system that supports the terror in the SBZ cannot be accorded any sort of trust under the rule of law."[139]

Of course, as Annette Weinke has pointed out, Kaul's support for Ormond's motion intentionally raised the already high political stakes involved, by directly implicating German-German relations.[140] Indeed, as early as April, Kaul had been informed by the East German government that the Polish authorities would approve any proposal for the court to examine Auschwitz.[141] Yet, as it turned out, the GDR played effectively no role in the negotiations concerning the proposed visit and neither did Kaul.[142] In

---

[132] Ibid., Bl. 2.

[133] Vermerk (June 5, 1964), HHA, HMJ III (IV-1076/59), Bd. 4, Bl. 123.

[134] Erlaß, HMJ to GStA (June 5, 1964), HHA, HMJ III (IV-1076/59), Bd. 4, Bl. 123R–24.

[135] BMJ Vermerk (June 11, 1964), BAK, B 141/22762, Bl. 5. The HMJ told the BMJ that because of this, it expected the court to reject Ormond's motion.

[136] See Renz, "Augenscheinobjekt," pp. 64–65.

[137] Laternser, Antrag, Anlage 2, HVP (June 22, 1964), FFStA 4 Ks 2/63, Bd. 99. Also in Hans Laternser, *Die andere Seite im Auschwitz-Prozeß, 1963/1965* (Stuttgart: Seewald Verlag, 1966), pp. 411–13.

[138] Ibid.

[139] Ibid. Kaul had filed a supporting motion on June 11. See Kaul, Antrag (June 11, 1964), Anlage 2, HVP (June 11, 1964), FFStA 4 Ks 2/63, Bd. 99. See also "SED sichert Auschwitz-Angeklagten Integrität zu," FR, June 12, 1964.

[140] Weinke, "Strafverfolgung," p. 45.

[141] Rehan to Kaul (April 20, 1964), BAB, Nachlaß Kaul, N 2503, Bd. 198.

[142] This is not to say that in other matters, the East German government was not actively seeking to bolster its position within the Warsaw pact by using its leading role in "anti-fascist" propaganda against the FRG to reinforce "socialist solidarity." See Annette Weinke,

part, no doubt, this was due to the adamant insistence by the West German authorities that under no circumstances would the court be allowed to pass through East German territory, which effectively cut East Germany out of the loop.[143] It may also reflect a limited divergence between the East Germans, whose interest in Nazi trials was almost purely political, and the Poles, who, while certainly not above trying to gain political advantage from West German Nazi trials, also had a genuine interest in seeing justice done in this matter, irrespective of the political benefits. Weinke may also be right when she speculates that the brewing controversy surrounding the proposed statute of limitations for Nazi crimes may have made the West German government more receptive to the idea of legal cooperation with East Block states, but the documentary record provides no evidence for this.[144]

In any event, Kaul's support for Ormond's motion was by no means the most important. Much to everyone's surprise, on June 17, Breitwieser's attorney, Wolfgang Zarnack, also made a motion to have the court visit Auschwitz. Zarnack hoped, rightly as it turned out, that an official examination of Auschwitz would reveal that the only eyewitness to have seen his client participate in the first experimental gassing of Soviet POWs in 1941 could not possibly have witnessed the event from where he claimed to have been situated.[145] This move proved crucial for future developments.

The most immediate impact of Zarnack's motion was that it made it all but impossible for the prosecution to follow the directives of the HMJ and to oppose Ormond's motion. The day after Zarnack's motion, the prosecution wrote to the HMJ, notifying them that they intended to support Ormond's motion.[146] As the HMJ explained to a rather annoyed Federal

"Der Kampf um die Akten: Zur Kooperation zwischen MfS und osteuropäischen Sicherheitsorganen bei der Vorbereitung antifaschistischer Kampagnen," *Deutschland-Archiv* 32 (1999): 564–77. More generally, see Günther Wieland, "Die deutsch-deutschen Rechtsbeziehungen zur Ahndung von NS-Verbrechen zwischen Mauerbau und Wiedervereinigung," in Helga Grabitz et al., eds., *Die Normalität des Verbrechens: Bilanz und Perspektiven der Forschung zu den nationalsozialistischen Gewaltverbrechen* (Berlin: Edition Hentrich, 1994), pp. 386–407.

[143] See, e.g., Vermerk, BMI (July 23, 1964), BAK, B 106/102266, p. 3. Internal pagination.
[144] Weinke, "Strafverfolgung," pp. 46–47.
[145] Antrag, Zarnack (June 17, 1964), Anlage 1, HVP (June 18, 1964), FFStA 4 Ks 2/63, Bd. 99. The court's visit did indeed reveal to the court's satisfaction that the witness Walter Petzold could not have seen the events he described. See Urteil, in C. F. Rüter et al., eds., *Justiz und NS-Verbrechen: Sammlung Deutscher Strafurteile wegen nationalsozialistischer Tötungsverbrechen, 1945–1966*, vol. 21 (Amsterdam: University Press Amsterdam, 1979), pp. 750–51. Other defense attorneys subsequently also made motions for the court to visit Auschwitz. See Antrag Göllner (July 11, 1964), Anlage 2, HVP (July 13, 1964), FFStA 4 Ks 2/63, Bd. 100, and Antrag Gerhard (September 23, 1964), Anlage 3, HVP (October 15, 1964), FFStA 4 Ks 2/63, Bd. 103. These latter defense motions did not have the political or legal significance of Zarnack's initial motion, however.
[146] FFStA to HMJ (June 18, 1964), HHA, HMJ III (IV-1076/59), Bd. 4, Bl. 140–44. Bauer attached a note to this letter, pointing out that the BGH had ruled that, under some circumstances, the failure to examine the scene of the crime could constitute a violation of the

Justice Ministry (which had been expecting the whole affair to go away quietly after the prosecution opposed the motion), while the court could readily
reject a motion made by a civil counsel alone, it was less clear for procedural
reasons if it could so easily reject such a motion when made by a defense
attorney.[147] "This was the only reason the prosecution also declared that it
felt an official visit was necessary."[148] In their written comment, the prosecution took the high ground, claiming that they felt that an official investigation of the scene of the crime would be "particularly suited to providing
the court with precise knowledge of the general spatial situation and the
spatial relationships that touch on many witness statements."[149] A heated
exchange ensued when Laternser protested that Großmann was overstep-
ping his authority and making an independent motion, to which Großmann
responded, "You're always getting it wrong." Laternser was outraged. "You
should not make such inappropriate remarks. I won't tolerate it." Großmann
replied sarcastically, "You can tolerate whatever you like." It would, after all
have been "astonishing," Großmann concluded, if Laternser had supported
the motion, "given his previous conduct."[150]

At this point, Hofmeyer felt that he had been left hanging out to dry,
politically speaking. On the one hand, he could hardly dismiss Ormond's
motion out of hand, now that both the prosecution and at least one defense
attorney supported it. The court, after all, had an obligation to the truth,
and in that capacity, it now faced considerable pressure from other trial
participants to approve a visit to Auschwitz on precisely those grounds.
On the other hand, given the undeniable political delicacy of the matter,
Hofmeyer hardly felt the court was able to make a decision entirely on its
own. Consequently, he turned to the HMJ both for advice and for political
cover. In his letter, he noted that at the present time, the court would have

---

court's obligation to the truth. See Bauer note (June 22, 1964), HHA, HMJ III (IV-1076/59),
  Bd. 4, Bl. 145. This note may indicate that the Frankfurt prosecution's decision to ignore
  the directive from the HMJ was taken with Bauer's encouragement. It certainly shows that
  they had his support.

[147] BMJ Vermerk (June 25, 1964), BAK, B 141/22762, Bl. 6–7.

[148] Ibid. It is worth noting that in their letter to the HMJ on June 18, the prosecution made no
  mention of the fact, much emphasized by the HMJ in its conversations with the BMJ, that
  it felt that it could no longer oppose the Ormond's motion because of Zarnack's maneuver.
  Rather, they stressed what they felt to be the legal advantages of the visit, as well as the
  technical legal and political matters that still needed to be resolved. It is therefore possible
  that the HMJ was simply trying to justify their failure to foresee or prevent the prosecution's
  support for Ormond. See FFStA to HMJ (June 18, 1964), HHA, HMJ III (IV-1076/59),
  Bd. 4, Bl. 140–44.

[149] StA Stellungnahme (June 22, 1964), Anlage 1, HVP (June 22, 1964), FFStA 4 Ks 2/63,
  Bd. 99. The prosecution again pointed to a number of legal and political matters that would
  still have to be resolved before such a visit was actually possible, including a guarantee of
  safety and the opportunity for the participants to move about freely.

[150] Bernd Naumann, "Lokaltermin in Auschwitz oder nicht?" FAZ, June 23, 1964.

to reject the motions to visit Auschwitz on the grounds that the evidence in question was "unreachable."[151] An official examination of the scene of the crime could not be done by an external judge (*ersuchten Richter*) but would have to be done by the court. Given the limitations posed by state sovereignty, this required a "special state treaty."[152] Since the court was not "a legal subject under international law," it could not undertake such negotiations on its own authority, for example, via Ormond's mediation with Sehn. He then asked the HMJ whether they could undertake anything to address these issues, since the court had a legal obligation to attempt to make such "unreachable" evidence "reachable."[153]

The HMJ too felt in over its head in these matters and contacted the Federal Justice Ministry, saying that it felt that "the question as to whether a German court can conduct official business in Poland requires clarification through diplomatic channels."[154] At this point, virtually the entire federal government became involved. Initially, the Federal Justice Ministry simply passed the matter along to the Foreign Ministry, since these matters clearly fell within their bailiwick.[155] The Foreign Ministry arranged a high-level meeting for July 22 to resolve this difficult matter.[156]

The principle matter of concern that emerged at this meeting was the impact that such an official court visit might have on world opinion.[157] Ministerial Director Josef Schafheutle from the Justice Ministry pointed out that the real public relations disaster would be for the government to reject the idea entirely. "Such a position would create the impression that the government was not doing everything in its power to assist in the prosecution of Nazi crimes."[158] In the face of such concerns, the government ministers decided that, in principle, an official court visit to Auschwitz was legally, diplomatically, and politically feasible, but that first the court itself needed to provide more information on the "modalities" of such a visit, in particular, what it felt the legal and practical requirements would be.[159]

Hofmeyer was therefore asked to clarify the technicalities of a court visit.[160] In particular, the government wanted to know why Hofmeyer had

[151] Hofmeyer to HMJ (June 23, 1964), FFStA 4 Ks 2/63, Bd. 91, Bl. 17941–42 and HHA, HMJ III (IV-1076/59), Bl. 153–54.
[152] Ibid.
[153] In a subsequent letter to the HMJ, Hofmeyer pointed out that Judge Düx's unofficial visit to Auschwitz during the preliminary investigation had been intended in part to obviate the need for an official court visit. Hofmeyer to HMJ (June 29, 1964), HHA, HMJ III (IV-1076/59), Bl. 167.
[154] HMJ to BMJ (June 30, 1964), HHA, HMJ III (IV-1076/59), Bl. 171–72.
[155] Vermerk, BMJ (July 9, 1964), BAK, B 141/22762, Bl. 26–28.
[156] Vermerk, BMJ (July 21, 1964), BAK, B 141/22762, Bl. 31.
[157] Vermerk, BMI (July 22, 1964), BAK, B 106/102266, Bl. 1. (Internal pagination.)
[158] Vermerk, BMJ (July 23, 1964), BAK, B 141/22762, Bl. 43.
[159] Vermerk, BMI (July 22, 1964), BAK, B 106/102266, Bl. 3.
[160] BMJ to HMJ (July 31, 1964), BAK, B 141/22762, Bl. 54–56.

said in his letter that he felt it would be impossible to send an external judge (*ersuchte Richter*). Was this a mater of legal procedure or of practicality? Would it be possible for the court to conduct an inspection via a deputed judge (*beauftragter Richter*)?[161] They also demanded answers to a series of legal questions pertaining to the practical prerequisites of the trip, the most important of which was whether the court planned to go for certain if Poland gave the necessary guarantees or whether the court's decision depended on whether all trial participants were willing to attend.[162]

At the end of August, Hofmeyer completed his response. He reiterated that a visit by an external judge was pointless. The court, he said, had not yet decided whether an examination of Auschwitz should be done by the entire court acting officially or whether a deputed judge could be used, though he did note that that latter option was not "impossible."[163] In the first case, all the defendants would have to attend, whereas in the second case, they could choose not to. This was important because by early August, a number of the defendants not in investigative detention had announced in court that they would refuse to attend any session in Poland.[164] The main point in Hofmeyer's response, however, was that the court could not yet decide whether such an examination was necessary, since it was still taking evidence and new issues might arise at any time that would change the court's assessment of the matter.

In the eyes of the government, Hofmeyer's answers were wholly unsatisfactory.[165] As far as the government was concerned, Hofmeyer had not answered the most important question, namely, whether the court was certain it would undertake the journey to Auschwitz so long as the Polish authorities met the necessary practical requirements. The court and the government had reached a standoff.[166] Each was using delaying tactics to try to force the other to take responsibility for making the final decision. As far as the government was concerned, the Foreign Ministry in particular felt it would be "politically intolerable that Poland should make the requested guarantees, only to have the court decline to visit Auschwitz for other reasons."[167] The fact that the HMJ had sent along Hofmeyer's report without taking a

[161] See §§224, 225 StPO.
[162] They also wanted to know which trial participants would need guarantees of safe passage, which official actions the court would take while in Poland, whether a guarantee was needed that outstanding Polish arrest warrants would not be enforced, whether it was necessary for police officers to accompany the court, and how long the trip would take. Ibid.
[163] Hofmeyer, Stellungnahme (August 21, 1964), BAK, B 141/22762, Bl. 62–63, and also HHA, HMJ III (IV-1076/59), Bl. 214–15.
[164] Kurt Ernenputsch, "Acht Angeklagte wollen nicht mehr nach Auschwitz," FAZ, August 7, 1964.
[165] Vermerk, BMJ (September 22, 1964), BAK, B 141/22762, Bl. 65–69.
[166] Werner Renz has reached a similar conclusion. See Renz, "Tatort Auschwitz," p. 137.
[167] Vermerk, BK (July 22, 1964), BAK, B 136/3173.

position of its own gave the Federal Justice Ministry the impression that both the court and the HMJ were trying "to saddle the federal government with the responsibility for this politically very difficult matter."[168] The court, on the other hand, felt that it was being asked to make a decision that lay well beyond its competence, both legally and politically.

There was one possible way out of this impasse. Judge Heinz Düx had visited Auschwitz in the course of his preliminary investigation in July 1963, so that the trial court would not have to.[169] In a telephone conversation in September, Düx told the HMJ that he felt that in practical terms, a court visit to Auschwitz would be superfluous, as he could answer any technical questions regarding sightlines and the like. The main impact of such a visit would be "psychological."[170] Yet when Düx was called on by the court to testify in October regarding these matters, it turned out that in many specific instances, he was unable to answer the relevant questions.[171] The easy way out was unfortunately unavailable.

In the standoff between the court and the government, the court turned out to be in the weaker position. By this point, the government was losing patience and was even considering whether it could legally force the court to make a decision.[172] In late September, Ormond began making inquiries with the government regarding their stance on a court visit to Auschwitz. Hermann Meyer-Lindenberg of the Foreign Ministry informed him of the government's decision to support such a visit if the court itself made a final decision first.[173] The government fully expected Ormond to report this conversation to the court – and by extension to the press – and was using him to put pressure on Hofmeyer to make a decision. As expected, on October 15 Ormond informed the court in open session of his conversations with the government.[174] On October 16, lead prosecutor Großmann informed the Justice Ministry that he too had told Hofmeyer that the court would have to decide on its own whether a visit was necessary and permissible.[175] He also noted that he was of the opinion that the court could not reject Ormond's motion without creating grounds for appeal and that it was therefore likely to grant the motion.

---

[168] Vermerk, BMJ (September 22, 1964), BAK, B 141/22762, Bl. 65–69.
[169] Hofmeyer to HMJ (June 29, 1964) HHA, HMJ III (IV-1076/59), Bl. 167, and Vermerk, HMJ (July 21, 1964), HHA, HMJ III (IV-1076/59), Bl. 190–90R.
[170] Vermerk, HMJ (September, n.d.), HHA, HMJ III (IV-1076/59), Bl. 218.
[171] Renz, "Tatort Auschwitz," p. 138.
[172] See, e.g., Vermerk, BMJ (September 22, 1964), BAK, B 141/22762, Bl. 66, and Vermerk, BMJ (September 25, 1964), BAK, B 141/22762, Bl. 70–71.
[173] Vermerk, BMJ (October 16, 1964), BAK, B 141/22762, Bl. 77–80.
[174] See Bernd Naumann, "Noch keine Entscheidung über Lokaltermin in Auschwitz," FAZ, October 16, 1964, and "Bonn will Lokaltermin in Auschwitz unterstützen," FR, October 16, 1964.
[175] Vermerk, BMJ (October 19, 1964), BAK, B 141/22762, Bl. 84–85.

Under growing pressure from the government, the prosecution, and the press, the court was on the verge of surrender. On October 20, Großmann called the Federal Justice Ministry to inform them that, contrary to his earlier impression, Hofmeyer was in fact very interested in meeting with them.[176] The following afternoon, Hofmeyer met with representatives of the Justice Ministry, the Chancellery, and the Foreign Ministry. Hofmeyer explained that the court had not yet reached a decision regarding the motions for an examination of Auschwitz but that, given the time constraints, such a decision was likely to be made very soon. While he could "self-evidently not anticipate the court's decision," Hofmeyer said that for purposes of discussion, it could be assumed that the court would decide in favor of a limited examination of Auschwitz under the direction of a deputed judge. "While on the one hand, this form of examination had the disadvantage that the entire court could not get a direct impression of the spatial conditions, it could not be overlooked on the other hand, that an examination by the entire court could well create insurmountable difficulties."[177]

The government representatives, who had been trying to get the court to make a decision for nearly three months, were clearly relieved to hear this. The Foreign Ministry reiterated that, although Poland would undoubtedly seek to make political capital out of the visit and the negotiations could become quite complicated, they were more than willing to help.[178] The Justice Ministry stressed that it was important to keep negotiations with the Polish authorities as narrowly focused as possible, and to that end, the court should specify in its decision what the precise legal prerequisites for its visit would be.[179] At the end of the meeting, the Foreign Ministry asked the court, once it made its decision (which it should do quickly), to write a letter to the Polish Justice Ministry, stipulating the conditions necessary for it to undertake the examination.[180]

The following day, October 22, 1964, the court issued its decision.[181] In the event that the necessary diplomatic arrangements could be made, the court resolved that it would undertake an examination of Auschwitz by a member of the court serving as a deputed judge. As requested by the Foreign Office, Hofmeyer wrote a detailed letter to the Polish Justice Minister, in which he outlined the court's requirements, including a list of who would attend, what activities they would undertake at Auschwitz (on-site investigations in cooperation with Kazimierz Smoleń, the director

---

[176] Vermerk, BMJ (October 27, 1964), BAK, B 141/22762, Bl. 93–99.
[177] Ibid., Bl. 94. In particular, since all of the defendants would in that case have to be present, the refusal of any of them to attend would mean that the entire undertaking would collapse. Nor could those not in investigative detention be forced to go.
[178] Ibid., Bl. 95–96
[179] Ibid., Bl. 96–97.
[180] Ibid., Bl. 98.
[181] HVP (October 22, 1964), FFStA 4 Ks 2/63, Bd. 103, Bl. 827.

of the Auschwitz Museum, taking photos, sketches, measurements, etc.), and asking for free access to Auschwitz and safe passage for all participants in keeping with the power of attorney granted to Sehn the preceding March.[182]

Hofmeyer passed this letter along to the government, and on November 24, the Cabinet was informed and raised no objections.[183] In his memo for the Cabinet, Paul-Günther Pötz of the Justice Ministry stressed that in the interdepartmental meeting the preceding July, there had been a consensus that "for domestic and foreign political reasons" the government had to do everything in its powers to reach an agreement with the Polish authorities in this matter. While the success of such negotiations remained to be seen, "the government should not open itself to the criticism that it did not do everything possible to support the Auschwitz Trial."[184] The following day, the Foreign Ministry transmitted Hofmeyer's letter to the Polish authorities through the West German trade mission in Warsaw.[185]

On November 27, the Polish government gave Sehn a new power of attorney, again empowering him to negotiate on their behalf in this matter.[186] A meeting was arranged for December 2 between Sehn, one of his colleagues (Eugeniusz Szmulewski), Hofmeyer, and representatives from Bonn. The West Germans decided in advance to try to arrange for formal guarantees to be given directly to Hofmeyer, rather than to open interstate negotiations.[187] According to Pötz, who represented the Justice Ministry at the meeting, the conversation proceeded very graciously on all sides.[188] Hofmeyer began by explaining the court's conditions for an examination of Auschwitz as outlined in his letter of October 27. Sehn replied that the Polish government was convinced of the importance of such an investigation and had therefore declared its willingness to allow the court to visit Auschwitz months earlier. While the details still needed to be discussed, he suggested that an agreement between the Polish justice ministry and the West German

---

[182] Hofmeyer to Polish Justice Minister (October 27, 1964), FFStA 4 Ks 2/63, Bd. 92, Bl. 18150–53.

[183] Hofmeyer to BMJ (October 27, 1964), BAK, B 106/102266; BMJ to AA (November 6, 1964), BAK, B 141/22762, Bl. 116. The issue was placed on the Cabinet agenda already on November 11. See Vermerk, BK (November 6, 1964), BAK, 136/3173. For the notification, see Vermerk für die Kabinettsitzung, BK (November 21, 1964), BAK, B 136/3173; Vermerk, BMJ (November 24, 1964), BAK, B 141/22762, Bl. 122–25; and Note zu Punkt 2 der TO der 144. Kabinettsitzung (November 24, 1964), BAK, B 141/22762, Bl. 126.

[184] Vermerk, BMJ (November 24, 1964), BAK, B 141/22762, Bl. 123.

[185] Fernschreiben, AA (November 27, 1964), BAK, B 141/22762, Bl. 129.

[186] Vermerk, BMJ (December 4, 1964), BAK, B 141/22762, Bl. 137. See also Hofmeyer's much briefer account: Hofmeyer to BMJ (December 3, 1964), BAK, B 141/22762, Bl. 145–46.

[187] Ibid., Bl. 138–41.

[188] Ibid., Bl. 139. According to Pötz, Sehn did all the talking during the meeting, raising the possibility that Szmulewski was there as Sehn's political watchdog, though this cannot be confirmed from the documentary record.

government was the best way to proceed.[189] As already agreed, Hofmeyer and Pötz made the counter-suggestion that a simple written guarantee from the Polish Justice Ministry to Hofmeyer would suffice. At first Sehn was reluctant to agree, indicating that perhaps the Polish government had hoped to exploit a chink in the West German diplomatic armor to win tacit diplomatic recognition. However, after a long discussion, Sehn finally said that he "did not want to make difficulties over the form of the agreement."[190] One could view such an arrangement as a kind of legal aid among internal state agencies, Sehn noted. This was of course precisely what the West Germans wanted. In this way, they managed to avoid many of the foreign policy implications that an interstate agreement would have brought with it, while still enabling the court to go to Auschwitz. According to Pötz, Sehn's willingness to compromise in this and other matters showed "that the Polish government places extraordinary value" on the court's visit. This may account for the noticeable stubbornness with which the Germans negotiated throughout the remainder of the meeting. The Poles had revealed early in the negotiations that any apparent recalcitrance on their part was pure bluff.

There was further difficulty with the court's demand for a formal guarantee of safe conduct for all of the participants in the on-site investigation. Sehn verbally promised that the Poles would return everyone to Germany "without a scratch" (*ungeschoren*), but this was inadequate for the Germans, who insisted on a formal guarantee.[191] Eventually, Sehn acceded to this demand as well. Finally, after reaching full agreement on all technical questions, the Germans were adamant that Sehn get yet another power of attorney from the Polish Justice Ministry, since the one from November 27 technically empowered him only to discuss the situation, not to make legally binding guarantees. Sehn insisted that he had verbal permission from the Justice Minister to make such promises but in the face of German intransigence, once again capitulated and promised to ask Warsaw for an official statement empowering him to make formal guarantees.[192] At the end of the meeting, all of the participants together drafted a letter from Sehn and Szmulewski to Hofmeyer, in which they agreed to all of the conditions stipulated by Hofmeyer in his letter of October 27.[193] The letter also noted that the Polish Justice Minister had verbally confirmed these arrangements and would send a written statement to that effect immediately. That same day (December 2), the Polish Justice Minister sent a formal written statement to Hofmeyer in which he

[189] Ibid.
[190] Ibid.
[191] Ibid., Bl. 140.
[192] Ibid.
[193] On the drafting of this letter, see ibid. For the letter, see Sehn and Szmulewski to Hofmeyer (December 2, 1964), BAK, B 141/22762, Bl. 147.

specifically acceded to all of the arrangements specified in Hofmeyer's letter of October 27.[194]

On December 14, 1964, Judge Walter Hotz, accompanied by three of the prosecutors, all of the civil counsel, eleven of the defense attorneys, a translator, and a police photographer, arrived at Auschwitz for the first day of their three-day visit.[195] Only one of the least incriminated defendants, Dr. Lucas, agreed to accompany the court.[196] Two observers from the West German government, Rolf Vogel and Harald Kirchner, also accompanied the court.[197] Kazimierz Smoleń, director of the Auschwitz museum, accompanied the court as an official "information provider" (*Auskunftsperson*). Nearly a hundred journalists trailed the court at a discrete distance, since technically the court's proceedings in Auschwitz were closed to the public.[198]

Both of the government observers were struck both by the readiness with which the Poles dealt with all technical and practical matters, including such formalities as visas and customs, and by the general friendliness of both Polish officials and civilians.[199] More important, they both stressed that the

[194] Polish Justice Minister to Hofmeyer (December 2, 1964), BAK, B 141/22762, Bl. 156–59. As it happened, this letter did not reach Hofmeyer until December 16, two days after the court arrived in Auschwitz. See Hofmeyer to BMJ (December 16, 1964), BAK, B 141/22762, Bl. 154. Werner Renz errs slightly when, based on the trial files, he says that Sehn and Szmulewski had this letter with them already at the December 2 meeting. See Renz "Auschwitz als Augenscheinobjekt," p. 70, and Renz, "Tatort Auschwitz," p. 138. The letter is found, together with Hofmeyer's letter to the BMJ of December 3, in: FFStA 4 Ks 2/63, Bd. 92, Bl. 18269–72 and Bl. 18275–76, respectively.

[195] Richterliche Protokoll, Ortsbesichtigung, Anlage 6, HVP (January 7, 1965), FFStA 4 Ks 2/63, Bd. 106, p. 1. Internal pagination. The court was supposed to arrive on December 13 but was delayed because of bad weather.

[196] "Nur ein Angeklagter fährt nach Auschwitz: Lucas will teilnehmen," *Die Welt*, October 30, 1964.

[197] Vogel, winner of the 1971 Leo Baek Prize and publisher of *Deutschland-Berichte*, was a conservative Jew, a supporter of German-Jewish reconciliation, and an vehement opponent of left-wing influence in the Federal Republic. It is not clear from the files whether he accompanied the court at the request of the government, but in any case, he sent a report to the Chancellery on returning from Poland. See Vermerk, BK (December 21, 1964), BAK, B136/3173, and Vogel, "Politische Beobachtungen zur Ortsbesichtigung von Auschwitz" (December 19, 1964), BAK, B 136/3173. For his most important writings, see Vogel, *Israel: Staat der Hoffnung* (Stuttgart: Schwabenverlag, 1957), *Der Demokratischen Staat im Kampf gegen radikale Ausdrucksformen in der Bundesrepublik Deutschland: eine Dokumentation der Deutschland-Berichte* (Bonn, n.p., 1968), and *Ein Stempel hat gefehlt: Dokumentation zur Emigration deutsche Juden* (Munich: Droemer Knauer, 1977). Kirchner was a lawyer and amateur student of Nazism who had drafted earlier reports on race relations in the United States for the BPA. On December 5, he wrote to the BPA suggesting that they pay his expenses to Poland in exchange for a report on the court's activities, to which they agreed. See Kirchner to BPA (December 5, 1964), BAK, B 145/6624, and BPA to Kirchner (December 8, 1964), BAK, B 145/6624. For his report, see Kirchner, "Bericht über den Termin des Schwurgerichts Frankfurt in Auschwitz" (February 25, 1965), BAK, B 145/6624.

[198] Kirchner, "Bericht," p. 1. Internal pagination.

[199] Ibid., p. 1. Vogel, "Politische Beobachtungen," pp. 2–3.

Poles had not taken the court's visit to Auschwitz as an opportunity for political speechifying. This apolitical stance, said Kirchner, was "typical for the authorities there throughout the time in Poland: renunciation of any attempt at influence, every possible help in technical matters."[200] Vogel was particularly impressed when, shortly before the return journey, Hotz was taken to meet with the Polish Justice Minister in Warsaw, and even the minister avoided any political comments, merely thanking the court for its hard work and expressing his confidence that the court would reach a just verdict. The closest the Poles came to a political declaration was when, in his farewell speech at the airport, Sehn said that he was glad that "despite the lack of international relationships, this investigation was possible. This was a precedent. May it smooth the way for closer relations between the two peoples. Such cases...create clarity and the preconditions for the development of normal ties."[201]

The journalistic observers of the court's visit were less concerned about the political implications than they were by the striking image of a *German* court investigating Auschwitz. Clearly, the court's visit was one of the most photogenic moments in the trial. As Gerhard Mauz, reporting for the newsmagazine *Der Spiegel* put it, despite the more than 250 witnesses who had testified to date, "It was diagrams, photos and words that represented the unatoned reality of the camp for the court and the public. So Auschwitz and its adjunct camps remained in half-darkness, against which one's self-consciousness could rebel, against which the defendants could defend themselves with words against words."[202] In principle, then, the point of the examination was to dispel this half-darkness, to pit brute physical reality against the torrent of "mere" words in the trial.

As far as the court itself was concerned, after all the political maneuvering and controversy, the main function of the local examination was to ascertain beyond a reasonable doubt certain physical facts about the camp. How far was it from the pits where bodies were burned to the train tracks? 5.4 meters.[203] "In the right-hand room of Block 20 in front of Block 11, the entry-steps (main entrance) of Block 11 were clearly visible from the windows in the front and the right front walls."[204] "The distance between Block 20 and Block 21 was ascertained to be twelve meters."[205] The "new

---

[200] Kirchner, "Bericht," p. 9.
[201] Vogel, "Politische Beobachtungen," p. 3. The quote is a paraphrase, not verbatim. Early in the court's visit, Sehn had been truly horrified to learn that the court's translator, Wera Kapkajew, thought he was a member of the Polish secret police. "He only wanted the best," he said tearfully over drinks that night. Ibid., p. 1.
[202] Gerhard Mauz, "'Wo ist unser Angeklagter?'" *Der Spiegel* 52 (December 1964): 88.
[203] "Ortsbesichtigung," p. 2.
[204] Ibid., p. 8
[205] Ibid., p. 11.

laundry" "completely blocks the view of the 'Black Wall'" from the windows on the first floor of Block 28.[206] And so it went.

For the sake of juridical precision, the court was forced to play out scenes at once absurd and grotesque. On the afternoon of December 15, the court checked the veracity of testimony by Georg Severa to the effect that he had been able to hear an inmate in one of the standing cells in Block 11 sing popular songs.[207] To verify this testimony, a bailiff crawled through the small opening at the base of a standing cell and stood inside. "Now the bailiff, after crawling with difficulty into the cell, had to sing a song – reverence forbade him from singing the same popular song. So instead, one heard the old folksong, which he must have remembered from kindergarten: '*Sah ein Knab ein Röslein stehen*' – and the court determined that the witness had been correct. Just as it turned out during the investigation of Auschwitz that the statements by witnesses who had been here as inmates were in almost every case correct." [208]

There was something more than a little macabre about conducting this kind of detailed forensic investigation at Auschwitz, twenty years after over a million human beings had been exterminated there. Even the reporter for the boulevard magazine *Quick* noticed this. "At the bottom of the ditch lie yellow-gray lumps, sunk in fine, dark sand. 'The ashes of burnt people. The lumps are cinders that were not completely burned-up. There – that is a charred bone.' It all sounds like the spiel of a tour guide: here in front of us is the October meadow, over there the Bavarian one.... One member of the group protests, 'That may be. But we should still have an expert examine the ashes.' A third voice pleads, 'Gentlemen, we should move on. We still have a lot to accomplish.'"[209]

It is difficult to imagine a more glaring example of the tension between the emotional and experiential truth of Auschwitz, which is undeniably central to its historical truth as well, and the quest for irrefutable factual truth at the heart of the juridical proceedings. The notion that it would be appropriate to have the human ashes, the sole remains of tens of thousands of human lives, scientifically verified is callow and grotesque from the one perspective, yet perfectly reasonable from the other. In the Auschwitz Trial, these

---

[206] Ibid.

[207] Langbein, *Auschwitz*, vol. 1, pp. 554–55. Severa said that that the inmate Herbert, a German artist, told him from the standing cell that the defendant Schlage had locked him in there and announced that he would die there. In the meantime, he sang songs to stay sane. Herbert eventually died of hunger.

[208] Kirchner, "Bericht," p. 7. For a detailed examination and critique of the use made by the court of the evidence gathered at Auschwitz with particular reference to Breitwieser's case where it proved decisive, see Renz, "Tatort," pp. 140–44.

[209] "Wer zählt die Toten, nennt die Namen? *Quick* mit dem Frankfurter Schwurgericht in Auschwitz," *Quick* 18 (January 10, 1965): 17.

incompatible perspectives were not, and could not have been, reconciled. Nowhere does this irreconcilability emerge more clearly than in the following exchange. Judge Hotz, in discussing the draft protocol of the visit, mentioned the ditch where the bodies were burned. He was interrupted by one of the defense attorneys: "'*allegedly*, were *allegedly* burned.'" Hotz agreed: "'were *allegedly* burned, please write, allegedly....'"[210]

The Politics of the Past and the Politics of the Present

The deep tension between the needs of the witnesses and the needs of the court that emerged in the evidentiary phase of the Auschwitz Trial was thus further exacerbated by the intrusion of political imperatives into the trial. However much tension there was between them, at least the witnesses and the court shared a basic commitment to justice, even if they often seemed to understand that term in very different ways. But the imposition of Cold War political concerns on the trial had little to do with justice, in any sense of the term. Cold War politics entered the trial for two reasons. Most obviously, they could be tactically useful, especially to the defense. By linking the fate of their clients to the Cold War, rather than to the Nazi past, the defense tried to shift the terms of the proceedings to more favorable terrain, where their clients might look like (nearly) innocent victims of a communist inspired witch-hunt.

Not quite so obvious but equally important is the fact that Cold War politics entered into the trial because the trial was always already a *political event*. All rhetoric about the Auschwitz Trial being an "ordinary" trial aside, it was from the start a political trial, in the dual sense of both being *about* political events and itself *being* a political event. For Fritz Bauer and for much of the liberal press in West Germany, the Auschwitz Trial was clearly an exercise in moral and historical pedagogy. And the lessons it was supposed to teach were preeminently political. Auschwitz taught the value of democracy.

The difficulties such a political and pedagogical agenda posed in the context of the Cold War, however, can be gleaned from the controversy surrounding the exhibit "Auschwitz: Pictures and Documents," organized by the Frankfurt Bund für Volksbildung (BVB) that opened in the Paulskirche on November 18, 1964.[211] The purpose of the exhibit was, according to its organizer Carl Tesch, to serve as a "reminder, simply a reminder, especially for young people. The youth should understand Auschwitz so that something

---

[210] Ibid., p. 61.

[211] See Cornelia Brink, *"Auschwitz in der Paulskirche": Erinnerungspolitik in Fotoausstellungen der sechziger Jahren* (Marburg: Jonas Verlag, 2000). Arrangements for the exhibit were made as early as April 1964. See BVB to Stadt, FF/M (April 8, 1964), SAFF, Magistratsakten, Zugang III/2-1979, Sig. 61.

like that can never happen again."[212] To that end, staging the exhibition in the "home" of German democracy was clearly intended to add political weight to this message.[213] Mayor Willi Brundert (SPD) of Frankfurt made the same point in his opening address. He thanked the prosecution and the court for conducting the trial "with judicial correctness and political understanding" but added that such long trials risked exhausting the public and thereby losing their effectiveness. "Therefore we were grateful when Attorney General Bauer made the suggestion to make the actual stuff of the trial, which should enter the consciousness of every politically thoughtful person, visible through an exhibit."[214]

Of course, matters could not be so easy – either politically or legally. In legal terms, at least according to Rolf Vogel's report to the government, the judges in the trial worried that the exhibit might provide the defense with grounds for appeal, especially because photos of the defendants appeared in the exhibit along with excerpts from the indictment.[215] Indeed, at Bauer's insistence, these photos and documents were removed shortly after the start of the exhibit.[216] In their place, the organizers placed a sign reading: "In this place hung pictures of the accused in the Auschwitz Trial currently taking place in Frankfurt am Main, as well as descriptions of their functions in the camp and their crimes. At the request of the prosecution, we have removed this portion of the exhibit for the duration of the trial, in order to avoid any inappropriate influence on the proceedings."[217] Certainly, the defense objected strenuously to the exhibit.[218] Hermann Stolting II, representing Mulka, Höcker, and Bednarek, declared that, while such exhibits were in principle permissible, "'in connection with the massive attention in the press, it can only be seen as massive pressure from the outside on the defense.'"[219] Laternser went so far as to complain to the HMJ that Bauer had violated his office by supporting the exhibit.[220] In the end, however, this turned out to be so much legal bluster; none of the defense attorneys appealed on the basis of the exhibit.[221]

Equally important, however, was the Cold War controversy surrounding the exhibit. Professor Robert Waitz of Strasbourg, president of the IAC,

---

[212] Tesch press conference, cited in Rolf Vogel's report to the BMI. Vogel, "Die Auschwitz-Ausstellung in der Frankfurter Paulskirche" (November 18, 1964), BAK, B 106/71044, p. 1. Internal pagination.

[213] The Paulskirche was the seat of the first all-German parliament in 1848.

[214] Vogel, "Auschwitz-Ausstellung," p. 2.

[215] Ibid., p. 9.

[216] Laternser, *Die andere Seite*, p. 418.

[217] Brink, *"Auschwitz in der Paulskirche,"* p. 22.

[218] Bernd Naumann, "Capesius: Nie auf der Rampe," FAZ, November 20, 1964.

[219] Ibid.

[220] Laternser, *Die andere Seite*, pp. 417–18. The HMJ rejected Laternser's protest.

[221] See the BGH ruling on all appeals, in Rüter, ed., *Justiz und NS-Verbrechen*, pp. 838–86.

was invited by the BVB to speak at the exhibition's opening ceremony.[222] This raised hackles among other survivor organizations. The German-based Union Deutscher Wiederstandskämpfer- und Verfolgtenverbände (UDWV) wrote to Frankfurt's mayor on November 2, complaining that they had gotten the impression from the press that the IAC was practically running the exhibition. "We have the impression that the authorities have taken little notice of the infiltration by the East and we would like to protect the city of Frankfurt from becoming viewed a port of entry for communism. Perhaps it is not too late to save the Auschwitz Exhibit in the Paulskirche from becoming a communist rally."[223] Frankfurt's police chief also informed the mayor of similar concerns.

On November 11, barely a week before the opening ceremony, Mayor Brundert and Fritz Bauer wrote to Waitz asking him not to speak at the opening ceremonies after all.[224] Brundert and Bauer said that while the BVB would continue to manage the exhibit itself, once the mayor had been invited to speak, the opening ceremony had become a matter for the city administration. In a meeting between Brundert, Bauer, and Tesch, it was decided that this ceremony should be a strictly German affair; only Germans should speak to remind Germany of its responsibility for what happened. While the mayor hoped that Waitz would still attend, he felt it best that he not speak so as to avoid giving the impression – "certainly false" – of foreign influence over the exhibit. The following day, Tesch visited Waitz in Strasburg to convey the same message in person.[225]

Waitz was furious. In a scathing response, which he sent to the *Frankfurter Rundschau* as well as the mayor, Waitz said that the city had reneged on a promise, and he asserted, "The constitutional police [*Verfassungsschutz*] got involved, groundless suspicions found ready ears and, in order to save the exhibit, the BVB had to cave in to the pressure. In the city of the Auschwitz Trial, a representative of the survivors of this camp was not allowed to speak. Boger, Kaduk, Mulka and their comrades will rub their dirty hands

---

[222] Waitz was probably invited sometime in mid-October. At any rate, his name is included in a list of invitees sent to Brundert on October 16. See BVB to Brundert (October 16, 1964), SAFF, Magistratsakten, Zugang III/2-1979, Sig. 61.

[223] UDWV to Brundert (November 2, 1964), SAFF, Magistratsakten, Zugang III/2-1979, Sig. 61. The letter was signed by Alfred Dietrich, who had organized an exhibition on the Warsaw ghetto in the Paulskirche the preceding year. See Brink, *"Auschwitz in der Paulskirche,"* pp. 12–18. Dietrich made similar protests through other organizations he was involved in. See, e.g., Verband für Freiheit und Menschenwürde (VFM) to FF Police (November 2, 1964), SAFF, Magistratsakten, Zugang III/2-1979, Sig. 61. The VFM was a right-wing organization with roots in the Nazi propaganda ministry. See Marc von Miquel, *Ahnden oder amnestieren? Westdeutsche Justiz und Vergangenheitspolitik in den sechziger Jahren* (Göttingen: Wallstein, 2004), p. 50.

[224] Brundert to Waitz (November 11, 1964), SAFF, Magistratsakten, Zugang III/2-1979, Sig. 61.

[225] Brink, *"Auschwitz in der Paulskirche,"* p. 20.

with glee."[226] Waitz also pointed out that he had been the only Jewish person scheduled to speak at the opening ceremony.[227] "We are ashamed in the face of this humiliating turn of events," remarked the *Frankfurter Rundschau.* "We are certain that all the citizens of goodwill in our city…share our feelings."[228] To drive this point home, the paper published Waitz's intended speech as well.

The mayor had clearly been placed in a rather embarrassing position. Publicly, it looked as though he was censoring Waitz, hardly the pedagogical message the Auschwitz exhibit was intended to convey. Brundert promptly fired off a letter to the *Frankfurter Rundschau* in which he reiterated that the real reason Waitz was asked not to speak was not censorship but rather to make it clear that "Germans should acknowledge German historical guilt and draw the proper political conclusions from it."[229] The *Frankfurter Rundschau*'s response was to publish an even more damaging report in which it was claimed, in effect, that the mayor was lying.[230] The paper alleged that Waitz was excluded from the opening ceremony primarily because he and the IAC were suspected of communist sympathies, that Langbein and the CIC had pressured the city to uninvite him, and, in particular, that there had been a "secret meeting" between Brundert, the Frankfurt police chief, and representatives from the BVB – "supposedly regarding expected traffic problems!" – but in reality to discuss the communist threat purportedly posed by Waitz. Allegedly, the mayor had threatened the BVB at this meeting with a withdrawal of city funds if they insisted on inviting Waitz. The whole thing was political censorship of the crassest sort and the mayor did not even have the courage to admit it, according to the paper.

Not all responses to the Waitz affair were critical of the mayor. Langbein wrote an open letter to the *Frankfurter Rundschau* condemning Waitz and the IAC, and the UDWV sent a letter of support to the mayor applauding his "rescue" of the Auschwitz exhibit.[231] Of course, not all of the support for the mayor's position came from such reputable sources. Among the scores

---

[226] "Wir geben professor Robert Waitz das Wort," FR, November 21, 1964. Curiously, this letter does not appear to be in the mayor's files in the SAFF.

[227] Ironically, Waitz himself would resign from the IAC a few years later in the face of another controversy over who could speak for the dead of Auschwitz. On April 21, 1968, Polish authorities opened a new pavilion to honor the dead of Auschwitz. Only one foreign Jew was invited to attend, and Waitz resigned in protest. See Benjamin B. Ferencz, *Less than Slaves: Jewish Forced Labor and the Quest for Compensation* (Bloomington: Indiana University Press, 2002), pp. 65–66.

[228] "Wir geben professor Robert Waitz das Wort," FR, November 21, 1964.

[229] Brundert to FR (November 21, 1964), SAFF, Magistratsakten, Zugang III/2-1979, Sig. 61. Reprinted as "Wirklich Redeverbot in Frankfurt?" FR, November 23, 1964.

[230] "Es gibt Hintergründe," FR, November 24, 1964.

[231] Langbein, "Denkmal für Ermordete – Maulkorb für Überlebende," FR, November 27, 1964 and UDWV to Brundert (December 25, 1964), SAFF, Magistratsakten, Zugang III/2-1979, Sig. 61.

of anti-Semitic letters and threats received by the mayor's office with regard to the Auschwitz Trial, at least one praised the mayor's decision to uninvite Waitz as an act of "courage," given the enormous power the letter writer assumed that Jews possessed in the world.[232] While it would be utterly unfair to imply that the mayor in any way shared such anti-Semitic sentiments, the potent combination of Cold War politics and the politics of memory clearly made for some strange bedfellows in the mid-1960s.

Indeed, while there is no reason to doubt that the mayor was sincerely committed to the public value of the Auschwitz exhibit and the Auschwitz Trial, it is also clear that the *Frankfurter Rundschau* was not simply being paranoid when it implied that there was much more at work in the Waitz affair than this. When the mayor was invited to speak, he apparently asked the police to investigate Waitz and the IAC.[233] On October 29, he received a report in which the Frankfurt police concluded that the IAC was indeed a "communist oriented organization."[234] The police also noted that a number of prominent organizations and individuals were withdrawing their support for the exhibit.[235] The following day, the police chief wrote directly to the mayor urging him to cancel the exhibit altogether: "[I]t is my opinion that the entire event – opening ceremony and exhibition – ought not under any circumstances be allowed to take place in the Paulskirche in its present form. Otherwise, we can expect extremely unpleasant political reactions among the public. It is my opinion that there can be no doubt that considerable damage has already been done, since the representatives of the communist IAC will doubtless attempt to keep you away from this exhibition and the opening ceremony, in order to be able to claim that this shows that the city of Frankfurt obviously identifies itself with the crimes committed in Auschwitz."[236]

A few days later, Bauer, apparently having gotten wind of the controversy brewing in the mayor's office, wrote to Brundert defending the exhibition.[237] The idea for such an exhibit, he said, was entirely his. The idea had been hatched at a time when the prospects of a court visit to Auschwitz seemed

[232] Anonymous to Brundert (February 25, 1965), SAFF, Magistratsakten, Zugang III/2-1979, Sig. 61.
[233] BVB to Brundert (October 16, 1964), SAFF, Magistratsakten, Zugang III/2-1979, Sig. 61. There is a handwritten red question mark next to Waitz's name in this letter of invitation, though it is not clear if it is from the mayor himself or one of his subordinates.
[234] Police Report re: IAC (October 29, 1964), SAFF, Magistratsakten, Zugang III/2-1979, Sig. 61.
[235] Thus the Landeszentral für Heimatdienst, Hesse withdrew its 5000 DM contribution. The Gewerkschaft IG-Metall (steel workers union) also withdrew its support, and its head, Otto Brenner, declined to speak at the opening. The president of the Bundestag, Eugen Gerstenmeier, likewise declined an invitation to speak. Ibid.
[236] Police Chief Littmann to Brundert (October 30, 1964), SAFF, Magistratsakten, Zugang III/2-1979, Sig. 61.
[237] Bauer to Brundert (November 4, 1964), SAFF, Magistratsakten, Zugang III/2-1979, Sig. 61.

remote, so he had suggested to Sehn, Ormond, and the prosecution that part of the Auschwitz museum be brought to Frankfurt instead. It was his idea to have the BVB organize the exhibit. Sehn helped to get the materials from the Auschwitz museum; otherwise, there had been no attempt to influence the exhibit, either by the Auschwitz museum or the IAC. There were no "behind the scenes actors" arranging the exhibit. As for the IAC, as far as Bauer knew, it was in the hands of the communists in the East: "How could it be otherwise?" Yet while the leadership might be communist, this did not represent the entire organization, which had members in both East and West. "The regrettable rivalries between various survivor organizations should not disrupt our Frankfurt intentions."[238]

Under the circumstances, it seems likely therefore that the decision to ask Waitz not to speak was a compromise by the mayor, who was under pressure on the one hand from those who wanted to cancel the exhibit entirely and, on the other hand, from those who argued that it was an extraordinarily important public gesture. Like most compromises, it was hardly adequate to satisfy all parties, as the controversy in the *Frankfurter Rundschau* shows, yet it also reflected the reality of a complicated political situation in which the politics of the past and the politics of the present were often indistinguishable. This dual politicization of the Auschwitz Trial set the stage for an interpretive battle over the legal and historical meaning of the trial that emerged fully only during the closing arguments. But as the controversies surrounding Kuczynski's testimony, the court's visit to Auschwitz, and the Waitz affair show, the Auschwitz Trial was more or less permanently an object of contemporary political controversy throughout the evidentiary phase as well.

The Cold War and the Witnesses

The Cold War could be incorporated into the juridical logic of the courtroom itself as well. If the defense, together with civil counsel Kaul, were more actively engaged during the evidentiary phase in explicitly politicizing the trial, this was because they felt, rightly from their point of view, that the trial's narrative configuration was stacked against them. After all, the trial's basic structure was dictated by the indictment. The prosecution's hermeneutic interpretation was, in this sense, *built into* the trial. The historical account the trial provided was that Nazism was a *political* problem that supplanted the rule of law with the rule of power, that the SS had been largely responsible

---

[238] Ibid. Ormond also wrote a letter supporting the exhibition in which he likewise claimed that the problem was more one of personal rivalries between Langbein and Waitz than it was substantive. Ormond to Brundert (November 5, 1964), SAFF, Magistratsakten, Zugang III/2-1979, Sig. 61. The following day, Brundert received a memo indicating that the police had been mistaken about IG-Metall's withdrawal of support and Brenner's refusal to participate. See Vermerk (November 5, 1964), SAFF, Magistratsakten, Zugang III/2-1979, Sig. 61.

for this development, and that the defendants were deeply and criminally involved in this process. For the defense, the evidentiary phase offered them a preliminary opportunity to call this narrative into question. Above all, they articulated a presentist account of Auschwitz that situated it firmly in a view of the past as long gone, that privileged the perceived communist threat from the East over the long dead horrors of Nazism.[239] Auschwitz was simply one example among many of totalitarian barbarism, one whose lessons, properly understood, meant that it was far more important to combat the present incarnations of that barbarism than it was to punish its previous instantiations. This political reimagining of Auschwitz was linked with the defense's tactical endeavor to admit the horrors of Auschwitz, while dissociating their clients from them.

The symmetry of this mode of presentist political argumentation should be noted; by replacing the term "totalitarian" with the term "fascist," one arrives at the East German, rather than the defense position. For Kaul, the point was that the FRG was itself a neo-fascist state, governed by the same old monopoly capitalists. By deliberately provoking the defense, by calling witnesses with official positions in East Block countries, he further sought to highlight the ongoing hostility toward "people's democracy" in the "imperialist west." For Kaul, every setback, such as the court's rejection of Kuczynski's testimony or Hans Laternser's efforts to have East German Minister of Industry, Erich Markowitsch, arrested during his testimony (on February 4, 1965) for allegedly helping to build the Berlin Wall, could be recycled into a triumph.[240]

The defense tried to deploy Cold War politics in two ways. First, they found in the figure of Friedrich Kaul a lightning rod for their own political agenda. In attacking Kaul, the defense sought not so much to influence tactically the course of the Auschwitz Trial itself as to taint all Nazi trials with the implication that they merely served communist propaganda. While this was unlikely to be of much help to their clients in *this* trial, they seemed to

---

[239] In this, the defense partook of a widespread sensibility in the Federal Republic's first decades. See, e.g., Norbert Frei, *Vergangenheitspolitik: Die Anfänge der Bundesrepublik und die NS-Vergangenheit* (Munich: C. H. Beck, 1996); Herf, *Divided Memory*; and von Miquel, *Ahnden oder amnestieren*.

[240] The East Germans had planned Markowitsch's testimony from the very beginning; indeed, his name is explicitly mentioned in the Politburo decision regarding the trial. See Beschluß des Politbüros (November 19, 1963), BAB, SAPMO, DY 30/J IV 2/2 A-999. Laternser moved to have Markowtisch arrested because of his ostensible role in building the Berlin Wall and the subsequent murder of people trying to flee to the west. The prosecution opposed Laternser's motion, saying they felt that it was not within the court's jurisdiction and that, anyway, Laternser was merely being provocative. See Vermerk, Großmann (February 5, 1965), FFStA HA 4 Ks 2/63, Bd. 22, Bl. 4401–3. Based on the prosecution's opposition, the court rejected Laternser's motion. See Bernd Naumann, "Der Herr Minister im Zeugenstand: Rechtsanwalt Dr. Laternser empfiehlt die vorläufige Festnahme," FAZ, February 5, 1965.

hope that it would stoke the mood of animosity toward Nazi trials in general. This would presumably aid the widespread efforts to achieve a direct or indirect amnesty for Nazi crimes.[241]

Second, the defense sought to mobilize a generalized distrust of the communist "East" to undermine the credibility of many witnesses. A great many of the witnesses from East Block countries were subjected to insulting tactics, their motives impugned and the veracity of their testimony questioned. This was particularly true for East Block witnesses who worked in any official capacity.

On September 24, 1964, Alois Eisenhändler, a major in the GDR army and former Jewish inmate at Auschwitz, was called to testify at Kaul's request. His testimony quickly ran into trouble, as when he claimed to have seen flames rising from the crematoria in January 1943 when these had not been built until March of that year.[242] But the real trouble began when Laternser rose to cross-examine the witness. Interrogating the major about his military career, Laternser sought to bring to the court's attention that Eisenhändler served in the East German border police and was thus at least indirectly implicated in the murder of civilians trying to flee the GDR.[243] The point of Laternser's attack here was not just to undermine Eisenhändler's credibility as a witness, which was hardly necessary, given that he had little to contribute to the proceedings anyway, but also to stage a polemical attack on the GDR. The implication was that any trial that allowed such tainted (i.e., communist) testimony was not a legitimate trial at all.

If Laternser's repeated attacks on witnesses from the East Block won him propaganda points, it was a dangerous game because it also allowed Kaul to position himself as the noble defender of unfairly insulted witnesses. When the very first Polish witness, Wojciech Barcz, came to testify on April 9, 1964, Laternser attacked him for having had a conversation with Hermann Langbein. Laternser claimed that this constituted witness tampering. Kaul leapt to Barcz's defense, asserting, quite rightly, that it was only natural that survivors should meet with one another and that Laternser was pursuing "systematic discrimination" against prosecution witnesses.[244] Laternser retorted that only an East Berlin lawyer, "'who has a different agenda than finding the truth,'" could say that.[245]

The political controversies surrounding East Block witnesses reached a fever pitch in two instances. The first concerned allegations that, while in the camp, the witness Josef Kral had instigated the murder of two Ukrainian

[241] Von Miquel, *Ahnden oder amnestieren*, pp. 186–207, and Herbert, *Best*, pp. 454–55.
[242] "'Auch an der Mauer gibt es Mord': Zwischenfall im Auschwitz-Prozeß um Zeugen aus der Zone," FNP, September 25, 1964.
[243] Ibid.
[244] "Zählfehler rettete ihm das Leben," FNP, April 10, 1964.
[245] Ibid.

nationalist leaders, Wassil and Olek Bandera.[246] Kral had earlier testified to great effect against various members of the Political Section, and the defense was particularly concerned to discredit his testimony. They called numerous Ukrainian witnesses, mostly nationalist émigrés living in West Germany, who claimed that Kral had been responsible for the deaths of the two brothers, while the prosecution called a number of Polish witnesses who denied the allegations. As a result, the court was never able to satisfactorily determine whether Kral had actually been involved in the murder of the Bandera brothers or not. Ukrainian witnesses said yes; Polish witnesses said no.

In any event, the defense had achieved its goal. The court treated Kral's testimony with great skepticism in its verdict. In particular, the court declined to convict Stark on one count where the sole evidence was Kral's testimony, noting that Kral may have projected his own crimes onto Stark, who was the camp supervisor for the Bandera group.[247] Above all, what this controversy revealed was the fractious nature of relations among inmates in Auschwitz, that although they were all victims, some of them had also been perpetrators. It was unfortunate that the defense was able to treat this profound tragedy only with tactical cynicism.

The second major political explosion came near the end of the trial. The defense alleged that the Polish authorities were deliberately preventing defense witnesses from traveling to Frankfurt.[248] They particularly highlighted the case of Barbara Pozimska and her husband Jerzy Pozimski. Jerzy Pozimski had testified earlier in the trial, on October 9, 1964, on behalf of Emil Bednarek. He had lived in the Block where Bednarek served as *Blockältester* and had said that he had personally never seen Bednarek kill anyone. Although he did add, "Admittedly, I was not there day and night."[249] On April 30, 1965, his wife testified for the second time in the trial (the first was on March 4, 1965), also on Bednarek's behalf. She claimed that when her husband returned to Poland after his testimony, he was fired from his job because he had testified on Bednarek's behalf. She further asserted that other potential witnesses were refused travel permits because they might exonerate the defendants. She refused to say more than that because she feared

---

[246] See the fairly detailed account in Langbein, *Auschwitz*, pp. 473–84. For a fuller analysis, see Franziska Bruder, "'Die Gerechtigkeit zu dienen': Die ukrainischen Nationalisten als Zeugen im Auschwitz-Prozess," in Irmtrud Wojak and Susanne Meinl, eds., *Im Labyrinth der Schuld: Täter-Opfer-Ankläger* (Frankfurt: Campus Verlag, 2003), pp. 133–62. It was the assassination of the third Bandera brother, Steffan, which led to the Staschynskij case discussed in chapter 2.

[247] Rüter, *Justiz und NS-Verbrechen*, pp. 794–96.

[248] "Neue Zeugenvernehmungen in Polen: Urteile im Auschwitz-Prozeß weiter verzögert," *FNP*, March 30, 1965.

[249] Langbein, *Auschwitz*, p. 798.

official retaliation back home.[250] The defense, as well as the conservative press, trumpeted this as decisive proof of witness tampering by the communist authorities.[251]

As it turned out, however, by the end of the month, prosecutor Kügler was able to announce that Mrs. Pozimska had committed perjury. Her husband had been fired not because of his testimony in Frankfurt but because of repeated criminal infractions.[252] This was confirmed in a deposition by Mr. Pozimski himself taken in Poland.[253] Kaul responded by demanding that Bednarek's attorney Rainer Eggert be questioned concerning his contacts with Mrs. Pozimska. While he denied any attempt to influence her testimony, Eggert did admit to having talked with Pozimska privately while she was in Frankfurt. Kaul concluded that the defense had taken the opportunity presented by the court's visit to Auschwitz to make contact with Polish witnesses to try to steer their testimony.[254] On questioning by the court, Kaul's associate Joachim Noack said that Pozimska had told him that she felt "overwhelmed" by Eggert but that she also worried about "unpleasantness" back home in Poland. He had informed her that so long as she told the truth, there would certainly be no difficulties in Poland.[255] Nonetheless, the court ordered that further depositions be taken from witnesses in Poland, in order to ensure that all of the defense witnesses had the opportunity to be heard, if only indirectly. Although this controversy did not achieve the same tactical success as the Bandera affair, it nonetheless did allow the defense to highlight their concerns about any legal proceedings that relied on "communists" for evidence. Indeed, Kaul told Sehn that the Pozimska affair "has hurt us considerably."[256]

---

[250] Bernd Naumann, "'Ja, was meinen Sie? Die hätten mich ja direkt eingesperrt,'" FAZ, March 5, 1965.

[251] See, e.g., "Schwarzer Tag," *Die Welt*, March 6, 1965. This conservative daily referred to Barbara Pozimska's allegations as "judicially acknowledged" (*gerichtsbekannt*).

[252] "Neue Zeugenvernehmungen in Polen: Urteile im Auschwitz-Prozeß weiter verzögert," March 30, 1965.

[253] Langbein, *Auschwitz-Prozeß*, p. 862.

[254] Kaul to Sehn (May 3, 1965), BAB, Nachlaß Kaul, N 2503, Bd. 197, p. 3. Internal pagination.

[255] Ibid., p. 4.

[256] Ibid. A definitive answer as to whether the Polish authorities interfered with witness testimony in the trial awaits an examination of the relevant Polish archives. On at least one occasion, the East Germans did prohibit two witnesses from testifying for the defense. See Kaul, "Verhandlungsbericht" (January 7, 1965), BAB, Nachlaß Kaul, N 2503, Bd. 197, and Kaul to Rehan (January 9, 1965), BAB, Nachlaß Kaul, N 2503, Bd. 197. There is, however, no evidence that any witnesses were coached or their testimony vetted in advance.

7

Closing Arguments, May 7, 1965, to August 12, 1965

On May 6, 1965, the evidentiary phase of the Frankfurt Auschwitz Trial came to a close.[1] As we have seen, it is extremely difficult to summarize the results of the nearly 140 days of testimony in the trial. And yet that was precisely the task now confronting the attorneys in their closing arguments (*Plädoyers*), which lasted twenty-six days, from early May through early August 1965. Per §258 StPO, the prosecution had the first word, followed by the civil counsel, then the defense.[2] The final word was reserved for the defendants themselves, if they so chose.

The attorneys' job in their closing arguments was both to *summarize* and to *interpret* the results of the evidentiary phase for the trial.[3] It was here that the prosecutors, defense counsel, and civil counsel intervened most directly in the proceedings. If the evidentiary phase belonged, in a very real sense, to the court and to the witnesses, then the closing arguments belonged to the lawyers. They sought to articulate, in as persuasive a manner as possible, their competing interpretations of law, evidence, and history. If the evidentiary phase was at least nominally a cooperative endeavor in pursuit of the truth, the closing arguments were a battleground.

Broadly speaking, four distinct interpretive positions emerged in the closing arguments. The prosecution articulated a vision of Auschwitz as the outcome of a deliberate, conscious policy of extermination, ordained by the Nazi leadership, but willingly implemented by the defendants. History here provided the necessary *context* for individual criminality but could hardly be said to have *caused* it in any strong sense. Indeed, history itself was nothing more than the dynamic outcome of individual decisions, which nevertheless

---

[1] The evidentiary phase was briefly reopened for two days, July 23 and 29, 1965, to interrogate the witness Franz Ruprecht again and to read two further witnesses' depositions.

[2] §258 StPO, p. 364.

[3] These were also termed *Schlußvorträge* (concluding remarks). In addition, some attorneys chose to make rebuttals (*Replike*) to the *Plädoyers* of competing attorneys.

remained independent. Agency, and hence guilt, remained squarely at the level of the autonomous individual. Such a historical interpretation was all but mandated, given the prosecution's hope to convict the defendants as perpetrators, that is as agents who had willfully acted to operationalize their own internal desires, who operated in a bureaucratic context but whose actions were in no way subjectively dictated by that context.

The civil counsel articulated two distinct visions of history and law. Henry Ormond and Christian Raabe stood in broad agreement with the prosecution's account. They too insisted on the individual agency of the defendants. However, they stressed even more vigorously than the prosecution the suffering of the victims and the extreme demands this made on the claims of justice. A just sentence had to be, on their account, a harsh sentence. Friedrich Kaul, by contrast, articulated a much more deeply structural interpretation of history. On his account, monopoly capitalism bore final and direct responsibility for Auschwitz. That he felt that this "monopoly capitalism" continued to dominate the Federal Republic hardly needed to be added. However ideological and one-sided it may have been, Kaul's interpretation was also one of the few instances where the broad social history of the Third Reich entered the courtroom at all.

The defense, as one might expect, vehemently contested the prosecution's agentive view of history. According to the defense, agency stopped at the highest levels of the state and party. Only the top leadership was in a position to dictate policy, and in a totalitarian state, once policy was set, those charged with its implementation had essentially no room for maneuver. For one thing, state directives had the force of positive law. Failure to obey, however morally justified, would have been a violation of one's civic obligation as a citizen. Furthermore, because this was a terrorist state, refusal to obey was also sure to bring swift and deadly sanction on anyone so brave or foolhardy as to undertake the effort. Thus, their clients had only done what they had to do. What is more, they had sincerely believed their actions to be legally sanctioned at the time. Furthermore, the defense contended that the evidence of specific criminal activity by any of the defendants was in almost every case highly suspect at best, stemming as it did from witnesses whose memory was often faulty, who were largely motivated by hatred and the desire for vengeance, and many of whom were communists as well.

Far more clearly than in the evidentiary phase, the closing arguments revealed the diverse interpretive and tactical agendas of the actors in the Auschwitz Trial. At the same time, though, they also revealed the juridical *boundedness* of these agendas, in that even the most explicitly historical arguments put forth in the closing arguments were constantly in dialogue with legal categories. None of the closing arguments was a purely representational exercise; in all of them, the interpretation of history necessarily took place through a juridical lens.

The Prosecution

Nowhere is this more apparent than in the very first closing argument, delivered on May 7, 1965, by Oberstaatsanwalt Großmann. Unlike his three subordinates – Kügler, Vogel, and Wiese, who were charged with evaluating the cases against individual defendants – Großmann choose to focus his closing argument exclusively on general considerations of history and law. It is thus worth examining in some detail, as it lays out with particular clarity the prosecution's interpretation of what was at stake in the trial. Großmann opened by quoting a speech by Bundespräsident Heinrich Lübke (CDU) on the twentieth anniversary of the liberation of Bergen-Belsen a few days previously. The president had said: "None of those who say that it is time to finally be done with this magical subordination to the shadows [*Schattenbeschwörung*] of a terrible past do us any favors. It is not *we* who conjure the shadows, it is the shadows which conjure *us,* and it does not lie in our power to break their spell."[4] Großmann added, "*The shadows conjure us – and they do so daily, also and especially here in these proceedings. Nor will these shadows of the past yield to the judgment that you, ladies and gentlemen, are about to pass.*"[5] From the very start, Großmann made it clear both that the stakes in the trial were nothing less than the status of the German past as an almost mystic burden on the German present and also that the power of the court to dispel these burdens was very limited indeed. On this account, the trial was in dialogue with the broader process of *Vergangenheitsbewältigung* but could not supplant it entirely.

Großmann took as his task the clarification of certain general issues relating to the trial. He noted preliminarily that the indictment and the *Eröffnungsbeschluß* had differed in their evaluation of whether certain defendants had been perpetrators or accomplices and that the prosecution felt that in all but two cases (Breitwieser and Schoberth), the evidence in the trial had in fact shown them to be perpetrators. But the real focal point of his remarks would be two sets of historical and legal issues: first, the cause, extent, and time frame of the alleged crimes and, second, the need to establish a general personality profile for the defendants. In other words, Großmann wanted to clarify both the objective and subjective issues pertaining to the case.

As far as the cause and extent of the crimes on trial were concerned, Großmann noted that it was important not to be misled by the juridically necessary but decidedly vague formulations in the indictment and the *Eröffnungsbeschluß,* which repeatedly charged the defendants with murder "in an unknown number of instances."[6] One must not forget, he insisted,

---

[4] Großmann, "Schlußvortrag," FBI SAP: FAP1/StA 1, Nachlaß Großmann, p. 1.
[5] Ibid.
[6] Ibid., p. 4.

that upward of 2.5 million people were killed at Auschwitz.[7] The "incomprehensibility of this mass murder" might lead some people, even those of good will, to misinterpret the cause of these murders in ways that were "wrong and, in addition, not without their dangers."[8] In particular, there were those who claimed that, because these crimes were committed in wartime, they could not be prosecuted, just as the attacks against civilians by the other side had not been prosecuted. It was but a short step, Großmann warned, from this argument to the one that held that anti-Semitism and the persecution of the Jews were legally sanctioned "reprisals," because of, for example, Chaim Weizmann's "declaration of war" on Germany. To refute such claims, it was not even necessary, Großmann said, to note that wars occur between states and there had been no Jewish state at the time. Rather, the simple fact that this had been not an armed conflict but the systematic murder of unarmed civilians gave lie to the thesis that the Final Solution was an act of war. The particularity of the persecution of the Jews was that it was the "realization of a programmatic goal established by National Socialism," one merely "accelerated," not caused by the war.[9]

As for the issue of time frame, Großmann said that this raised the central questions: Why are such trials taking place only now? And why are such trials still taking place at all? Großmann answered the first question with reference to a variety of "interrelated" factors.[10] These included the total collapse of Germany after the war, the difficulties of reconstruction, the fact that the large number of Allied trials made German trials seem superfluous, the jurisdictional problems that plagued prosecutions prior to the founding of the Central Office, the inaccessibility of foreign archives, and so on. Großmann did admit that these various factors could not satisfactorily explain every single instance of delay, implicitly acknowledging that there may also have been a lack of political will at work, but only in a few isolated cases.

The second and, from Großmann's point of view, more important question was why these trials did and should continue into the present. The initial,

---

[7] The Auschwitz Trial worked with Rudolph Höß's figure of 2.5 million victims. Recent scholarship estimates the number of persons killed at Auschwitz at between 1.1 and 1.5 million. See Franciszek Piper, "The Number of Victims," in Yisrael Gutman and Michael Berenbaum, eds., *Anatomy of the Auschwitz Death Camp* (Bloomington: Indiana University Press, 1994), pp. 61–76. Cf. Robert Jan van Pelt, *The Case for Auschwitz: Evidence from the Irving Trial* (Bloomington: Indiana University Press, 2002), pp. 106–18. Van Pelt settles on the figure of 1.1 million.

[8] Großmann, "Schlußvortrag," p. 1.

[9] Ibid., p. 6. In recent years, the military context of the decision for the final solution has become a topic of considerable controversy. For perhaps the most up-to-date summaries of the debates, see Christopher Browning, *Nazi Policy, Jewish Workers, German Killers* (Cambridge: Cambridge University Press, 2000), pp. 26–57, and Konrad H. Jarausch and Michael Geyer, *Shattered Past: Reconstructing German Histories* (Princeton: Princeton University Press, 2003), pp. 111–48.

[10] Großmann, "Schlußvortrag," p. 8.

"procedural" answer was that the legality principle underlying German law mandated that such trials continue. But there was a more important political answer to this question as well. "All of us who have tried over the years to legally master these most serious crimes know only too well the reluctance, indeed the aversion, these efforts encounter in some circles. We don't need the recent survey data to tell us this. And we sense quite clearly the substantial cause of this reluctance and aversion, even if this cause remains largely hidden in silence. *I mean that – conscious or unconscious – inner entanglement* with all the events of those days, including the actions at Auschwitz, which particularly afflicts members of the older generation."[11]

Großmann was careful to note that this "inner entanglement" did not constitute collective criminal guilt.[12] "Despite Auschwitz," Germany was not a nation of murderers. Rather, this was an entanglement of "errors and omissions," as the *Wort des Rates der evangelischen Kirche in Deutschland zu den NS-Verbrecherprozessen* had put it on March 13, 1963.[13] Clearly, Großmann added, this court could not accomplish "something like a purification of our entire people."[14] But it could, indeed must, serve to accomplish the fundamental task set for the courts by the Evangelical Church: "It is the high office [of the courts] to rebuild among our people that commitment to law which was destroyed in the past and thereby to contribute decisively to the inner recovery of our people."[15]

This "primacy of criminal law" also linked directly with the necessity for incorporating historical research into the proceedings; this was the point of the historical testimony. Without this knowledge, "the cause and extent, as well as the time frame of the [criminal] acts could be as little recognized as . . . the personality profiles of the defendants."[16] Without history, one could not hope to understand either the perpetrators or their crimes; and without such an understanding, one could not possibly hope to reconstruct the legal solidarity that was imperative for the nascent German democracy. This shift from the inner entanglement of the older generation to the need to reconstitute the rule of law in the Federal Republic elides the fact that these are in fact different order problems, the former an issue of collective memory, the latter, a matter of legal and political education.

As far as the personality profiles of the defendants were concerned, Großmann noted that, as was so often the case, these could not be typified according to criminological categories. There were no "Auschwitz

---

[11] Ibid., p. 10. Emphasis in the original.
[12] Jan Friedmann and Jörg Später, "Britische und deutsche Kollektivschuld-Debate," in Ulrich Herbert, ed., *Wandlungsprozesse in Westdeutschland: Belastung, Integration, Liberalisierung 1945–1980* (Göttingen: Wallstein Verlag, 2002), pp. 53–90.
[13] Großmann, "Schlußvortrag," p. 10.
[14] Ibid., p. 11.
[15] Ibid., p. 12.
[16] Ibid., p. 13.

perpetrators per se," certainly not in this trial.[17] However, certain generalizations were possible. In particular, the personality profiles of the defendants depended on their "commitment [*Bindung*] to National Socialism
and the SS."[18] Without this commitment, the defendants would never have
made themselves criminally culpable. In particular, none of the defendants
had denied his general participation in the "production line of mechanized
death" at Auschwitz, even if his degree of involvement varied. Consequently,
the defendants' actions "should thus already be deemed psychological co-
perpetratorship and/or accessory to *Mord*; it comprises a natural unity of
action per §73 StGB."[19]

Here, Großmann touched on an issue that was of decisive importance for
the prosecution's interpretation of the defendant's crimes at Auschwitz. The
historian Werner Renz has rightly pointed to the centrality of the legal concept of "concurrence" to the prosecution's ultimately unsuccessful attempt
to argue that almost all of the defendants had been perpetrators, not accomplices.[20] Under German law, there are two ways of characterizing individual activities in collective crimes: ideal and real concurrence. The former
stresses the unitary nature of a complex activity, wherein all participants
are held responsible in effect for the entirety of the undertaking, not simply their specific individual actions; the latter focuses on the specific actions
of individuals within that more general activity.[21] Traditionally, Nazi trials
had adhered strictly to the category of real concurrence. Fritz Bauer was
deeply critical of this, arguing that it was a major contributing factor to
the tendency of German Nazi trials to dissect the unitary activity of the
Holocaust into discrete "episodes."[22] Consequently, at Bauer's urging, the
prosecution had moved on the final day of the evidentiary phase to have
the court inform the defendants that "their presence in Auschwitz might
be construed as a naturally unitary act per §73 StGB, which, depending
on the subjective conditions of the individual case, could qualify as psychologically aiding and abetting or co-perpetrating a unitary extermination
program."[23]

[17] Ibid., p. 14.
[18] Ibid. Cf. Kerstin Freudiger, *Die juristische Aufarbeitung von NS-Verbrechen* (Tübingen:
Mohr Siebeck, 2002), pp. 138–42.
[19] Großmann, "Schlußvortrag," pp. 15–16.
[20] Werner Renz, "Der erste Frankfurter Auschwitz-Prozess: Völkermord als Strafsache," *1999:
Zeitschrift für Sozialgeschichte des 20. und 21. Jahrhunderts* 15 (2000): 20–26.
[21] §§73, 74 StGB.
[22] Fritz Bauer, "Ideal- oder Realkonkurrenz bei nationalsozialistischen Verbrechen?" *Juristenzeitung* 22 (1967): 627.
[23] HVP, Anlage 1 (June 5, 1965), FFStA 4 Ks 2/63, Bd. 111. Former prosecutor Gerhard Wiese
confirmed Bauer's role in the prosecution's decision to pursue this line of argumentation in
an interview with the author in Frankfurt on August 30, 2001. This is also confirmed in
FFStA to HMJ (June 24, 1966), FFStA HA 4 Ks 2/63, Bd. 25, Bl. 5191.

One can get a sense of the value of this approach to the prosecution from the criticisms leveled against it by other trial participants. Ormond's associate Christian Raabe cited a BGH decision, which held that German law did not recognize "a general concept of mass crimes as unitary actions" and concluded that "a just differentiation of the guilt of individual defendants is practically impossible simply on the basis of their function in the camp."[24] The defense was even more critical. Laternser's associate Fritz Steinacker asserted that the theory that mass crimes constituted unitary actions would lead to a "boundless expansion of the proceedings" and a "complete watering down" of the law.[25] Laternser himself argued that the prosecution's theory implied that "simply being present at the ramp – without actually doing anything – already constituted a form of co-perpetratorship [and thus] cannot be sustained . . . in the slightest."[26] In other words, applying ideal concurrence to the actions of the accused would make the prosecution's attempt to demonstrate their guilt by "reading" the camp's functional division of labor infinitely easier. Since the act of extermination would have to be viewed as a single, indivisible crime, any participation in that crime whatsoever would constitute at a minimum aiding and abetting and, if a perpetrator's will could also be demonstrated, co-perpetratorship. Such an interpretation would relieve the prosecution of the burden of demonstrating that individual defendants actually carried out criminal orders, since such activity could then be taken as given, based on the unitary nature of the exterminatory act. However, to no one's great surprise, including the prosecution's, the court did not agree with the prosecution in this matter.[27]

In dealing with the defendants' personalities, Großmann also tried to refute, in advance, the defense of higher orders and duress, which he knew full well would form a central theme for the defense. The defense of duress by higher orders (*Befehlsnotstand*) argues that a defendant cannot be found guilty if he had reason to fear for his life and safety if he refused to obey criminal orders. Großmann pointed out, however, that prior legal precedent had established that this threat must be "probable," not merely "possible."[28] Furthermore, a defendant's criminal actions were excused only if he had made every reasonable effort to avoid the threat in some other way first. "The law does not excuse the commission of a crime as the means to avert a threatened danger simply because this is the easiest and most comfortable

---

[24] Raabe, Plädoyer (May 21, 1965), FBI SAP FAP1/NK-11, p. 84. See BGHSt 1 (1951), pp. 219–22.

[25] Fritz Steinacker, Plädoyers, Dylewski und Broad (June 11/14, 1965), FBI SAP: FAP 1/V4, p. 15.

[26] Hans Laternser, *Die andere Seite im Auschwitz-Prozeß, 1963/65* (Stuttgart: Seewald Verlag, 1966), p. 189.

[27] Wiese confirmed that the prosecution was not terribly optimistic about the prospects for the success of this mode of argumentation: Interview with the author, Frankfurt, August 30, 2001. On the court's position, see chapter 8 below.

[28] Großmann, "Schlußvortrag," p. 19.

solution for the perpetrator."[29] He asserted that on these legal bases alone, most of the defendants' claims of *Befehlsnotstand* were invalid. The fact that almost none of them was able to point to specific instances where he had felt that his life was directly threatened merely confirmed this. The defendants' retreat into generalities and a nonspecified obligation to obedience did not constitute evidence of duress. Nor had defense witnesses provided any clear evidence that disobedience brought with it any penalties worse than transfer.

Given the interconnection between historical and legal issues in the trial, Großmann also addressed the historical problem he took to be most central: the Final Solution. Because this was an *Auschwitz* trial, one concerned with the extermination of millions of human beings in the course of the Nazi genocide of the Jews, Großmann felt that such an effort could not be omitted. Tracing the stages of Nazi anti-Jewish policy – ideology, discrimination, forced emigration,[30] ghettoization, and, finally, extermination – he outlined the Final Solution as the implementation of a long-standing plan. "There can be *no doubt* that the *National Socialist leadership,* with Hitler, Himmler, Göring and Heydrich at the top, *had decided upon a radical Final Solution to the Jewish Question, in the sense of the physical extermination of all European Jews, before the start of the campaign against the Soviet Union in 1941.* The measures undertaken before the outbreak of the Second World War, which I have outlined, do nothing to change this."[31] The intention to murder Europe's Jews had been firm in Hitler's mind from the very beginning of his political career, and in this sense, he could properly be considered, as German jurisprudence did, the principle perpetrator of the Holocaust.

While it was thus clear, according to Großmann, that the events at Auschwitz did not come from nowhere, it was not the court's job to decide whether Hitler or Auschwitz were "merely an 'industrial accident' of German history" even if "the question hangs in the air – in this courtroom as well."[32] The court's job was to reach a verdict, based on the "macabre and disheartening" knowledge it had gained over the preceding seventeen months. The extent and thoroughness of this knowledge, however, was sure to protect them from error. "In Auschwitz," Großmann concluded, "millions were murdered, without judicial sentence, indeed, without the least possibility

---

[29] Ibid.

[30] There is an emerging consensus in the scholarly literature that these stages – ethnic cleansing and genocide – need to be viewed as lying on a continuum, rather than as radically distinct undertakings, since much of Nazi population politics in the late 1930s already had genocidal implications. See Götz Aly, *"Final Solution": Nazi Population Policy and the Murder of the European Jews* (London: Arnold, 1999); Magnus Brechtken, *Madagaskar für die Juden: Antisemitische Idee und politische Praxis, 1885–1945* (Munich: Oldenbourg, 1997); Peter Longerich, *Politik der Vernichtung: Eine Gesamtdarstellung der Nationalsozialistische Judenverfolgung* (Munich: Piper, 1998); and Norman M. Naimark, *Fires of Hatred: Ethnic Cleansing in Twentieth-Century Europe* (Cambridge: Harvard University Press, 2001).

[31] Großmann, "Schlußvortrag," p. 38. Emphasis in the original.

[32] Ibid., p. 48.

for such a judicial sentence. You, judges and jurors of this court, should now pass just sentence, *according to today's principles of the rehabilitated Rechtsstaat, on the murderers of yesterday.*[33]

Großmann's three subordinates, Kügler, Vogel, and Wiese, were charged with the more difficult task of evaluating the evidence against the individual defendants and recommending specific sentences. Vogel began his closing argument with the thorny issue of witness credibility.[34] There were, he said, four possible reasons to question the credibility of the witnesses. The first was the long time span between the alleged crimes and the trial. The second was the physical and organizational circumstances in Auschwitz. The third was the biographical background, character, and educational level of individual witnesses. These were all legitimate sources of concern. However, the fourth concern, raised by some members of the defense, alleging that witness testimony had been tampered with, was not so legitimate. There was, according to Vogel, absolutely no foundation to such allegations. Such charges were nothing more than "insolence." "In describing what happened in Auschwitz, it is hardly necessary to exaggerate because the truth in this case is the most severe indictment!"[35]

As for the three legitimate concerns, Vogel argued that while each of them had some merit, they did not suffice to undermine the credibility of the vast majority of witnesses. Vogel admitted that the problems posed by the long time span between the crimes and the trial were considerable, particularly given the witnesses' extreme emotional involvement in the events and the fact that many stories concerning Auschwitz had since been widely publicized. This was why it was imperative for the court to "evaluate their testimony with particular care."[36] It was especially important to establish in each case whether the witness was testifying on the basis of his or her own experience or on the basis of hearsay, and whether the testimony may have been influenced by psychological "baggage" (*Nachlassen*) or other external factors, such as published accounts. If the court weighed the testimony carefully, Vogel was convinced that they would find the vast majority of witnesses credible. Vogel also acknowledged that many of the witnesses had been under considerable emotional strain during their testimony. "Insofar as certain witnesses, were upset by having to testify regarding the personal injustices they had suffered and the fate of good friends, and [therefore] had to fight back tears; or insofar as, in isolated cases, witnesses made somewhat personal attacks against

---

[33] Ibid., p. 49.
[34] Unfortunately, as with all of the *Plädoyers*, these were considered private, not official, documents, and were thus not preserved in the official trial records. A handful of the *Plädoyers* were published in various venues. In addition, Werner Renz, archivist for the Fritz Bauer Institute, has collected several more *Plädoyers* from surviving trial participants. To date, the Fritz Bauer Institute has been able to acquire only two sets of prosecution *Plädoyers*: that of Großmann and those of associate prosecutor Georg Vogel.
[35] Vogel, "Schlußvortrag," FBI SAP: FAP1/StA 2, p. 3. Internal pagination.
[36] Ibid., p. 4.

the defendants for the same reasons, they nevertheless did not, in my view, deliberately or unconsciously falsify their recollections on the basis of hatred or the desire for revenge. They were far more able to immediately master their very understandable anger and to earnestly try to testify in a sober and objective manner."[37]

Finally, Vogel reiterated Großmann's point that while the primary function of this trial was to ascertain the guilt of the defendants, this juridical function was not entirely independent of its broader representational function: "We ought not try to master the German past here, at the expense of a small group of defendants. In this sense, this trial can and should only provide the impetus for a broader public discussion. The defendants, however, should be convicted for their demonstrable crimes of murder – or accessory to murder – at Auschwitz, *according to the measure of their personal guilt.*"[38]

Still, Vogel felt it necessary to address certain historical issues omitted from Großmann's closing argument, particularly the history of the camp itself and the various bureaucratic subgroups within the camp, such as the Political Section and the protective custody camp leadership. Vogel's history of Auschwitz reiterated, often almost verbatim, that outlined in the indictment. Most important, he noted that the camp served three distinct, if related, functions. First, it was a work camp, used to exploit the slave labor of people from all over Europe for the benefit of the German war effort. Second, it was an extermination *camp* (*Vernichtungslager*), which served the Nazi regime of terror by working hundreds of thousands of people to death, officially sanctioned as "extermination through work." Finally, it was an extermination *institution* (*Vernichtungsanstalt*), one where, in the context of the Final Solution, millions were murdered outright, simply because of who they were, as Jews, with no connection to the camp's other functions.

Two things are worth noting about this tripartite categorization of Auschwitz. First, Vogel argued that every one of the camp's functions was lethal; the only difference was how long inmates were exploited before they were killed, either by the harsh living conditions or by more directly murderous means. Murder *was* the function of Auschwitz, and even the exploitation of labor was merely one more means to that end. Second, the camp's lethality was deliberate and intentional. The entire bureaucratic apparatus at Auschwitz was organized around the simple and deliberate principle that the inmates should eventually die. This basic interpretation of Auschwitz conforms not only to the "intentionalist" interpretation of the Holocaust previously outlined by Großmann but also to the prosecution's legal emphasis on subjective autonomy among the defendants. No one, Vogel implied, could have long worked at Auschwitz, who did not in some measure internally

[37] Ibid., p. 6.
[38] Ibid., p. 10.

"approve" of its exterminatory function because no one who worked there was exempt from participation in murder in one way or another. Finally, the claim that every aspect of Auschwitz was murderous corresponded with the prosecution's claim that murder in the camp had to be interpreted legally as a unitary act under ideal concurrence. Vogel, however, did not, and within the confines of German law could not, draw the logical conclusion from this that everyone who served in Auschwitz was a murderer. Legally speaking, they were not, and even the theory of ideal concurrence was not intended to change this.

This tension, between a generalized interpretation of Auschwitz as a site of pure lethality, where all of the inmates were doomed to die sooner or later, and the legally necessary fiction of fully autonomous agency on the part of the defendants, also pervades Vogel's historical introductions to the Political Section and protective custody camp leadership. Of the Political Section, for example, Vogel remarks, "[Its] activities were of decisive importance for the fate of concentration camp inmates."[39] Here, the agentive principle is highlighted. The Political Section and, by extension, its individual members, could "decisively" influence the fate of the inmates. And yet, Vogel had just remarked that the concentration camps as a whole were part of a vast system of organized terror, a means of operationalizing the Nazis' "psychologically accurate recognition that a minority can only dominate a majority in the long term by means of terror."[40] In other words, the concentration camps were simply one aspect of a larger *system* of terror, which allowed the Nazi "minority" to dominate a larger, presumably German, "majority." The tension between systematicity and (minority) agency is almost palpable.[41]

In his closing arguments against the individual defendants, Vogel addressed three broad themes: (1) the biography of the defendant and his subjective disposition toward his crimes, (2) his bureaucratic function inside the camp and what his duties would ordinarily have been, and (3) the specific evidence against him for various counts in the indictment.[42] Once again, we see a dual consideration emerge in this general structure; it considers both the objective and subjective aspects of the case against the defendants, with the subjective side ultimately being the more important. What did the defendant do? And why did he do it?

One may take the charge that Hans Stark both supervised and participated in executions in the "Old Crematorium" as indicative.[43] Objectively,

[39] Ibid., p. 26.
[40] Ibid.
[41] Recent scholarship makes it clear that the Nazis enjoyed far greater popular support than this. See Eric A. Johnson, *Nazi Terror: The Gestapo, Jews, and Ordinary Germans* (New York: Basic, 1999), and Robert Gellately, *Backing Hitler: Consent and Coercion in Nazi Germany* (Oxford: Oxford University Press, 2001).
[42] Vogel pled against Broad, Hofmann, Schoberth, and Stark.
[43] Vogel, "Schlußvortrag gegen Stark," FBI SAP, FAP1/StA 2, pp. 8–12.

Vogel first outlined the historical and bureaucratic context of these executions. In addition to the large transports destined for the gas chambers, Vogel
noted that occasionally smaller transports would arrive for immediate execution. Like those gassed to death, the victims of these executions were never
officially registered in the camp. Instead, Stark would take them to the Old
Crematorium, where the victims were told to undress because they would
be showering. Stark would then lead them one by one into another room,
where another SS man was waiting with a gun behind his back. The victim
would be told to look in a certain direction, and then the SS man would
shoot them in the back of the neck. During the course of the trial, Stark had
admitted to participating in such activity on two occasions.

   In addition, Kazimierz Smoleń, the director of the Auschwitz Museum
and a former inmate himself, had testified on May 21, 1964, that he had
on one occasion seen Stark escort a woman with two small children to
the Old Crematorium on his own. A short while later, he had seen Stark
return alone. Smoleń subsequently heard another SS man remark that it was
"'an irresponsible crime'" to shoot this woman and her children for the
petty offense of stealing a rabbit.[44] Smoleń also noted that Stark was very
"agitated" on his return. The character of the "objective" evidence in this
case was, as can be seen, somewhat shaky. No witness had actually seen
Stark shoot the woman; this could only be inferred from hearsay. And in
the other executions, Stark had not actually shot the victims himself, but
merely escorted them to their deaths. Here, as elsewhere, the prosecution
was forced to rely on circumstantial evidence, on an account of what the
defendant must have done, given the prevailing conditions in the camp.

   Vogel then turned to a much more lengthy consideration of the legal
issues involved, which hinged on Stark's subjective disposition toward the
crime. "This boundless contempt for human life – as the motive for the
killings and the orders to kill by a political system of terror oriented toward
the extermination of real or potential opponents – constitutes, from the
perspective of a rational and moral human being, a particularly base motive,
per §211 StGB."[45] Vogel also argued that such executions were not justified
by the fact that they were conducted on the basis of higher orders. Such orders
were not, on Vogel's view, legal in the first place. Regardless of what one
thought of the concept of natural law, he maintained that orders to commit
murder could never be legally valid. As for the objection that such deaths
were inevitable, since the Nazis would have killed these people one way
or another, Vogel dismissed this claim as legally irrelevant. "This *historical*

[44] Ibid., p. 8. The woman was accused of having stolen a rabbit belonging to the Germans so
her child could play with it. See Hermann Langbein, *Der Auschwitz Prozeß: Eine Dokumentation* (Frankfurt: Verlag Neue Kritik, 1995), p. 447. According to Smoleń's testimony
as recorded by Langbein, the woman had only one child.
[45] Vogel, "Schlußvortrag gegen Stark," p. 10.

inevitability does *not* suffice to justify *individual* criminal acts in the context of the National Socialist extermination program."[46] Each case had to be evaluated individually, because in every case, there were moments where, had the accused not acted in the way that he did, then the victim either would not have died or, at least, would not have died in this way. "If every person in the chain of command had refused to carry out illegal orders to kill, then the death of the victims could have been avoided. Therefore, one cannot speak of inevitability [*Unvermeidbarkeit*] in the strict sense of the term."[47]

In arguing that Stark should be convicted as a perpetrator, Vogel offered a very interesting reinterpretation of the BGH's Staschynskij decision.[48] Vogel stressed the BGH's assertion in previous rulings that, *ordinarily*, anyone who directly and personally kills another human being ought to be considered a perpetrator. Vogel claimed that the Staschynskij decision did nothing to change this because what was decisive in that case was that Staschynskij had shown remorse, which revealed that he had not internally affirmed the criminal motives of his superiors. Vogel quoted the Staschynskij decision at great length, placing particular emphasis on the BGH's caveat that, in some cases, subordinates could be perpetrators in instances of state-organized mass murder if they internalized the criminal motives of the state or if they showed "'*particular zeal*'" in carrying out their duties.[49] In Stark's case, Vogel contended, he had both internalized the state's criminal motives and had demonstrated considerable zeal in carrying out his orders. Consequently, he ought to be considered a perpetrator or co-perpetrator, and not an accomplice. Similar considerations, the prosecution contended, applied to almost all of the other defendants as well. Here one sees that the prosecution, aware that the theory of ideal concurrence was unlikely to be applied by the court, was articulating a fall-back argument: Even if the crimes of Auschwitz were not a unitary act, the individual defendants were *still* perpetrators under the law because they evinced a perpetrator's will through their particular zeal.

The Civil Counsel

In contrast to the prosecution, the civil counsel in the trial represented private citizens. This meant that, although their task was technically to assist the prosecution in the trial, they were not bound by the prosecution's arguments and could interpret both the facts of the case and the law differently.

---

[46] Ibid., p. 11.
[47] Ibid., p. 12.
[48] See chapter 2.
[49] Vogel, "Schlußvortrag gegen Stark," p. 14. Vogel's emphasis. Citing BGHSt 18 (1963), p. 94.

Ormond and Raabe represented fourteen clients in the trial, who had been specifically selected to "represent" Nazi victims from throughout occupied Europe.[50] According to Ormond, "The task of the prosecution is to pursue the state's right to punish; the task of the civil counsel is to make sure that the voice of the victims is heard. Our clients seek to achieve personal satisfaction for the suffering and injustice they suffered due to the death of their immediate family members through the punishment of the guilty perpetrators."[51]

In addition to examining the specific cases against the defendants Broad and Capesius in some detail, Ormond took as his task in his closing argument the refutation of seven general defense claims frequently made in this and other Nazi trials. These he universally dismissed as "fairy tales," "legends," or "myths." Specifically, he addressed "the fairy tale of the collective innocence of the Waffen SS," "the legend of the character of the Waffen SS as a military elite," "the myth of iron discipline among the Waffen SS in Auschwitz," "the myth of *Befehlsnotstand*," "the fable of the failed effort to be transferred to the front," "concocted testimony [by the defendants]" and "the legend of having helped concentration camp inmates." As one can see from the labels he gave these various defense tactics, Ormond felt that there was hardly a word of truth to any of them. He asserted that the evidence in the trial, from both eyewitnesses and expert witnesses, had utterly destroyed any plausibility that these various legends and myths might once have had.

Take Ormond's discussion of "the fable of the failed effort to be transferred to the front," for example. He noted that almost all of the defendants told one version or another of this story during the course of the trial. In other words, they almost all claimed that they had not wanted to serve at Auschwitz and had made every effort to get a transfer elsewhere, even to the battlefront. It seemed odd to Ormond that no record of these efforts survived the war. "Everything conceivable is in their files, except precisely this."[52] It was also strange that their efforts "failed," given that as war loses mounted, practically every able-bodied male was drafted into service. The Germans even began to replace concentration camp personnel with troops no longer fit for combat duty, especially if these had some prior connection with Nazi organizations. It was particularly important, he noted, to keep in mind that of the defendants, only Mulka was over forty at the time of their service in Auschwitz. So their age certainly did not disqualify them for frontline duty. Both documentary evidence and eyewitness testimony confirmed

[50] They originally represented fifteen clients, but one died during the course of the proceedings. Henry Ormond, "Plädoyer im Auschwitz-Prozeß," *Sonderreihe aus Gestern und Heute* 7 (1965): 2.
[51] Ibid., p. 1.
[52] Ibid., p. 28.

that transfer to the front was both possible and easily obtained. Therefore, Ormond concluded, it was "demonstrably untrue" that the defendants had tried and failed to escape Auschwitz.[53]

On the other hand, they certainly had no difficulties killing Jews and other inmates. "Ideologically [*Weltanschaulich*], they found it quite congenial to translate the solution, 'Jews die,' into action, to exterminate 'Jewish parasites' and – to follow the hateful song of the Nazi formations – to let Jewish blood spill from their knives."[54] They consistently considered the inmates, Jews especially, but others as well, to be racially inferior. It might be hard to believe today, Ormond said, that they ever seriously considered themselves to be racially superior. "But somehow, these gentlemen, who after all conformed to the average, must have felt themselves to be superior human beings in their uniforms and their high boots. They gave into this racial insanity. After all, they practiced this superiority to its ultimate conclusion; they were, in fact, masters over life and death, however grotesque that may sound, for thousands, tens of thousands, hundreds of thousands."[55] Indeed, they benefited enormously from this "superiority." They were safe from the risks of combat and the Allied air war against Germany. They got better rations, extra cigarettes, liquor, and so on. They had inmate servants to attend to their needs. They could even bring their families to live with them at the camp. Why, then, would they want to transfer to the front?

As it happened, transfer to the front was not something for which the SS strove but something that was imposed on them as punishment. This was, in fact, the worst punishment ever imposed on SS men who refused to obey illegal orders. So, had the defendants really preferred combat duty to serving in Auschwitz, all they need have done was to refuse to follow the illegal orders they were now charged with having obeyed. Clearly, then, they had not made any real efforts at transfer.

Ormond delivered similarly devastating critiques of the various other defense tactics he analyzed. These critiques served as a prelude to the most important part of his closing argument, which was his account of the internal motives of the defendants. Given that objectively they had shown no reluctance whatsoever to participate in extermination whenever they were ordered to do so, "their cooperation was conscious and deliberately [*gewollt*] in full accordance with the will of their Führer, the Reichsführer SS [Himmler] and the world view they believed in, had made their own, and to which they felt obligated."[56] These "fanatical followers" had not had to overcome any "scruples" in order to participate in the killing operations at Auschwitz; they

[53] Ibid., p. 29.
[54] Ibid.
[55] Ibid., p. 30.
[56] Ibid., p. 43.

had participated "body and soul."[57] Given this, the defendants had to be considered perpetrators rather than accomplices.

To emphasize this point, Ormond stressed that the defendants had exercised controlling agency in the camp, that *they* had decisively directed the course of events. "They, the defendants, made the hell of Auschwitz, in itself barely tolerable, that much more unbearable, more hopeless, more cruel, more brutal for their victims."[58] Had they been the least bit humane, they could have made things better for the inmates. Indeed, the SS's own regulations stipulated that inmates were not to be arbitrarily mistreated; their laboring capacity was to be preserved (itself surely a perverse rule in a camp dedicated to extermination, but the operative regulation nonetheless). And yet the defendants regularly ignored these regulations. Here Ormond was painting the defendants as *Exzeßtäter*, as perpetrators who had exceeded their orders, who had demonstrated their ill will by independently and voluntarily abusing and killing inmates – acting above and beyond the call of duty, as it were. The point was to reinforce the image of the defendants as autonomous agents and, hence, perpetrators. If the prosecution had insisted that the defendants were perpetrators for obeying criminal orders, Ormond added that they were doubly so for exceeding them.

It was clear, according to Ormond, that the defendants were well aware that their actions in Auschwitz were illegal, in the sense that they had a "guilty conscience."[59] But when someone lies for years, it affects him or her. These defendants "were still today marked and determined . . . by the lie."[60] They may have had a guilty conscience in Auschwitz, but they no longer possessed even that. Their only concern now was to evade punishment. The evidence for this was above all their utter lack of remorse. "Sometimes when I looked at the face of Boger or Kaduk, but also Capesius and Klehr, during particularly incriminating witness testimony, I could not escape the feeling that they wanted to say: 'It was a mistake to have left you alive. We obviously forgot to gas you. Now that's coming back to haunt us.' Certainly, there was no trace, absolutely no trace of remorse."[61] Given this lack of remorse, the court was obligated to be particularly cautious in applying the maxim *in dubio pro reo*, because this trial was not a matter of "one person's statements against another's, but rather of lies against truth, against the most terrible, dreadful experience."[62] Here, Ormond pitted the incontrovertible experiential truth of the survivor witnesses against the eminently contestable factual truth of

[57] Ibid.
[58] Ibid., p. 46.
[59] Ibid., p. 49.
[60] Ibid.
[61] Ibid., p. 41.
[62] Ibid., p. 50.

a distant past; the only problem was that such experiential truth fell outside the proper range of juridical truth. It is not clear that Ormond recognized that the opposition of lies and truth he insisted on was also an opposition of different registers of truth.[63] Nonetheless, he maintained that the court should decide, as the law required, in favor of the defendants in cases of doubt, but only when that doubt was very well founded. "None of us, who listened with growing horror to the witness testimony in this courtroom, can seriously still doubt the guilt of those defendants whose punishment is being demanded."[64]

Like Ormond, Friedrich Karl Kaul, representing civil plaintiffs living in the GDR, chose to focus on the significance of the victims' experience in Auschwitz; unlike Ormond, however, he very clearly had an ulterior motive as well. After all, Kaul's main goal in the trial had all along been to use it as a propaganda weapon against the Federal Republic. His closing argument was his best opportunity to push that agenda. According to Kaul, the extraordinariness – "in fact, uniqueness" – of this trial stemmed from the urgent need to hear the truth about Auschwitz from witnesses from all over the world.[65] Such testimony made it "oppressively obvious" that the whole world had had to pay for the crimes of Nazism. The civil plaintiffs in this trial were thus in a very real sense the representatives of all mankind, and the point of the trial was to help to protect the "public in general" from a "repetition of this horror, in whatever form it might appear."[66]

In the end, though, Kaul's universalism was not nearly so universal as all that. Instead, it was a weapon with which to attack the Federal Republic as a country largely unconcerned with the Auschwitz survivors' community of suffering. He himself, he added, had been sent to a concentration camp in early 1934. He agreed with Großmann that history was the key to the Auschwitz Trial, but he felt it imperative to remind the court that murder had been a "state doctrine" prior to 1933 as well. As examples, he named

---

[63] Devin O. Pendas, "Truth and Its Consequences: Reflections on Political, Historical and Legal 'Truth' in West German Holocaust Trials," *traverse: Zeitschrift für Geschichte/Revue d'Histoire* 11/1 (2004): 25–38.

[64] Ormond, "Plädoyer," p. 50.

[65] Friedrich Karl Kaul, *Schlußvortrag und Erwiderung des Prof. Dr. Friedrich Karl Kaul Prozeßvertreter der in der Deutschen Demokratischen Republik ansässigen Nebenkläger im Strafverfahren gegen Mulka u.a. vor dem Schwurgericht beim Landgericht Frankfurt am Main* (Herausgegeben von der Arbeitsgruppe der ehemaligen Häftlinge des Konzentrationslagers Auschwitz beim Komitee der Antifaschistischen Widerstandskämpfer in der Deutschen Demokratischen Republik und dem Nationalrat der Nationalen Front des demokratischen Deutschlands, 1965). Translated as Friedrich Karl Kaul, *Auschwitz Trial in Frankfurt-on-Main: Summing up and reply of Professor Dr. Friedrich Karl Kaul, legal representative of the co-plaintiffs resident in the German Democratic Republic in the criminal proceedings against Mulka and others before the criminal court at the Provincial Court in Frankfurt-on-Main* (n.p., 1965). All citations will be to the English translation. Here p. 6.

[66] Ibid., p. 7.

the murders of Rosa Luxemburg and Karl Liebknecht, among others. The "forces" that had driven Germany down the murderous road to Auschwitz "always remained the same."[67] He pointed out that the defendants were not entirely mistaken when they complained that they were being punished for carrying out orders, while those who gave the orders "got off scot-free." Although these complaints did not excuse the defendants of their guilt, they were hardly unjustified. The fact that Nazi luminaries had again acquired positions of influence and authority in the FRG was even borne out by the fate of the SS witnesses in the trial, many of whom now occupied respected positions in West Germany. This was an offense against "general justice."[68]

The GDR's interest in the trial was thus twofold. First, it had an interest in securing justice for all mankind; second, it had a political interest in safeguarding the world against a recurrence of Auschwitz by prosecuting the crimes committed there. Until all too recently, similar efforts had been rare in the FRG, as evinced by the opposition to any change in the statute of limitations for Nazi crimes. Any "political rapprochement" between the two Germanys would depend in part on "bilateral contacts between prosecuting authorities."[69] Hence the need for a joint prosecutorial commission, "as has been repeatedly proposed by the GDR." Such cooperation would depend, needless to say, on the formal recognition "that different political and especially juridical conceptions exist" in the two Germanys. Kaul thus parlayed, at least rhetorically, his accusations against the FRG into a plea for the official recognition of the GDR as an independent state. A better example of the co-mingling of Kaul's presumably sincere demands for justice and his perhaps equally sincere desire to push the East German political agenda in the trial would be hard to come by.

In his brief consideration of the specific charges against the defendants, Kaul supported the prosecution's application of ideal concurrence to Auschwitz, arguing that all three categories of crimes with which the defendants were charged (selections and gassings on arrival, selections within the camp, and murders done on their own initiative) formed an interrelated and unitary whole. "Thus all SS members who were functionally active in Auschwitz concentration camp... formed a community of co-perpetrators whose contributions to the crime were objectively different, whereas the subjective will to [commit the] crime was aimed at the same goal: mass murder."[70] Kaul here strongly argued that, on the basis of the unitary character

---

[67] Ibid., p. 9.

[68] Ibid., p. 10.

[69] Ibid., p. 11. Translation modified. The East Germans had long sought to win back-door diplomatic recognition from the FRG by pushing for such a joint commission. See Marc von Miquel, *Ahnden oder amnestieren? Westdeutsche Justiz und Vergangenheitspolitik in den sechziger Jahren* (Göttingen: Wallstein, 2004), p. 76.

[70] Kaul, *Auschwitz Trial*, p. 45. Translation modified.

of the crimes at Auschwitz, all of the defendants *had* to be considered
co-perpetrators.

Finally, Kaul argued that the court had to consider the broad historical background to these crimes. In this, the distinctive character of Kaul's
Plädoyer, the complicated interaction between historical insight and political propaganda that characterized his argumentation, becomes particularly
apparent. He noted that almost all of the historical experts who testified in the
trial (and he could cite only the West German experts, as Jürgen Kuczynski's
testimony had been disallowed by the court) had agreed that Auschwitz and
its crimes "were firm components of general National Socialist policy and
could therefore be judged only against this background."[71] The historians
all pointed, "though unfortunately only superficially," to the key features of
this policy, in particular that it was a "policy of aggression."[72] This policy
consisted in the "forcible suppression" of the "peace-loving population" of
both Germany and any other country that dared resist Nazi expansion.[73]
In particular, Kaul pointed out that this expansionist zeal was part of a
broader "will to destruction," which manifested itself above all in the extermination of the Jews.[74] Kaul particularly stressed that both the German
state bureaucracy and the regular army had been deeply implicated in the
crimes of Auschwitz.[75] "By way of summary it can thus be stated that the
evidence indicates that the mass destruction which took place in the Nazi
concentration camps was introduced in close cooperation with the ministerial bureaucracy and the supreme command of the Wehrmacht of the Nazi
state."[76]

Kaul did not rest content, however, with pointing far more explicitly to
the broad institutional context of the Holocaust than did any other trial
participant. Given his ideological agenda, it was imperative that he point

---

[71] Ibid., p. 47.

[72] Ibid.

[73] Ibid., pp. 47–48.

[74] Ibid., p. 48.

[75] Kaul here anticipates an argument about the role of the military in Nazi crimes, including the Holocaust, that it would take mainstream western historiography another thirty
years to develop fully. See, e.g., Christopher Browning, "Wehrmacht Reprisal Policy and the
Mass Murder of Jews in Serbia," *Militärgeschichtliche Mitteilungen* 33 (1983): 31–47; Mark
Mazower, "Military Violence and National Socialist Values: The *Wehrmacht* in Greece,
1941–1944," *Past and Present* (February 1992): 129–58; Omer Bartov, *Hitler's Army: Soldiers, Nazis, and War in the Third Reich* (Oxford: Oxford University Press, 1992); Till
Bastian, *Furchtbare Soldaten: Deutsche Kriegsverbrechen im Zweiten Weltkrieg* (Munich:
C. H. Beck, 1997); Wolfram Wette, *Die Wehrmacht: Feindbilder, Vernichtungskrieg, Leg-
enden,* 2nd ed. (Frankfurt: Fischer Verlag, 2002); and Johannes Klotz, "Die Ausstellung
'Vernichtungskrieg. Verbrechen der Wehrmacht 1941 bis 1944': Zwischen Geschichtswis-
senschaft und Geschichtspolitik," in Detlef Bald, Johannes Klotz, and Wolfram Wette, eds.
Mythos Wehrmacht: Nachkriegsdebatten und Traditionspflege (Berlin: Aufbau Taschenbuch
Verlag, 2001), pp. 116–76.

[76] Kaul, *Auschwitz Trial,* p. 50. Translation modified.

to the underlying economic factors that he viewed as driving the entirety of Nazi policy. "Further," he stated, "the evidence has shown that there was an internal connection between the program of exterminating so-called 'worthless life' through work, which was realized in the concentration camps, and the needs of the trusts for manpower."[77] Martin Broszat had indicated the extent to which the concentration camps became "collection centers" for slave labor.[78] On *Kaul's reading*, Broszat had argued not only that the existence of armaments factories had been decisive for the establishment of concentration camps in certain locales, but also that there was a "direct connection between industry's demands for manpower and the deportation actions."[79] For instance, he cited the witness Ella Lingens, who had described the way that civilian personnel directors accompanied the SS into the camp to select workers. "'It looked like a cattle market,'" she had said.[80]

Kaul concluded: "The cooperation of the SS, ministerial bureaucracy, army leadership and industry, as set forth in the evidence, provided the initial basis for mass murder in Auschwitz, for the extensive destruction of 'economically no longer valuable life,' as Public Prosecutor Vogel called it. Without this basis none of the accused could have continued to commit for many years those crimes with which he is now charged."[81] Kaul thus managed to combine both the most sophisticated analysis by far of the institutional framework of genocide presented anywhere in the Auschwitz Trial with the crudest analysis by far of its underlying social conditions.

The Defense

Not surprisingly, the portrait of Auschwitz painted by the defense in their closing arguments diverged considerably from that presented by either the prosecution or the civil counsel. The defense took its own course in interpreting both matters of fact and matters of law. It is difficult to make sweeping generalizations about the defense's position in their closing arguments, because naturally not all of the defense attorneys conformed to a uniform set of interpretations. The legal situation confronting the various defense attorneys differed depending on the evidence and specific charges against their clients, and so too did their closing arguments. Similarly, the political and legal orientation of the various attorneys varied to one degree or another. Nevertheless, certain key themes do emerge, which are certainly indicative of the general argumentative approach of the defense as a whole.

Four themes emerge in the defense's closing arguments: (1) that the defendants had operated under very restrictive circumstances in Auschwitz and

---

[77] Ibid. Translation modified.
[78] Ibid.
[79] Ibid.
[80] Ibid., p. 52.
[81] Ibid., p. 55. Translation modified.

had not possessed decisive agency, (2) that the evidence pertaining to specific, concrete allegations against the defendants was inadequate and that their guilt had consequently not been proven, (3) that the defendants' actions at Auschwitz had not been crimes, in the strict legal sense, and (4) that certain procedural irregularities in the trial itself meant that the defendants had not received a "fair" trial and should thus be acquitted. Taken together, these four arguments had profound political and historiographic implications, not the least of which was that the defendants, like the German people as a whole, had been the first *victims* of Nazism and that convicting them would simply add to the injustice of the situation.

The defense's first, and in many ways most fundamental, argument was that their clients had possessed, at most, a very limited degree of agency during their time in Auschwitz. The defendants had not been in a position to influence decisively the course of events in the camp; they certainly could not have stopped the killing. What is more, given that the Third Reich was a totalitarian dictatorship, which brooked no resistance, any efforts by the defendants to interfere with or even merely to avoid participating in the extermination process would have brought down upon them swift and dire retribution. To deny this fact, as both the prosecution and the civil counsel had done, was to misrecognize fundamentally the terroristic quality of the Third Reich, according to the defense.

Eugen Gerhard, arguing on behalf of the defendant Baretzki, noted that since the defendants had not created Auschwitz, "[t]his already differentiates the Auschwitz Trial as it prepares to enter into history from every other criminal trial in daily life. Every criminal trial is characterized by the fact that the perpetrator seeks out his field of criminally punishable activity according to his own wishes and will. The defendant Baretzki was detailed to Auschwitz. Today the public knows the names of Kaduk and Baretzki; it could just as easily have been other names."[82] Therefore, Gerhard continued, it was imperative that the court take into account the historical context of these crimes, the "extermination policies pursued by the power elites in the Third Reich," in evaluating the individual guilt of the defendants.[83]

In a similar vein, Fritz Steinacker, arguing for the defendants Dylewski and Broad, maintained that in evaluating the mode of participation by the defendants, that is whether they were perpetrators or accomplices, it was important for the court to remember that Auschwitz was a case of bureaucratically organized, state-ordered mass murder. "A state order is something very different from the mere incitement to murder or the mere instructions by one co-perpetrator to another.... A bureaucratic organization is something quite different from the organization of a gangster band or the simple

---

[82] Eugen Gerhard, Plädoyer (Baretzki), HVP (July 2, 1965), Anlage 2, FFStA 4 Ks 2/63, Bd. 112, p. 1. Internal pagination.
[83] Ibid.

union of multiple murderers for the purposes of dividing their labor."[84] This was precisely what the prosecution had missed in their closing arguments, Steinacker contended. The prosecution had argued that the defendants were perpetrators under the doctrine of ideal concurrence, in that they participated, "in bits and pieces," in a "unitary program of extermination."[85] But one could not simply approach the problem of guilt according to the formula: "Was in Auschwitz, is a murderer."[86]

Rather, a perpetrator was someone who controlled the course of events. This would apply here only if the defendants had possessed "a certain room for maneuver," could have controlled the time, place, and manner in which the orders were carried out.[87] But this was not the case. The defendants were simply ordered to kill a certain number of inmates, at a certain time, in a certain manner. Their only choice was to obey or to refuse to obey (with all of the consequent risks). "The only possibility was either/or."[88] Thus, Steinacker concluded: "No objective control over the act and therefore no perpetrator."[89]

Defense attorney Hans Knögel extended this logic to the case of accomplices as well. Knögel's client, Scherpe, was charged only as an accomplice, and both the prosecution and the civil counsel had agreed with this charge. Nonetheless, Knögel felt it necessary to question whether even this charge applied. It was, he maintained, "uncontroversial" in cases of perpetration that the accused had to have a direct and immediate influence on the "if, when, and how" of the criminal act, that he must have a *causal* role in it.[90] After an extended technical discussion of the theory of causation in German law, Knögel asserted that it was proper to consider the role of accomplices in the Auschwitz Trial under the so-called theory of surpassed causation.[91] The classic example of this theory is a case where someone was murdered on his way to the airport, but the killer maintains his innocence because the victim's plane crashed and he would have died anyway. But Scherpe's case was different. In the airplane example, there were in fact two distinct events, two different causal sequences at work, each of which was causally indifferent to the other. In Scherpe's case, however, "the same successful result would have come about not as a result of other causes, but rather because of the same cause and at a temporally hardly later stage as well."[92] So, from the standpoint of causation, Knögel concluded, Scherpe could not even be considered

---

[84] Fritz Steinacker, Plädoyers (Dylewski und Broad), FBI SAP: FAP 1/V4, pp. 242–43.
[85] Ibid., p. 243.
[86] Ibid.
[87] Ibid., p. 245.
[88] Ibid.
[89] Ibid., p. 245.
[90] Hans Knögel, Plädoyer (Scherpe), FBI SAP: FAP 1/V11, p. 30.
[91] Ibid., p. 31.
[92] Ibid., p. 32.

an accomplice because he had not, in any meaningful sense, *caused* the death of the victims.

Thus the defense argued on three distinct levels – that of general historical context, the theory of perpetration, and the theory of causation as applied to accomplices – that the defendants were not guilty because *they* had not caused the deaths in Auschwitz. This theory was in essence the exact opposite of that articulated by the prosecution and civil counsel, which had stressed the agentive character of the defendants' actions, the fact that they had often exceeded their orders, that they could have, but did not, mitigate the conditions under which the inmates had suffered. The defense argued, on the contrary, that the defendants had not exercised any significant control over the events in Auschwitz. To put this argument in its crudest form, the defense argued that if the defendants had not killed these inmates, someone else would have, and that therefore the defendants could not be held criminally liable.

Here the defense tried to exploit a fundamental paradox in German criminal law. The principle of guilt meant that interchangeable perpetrators could, with some legal justification, see themselves as not culpable for their actions.[93] The unflinching Hans Laternser pushed this argument even further. It was a "historical fact," Laternser maintained in full agreement with Großmann, that "the Final Solution meant the murder of all Jewish persons living under German authority and that these tragic acts were to a considerable extent carried out in the gas chambers of Auschwitz."[94] Specifically, Hitler intended that no Jew should survive the war. It was in this context that the transports arriving at Auschwitz were sent to the gas chambers. As several witnesses testified, in some cases entire transports were sent to the gas chambers. Laternser continued: "If there had not been a selection at the ramp in Birkenau, that is the choosing of a previously determined number of persons capable of working, then in every case, the entire transport would have been exterminated. Without the selection of those capable of work for an always well-determined purpose, then more Jewish people would have been murdered than was actually the case. . . . The selections thus meant preserving the persons selected from being murdered immediately on arrival. Choosing which persons were admitted to the camp could thus not constitute participation in murder, either as an accomplice or as a co-perpetrator, because the persons chosen were not murdered."[95] In short, the selections were not murder but rescue.

---

[93] Peter Noll, "Die NS-Verbrecherprozesse strafrechtsdogmatisch und gesetzgebungspolitisch betrachtet," in Peter Schneider and Hermann J. Meyer, eds., *Rechtliche und politische Aspekte der NS-Verbrecherprozesse: Gemeinschaftsvorlesung des studium generale Wintersemester 1966/67* (Mainz: Gutenberg-Universität Mainz, 1968), p. 46.

[94] Laternser, *Die andere Seite*, p. 185.

[95] Ibid., p. 186.

As for why the accused had not then rescued more victims by selecting them, the answer was simple: Hitler had ordered the extermination of *all* Jews. The victims' fate was sealed long before they arrived at Auschwitz. Selections could thus be viewed only as a method for saving the lives of at least some Jews. Why had the defendants sought to avoid ramp duty, then, if not because of the pangs of a guilty conscience? Simply out of an innate human sympathy for the suffering of the victims.[96]

Thus, according to the logic of Laternser's terrifying sophistry, the sole agent of murder was Hitler, whereas the only agency retained by the defendants led directly to the saving of lives. Negative agency resided only at the top of the bureaucratic hierarchy; positive agency, by contrast, resided at the bottom. Failing to kill (for now) was transformed into life saving. Laternser did not mention that this "failure to kill," this life saving by omission, was simply an aspect of the broader *process* of extermination, that the selections were as essential to this process as the rounding up of Jews in the ghettos or the scheduling of the deportation trains. After all, the Jews "saved" by the selections were intended as labor to be exploited; their death was merely postponed, its mode altered, but their murder was not for the most part averted. Such an acknowledgment would have implicated not only his clients but much of German society as well. Clearly, that was not Laternser's goal. Because he deliberately avoided addressing the concept of extermination through work that had been so central to the prosecution's case, Laternser did not have to acknowledge the systematic interconnection between various kinds of murder in Auschwitz.[97]

In addition to arguing that the defendants could not be guilty because they had not exercised sufficient agency to be liable, the defense also reminded the court that under German law, the defendants could not be convicted merely for being present in Auschwitz. They could be convicted only for their own concrete and specific actions. There could be no doubt, according to defense attorney Hermann Stolting II, that what happened in Auschwitz, "about which the German people, with a few exceptions, knew nothing," was state-organized and implemented mass murder.[98] But those who organized this crime – Hitler, Himmler, Göring, Bormann, and Goebbels – were all dead. It was thus perfectly understandable that the survivors, who had after all

---

[96] Ibid., p. 188.

[97] Laternser did say, "If they [the persons selected for admission to the camp] later died in some other way, then the person who selected them on the ramp was only responsible if he established supplemental effective conditions for this potential subsequent death." Ibid., p. 186.

[98] Hermann Stolting II, *Plädoyer im Auschwitz-Prozeß in Frankfurt am Main* (n.d., n.p.), p. 8. Hermann Stolting II is not to be confused with his brother, Hermann Stolting I, whose political orientation could hardly have been more different, having helped Kaul during the Auschwitz trial. See Kaul, "Bericht Nr. 1, Zeitspanne 6 Januar 1964 bis 17 Januar 1964," BAB, Nachlaß Kaul, N 2503/198, p. 1.

suffered so horribly, had sought out those who were still alive, on whom they could take their revenge. "In the process, they miss, however, the fact that we live neither under a dictatorship nor during a revolution, and that therefore, one cannot simply label and condemn as a murderer, everyone who was in some way incorporated into this machinery of mass extermination."[99] Under the rule of law, no one could be declared a murderer simply because he or she was "a component [*Glied*] in a criminal, bankrupt system"; it had to be on the basis of his or her "own guilty contribution."[100]

In many cases, the defense contended, there was absolutely no evidence proving such culpable contributions on the part of their clients. The defense was particularly critical of the prosecution's tendency to take mere presence as evidence of participation.[101] The question was not what functional role the defendants were supposed to have played in Auschwitz. Rather, the question was, "Where is their personal contribution to the act, where is their personal guilt, where did they do more than they were obligated to under the given circumstances?"[102] "Contrary to what the prosecution said in similar cases," argued Hans Knögel, "along the lines of 'He was at the ramp and did nothing and that was murder' – the mere presence of an NCO medic at an event that was led by an SS medical officer does not constitute legally relevant behavior, unless he undertook some supplemental action as well."[103]

Even in cases where witnesses had testified that they had seen the defendants commit specific crimes, the defense argued that these statements were absolutely unreliable. This was their second major argument. One should not, Laternser argued, "reduce the requirement for strict evidence" just because twenty years had elapsed since the crime in question.[104] Not only did the defense maintain that this time lapse prima facie called into question the reliability of eyewitness testimony in such cases, the witnesses were per se unreliable because of what they had suffered in Auschwitz. It was only too understandable that the witnesses were bitter and angry, but this did not change the fact that their desire for revenge fatally undermined the credibility of their testimony. As Stolting put it, because of what they had suffered, survivors "*could* no longer be objective, even if they *wanted* to be and subjectively believed themselves to have *been* objective."[105]

In addition, the defense took great pains to undermine the credibility of as many individual witnesses as possible. In contrast to the prosecution and the civil counsel, who had contented themselves with an evaluation of

---

[99] Stolting, *Plädoyer*, p. 8.
[100] Ibid., p. 7.
[101] See, e.g., Laternser, *Die andere Seite*, p. 219.
[102] Stolting, *Plädoyer*, p. 9.
[103] Knögel, "Plädoyer," p. 4.
[104] Laternser, *Die andere Seite*, p. 141.
[105] Stolting, *Plädoyer*, p. 6.

the reliability of the witnesses in general, the defense examined the specific testimony against their clients in great detail. No doubt, this was because each defense attorney had only a limited number of cases to treat, whereas the prosecution especially had been obliged to consider all twenty cases and could not afford the luxury of such detailed exegeses of individual witness statements.

As a rule, the defense sought to undermine the credibility of witness testimony by pointing to internal inconsistencies and minor factual errors, a form of argumentation by nit-picking. Benno Erhard, for example, arguing on behalf of Stark, had the following to say regarding the testimony of Josef Gabis. Gabis had claimed to have seen Stark escorting a woman with an infant or toddler in the fall of 1942 to the Old Crematorium. Stark was carrying a carbine and returned a short while later alone.[106] According to Erhard, the court could not believe a word of this, "because this witness stated that he had gone from Auschwitz to Birkenau by himself already in 1942. He had a pass. This statement itself is already certainly false."[107] As one could tell from numerous issues of the *Auschwitz Hefte* (the official publication of the Auschwitz Museum), even *Funktionshäftlinge* had to be escorted whenever they went from Auschwitz to Birkenau. In addition, Erhard pointed out that the witness had claimed that the ramp itself had consisted of multiple rail lines, approximately 400 meters wide. But as the court well knew, this was not true; the ramp was "a dead-end rail head."[108] Therefore, because of these alleged errors in utterly unrelated matters, the witness could not be believed with regard to his testimony against Stark, either.

The defense also latched onto instances where the witnesses contradicted their preliminary testimony as evidence of their unreliability. The witness Erwin Bartel, for instance, had testified in his pretrial testimony that all members of the Political Section, including Broad, had done duty on the ramp. But defense attorney Steinacker pointed out that, while he had told essentially the same story during the main proceedings, he had had to admit, on direct questioning by Judge Hofmeyer, that he had never been to the ramp himself; he had only overheard the SS discussing the selections amongst themselves. "On the basis of this statement by the witness, one can clearly see that he can give no immediate information regarding whether Broad participated in selections at the ramp or not – as he had earlier maintained."[109]

The third basic defense strategy was far more radical. It was to attack the very foundation of postwar German Nazi trials. There were two versions of this argument, both of which led to the same conclusion: namely, that the

---

[106] For Gabis's testimony, see Langbein, *Auschwitz-Prozeß*, p. 448.
[107] Benno Erhard, Handakten RA Erhard, vol. 5, "Plädoyers (Stark)," FBI SAP, 1/V9, p. 8.
[108] Ibid., p. 9.
[109] Steinacker, "Plädoyer (Stark)," p. 168.

Frankfurt court had no jurisdiction in these cases. The first approach was to turn the principle of legal continuity between the Third Reich and the FRG, which enabled the prosecution of Nazi crimes under existing statutory law, against itself.

Hans Fertig, arguing on behalf of the defendant Klehr, advanced this argument most forcefully. Fertig pointed out that the court had authority over these crimes merely on the basis of "German jurisdiction."[110] Jurisdiction in the legal sense, however, was a function of the state. The jurisdiction of the courts extended temporally, personally, and factually only as far as the power of the sovereign state. But what were the temporal boundaries of the Federal Republic's sovereignty? Certainly, this extended at least as far back as the passage of the Basic Law. Whether this sovereignty extended back before 1945 depended on how one evaluated the relationship between the FRG and the Third Reich. While he noted that much ink had been spilled over this matter, Fertig argued correctly that the consensus view was that the German Reich had never disappeared, either in 1933 or in 1945, but had merely been transformed into the FRG, so that legal authority was presumed, according to the so-called continuance theory (*Fortbestandslehre*) or identity theory (*Identitätslehre*), to transcend the 1945 divide.[111] In this manner, the courts of the Federal Republic were granted jurisdiction over crimes committed prior to 1945.[112]

But the crucial question, according to Fertig, was whether this jurisdiction in fact applied to *all* crimes committed prior to 1945, particularly to those with which Klehr was charged. Klehr had acted not as a private citizen but as a state agent. "Therefore, according to the identity theory, he acted on the basis of the same state authority on whose basis you now sit here in judgment. The state authority which is here trying the defendant is identical with the state authority that created Auschwitz and that ordered the defendant to commit the actions which are the subject of this trial – indeed, which even gave him the *Kriegsverdienstkreuz* (military service cross) for his actions. By means of this trial, state authority thus contradicts its own previous conduct; it is practically putting itself on trial."[113] It was clearly absurd, according to Fertig, for the state to put itself on trial. Were this a civil case, it would be dismissed out of hand, according to the principle *venire contra factum proprium,* the inadmissibility of contradictory conduct.[114] To violate this principle was not an act of law but an abuse of law. The same principle applied to criminal law, according to Fertig. It would "contradict every legal order, indeed stand it on its head," for the state to try people

---

[110] Hans Fertig, Plädoyer (Klehr), FBI SAP: FAP1/V10, p. 3.
[111] Ibid.
[112] For more on the issue of continuity in German Nazi trials, see Pendas, "Truth."
[113] Fertig, Plädoyer (Klehr), pp. 4–5.
[114] Ibid., p. 5.

for obeying its own orders.[115] Therefore, Fertig concluded, the court did not have jurisdiction in these cases.

"The fact that a law formally continues to exist," Fertig stated in his closing argument for the defendant Schlage, "that is, is not explicitly abolished or changed, does not constitute absolute evidence that this law actually continues to apply as law."[116] One could, of course, appeal to principles of natural law, particularly in cases such as these, where human lives were at stake. Such an argument rendered these killings a violation of principles of justice. "However, a violation of justice [*Recht*] is not, *eo ipso,* punishable."[117] He urged the court to have the "courage" to draw the proper consequences from this fact, even if this meant that "in certain circles, the trial thus appeared to be without results."[118]

Fertig's colleague Erhard reached a similar conclusion by a slightly different path. He asserted that, while in his opinion what had happened in Auschwitz was a crime (and not merely unjust, as Fertig had maintained), this was not because it violated some "inner core of the law," which after all could be interpreted in many different ways, "but rather [because it was] illegal on the basis of norms that derive necessarily from state law."[119] In other words, the crimes of Auschwitz had been illegal according to positive law. However, in this case, this illegality in turn raised the question as to whether state orders constituted a legal excuse that excluded punishment (*Rechtsfertigungsgrund*), even when these orders were illegal under positive law. In this respect, he noted that per Article 237 of the French Penal Code, as well as according to both British and American military law prior to 1944, government orders directly excused an illegal homicide. The same applied to German law, he argued. Thus, the law held at the time that soldiers who violate the laws of war on government orders were not war criminals and could not be punished by the enemy as such. "That they could not thus be punished by their own government actually lies in the essence of the law, because what one does on the orders of one's own government, cannot be punishable."[120] These acts were clearly unjust and even illegal but could be deemed punishable only if there was a law above the state, not if law only existed within the state. Since the Frankfurt court could apply only German domestic law, the actions of the accused could not be considered to have been punishable at the time of their commission, and thus, the court had no jurisdiction.

Thus, both Fertig and Erhard argued, in effect, that the defendants' crimes were not *punishable* under German law. At least one attorney went

[115] Ibid.
[116] Hans Fertig, "Plädoyer (Schlage)," FBI SAP: FAP1/V10, p. 5.
[117] Ibid., p. 6.
[118] Ibid.
[119] Erhard, "Plädoyer (Stark)," p. 77.
[120] Ibid., p. 78.

even further, however. Rather than merely claim that the law had not been enforced, Hans Knögel argued that Nazi law had, contrary to current legal interpretation, in fact been legally valid in the first place. In other words, however abhorrent they might be from a moral point of view, the "crimes" with which the defendants were charged had not been *crimes* in any sense at all.

Knögel argued that while prior to the Third Reich, Germany had been a *Rechtsstaat*, this changed with the Nazi seizure of power. State power was bound up in the person of the Führer. There was no longer any clear distinction between law and administrative orders.[121] According to the BGH, legal norms were not invalid simply because they originated in a dictatorship.[122] Nonetheless, Knögel admitted, the BGH maintained that many of the rules and regulations passed by the Nazi regime had not constituted law, because they had violated the "demands of natural law or the generally valid ethical laws [*Sittengesetze*] of Christian-Occidental culture."[123] But, Knögel asked rhetorically, is the "nullity of an order, by virtue of its harm to the fundamental principles of all civilized peoples, sufficient to ground the continuance of a penal threat for murder?"[124] Clearly, from a positive law standpoint, the one in which Knögel and his compatriots on the court had been trained, the answer had to be no. The law was what was contained in legal statutes, nothing more, nothing less, and the Nazi state had legally ordained the murders at Auschwitz, thus rendering them legal.

None of these arguments was likely to prove very effective in the trial. It is difficult to imagine the Frankfurt court declaring itself incompetent to pass judgment, particularly as this would have been a radical departure from existing legal precedent regarding the jurisdiction of West German courts over Nazi crimes. The enormous political outcry that would have accompanied such a ruling made such a decision even less likely. It is possible that the defense attorneys failed to recognize the improbability of the court adopting these arguments, though this seems doubtful. It is more likely that the defense was hoping that these polemical legal arguments might possibly be taken up by other courts and applied at a later date, or at least that they would help to shape the course of the public debate regarding Nazi trials in general. In this regard, these arguments should be viewed as more political than legal in nature.

The defense further argued that, even if the court disagreed and found both that Nazi law had not in fact been valid law (and that the defendants' actions were thus legally actionable) and that, as crimes, these could be

---

[121] Knögel, "Plädoyer (Scherpe)," pp. 33–34.
[122] Ibid., p. 35. Citing *Entscheidungen des Bundesgerichtshofs in Zivilsachen* (BGHZ) 5, p. 95.
[123] Knögel, "Plädoyer (Scherpe)," p. 35.
[124] Ibid., p. 36. Citing Anton Roesen, "Rechtsfragen der Einsatzgruppen-Prozesse," NJW 17 (1964): 133–36.

legally punished by a contemporary German court, it still could not punish the defendants. After all, the defense maintained, the defendants had not, and could not have, *recognized* the "illegality" of their actions. Again, given that the Third Reich had been a totalitarian dictatorship and had controlled the educational system, the mass media, and every form of public and private association, the only message the defendants had ever received was that the Führer's will had the force of law. It would be unreasonable to expect these "small men" to see through this propaganda when even the German judiciary at the time had not.

Fertig noted with regard to his client Klehr, for example, that the trial had quite literally broken him, physically and psychologically. On this basis, one could only conclude, according to the defense attorney, that "this man has only now recognized how his 'duties,' of which he spoke repeatedly during the proceedings, are to be properly evaluated, that only now have his eyes been opened, that only now have the brown scales fallen from his eyes" and that in Auschwitz, he was "lacking in – had had stolen from him" the capacity to recognize right and wrong.[125] Fertig argued that the capacity to distinguish right from wrong, the legal from the illegal, is not evenly distributed among people. To support this claim, Fertig went so far as to cite Fritz Bauer's claim that conscience itself is a social effect, which depends on a person's social environment. In Klehr's case, all of those around him, most especially his superior officers, whom he looked up to and respected greatly, had felt these crimes to be legal. How could Klehr then have thought otherwise?

More particularly, the defense repeatedly argued that the defendants were excused in their actions under military law per §47 MStGB (*Militärstrafgesetzbuch*). Knögel in particular pointed out that this issue was identical with the question as to whether the defendants had known their actions were illegal. §47 MStGB states that a soldier is not obligated to obey superior orders if he *knows* those orders to be illegal. In other words, had the defendants known that the orders they received in Auschwitz were illegal, they could, indeed should, have disobeyed them. But, Knögel maintained, his client Scherpe, at least, had not known such orders to be illegal. The orders he received, specifically those pertaining to "injections," were *Dienstbefehle,* direct orders pertaining to his military duties. The fact that he had left the injection room in disgust on at least one occasion indicated that he "disapproved" of these orders.[126] But according to Knögel's interpretation of §47 MStGB, it was not enough that a subordinate suspect that an order was illegal, that it violate his own personal values; rather, he had to know for certain that the order was in fact illegal. Ordinarily, this would be determined on the basis of the rule and the exception. If an order exceeds the

[125] Fertig, "Plädoyer (Klehr)," p. 2.
[126] Knögel, "Plädoyer (Scherpe)," p. 38.

bounds of the legal system that the soldier is used to, then he may assume it is illegal. But what was "unique" about the situation in Auschwitz was that in this context, "crime was the rule and that, therefore, one cannot say he ought to have recognized that what was going on were crimes and misdemeanors."[127]

For the defendants, these events were not "excessive acts by individual groups" but rather "orders from the Führer and Reich Chancellor."[128] Knögel cited an article by Konrad Redeker in the *Neue Juristische Wochenschrift*, arguing that at least those at the head of the state apparatus and the judiciary were of the opinion that the orders for the Final Solution were legally valid.[129] The fact that these actions were never legally punished reinforced this perception. "As far as my client is concerned, he himself had no knowledge of these legal judgments. He simply fulfilled his orders, which were seen as legal at that time."[130] At the very least, the court could thus not exclude the possibility that, although Scherpe felt a "personal antipathy" to what was going on, he thought that it was in fact legal.[131]

The fourth and final general theme to emerge in the defense's closing arguments was their sense that there were certain serious procedural irregularities in the conduct of the trial itself, which would render any convictions unfair and invalid. Indeed, a conviction under such circumstances would merely add injustice to injustice, and thus would not be in keeping with the commitment to the rule of law in the Federal Republic. Two related issues in particular concerned the defense in this regard: first, what they took to be the undue influence exercised on the witnesses both by outside organizations such as the IAC and by East Block governments, and, second, the massive publicity attracted by the trial, which they felt also influenced the witnesses and made a truly fair verdict impossible. In effect, they argued that because this was a highly public trial, it was necessarily also an unfair one.

Stolting began his closing argument by claiming that the already considerable advantages exercised by the prosecution in criminal cases were even more exaggerated in this case.[132] The preliminary investigation, he noted, had lasted nearly five years. During this time, the prosecution had taken depositions from a huge number of witnesses, only a small percentage of whom had been called on to testify in the trial itself. Given the repeated public calls by "decisive personages in our public life" to use this trial to master the past, "one can well imagine the criteria used in selecting these witnesses

---

[127] Ibid., p. 39.
[128] Ibid., p. 40.
[129] Ibid., pp. 41–42. Citing Konrad Redeker, "Bewältigung der Vergangenheit als Aufgabe der Justiz," NJW 17 (1964): 1097–100.
[130] Knögel, "Plädoyer (Scherpe)," p. 42.
[131] Ibid.
[132] Stolting, *Plädoyer*, p. 1.

by the prosecution."[133] Although Stolting did stop short of "decisively asserting" that the prosecution had neglected to call exculpating witnesses, he did
note that an unusually high percentage of the witnesses had had nothing
to say about the personal guilt of the defendants, but had been called only
to "give an atmospheric account of the milieu, to report in general terms
on the blows, torture, martyrdom, to project the screams and suffering of
those martyred into the courtroom and, in this manner, to generally paint
the defendants as guilty before any personal guilt on their part... had been
proven beyond a shadow of a doubt."[134]

What was worse, according to Stolting, the press had attempted directly to
influence the course of the proceedings, when, for example, "they portrayed
statements by the defense in a satirical light."[135] All of this was merely exacerbated by the propaganda efforts by prosecutors and civil counsel in giving
numerous public lectures about the trial while it was still ongoing. Worst
of all was the Auschwitz exhibit: "I have to note here, that my critique of
the prosecution's mode of operation is not a polemic directed against the
prosecutors in the trial itself, but rather is a critique of the Hessian Attorney
General Dr. Bauer who, as a civil servant in a position of authority, had in my
view an obligation, to put it delicately, to prohibit any inappropriate efforts
to influence these proceedings as best as he was able."[136]

And yet, according to Stolting, the witnesses had clearly been influenced by outside agencies. While it was good and proper that the witnesses
were well cared for in Frankfurt by the Red Cross and that they had had
their transportation costs covered, the fact that they were "remunerated
[*entschädigt*] – I say remunerated because I want to avoid the word honorar-
ium [*honorieren*] – is unfathomable."[137] Other defense attorneys expounded
on this theme of alleged witness tampering in even greater detail in their closing arguments. Hans Laternser had registered with dismay, for example, the
fact that more than half of the witnesses came from foreign countries, and
thus could neglect the threat of prosecution for perjury at will.[138] Unsurprisingly, he neglected to mention that this was inevitable, given that the
vast majority of the victims in Auschwitz had likewise not been German citizens. Laternser further asserted that Polish witnesses had been allowed to
travel to Frankfurt to testify only after a "thorough screening" by the Polish
authorities.[139] He noted that according to the reimbursement applications of

[133] Ibid., pp. 1–2. It should be recalled that under German law, the prosecution has an obligation
to present exculpating as well as incriminating evidence. Stolting is here implying that they
did not adhere to this obligation.
[134] Ibid., p. 2.
[135] Ibid., p. 4.
[136] Ibid., p. 3.
[137] Ibid., p. 4.
[138] Laternser, *Die andere Seite*, p. 156.
[139] Ibid., p. 160.

several Polish witnesses, they had spent several days in Warsaw undergoing "preliminary questioning" prior to coming to Frankfurt.

Stolting expanded on Laternser's claims of witness tampering by the Polish authorities by noting that the close cooperation between the prosecution and the IAC ran throughout the proceedings like a "red thread."[140] The fact that the IAC, by now widely perceived as a communist front organization, had both put considerable pressure on the prosecution to arrest defendants and had been decisive in finding witnesses, constituted on Stolting's view an undue influence on the proceedings. This "red thread" continued with the "pre-examination" of witnesses in Poland, as Laternser had asserted. The defense's request to question officials from the Polish justice ministry had been rejected by Warsaw as "provocative." "Well," Stolting exclaimed, "the term 'provocative' belongs to the terminology of the East Block states."[141]

The connection the defense drew between alleged witness tampering and the general unreliability of witness testimony, between the trial's mass publicity and the alleged violations of due process, meant that their arguments led, directly or indirectly, to the claim that such trials were *in principle* unjust and ought to be terminated for the sake of the rule of law. The defense's insistent claim that the Third Reich had been a totalitarian regime, *just like* the communist regimes in Eastern Europe, served to connect this call for a termination of Nazi trials to a generic stance of anti-communism. Thus the defense argued, sometimes implicitly, sometimes explicitly, that the struggle against communism mandated a cessation of the obsession with the Nazi past. Correspondingly, the defense portrayed the defendants, and the German people, as themselves the victims of Nazism. Only the Nazi elite had truly born responsibility for the horrors of the Third Reich, only they had controlled the extermination process, only they were truly culpable. And since they were all dead, to continue such trials was at best superfluous, at worst an act of injustice.

The defense reached what they saw as the inevitable conclusion that this was a political show trial, not in keeping with the *Rechtsstaat*. Defense attorney Gerhard said in his *Plädoyer* for Baretzki, "You [ladies and gentlemen of the court] cannot escape the conclusion that the system of the Third Reich and the so-called wire pullers who animated that system were responsible for what happened in Auschwitz. Consequently, the theory of deterrence clearly does not apply to the defendant Baretzki. But precisely this proves that the successor state to the Third Reich has given you a task that cannot be fulfilled with the methods of traditional criminal law."[142]

Benno Erhard went further. This was a political trial, he declared, and worse. "It is not just the interests of the state, which are, consciously or

[140] Stolting, *Plädoyer*, p. 4.
[141] Ibid., p. 6.
[142] Gerhard, "Plädoyer (Baretzki)," p. 6.

unconsciously, on the table here. Rather an interest far beyond that of the state is in play here, the interest of worldwide, internationally known powers that seek to influence our state, our consciousness, our *Volk*."[143] That this tacit reference to a global Jewish conspiracy is a reiteration of the Nazi's own anti-Semitic idiom should be obvious. Erhard also maintained that this was not just a political trial but, indeed, a show trial. It was hardly the court's job, he asserted, to reconstitute the rule of law, as the prosecution had insisted. The court's task was to decide the guilt of the defendants, not to teach history.

In the end, then, the defense *Plädoyers* compose a curious admixture of insight and often deliberate, ideologically inspired blindness. On the one hand, the defense recognized to a far greater extent than either the prosecution or the civil counsel the paradoxical character of trying participants in state-organized genocide as isolated individuals acting on the basis of their own voluntary dispositions. Although they often took this argument to absurd lengths (as in Laternser's claim that selections constituted a form of life saving), the defense was quite right to point out that Auschwitz was only the final, fatal stop on a long road that implicated most of the German state, the Nazi party hierarchy, and indeed German society as a whole. The defense was also right to point to the deep problems posed for prosecuting Nazi crimes under statutory law by the fact that Nazi law had been widely interpreted at the time as valid law, up to and including secret verbal orders by Hitler.[144] Finally, the defense was by no means wrong to indicate the ambiguity of using the court to teach what were, in effect, state-sponsored history lessons.

On the other hand, the defense failed to draw from these observations the obvious conclusion that either Nazi trials needed to be greatly expanded – not, as the defense would have it, restricted – or, at the very least, that they had to be incorporated into a much more widespread political and cultural process of engagement with the legacies of Nazism, as Fritz Bauer proposed to do. Instead, the defense had, cynically or sincerely as the case may be, deployed their arguments for the sole purpose of exculpating their clients. While this is understandable from the standpoint of courtroom tactics, and hardly surprising given the apparent political inclinations of many of the defense counsel, it nevertheless had the direct consequence of transforming the defense's occasional insights into mere legal ploys. Given the way that many of the defense attorneys sought explicitly to politicize the proceedings, both by linking their historical assessment of Nazi totalitarianism with a polemical critique of East Block totalitarianism and by explicitly claiming

[143] Erhard, "Plädoyer (Stark)," p. 2.
[144] Rebecca Elisabeth Wittmann points to the paradoxes this had created for the prosecution as early as the indictment. See Wittmann, "Indicting Auschwitz? The Paradox of the Frankfurt Auschwitz Trial," *German History* 21 (2003): 505–32.

that the witnesses had been influenced by communist agents, it is hardly surprising that they failed to expand their analysis into a general analysis of the social basis of Nazism and the Holocaust.

However, because the defense chose to take the easy way out, to content themselves with partial insights and cynical attempts to manipulate the criminal code, they actually ultimately undermined the efficacy of their own arguments. The court largely rejected their arguments, save in a few cases, where it did deem specific witnesses unreliable. Nor were the defense's arguments given much credence by the mainstream press. Only the nationalist press, ideologically predisposed to agree with the defense, was at all persuaded by any of their arguments. The defense thus failed both to win their case and to persuade the public. Nor did they have the courage, perhaps unavoidably but nonetheless unfortunately, to draw the real lessons from their own arguments and argue for an expanded, rather than a restricted, understanding of agency in the Holocaust.

8

Judgment

In many respects, the most important phase of the Auschwitz Trial was the court's final judgment. From a strictly legal perspective, this is obviously the case, because it was here that the fate of the accused was determined. But in a deeper sense, this was also true because the final judgment did much more than merely pass sentence on the defendants. Unlike Anglo-American verdicts, where the jury simply announces the guilt or innocence of a given defendant, and the judge (or sometimes the jury) decides the sentence to be imposed, German courts articulate the legal and evidentiary *reasons* for their decisions in some detail. German judgments are thus not merely juridical announcements of a *decision*; they are also representational articulations of an *interpretation*. What is more, they are final, authoritative interpretations. In contrast to all prior interpretations in the trial, whether articulated by the prosecution in the indictment, by witnesses in their testimony, or by lawyers in their closing arguments, the court's interpretation in the final judgment has nearly the full force of law, pending the appeals process. In the Auschwitz Trial, only one sentence, that of Dr. Lucas, was reversed on appeal.[1]

Oral Verdict

On August 19 and 20, 1965, Judge Hofmeyer announced the verdicts in the Auschwitz Trial and provided the requisite "oral justification" for the judgment. Prior to his detailed analysis of the verdicts against the individual defendants, Hofmeyer began by considering several general issues raised by the trial. He noted that it was "understandable" that many people hoped that this trial would lay the foundations for a "comprehensive historical

---

[1] BGH 2 StR 280/67 (February 20, 1969), in C. F. Rüter et al., eds., *Justiz und NS-Verbrechen: Sammlung Deutscher Strafurteile wegen nationalsozialistischer Tötungsverbrechen, 1945–1966*, vol. 21 (Amsterdam: University Press Amsterdam, 1979), pp. 869–73.

presentation of the events of that time."[2] To this end, the court had received extensive reports by historians serving as expert witnesses. However, the court could not allow itself to be distracted by the almost infinite number of questions raised by such historical issues. Nor was it relevant to the court's decision to answer the question posed by the prosecution at the start of their *Plädoyers* as to why such Nazi trials were only now taking place or whether they should continue. The court's sole task was to evaluate the prosecution's charges against the defendants. "It is certain that this is a normal criminal trial, whatever its background. The court could only pass judgment according to the laws it has sworn to uphold. And these laws demand on both the subjective and objective sides, an exact determination of the concrete guilt of the defendants."[3] If for the public this was the "Auschwitz Trial," for the court it remained a "trial against Mulka and others."[4] "The court was not called in order to master the past, nor does it need to determine whether this trial was advisable [*zweckmäßig*] or not. The court could not conduct a political trial, much less a show trial."[5]

Indeed, Hofmeyer regretted that the phrase "show trial" had been used at all. Anyone who had followed the proceedings closely knew full well, he insisted, that "the discovery of the truth alone has formed the core of this trial."[6] Moreover, the court was concerned with the truth regarding the *criminal* guilt of the accused, not their moral or political guilt, which fell outside the court's purview. Nor did the oft-repeated accusation that only "small fry" were on trial, even if true, make any difference, since their guilt was not diminished just "because they themselves had not initiated the entire course of events. They were as necessary for the implementation of the plan for the extermination of people in Auschwitz as those who drafted this plan at their desks."[7]

With regard to this guilt, Hofmeyer noted, the defense was well within its rights to call into question the court's jurisdiction over the alleged crimes of the defendants. On the one hand, the defense had argued that the court could not pass judgment on these crimes because a state cannot pass judgment on actions that it has itself mandated at an earlier time. On the other hand, others in the defense had maintained that the Third Reich had been an independent, sovereign state, whose laws and "state morality" had an autonomous, positive validity and were not subject to the jurisdiction of West German courts. "These legal interpretations," Hofmeyer concluded, "are mistaken."[8]

[2] TR, August 19, 1965, 182nd Session, FBI SAP, CD AP357, T10–11.
[3] Ibid., T39.
[4] Ibid., T13.
[5] Ibid.
[6] Ibid., T14.
[7] Ibid., T14–15.
[8] Ibid., T17.

To begin with, the German Reich had been a continuous state entity since 1871, one whose criminal laws had remained in effect throughout its history. Hofmeyer here reasserted the continuity thesis that had governed German jurisprudence with regard to the Third Reich since the inception of the Federal Republic. This might seem to confirm the defense's critique – that a state could not pass judgment on its own earlier actions – but this was not the case, according to Hofmeyer. "It is true that the entire power of the German Reich was at the disposal of National Socialism but this did not place it in a position to transform illegality into legality [*Unrecht Recht zu machen*]."[9] Even National Socialism was subordinate to the "core of law."

This was particularly true of the so-called Final Solution. This was based on a criminal order, originating with Hitler and passed on to the SS. Himmler and his subordinates, including the defendants, had known this order to be illegal, as they themselves had indicated during the trial.[10] If the defendants nonetheless obeyed these criminal orders, it was because of their ethic of "unquestioning obedience." It was true that in a totalitarian dictatorship, the dictator could prevent any criminal investigation into such activities. This did not make them legal; it meant only that the defendants had acted under the assumption that they would not be held accountable for their actions, which was not the same thing. But this raised the question – repeatedly posed by the defense – as to why the courts in the Third Reich had not in fact investigated this criminality, if indeed it had been illegal all along.

Hofmeyer here took the opportunity to defend the conduct of the German judiciary and, by implication, himself during the Third Reich. "The NSDAP and its organizations had the power in their hands to bend the courts to their will."[11] The courts, he asserted, had stood under a direct threat from Hitler. (He cited as evidence the *Reichstag Beschluß* of April 25, 1942, which gave Hitler the power to punish any German, regardless of official position, if they failed to carry out his orders, as well as a speech by Hitler to the Reichstag, in which Hitler said that the task of the courts was to serve the nation, not the law, and that he would remove from office any judge who did not understand this.)[12] The fact that Hitler had not just been the head of state but also the *Oberster Gerichtsherr* (supreme judge) had effectively terminated the separation of powers in Germany and eliminated the independence of the judiciary. Since most courts were not, however, willing to act only in accordance with state policy, despite these threats from Hitler, he had used his authority as *Oberster Gerichtsherr* simply to prevent political crimes from

---

[9] Ibid., T18.

[10] As evidence, Hofmeyer cited the defendant Hofmann's outburst, "It is horrible what people can demand of other people!" Ibid., T21.

[11] Ibid., T22.

[12] Ibid., T24. It is worth noting that, with reference to Hitler's order of April 25, Hofmeyer calls it "this law [*Gesetz*] and threat." But if this was a *law*, then it must have had some legal force. Perhaps Hofmeyer is here arguing implicitly that there was a distinction between law and justice, but he does not say so explicitly.

coming before the courts at all. Since courts can judge only crimes brought
before them, the fact that, for instance, none of the crimes that were committed in Auschwitz was ever indicted during the Third Reich (because Hitler
would not allow it) explained why the courts had never passed judgment on
them. In short, far from representing a craven moral surrender, the courts'
failure to investigate Nazi crimes during the Third Reich was reinterpreted
by Hofmeyer as a form of principled "inner emigration."

It is worth noting that – without the slightest trace of irony – Hofmeyer
here effectively replicated precisely the kind of defensive tactics he disallowed when practiced by the defendants in the trial. He argued that the
courts essentially operated under a form of duress, because Hitler would
have punished any efforts on their part to prosecute SS crimes. In addition,
he shifted the blame for their crimes of omission onto others. The courts
would have passed judgment, if only the prosecutors had brought indictments; the prosecution, in turn, would have brought indictments if only they
had not been prevented by Hitler's overweening power from doing so. Neither the courts nor the prosecutors had *approved of* Hitler's actions, but
they had been powerless to resist them. The defendants on trial, down to
the lowliest of them, the inmate Bednarek, may have exercised a degree of
controlling agency in Auschwitz, according to Hofmeyer, but the vastly more
powerful German judiciary had apparently been powerless to confront or
resist the will of Adolf Hitler.

The very secrecy of Hitler's extermination order, designed to protect the
Nazi genocide from public scrutiny, also meant that any possible argument
for the legal validity of such orders was mistaken. At a minimum, such orders
would have had to have been published in order to acquire legal force.[13]
Furthermore, according to Hofmeyer, this secret order for the extermination
of millions was given to the SS, not to the Wehrmacht, the citizenry, or
the judicial authorities, because the Nazis felt that "only the SS, with their
unconditional obedience and their absolute loyalty to the Führer, were ready
to commit this crime without asking questions" about either its morality or
its legality.[14]

After this self-justificatory excursus into German legal history, Hofmeyer
returned to the main theme of the judgment: the guilt of the individual defendants. Had this question been posed twenty years earlier by an SS *Standes-
gericht* in Auschwitz, the question would have been easily answered. All of
the defendants had been in Auschwitz and had been members of the SS. That
would have sufficed for a conviction in an SS court, but that was precisely the
difference between the Nazis and "judicial decision making under the rule
of the law."[15] Guilt by association was a Nazi concept, not a legally just one.

[13] Ibid., T30.
[14] Ibid., T31–32.
[15] Ibid., T33.

Legal guilt had been exceedingly difficult to ascertain in these cases because the court had been forced to rely almost exclusively on eyewitness testimony, which, as criminologists had long recognized, was one of the least reliable sources of evidence. The difficulties with eyewitness testimony were only exacerbated in this instance by the long time span involved and the tremendous suffering the witnesses had endured. For this reason, the defense had been quite right to question closely the reliability of the witnesses. "It must certainly have been an imposition on the witnesses, to ask them today about all of the details of their experiences."[16] Some would say that it was "expecting too much" to ask them to recall "specifically when, where and how, who did what."[17]

However, it would be completely unjust to accuse the defense of wanting to ridicule the witnesses by asking such questions. In the absence of the kind of forensic evidence on which most modern murder trials rely, it was imperative to be as certain as possible of the veracity of the witness testimony. Often, the only way to determine this was through precisely this kind of detailed interrogation, however difficult it may have been for the witnesses. After all, there were no calendars or watches in Auschwitz, Hofmeyer acknowledged.[18] It was precisely in the details of time and place that testimony could be cross-checked and compared with the limited documentary evidence, thus establishing its veracity. Because of these evidentiary limitations, the court had had to be particularly cautious in reaching its verdict.[19] Any mistakes would undermine the faith of the German people in the rule of law. Thus, the court had examined every witness statement with the utmost care, and "in a whole series of instances, the court was unable to convict [the defendants] of certain charges against them in the indictment, because the requisite certainty for such a judgment was lacking."[20]

The defense can thus be said to have won one round in the final judgment and to have lost one. The court did not find their legal argumentation concerning the court's jurisdiction over Nazi crimes the least bit plausible. This could hardly have been unexpected. The likelihood that the Frankfurt court would, contrary to all legal precedent in the Federal Republic, declare itself incompetent to sit in judgment on Nazi crimes could never have been very great. However, the court seemed far more persuaded by the defense's specific and detailed attacks on the reliability of eyewitness testimony than it did by the prosecution's generic defense of the witnesses. It is true that the

---

[16] Ibid., T35.
[17] Ibid.
[18] Ibid., T38.
[19] Ibid. As an example of what could go wrong in such cases, Hofmeyer cited a case where a defendant had been convicted of murdering an inmate in Buchenwald, only to have it turn out later that the alleged victim was in fact still alive.
[20] Ibid., T40–41.

court did not reject all eyewitness testimony out of hand. Had it done so, no convictions would have been possible at all. But, as Hofmeyer indicated, it did treat this testimony with a high degree of skepticism. It was far better, on the court's reasoning, to acquit a guilty defendant than to convict an innocent one. As we shall see in examining the written verdict, the court did indeed reject as unreliable much (though not all) of the witness testimony that the defense had found particularly onerous.[21]

Hofmeyer concluded his introductory comments by defending the sentences imposed, which ranged from three years and three months to life in prison. No mathematical formula could provide adequate criteria for determining sentences in such cases, he insisted. Even life sentences, if divided by the number of victims, were not adequate to the demands of justice. "Human life is much too short for that."[22] According to Hofmeyer, then, the court's sentences could not be measured by the standard of justice as such, because in the face of Auschwitz's unprecedented and unimaginable crimes, such justice eluded the grasp of human courts. This was a neat rhetorical trick. Since it was undeniably true that human justice could not hope to match completely the human evil of Auschwitz, Hofmeyer sidestepped any criticism that the sentences in the trial were too mild. Of course they were too mild, he in effect said, all of them, even the life sentences; nothing more was possible. The very real difference between a three-year sentence and life were elided in the face of the almost metaphysical enormity of Auschwitz.

At the very end of his oral verdict, Hofmeyer paused to consider the consequences of the trial for its participants. In a voice choked with emotion, he said: "During the course of the trial's twenty months, the court had to once more experience in the mind's eye all of the suffering and torments that the people there suffered and which will forever be connected with the name of Auschwitz. There will probably be many among us who, for a long time to come, will no longer be able to look into the happy and trusting eyes of a child without seeing in the background, the hollow, questioning and uncomprehending, fear-filled eyes of those children who went their final way in Auschwitz."[23]

Written Verdict

The court's written judgment, drafted immediately after the conclusion of the trial, is an exhaustive 457-page document.[24] It is divided into three main

---

[21] Though it should be pointed out that Hofmeyer explicitly rejected the charges of witness tampering with regard to the monetary compensation witnesses received. See ibid., T42.

[22] Ibid., T47.

[23] TR, August 20, 1965, 183rd Session, AP 365, T66–67.

[24] Urteil, in Rüter et al., eds., *Justiz und NS-Verbrechen*, vol. 21. Cf. the critical edition of the verdict: Friedrich-Martin Balzer and Werner Renz, eds., *Das Urteil im Frankfurter Auschwitz-Prozeß (1963–1965)* (Bonn: Pahl-Rugenstein, 2004). The verdict can also be found in FFStA 4 Ks 2/63, Bd. 114–19. Since the Rüter volume is the most readily accessible, I have chosen to quote from this version.

parts: an excursus on the history of the concentration camp system and Auschwitz in particular, a consideration of the cases against the individual defendants, and, finally, a consideration of procedural issues. The consideration of the cases against the individual defendants is by far the most extensive section in the written judgment, consuming 405 pages. The historical excursus, by contrast, is a mere forty pages long, and the consideration of procedural issues occupies a perfunctory seven pages. Clearly, as was to be expected, the court's emphasis was on the individual cases under consideration. Of the general questions considered by Hofmeyer in his oral verdict, only the issue of witness reliability found its way into the written verdict.

The court's historical excursus, which opens the written judgment, was based heavily on the reports from the Institute for Contemporary History, although it also incorporated information derived from eyewitness testimony, historical documents, and the memoirs of the first camp commandant, Rudolf Höß. It focused even more narrowly than the indictment on the history of Auschwitz itself as the relevant contextual frame for the defendant's actions, though it did consider briefly Nazi policy in Poland and the general course of the Final Solution.

The court's historical excursus was designed, first, to demonstrate the organizational typology of Auschwitz, the administrative context within which the defendants had acted. To a greater extent than the indictment, the verdict concentrated on Auschwitz as an extermination center, while downplaying its role as a labor camp (and consequently, the connection between the gas chambers and extermination through work that had been so central to the prosecution's case). Second, the court traced a direct line of intentionality for the Final Solution from Hitler through Himmler and Eichmann to Höß and thence to the defendants. Finally, the court did note that many of the victims executed by members of the Political Section at the Black Wall had in fact been tried by an SS *Standgericht* in Block 11 prior to being killed. Although the court did not accord these "trials" the status of full legal proceedings, it nonetheless did treat the defendants less harshly on these counts than others.

The court's concern with history was necessarily instrumental, as was true of almost all the legal actors in the Auschwitz Trial. How could it be otherwise? The point of the trial was, as almost everyone involved insisted, to determine the criminal guilt of the defendants and to impose an appropriate sentence on them. History here had to be placed in the service of law. But there was a price to be paid for this service. This price was paid above all in the questions not asked, the avenues of inquiry not followed.

The court rightly noted that it was not its task to examine "in detail the organizational implementation of . . . the so-called 'Final Solution of the Jewish question,' the various arenas of competence and responsibility."[25]

---

[25] Rüter et al., eds., *Justiz und NS-Verbrechen*, vol. 21, p. 419.

But how much more fragmentary and arbitrary does the Holocaust appear when viewed almost exclusively through the lens of Auschwitz? And, perhaps more important, how much narrower does the realm of responsibility and culpability become when restricted to one killing center, even if it was the most significant one? For the court, this was not even really an *Auschwitz* trial; it was a trial against "Mulka and others." History was ultimately only of interest, as Hofmeyer had said in his oral judgment, to the extent that it pertained directly to this handful of individuals. Hofmeyer was probably quite right that the court had no choice but to restrict its historical inquiries in this way, lest it "wind up in a boundlessness that rendered any decision impossible."[26] But in avoiding the boundlessness of history, the court perpetuated a restrictive reading of German history and the Holocaust that systematically devalued the structural relationship between the Holocaust and German society.

The court's true and proper interest was, as it had to be, in the cases against the individual defendants, which is why these comprise the vast bulk of the written judgment. In evaluating the cases against the twenty remaining defendants, the court faced three questions: What had the defendant done? Was it *Mord*? And why had he done it, that is, was he a perpetrator? The first question was, in the first instance, "objective." It was a question of evidence. What had been proven beyond a reasonable doubt about the defendant's actions? In particular, had it been shown that the defendant had participated in homicide? This immediately raised a second question, which was whether this homicide, if demonstrated, constituted *Mord* under German law.

If the court felt that the evidence in fact demonstrated that a given defendant had participated in *Mord*, then the court faced a third question. Had the defendant acted as a perpetrator or an accomplice? The answer to this question was necessarily subjective, depending on whether the defendant had made the criminal motives behind the crime "his own" or whether he had merely aided and abetted a foreign deed. In seventeen cases, the court found the defendants guilty; seven as perpetrators and ten as accomplices (Table 4).

In considering the individual cases, the court briefly recapitulated the biographies of the defendants but was mainly concerned with the charges against them and the evidence pertaining to these. The primary issue here was what could be objectively proven against the defendants. The court went into great detail, describing exactly what the defendant was found to have done, on how many occasions, against how many victims, whether this was done under orders or on the defendant's own initiative, and so on.

Defendants could either be convicted of indirectly participating in killing operations at Auschwitz, most commonly in the form of taking part in

[26] TR, August 19, 1963, 182nd Session, FBI SAP, CD AP357, T12.

TABLE 4. *Charges, final verdicts, and sentences against Auschwitz Trial defendants*

Name	Charges per order to Convene	Verdict	Sentence
Mulka	Accessory to *Mord*	Accessory to *Mord*	14 years
Höcker	Accessory to *Mord*	Accessory to *Mord*	7 years
Boger	*Mord*	*Mord* and accessory to *Mord*	Life + 5 years
Stark	Accessory to *Mord*	*Mord*	10 years' juvenile sentence
Dylewski	*Mord* and accessory to *Mord*	Accessory to *Mord*	5 years
Broad	*Mord* and accessory to *Mord*	Accessory to *Mord*	4 years
Schoberth	Accessory to *Mord*	Acquitted	–
Schlage	Accessory to *Mord*	Accessory to *Mord*	6 years
Hofmann	*Mord*	*Mord*	Life
Kaduk	*Mord*	*Mord*	Life
Baretzki	*Mord*	*Mord* and accessory to *Mord*	Life + 8 years
Breitwieser	Accessory to *Mord*	Acquitted	–
Lucas	Accessory to *Mord*	Accessory to *Mord*	3 years, 3 months
Frank	Accessory to *Mord*	Accessory to *Mord*	7 years
Schatz	Accessory to *Mord*	Acquitted	–
Capesius	*Mord*	Accessory to *Mord*	9 years
Klehr	*Mord*	*Mord* and accessory to *Mord*	Life + 15 years
Scherpe	Accessory to *Mord*	Accessory to *Mord*	$4\frac{1}{2}$ years
Hantl	Accessory to *Mord*	Accessory to *Mord*	$3\frac{1}{2}$ years
Bednarek	*Mord*	*Mord*	Life

"selections," either at the ramp or within the camp itself, or they could be convicted of having directly killed inmates themselves, through torture, other forms of physical abuse, so-called injections, or during executions. The evidence supporting these convictions, in turn, could take one of two forms. It could be circumstantial, in the sense of deriving from the defendant's bureaucratic position within the camp, or it could be specific, in the sense of deriving from direct eyewitness testimony implicating the defendant in a given action, sometimes, though not often, supported by documentary evidence.

At the most basic level, the court's evaluation of the evidence was the decisive factor in each case. Without sufficient evidence, there was no case. All three of the defendants who were acquitted were acquitted for lack of evidence.[27] In no case was a defendant acquitted on the basis of the kinds of secondary arguments advanced by the defense in their *Plädoyers*. It is true that the defendant Schoberth was acquitted, despite the fact that the court considered it proven that he had participated in executions in the small crematorium. It had not been proven either that these executions had been illegal or, if they were illegal, that Schoberth had known them to be illegal.[28] In other words, he still was acquitted for lack of evidence, not on the grounds of legal interpretation.

As a rule, none of the defendants was convicted solely on the basis of circumstantial evidence, though it often formed the primary basis for conviction. This was particularly true for those defendants (the two adjutants and the higher ranking medical personnel) charged exclusively with having participated in the genocidal killing of arriving transports, that is, with indirect killing. Thus, for instance, Robert Mulka was convicted of having participated in and having supervised (on at least one occasion) ramp selections. Although the court could not determine whether Mulka had ever directly selected inmates for the gas chambers himself, it did determine that he had been present at such selections. The court stated that it was well known that the camp commandant Höß had regularly supervised Ramp selections personally. "It seems likely, simply on the basis of common experience, that the defendant Mulka, who as adjutant was supposed to be the commandant's closest confidant, accompanied him at least now and then."[29] In addition, as head of the camp motor pool, Mulka had arranged for motor transport to take the sick and weak to the gas chambers for extermination. And on at least one occasion, he had made the bureaucratic arrangements for procuring Zyklon B for the gas chambers. In these last two instances, Mulka's bureaucratic duties came back to haunt him, as his signature was found on documents pertaining to both the motor pool and the procurement of Zyklon B.[30]

However, even in Mulka's case, where the circumstantial evidence was the strongest against any of the defendants, the court also relied extensively on eyewitness testimony. "In so far as the defendant Mulka denies having

---

[27] Rüter et al., eds., *Justiz und NS-Verbrechen*, vol. 21, pp. 745–57.

[28] Ibid., pp. 746–47.

[29] Ibid., pp. 436–37.

[30] Ibid., pp. 431, 440. It is worth pointing out that in these cases, documents provided by the East Block often proved crucial. Sehn, for instance, provided the prosecution with the decisive document with Mulka's signature on it arranging transport for victims going to the gas chambers. So whatever the political calculus behind such cooperation – on either side – the fact remains that this East-West cooperation was often essential for the trial. See Vermerk, Kügler (June 29, 1960), FFStA HA 4 Ks 2/63, Bd. 3, Bl. 424–25.

participated in the killing of so-called RSHA Jews and denies any knowledge of these things and events, his statement is in itself unbelievable, given his position as adjutant, the physical circumstances and the general relationships in the camp. However, it was also contradicted in many points by the evidence."[31] In other words, the mere fact that his position as adjutant rendered his denials implausible was not, in itself, sufficient for the court to reject them. Only the availability of direct eyewitness testimony to the contrary sufficed to refute Mulka's denials decisively.

In particular, the court made use of eyewitness testimony to establish that Mulka had indeed been on the ramp, as was to be expected given his duties as adjutant. It noted that the witness Rudolf Vrba had testified to seeing Mulka at the ramp on numerous occasions.[32] While the court acknowledged the difficulties posed for identification after twenty years, it felt that Vrba had "made an excellent and intelligent impression." In addition, he had had good reason to be observant, since he was planning the escape that would allow him to first inform the world of the mass murders taking place at Auschwitz.[33] Therefore, the court found Vrba's testimony convincing and concluded that Mulka had, in fact, been on the ramp on more than one occasion.

In most cases, the court was even more reliant on eyewitness testimony than in Mulka's case. Indeed, in every instance where a defendant was charged with having directly killed his victims, the sole evidence was eyewitness testimony. Consequently, the single most decisive "objective" factor affecting the court's decision in any given case was how it evaluated the eyewitness testimony against the defendant in question. In his oral verdict, Hofmeyer had conceded that the defense had been right to point to the enormous difficulties posed by relying so heavily on eyewitnesses and that the court had had to evaluate individual testimony with great care. The full extent of this caution emerges in the written judgment.

Two factors in particular were decisive for the court's evaluation of witness reliability. The first was whether a witness's testimony was both internally and externally coherent, that is, whether it contradicted itself or other previously established facts about life and operations in the camp. The witness Erwin Olszówka, for example, claimed to have seen Mulka participate in executions at the Black Wall. However, the court acquitted Mulka on this count because it did not believe Olszówka's testimony to be reliable.

---

[31] Rüter et al., eds., *Justiz und NS-Verbrechen*, vol. 21, p. 435.

[32] Ibid., p. 438. The Rüter edition of the judgment gives only the initials of witnesses and defendants who were acquitted or who, for some other reason, had a legal right to have their privacy protected. Since the names of all the witnesses and defendants have now been published elsewhere and over thirty-five years have passed, this is now superfluous. For Vrba's testimony, see Langbein, *Auschwitz-Prozeß*, p. 198.

[33] Rüter et al., eds., *Justiz und NS-Verbrechen*, vol. 21, p. 438.

He had failed to differentiate sufficiently between his own experiences and mere hearsay, and worse, he was "inclined to exaggerate."[34] Specifically, the court distrusted the witness as the result of other statements he had made against the defendant Boger. Olszówka had claimed to have witnessed the hanging execution of twelve inmates for attempted escape, an action that he attributed to Boger.[35] But the court found this attribution implausible. It rested primarily on the fact that the execution had allegedly taken place immediately after the escape attempt, leaving too little time for an official order for the execution to come from the RSHA in Berlin. Olszówka took this to mean that the Political Section had ordered the hangings on his own authority.

"This conclusion by the witness is not persuasive," remarked the court.[36] It noted that Berlin could have sent a telex very quickly, and the simple fact that the inmates were hanged, rather than being quietly shot, pointed to the likelihood of an order from Berlin. Executions undertaken without higher orders were generally done in secret. The public character of this particular execution thus indicated the likelihood that Berlin had ordered it. Furthermore, another witness had contradicted Olszówka's claim that Boger and Kaduk had beaten and abused the victims during the execution, saying that it had been a Kapo who beat them, thus further undermining Olszówka's reliability as a witness.

Both because Olszówka's testimony in the hanging case contradicted the ordinary practice of the Political Section of simply shooting inmates if there was no order from Berlin and because it did not mesh with other witness testimony, the court found it unreliable. And because Olszówka was unreliable in this instance, the court was strongly disinclined to believe him with regard to his allegations against Mulka, also. Thus the court's sense of bureaucratic history, of how Auschwitz operated on a day-to-day basis, formed one of the central yardsticks by which it measured the reliability of eyewitness testimony, as did agreement between the testimony of different witnesses.

The second major factor that influenced the court's assessment of witness reliability was a witness's emotional demeanor during his or her testimony. One can contrast the court's evaluation of the testimony of Józéf Kret against Stark with that of Dr. Czesław Głowacki against Dylewski in this regard. Of Kret, the court said that he had "made an excellent impression on the court and had testified with great calm, a deep understanding for human weakness and a certain wise composure."[37] The court took Kret's assessment of Stark's character as foundational for its own. By contrast, the court noted that

[34] Ibid., p. 759.
[35] For Olszówka's testimony in this matter, see Langbein, *Auschwitz-Prozeß*, p. 228.
[36] Rüter et al., eds., *Justiz und NS-Verbrechen*, vol. 21, p. 760.
[37] Ibid., p. 506.

Głowacki, who had worked as a *Leichenträger* (corpse carrier), "still suffered a great deal emotionally from those bloody events. They were obviously still on his mind, with all their attendant terrible side-effects, during his testimony."[38] As a result, and because of a degree of hesitancy in identifying the SS men he alleged to have executed victims at the Black Wall, the court chose not to rely on Głowacki's testimony.

So, for the court, only those witnesses who were not visibly shaken by their experiences could be considered reliable. Suffering itself became a disqualifying factor for the witnesses. This, together with the demand for internal and contextual coherence, formed the court's core criterion for evaluating the reliability of witnesses. Strikingly absent from the court's criteria are the kinds of political concerns raised by the defense.[39] It is true that the court found Josef Kral's testimony to be unreliable in part for political reasons. The defense's contention that Kral himself was guilty of murdering the Bandera brothers was not without impact, but it was not the only factor in the court's skepticism.[40] The court also found Kral's testimony dubious for the conventional reasons: that he was overly emotional and that his testimony was internally inconsistent. Thus, the court noted that Kral himself had said that he became physically ill whenever he thought about his time in Auschwitz and that, consequently, he tried not to think about it too often. "For this reason alone," the court asserted, "there is a risk that the witness Kral, who undoubtedly suffered greatly in Auschwitz and suffers greatly still, unconsciously associated experiences with the defendants in his recollections, in which they were in fact not involved."[41]

Furthermore, the court noted, there were inconsistencies in Kral's testimony, as when he testified during the trial to having personally seen Boger shoot the inmate Zdzisław Wróblewski, whereas he had earlier told a comrade that he had merely heard the shot but not seen the execution directly.[42] It turned out, then, that the defense's highly politicized deployment of Ukrainian witnesses to discredit Kral was probably superfluous, as the court would most probably have rejected his testimony anyway. Whether the anti-Kral defense witnesses would have been sufficient to discredit his testimony on their own is impossible to say. In any event, the court clearly strove, in evaluating the witnesses, to minimize its consideration of purely political factors.

Once the court had determined what could be proven against a given defendant, it then had to determine how to "subsume" this activity in legal

[38] Ibid., p. 519.
[39] Indeed, in his oral verdict, Hofmeyer had explicitly rejected such arguments. TR, August 19, 1963, 182nd Session, FBI SAP, CD AP357, T42–44.
[40] Rüter et al., eds., *Justiz und NS-Verbrechen*, vol. 21, p. 531.
[41] Ibid., p. 530.
[42] Ibid., pp. 531–32.

terms. The first issue was whether a given killing constituted *Mord*. The court concurred with the standard legal interpretation and declared that the main perpetrators of the crimes committed in Auschwitz had been Hitler, Himmler, Göring, Heydrich, and others, "whose identity it was not the task of this court to ascertain."[43] They had acted from base motives, in particular, on the basis of racial hatred, which was viewed by the court as "cruel and reprehensible."[44] Furthermore, the court declared that the killings were treacherous and malicious. The court acknowledged that the killings in Auschwitz manipulated the defenselessness and innocence of the victims, and were thus treacherous; it also acknowledged that the killings imposed "particularly severe suffering," both physical and psychological, on the victims, and were thus malicious in the legal sense.[45] In the final analysis, however, the base motives of the main perpetrators remained the decisive factor in the court's determination that most of the homicides committed at Auschwitz were *Mord* and not *Totschlag*.

Once the court had declared that, in fact, all of the killings of which the defendants were convicted constituted *Mord*, it had to determine whether a given defendant had been a perpetrator or an accomplice. Two factors were decisive for the court's decision in this matter: whether the defendant had directly killed the victim himself and whether the court felt it could be demonstrated that he had subjectively affirmed the criminal motives of the main perpetrators. In reality, these are simply two forms of the same question. The fact that, generally, defendants who directly killed their victims were considered to be perpetrators (see Table 5), merely confirmed the BGH's finding that "as a rule, whoever kills by his own hand, is a perpetrator."[46] This had nothing to do with the objective quality of killing, however. Rather, it was simply that directly killing constituted prima facie evidence that the defendant's motivations were "morally objectionable."

This point becomes somewhat clearer when one compares cases where defendants were treated differently by the court for similar crimes, that is, where one was convicted as a perpetrator and another as an accomplice. Wilhelm Boger was convicted as a perpetrator for his role in so-called *Bunkerentleerungen* (emptying the Bunker) and the subsequent execution of the victims. Two factors were decisive for the court's decision in this instance. First, Boger evinced a particular hatred for Polish inmates: "goddamned Polacks," he called them.[47] Second, the court found that Boger had been "particularly zealous" in participating in such killings, which precluded

---

[43] Ibid., p. 442.
[44] Ibid. For racism as a base motive in Nazi cases, see Kerstin Freudiger, *Die Juristische Aufarbeitung von NS-Verbrechen* (Tübingen: Mohr Siebeck, 2002), pp. 140–42.
[45] Rüter et al., eds., *Justiz und NS-Verbrechen*, vol. 21, p. 443.
[46] BGHSt, vol. 18 (1963), p. 87.
[47] Rüter et al., eds., *Justiz und NS-Verbrechen*, vol. 21, p. 488.

TABLE 5. *Perpetratorship by defendant and type of crime.*

Defendant	Selections (both "in-camp" and on the ramp)	Injections	Executions	Exzeßtaten (torture/ abuse)	Gassings
Mulka	Accomplice				
Höcker	Accomplice				
Boger	Accomplice		Perpetrator	Perpetrator	
Stark			Perpetrator		Perpetrator
Dylewski	Accomplice		Accomplice		
Broad	Accomplice		Accomplice		
Schlage			Accomplice		
Hofmann	Perpetrator		Perpetrator	Perpetrator	
Kaduk	Perpetrator			Perpetrator	
Baretzki	Accomplice			Perpetrator	
Lucas	Accomplice				
Frank	Accomplice				
Capesius	Accomplice				
Klehr	Perpetrator	Perpetrator			
Scherpe	Accomplice	Accomplice			
Hantl	Accomplice	Accomplice			
Bednarek				Perpetrator	

any possibility that he had acted merely on the basis of superior orders.[48] The fact that Boger had directly participated in the executions, that is, the fact that he had himself shot a number of inmates in the back of the neck, was merely an indication of this zeal.

By contrast, the defendant Broad, who was likewise convicted of participating in *Bunkerentleerungen* and the subsequent executions, was found to have been an accomplice. Unlike Boger, the court had been unable to prove that Broad had ever personally shot any of the victims or that he had decisively influenced the course of the selections in the Bunker. He had merely been present during the selections and executions, helping to guard the prisoners and preventing any panicked resistance. The court declared: "It cannot be proven that the defendant Broad made the killing of these inmates into his own affair, and therefore acted on the basis of a perpetrator's will. According to our findings, the defendant Broad did not demonstrate any particular zeal. Nor could it be demonstrated that he had been especially eager to take part in the executions or that he exercised decisive influence on the selection of the victims in some other way. Nor does the defendant Broad's general

[48] Ibid., p. 490.

demeanor indicate that he possessed a perpetrator's will."[49] In other words, the fact that Broad had not shot, while Boger had, was taken by the court to indicate objectively that each had had a distinct subjective orientation toward the executions in question.

The centrality of subjective factors becomes even clearer if one examines cases where even this minimal objective difference is lacking. Robert Mulka and Franz Hofmann were both convicted of participating in the liquidation of Jews arriving at Auschwitz, Mulka as an accomplice, Hofmann as a perpetrator. In both cases, the defendants were essentially convicted for having sustained these operations through their presence as high-ranking officers on the ramp and by taking care of the requisite bureaucratic procedures involved in the operation. In neither case could it be proven that the defendants had personally selected the inmates to be killed in the gas chambers. In other words, they were both convicted for their indirect, supervisory contributions to the genocide. Their objective contributions to the killing were substantially identical.

And yet Mulka was declared an accomplice, whereas Hofmann was found to have been a perpetrator (the only defendant convicted as a perpetrator for his role in the ramp selections). The court very nearly convicted Mulka as a perpetrator but, in the end, decided that, in accordance with the principle *in dubio pro reo*, it could not be demonstrated beyond a reasonable doubt that he had internally affirmed the criminal motives of the main perpetrators in the genocidal killing of the Jews.[50] Since Mulka himself had given no reliable indications during the trial regarding his subjective orientation while in Auschwitz, the court was forced to rely on "external circumstances" and his behavior during the extermination actions as indicators.[51] The court pointed out that it was particularly difficult in this trial to determine the issue of perpetratorship, because the original criminal impulse had come from the highest state authorities, and the defendants, like Mulka, had been only a "cog in the total 'extermination machine,' which 'functioned' through the cooperation of numerous people."[52]

Despite these difficulties, the court had to make a final determination. In Mulka's case, what was decisive was his limited ability to control the course of events. By the time the RSHA transports arrived in Auschwitz, the court noted, the fate of the victims' was already sealed. In this, the court agreed with the defense, though it did not go so far as to concur with Laternser that because the victims were predestined to die, the defendants could not be said to have killed them. During the selections themselves, the defendants were left with only "limited room for maneuver"; they "hardly still controlled the

[49] Ibid., p. 545.
[50] Ibid., p. 450.
[51] Ibid., p. 447.
[52] Ibid., pp. 447–48.

events."[53] This was as true for the adjutants as for the other SS men at the ramp, as indicated by the fact that the commandant was himself generally present to supervise the operations.

The court did admit that there were some indications that Mulka may well have been a perpetrator. The court found his decision to volunteer for the Waffen SS in 1941 at the age of forty-six – that is, at an age when such an action was by no means necessary – highly suspicious. By this point, it was obvious to everyone that the SS was deeply implicated in the oppression of the Jews, even if not everyone knew the full extent of this. Anyone who joined the SS had to know that he might be expected to "unreservedly" contribute to the goals of the Nazi leadership, even those that were criminal. Mulka's decision to volunteer for the SS might thus indicate that he had internally approved of these goals. But this could not be determined for certain. The fact that he had been an army officer in World War I but was not allowed to serve as an officer in the Wehrmacht because of his prior criminal conviction might have played a role in his decision to join the SS. After all, he also knew that the Waffen SS served at the front, so it was possible that he was simply motivated by patriotism, itself hardly a "base motive."

Similarly, the fact that Mulka served as adjutant for some time and had in fact been acting adjutant prior to his official promotion to the job meant that he knew that this position entailed participation in criminal activity. The fact that he nonetheless accepted the job might indicate that he internally approved of these crimes. But again this could not be determined for certain. It was possible that Mulka had accepted the promotion on the basis of the "blind obedience" expected of all SS men. This did not, in itself, necessarily indicate that he approved of the killings.[54] "In considering all these factors," the court concluded, "there remains a considerable suspicion that the defendant Mulka, as adjutant, internally affirmed the mass murder of the Jews and supported these quite willingly, and thus acted with a perpetrator's will."[55] But this could not be proven beyond a doubt, and consequently, Mulka could be convicted only as an accomplice.

The case of Franz Hofmann played out quite differently. Like Mulka, Hofmann had been convicted of helping to implement the genocidal mass murder of the Jews. But in his case, the court was convinced that he had "internally affirmed [these killings] and made them into his own affair."[56] As evidence for this, the court cited two factors above all. First, not only had Hofmann been a "fanatical Nazi" who had joined both the party and the SS before Hitler's seizure of power, but, even more significant on the court's view, he had been posted as a guard to Dachau from 1933 and had served

[53] Ibid., p. 448.
[54] Ibid., p. 450.
[55] Ibid.
[56] Ibid., p. 564.

exclusively in concentration camps for the next twelve years.[57] In 1933, the Nazis had accepted only the most eager and reliable "fighters" for concentration camp duty. Second, after his transfer to Auschwitz, particularly when he was made first leader of the protective custody camp at Birkenau in early 1943, he had exercised a considerable degree of agency in the camp. As camp leader, he had been in a position to see that sick inmates were adequately cared for and could have omitted the various "in-camp" selections that he conducted. But he had not. "This clearly indicates that was in full agreement with the race teachings and goals of the Nazi authorities with regard to the Jews arriving on RSHA transports as well and desired their extermination on the basis of his own internal motives."[58]

In the end, the court's final judgment confirmed elements of both the prosecution's and the defense's arguments. The court agreed with the prosecution that the killing operations in Auschwitz had been illegal, whatever their administrative authorization and that, furthermore, these killings had been *Mord*. It also agreed that the vast majority of the defendants had been perfectly aware of the illegality of these measures and had participated anyway, thus making themselves criminally liable. However, the court also disagreed with the prosecution on several key points. In particular, the court agreed with the defense that the defendants had often exercised only very limited agency in the camp and had not been in a position to influence the course of events decisively. While the court did not agree with the defense that this constituted sufficient grounds for acquittal, it was decisive for the court's decision to convict a large number of the defendants only as accomplices. Because the defendants had not controlled the course of events, the possibility that they had simply been aiding a foreign deed could not be ruled out. The court also agreed with the defense that in many instances, the testimony of the eyewitnesses had been an unreliable source of evidence. The court rejected the prosecution's vague contention that the witnesses could be held, as a group, to have given objective and accurate testimony. Instead, it chose to evaluate all of the testimony on a case-by-case basis, rejecting testimony when it seemed inconsistent or emotionally biased and accepting it when it "fitted" the previously established facts and when the witness had seemed cool and sober during the trial.

The court also agreed with the defense in rejecting the prosecution's proposal to apply the doctrine of ideal concurrence to defendants' crimes in Auschwitz.[59] The court declared: "While the mass murder of Jews, which took place over the course of several years, was based on a willed decision and willed statements by Hitler, the total extermination process could not be viewed as a unitary action. German criminal law does not recognize the

[57] Ibid.

[58] Ibid., p. 565.

[59] Werner Renz, "Der erste Frankfurter Auschwitz-Prozess: Völkermord als Strafsache," *1999: Zeitschrift für Sozialgeschichte des 20. und 21. Jahrhunderts* 15 (2000): 22–24.

concept of mass murder."[60] It was true, the court noted, that in principle multiple individual criminal actions, deriving from individual decisions, could sometimes be viewed as a "unitary whole."[61] However, the court insisted that these were actions that derive from "a *single* willed decision – [that are] temporally and spatially closely and immediately related, that blur into one another without clear divisions."[62] According to the court, these conditions did not obtain in the case of the Final Solution. The various actions in diverse European countries, carried out by a plurality of persons, each acting on the basis of an independent decision, the diverse methods of killing, and the long duration of the process all meant that the mass extermination of the Jews could not be regarded as a naturally unitary act. Even discrete elements, such as the gassing of Jews in the crematoria of Auschwitz, "required in every instance a discrete decision and a specific confirmation by the will on the part of the participants."[63] With that, the prosecution's best hope of overcoming what Fritz Bauer had called the legal "dissolution" of the Holocaust into "discrete episodes" was defeated.[64]

Because of the way perpetrators were distinguished from accomplices, the judgment ended up inadvertently privileging atrocity over genocide in its assessment of Auschwitz. That this was inadvertent is apparent from the court's own historical excursus, where torture and other atrocities are clearly subordinated to the camp's exterminatory functions. However, in the consideration of the individual cases, that is, in the bulk of the judgment, these priorities were reversed.

While it is important to note that three defendants (Hofmann, Kaduk, and Stark) were convicted as perpetrators for obeying criminal orders, not for exceeding them or acting on their own initiative, excessive brutality and personal initiative were commonly taken as a strong indicator of a perpetrator's will. In Nazi trials more generally, what were called "excessive acts" became a primary objective indicator of a perpetrator's will. An excessive act, as the name implies, was a criminal act that exceeded the strictly necessary components of the crime. For Nazi crimes, murder alone, even if done for political reasons, was not held to constitute an excessive act in and of itself, since it might have been done simply in compliance with an order, that is, as a "foreign deed." In the case of Nazi trials generally, then, simply killing Jews in a regular and regulated manner did not serve to indicate that the defendant had a perpetrator's will.[65] On the other hand, in cases where the

[60] Rüter et al., eds., *Justiz und NS-Verbrechen*, vol. 21, p. 445.
[61] Ibid.
[62] Ibid.
[63] Ibid.
[64] Fritz Bauer, *Die Humanität der Rechtsordnung: Ausgewählte Schriften*, ed. Irmtrud Wojak and Joachim Perels (Frankfurt: Campus Verlag, 1998), p. 83.
[65] As Friedrich puts it: "In the major Nazi trials, simply operating the conveyor belt of a death factory was held to be a minor infraction; the real criminals were the ruthless tyrants who simply saw in the mass exterminations a suitable environment for their own private

killing was clearly undertaken on the defendant's own initiative or where a degree of cruelty was inflicted on the victims above and beyond that inherent in murdering them, the crime was considered to be an excessive act and served to indicate a perpetrator's will. Torturing someone to death, as can well be imagined, came to be viewed by the German courts as an excessive act *par excellence.*

In the case of Wilhelm Boger, this legal framework meant that his role as the chief torturer in Auschwitz loomed far larger in the final judgment than his participation in genocide. The court held Boger to be far more accountable for torture than genocide. For his participation in at least one selection of an arriving transport, in which at least 1,000 people were gassed, the court convicted Boger as an accomplice. The court wrote: "Since it also could not be determined that Boger was, during his duty on the ramp, particularly eager or brutal or ruthless vis-à-vis Jewish persons, the court could not ascertain his 'perpetrator's will' beyond a reasonable doubt. The possibility could not be excluded that he merely wanted to support and further, if quite willingly, the crimes of the principle perpetrators. His contribution to the killing of at least 1000 persons from a RSHA transport can therefore only be considered aiding and abetting under §49 StGB."[66] On this count, Boger was sentenced to four years in prison.

On the other hand, there were five instances where it could be proven beyond a reasonable doubt that Boger had tortured inmates to death. The court wrote: "The established killings by Boger during 'intensive interrogations' meet the definition of murder. They were savage. Simply being hung on the Boger Swing was painful for the victim. By means of blows from a bullwhip or a club, Boger inflicted extraordinary physical pain on the victim, particularly because he not only delivered blows to the buttocks but to other body parts as well.... From the style and manner in which Boger conducted these so-called intensive interrogations, it can clearly be determined that he could only have inflicted such pain and suffering on his victims out of a cold-hearted, merciless sensibility."[67] For torturing people to death, Boger was convicted as a perpetrator on five counts of *Mord* and sentenced to five life sentences. The disproportion between the number of victims and the severity of the sentences in the two instances is striking and clearly indicates that the weight attached by the court to torture as an indicator of subjective motivation far exceeded that which it gave to genocide.

Although the disparity in the sentences was to an extent mandated by law, one should not make too much of this. Remember that the court was in

---

murderous impulses. Absurdly enough, disciplined, mechanized extermination was rewarded and the pathological killers were punished." Jörg Friedrich, *Die kalte Amnestie: NS-Täter in der Bundesrepublik*, rev. ed. (Munich: Piper, 1994), p. 356.

[66] Rüter et al., eds., *Justiz und NS-Verbrechen*, vol. 21, p. 486.

[67] Ibid., pp. 490–91.

principle free to impose the same sentence on accomplices as on perpetrators. That, like the courts in virtually every other Nazi case, it never once chose to do so is thus highly instructive. Although the court acknowledged the *historical* centrality of genocide in Auschwitz, its *legal* assessment was radically biased toward considering torture and other atrocities as, in a sense, *more criminal.*

In Boger's case, the sheer brutality of his actions leaves little doubt as to his sadistic character, making him actually atypical of many Nazi perpetrators. The defendant Dr. Lucas may be more representative in this regard. Lucas was able to produce a great many witnesses who testified to his decent conduct and generally humane treatment of inmates. Certainly, he never tortured anyone or inflicted any "excessive" suffering on the inmates. Like Boger, however, Lucas also participated in the selection of victims for the gas chambers. Indeed, as a physician, he was far more centrally involved in that process than Boger, since it was the camp's medical personnel who regularly supervised the ramp and hospital selections. In that sense, Lucas was indispensable to the killing operation in a way that Boger was not. Lucas was convicted as an accomplice to murder on four counts, each involving at least 1,000 victims. He received three and a half years in prison. In other words, despite having participated in at least four times as many murders as Boger, Lucas received even less prison time for his role in genocide than Boger did.

What the two cases reveal is that the efficient functioning of the apparatus of murder in Auschwitz did not centrally depend on sadists such as Boger. It could function equally well with the help of "good Germans" such as Lucas. In the final analysis, because subjective motives can never be objectively determined with any certainty, an undue focus on them calls into question the veracity of the entire juridical process. The defense was certainly aware of this fact and tried to use it to their advantage, when they emphasized the "accidental" manner in which their clients had been assigned to Auschwitz. That this tactic failed to win acquittal for the defendants should not distract from the fact that the court often concurred with the defense that the defendants had not evinced a perpetrator's will while in Auschwitz. If the defense generally failed in its primary goal of securing acquittal, it was far more successful in its fall-back tactic of securing conviction only as an accomplice.

In interrogating Boger's motives, the court neglected or suppressed several key questions concerning the broader social and institutional context of Auschwitz, relegating them to a historical excursus that was in many ways disconnected from the court's main purpose. In evaluating the cases against the individual defendants, particularly those, such as Boger, convicted of individual atrocities, it is often almost as if the court had forgotten its own previous examination of the historical context. In particular, because the court only tacitly picked up the prosecution's distinction between an extermination camp and an extermination institution, the court fundamentally missed the connection between working inmates to death and gassing them, both integral elements in the Nazis' larger genocidal project.

However, to integrate the centrality of Nazi genocide into the individual cases and, even more, to acknowledge the role played in it by "ordinary" Germans would have been, in the context of a German court, to give expression to the intimate relation between the present reality of Germany and its past reality at Auschwitz. To express such an intimate relation between past and present openly would have been difficult, to say the least. In this context, it is an open question whether Kaul's efforts to thematize this very issue were not more harmful than beneficial. After all, since his ideological agenda was plain for all to see, there must have been many in West Germany who were unwilling to concede such a close connection to the past precisely because that would have meant admitting that the communists had a point, on this issue at least. It was easier by far – legally, psychologically, and politically – to focus on Wilhelm Boger's whips, his "swing," his brutal but foreign physiognomy. In adhering to the letter of the law, with its intense subjective focus, the Auschwitz court unintentionally but also unavoidably engendered a degree of historical distortion: the repression of the centrality of genocide to the Nazi past and the substitution of a more conventional image of sadism and barbarism.

9

Public Reaction

The Frankfurt Auschwitz Trial presented a complicated, polyvalent, and contested narrative of what would come to be known as the Holocaust, one that proved in many ways inadequate to the historical reality of that event. It remains to be seen what impact this had on the West German public sphere.[1] Obviously, judges are not historians.[2] Nor are lawyers or even witnesses. Nor can such legal actors be expected to supplant teachers, academics, or public intellectuals when it comes to educating the public about the past. And yet very clearly many hoped the Auschwitz Trial would serve precisely that role. There are those who argue that in the aftermath of mass atrocity, only trials can properly serve a public pedagogical function, because under such circumstances, the need to learn cannot be separated from the need for justice.[3] Clearly, Fritz Bauer was not alone among the Auschwitz Trial participants in actively striving to ensure that the trial played such a pedagogical role. In their own ways, Henry Ormond, Friedrich Karl Kaul, and even Hans Laternser wanted the trial to be about more than simply the defendants. For them, the Auschwitz Trial was about the *past in relation to the present*, it was about the history of politics and the politics of history. Even those most vehemently opposed to the notion that trials could or should serve such ulterior purposes, Hans Hofmeyer foremost among them, were forced to concede that in this case at least, the trial could not be kept firmly within the boundaries of the courtroom.

---

[1] In general, see Devin O. Pendas, " 'I didn't know what Auschwitz was': The Frankfurt Auschwitz Trial and the German Press, 1963–1965," *Yale Journal of Law and the Humanities* 12 (Summer 2000): 101–50.

[2] See Carlo Ginzburg, *The Judge and the Historian: Marginal Notes on a Late-Twentieth-Century Miscarriage of Justice* (London: Verso, 1999), and Norbert Frei, Dirk van Laak, and Michael Stolleis, eds., *Geschichte vor Gericht: Historiker, Richter und die Suche nach Gerechtigkeit* (Munich: C. H. Beck, 2000).

[3] See Mark Osiel, *Mass Atrocity, Collective Memory and the Law* (New Brunswick: Transaction, 1997).

Whatever else it was, then, the Auschwitz Trial was a public history lesson. While it would be anachronistic to expect the trial to have articulated an
interpretation of the Nazi past, the Holocaust in particular, that went beyond
the state of historical knowledge at the time, it is not unreasonable to examine how the West German public reacted to the Auschwitz Trial in order to
understand better its public pedagogical role in 1960s West Germany.[4] This
is all the more true given that the Auschwitz Trial did not merely articulate existing historical knowledge about the Nazi past; it quite deliberately
expanded it.

So what kind of history did the public learn from the trial? Writing at
the very beginning of the Frankfurt Auschwitz Trial, the novelist, critic,
and cultural gadfly Erich Kuby worried that the trial would encounter little
more than "inner resistance" among the general population. "Nothing can
be changed about that," he wrote. "Social reality is the way it is and it
would be utopian to expect that the public would not seek to repress this
trial just like it represses everything uncomfortable to it."[5] Therefore, he
continued, if the trial was to have any lasting significance at all, it would
have to serve as a form of moral pedagogy. It would have to make use of
whatever temporary interest it might attract to teach a lesson to the German
people about their responsibility for Auschwitz. "You didn't just say yes to
this. In your overwhelming majority, you participated."[6]

In a similar vein, the novelist and playwright Martin Walser, writing in
the first issue of Hans Magnus Enzensberger's seminal journal *Kursbuch*,
argued that the true significance of the trial lay not in the judicial proceedings
but in "the education [*Aufklärung*] of a population, which obviously could
not be brought to recognize what had happened in any other way."[7] The
problem, according to Walser, was that the nature of the *Aufklärung* being
offered was inadequate. The detailed, often almost voyeuristic recounting of
atrocity stories in the press allowed the public to distance themselves from
what had happened and, perhaps more significantly, from the perpetrators
of these atrocities; it all came to appear as "hideousness as such, as pure

[4] The term "Holocaust" was first used with regard to the Nazi genocide of the Jews in the late
1950s and early 1960s, though initially primarily by Jewish scholars. See Ian Kershaw, *The
Nazi Dictatorship: Problems and Perspectives of Interpretation*, 4th ed. (London: Arnold,
2000), p. 93. It gained widespread usage in Germany in the late 1970s, especially after the
screening of the American miniseries *Holocaust* in 1979.
[5] Erich Kuby, "Auschwitz und die bundesdeutsche Gegenwart," in Ulrich Schneider, ed.,
Auschwitz – Ein Prozeß. Geschichte-Fragen-Wirkungen (Cologne: PapyRossa Verlag, 1994),
p. 7. The article was initially published in the Hamburg student magazine *konkrete*
in 1963.
[6] Ibid., p. 9.
[7] Martin Walser, "Unser Auschwitz" *Kursbuch* 1 (June 1965): 189. This was an expanded
version of an essay first published in the Frankfurt *Abendpost*: Martin Walser, "Die Teufel
von Auschwitz waren eher arme Teufel," *Abendpost*, March 13/14, 1965.

brutality."[8] A psychological dynamic developed in which Germans were simultaneously repelled and fascinated by the brutality on display. Walser feared that, detached from any historical context, this fascination would prove short-lived at best: "And because neither Höß, nor Heydrich, nor Himmler, nor some racial ideologue or IG-Farben general director sits on the dock, it would still be conceivable for the Auschwitz Trial to become a monstrous jumble of murder trials for us; that would involve us merely as consumers of shrill headlines. And these are forgotten as soon as they are replaced by new headlines."[9]

If this trial and others like it went no further than awakening a fleeting fascination with brutality, if no political consequences were drawn from it, contemporary Germans would be able to maintain a comfortable distance from what had happened, as if they had not been responsible for it. "Our" culpability as "co-liable" (*Mitgewisser*), as part of the historical context that generated such brutality, would be all the more effectively hidden by our fascination with that brutality as such.

Both of these essays highlight the concern among contemporary Germans with the extra-juridical significance of the Auschwitz Trial, its status as a public event. All of the lightning and thunder generated during the trial, the shrill, tragi-comic battles between Laternser and Kaul, Judge Hofmeyer's dignified yet somehow merciless cross-examination of the witnesses, the brutal struggle between memory and legality, even the war of maneuver concerning the place of Nazi trials in the Cold War context – all of these conflicts would have had only a parochial significance had the trial remained an isolated juridical event, one whose significance exhausted itself in the conduct of the trial *as such*, in the conviction of certain defendants and the acquittal of others; in short, had the trial been merely a *trial*, its internal battles would not have amounted to much – except of course for the defendants.

Instead, much of the significance of the Frankfurt Auschwitz Trial arose from its public reception, from the fact that it proved to be very much more than simply a trial. It was a cultural watershed. It was both a focal point and a wellspring for the politics of memory in the Federal Republic. The Auschwitz Trial would have remained simply one more German Nazi trial in the long line of such trials were it not for the enormous public attention it attracted. Like the Eichmann trial two years previously and the TV miniseries *Holocaust* a decade later, the Auschwitz Trial served to crystallize a specific set of public images of Nazism, the Holocaust, and, by extension, the German present. The fascination with the Auschwitz Trial was translated into a variety of discourses that continued to provide the cultural vocabulary of Holocaust remembrance in the Federal Republic until at least the late 1970s, and in some cases well beyond. And what is more, unlike other forms

---

[8] Walser, "Unser Auschwitz," p. 192.
[9] Ibid., p. 195.

of cultural memory, the Auschwitz Trial placed the issue of justice squarely at center stage. It claimed not simply to memorialize Auschwitz but to render justice on it. The public reaction to the Auschwitz Trial was thus a reaction to both the "truth" of Auschwitz and to the "guilt" of Auschwitz as well.

But what was the exact character of this public reaction? Did the Auschwitz Trial encounter the kind of inner resistance Kuby feared? Was it as pedagogically questionable as Walser claimed? Or ought one to claim, as Hermann Langbein did some months later, that "these court proceedings also have a fundamental significance for political education"?[10] Was it, as Ian Buruma has claimed, "the one history lesson...that stuck"?[11] What, if anything, did Germans learn from the Auschwitz Trial, and did they feel that justice had been done?

In fact, all contrary claims aside, the public reaction to the Auschwitz Trial can best be characterized as ambivalent. On the one hand, much of the general public reacted to the trial with discernible hostility, while, on the other hand, the trial itself exercised a clear fascination for the German public sphere. Günther Leicher captured something of this ambivalence reporting on the trial's opening day for the *Allgemeine Zeitung/Neuer Mainzer Anzeige*: "A huge mass of journalists, photographers and camera people from all over the world and half-empty seats in the visitors' gallery: these are the contradictory emblems of the public interest in the Auschwitz Trial...."[12]

The Public Reaction to the Auschwitz Trial

The Frankfurt Auschwitz Trial proved to be one of the genuine media sensations of the 1960s in the Federal Republic. In the national press alone (*Die Welt, Frankfurter Allgemeine Zeitung, Frankfurter Rundschau,* and *Süddeutsche Zeitung*) there were 933 articles about the trial between November 1963 and September 1965.[13] Almost every newspaper in the Federal Republic – including most of the local press – carried at least sporadic reports on the trial.[14] In terms of published opinion, then, the Frankfurt Auschwitz Trial would have been a virtually inescapable topic in Germany in the years 1963–65.

There were two significant concerns that emerged among West German intellectuals regarding the public reaction to the Auschwitz Trial, expressed

[10] Herman Langbein, "Stimmen der Bevölkerung zum Auschwitzprozeß: Protokoll eines Referates," *Hessische Blätter für Volksbildung* 16 (1966): 323.
[11] Ian Buruma, *The Wages of Guilt: Memories of War in Germany and Japan* (New York: Farrar, Straus and Giroux, 1994), p. 149.
[12] Günther Leicher, "Auschwitz Prozeß vor halbleeren Zuschauerbänken," *Allgemeine Zeitung/Neuer Mainzer Anzeiger,* December 21, 1963.
[13] Jürgen Wilke et al., *Holocaust und NS-Prozesse: Die Presseberichterstattung in Israel und Deutschland zwischen Aneignung und Abwehr* (Cologne: Böhlau Verlag, 1995), p. 53.
[14] My own data base includes over 1,400 articles about the trial from 85 German periodicals.

by Kuby and Walser, respectively. The first was that the trial would simply be ignored by the public, a victim of massive "inner resistance." The second was that even those people who did pay attention to the trial would simply learn the wrong lessons from it, in other words, that the trial would be a pedagogical failure.

To begin at the broadest level: Was there significant "inner resistance" among the German population to this trial? A great many contemporary observers clearly felt that there was. This impression is largely borne out by the available survey data. A *DIVO-Institut* survey revealed in June 1964 that 40 percent of those surveyed had not followed the Auschwitz Trial in any of the media (press, radio, or TV).[15] This may indicate at least significant indifference to the trial, particularly when contrasted with the 95 percent of Germans who had followed the Eichmann Trial two years earlier.[16] However, another survey a month later, this one conducted by the *Institut für angewandte Sozialwissenschaft* (*Institute for Applied Social Sciences*), indicated that 83 percent of Germans had heard of the Auschwitz Trial and 42 percent were able to specify that it was taking place in Frankfurt.[17] This approaches the Eichmann Trial in resonance: 87 percent of Germans had heard of the Eichmann Trial and 46 percent had known it was in Israel.[18]

There is also some survey data on the public stance toward Nazi trials in general. At the beginning of 1965, a survey by the Allensbach-based *Institut für Demoskopie* (*Public Opinion Research Center*) found that 57 percent of the German population opposed any *further* Nazi trials.[19] Of course this does not necessarily mean that they were opposed to the Auschwitz Trial in particular, although this might be a plausible inference. More significant, perhaps, is the fact that 1965 represented a high point of opposition to Nazi trials. Thus, in 1958 only 34 percent of the public had opposed further trials, while by 1966 the number of people opposed had again dropped to 44 percent.[20] This means that 1965 was the only year for which data is

[15] Regina Schmidt and Egon Becker, *Reaktionen auf politische Vorgänge: Drei Meinungsstudien aus der Bundesrepublik*, Frankfurter Beiträge zur Soziologie, vol. 19, with a preface by T. W. Adorno and L. v. Friedenburg (Frankfurt: Europäische Verlagsanstalt, 1967), p. 111. The Deutsche Institut für Volksumfragen (German Institute for Public Surveys) was founded by the Americans after World War II to conduct public opinion research in their occupation zone and later became the official government survey organization.

[16] Ibid., p. 108.

[17] *Die Welt*, July 9, 1964.

[18] Ibid.

[19] Institut für Demoskopie, *Verjährung von NS-Verbrechen. Ergebnisse einer Schnellumfrage* (Allensbach am Bodensee: Institut für Demoskopie, 1965). Cited in Ulrich Kröger, "Die Ahndung von NS-Verbrechen vor Westdeutschen Gerichte und ihre Rezeption in der deutschen Öffentlichkeit 1958 bis 1965 unter besonderer Berücksichtigung von 'Spiegel,' 'Stern,' 'Zeit,' 'SZ,' 'FAZ,' 'Welt,' 'Bild,' 'Hamburger Abendblatt,' 'NZ' und 'Neuem Deutschland,' (Ph.D. diss., University of Hamburg, 1973), p. 276.

[20] Kröger, "NS-Verbrechen und Öffentlichkeit," p. 277.

available in which a *majority* of Germans opposed further Nazi trials. The June 1964 *DIVO-Institut* survey confirms this trend, though it gives much lower total figures for the opposition to Nazi trials than the Allensbach survey. The *DIVO-Institut* survey indicates that in 1961, only 15 percent of those who were aware of the Eichmann trial felt it would be better not to have Nazi trials at all, while in 1964, 39 percent of those who had heard of the Auschwitz Trial were opposed to such trials.[21] The discrepancy between these two surveys can in part be accounted for by the fact that, since any ignorance of the Auschwitz Trial must have been somewhat willful in the face of the ubiquitous media coverage, those who were *aware* of the trial were also the people more likely to support such trials as well. One can assume that among those who had not even heard of the Auschwitz Trial, the number disapproving of Nazi trials was in general higher.

Of those who had heard of the Auschwitz Trial, just over half (53%) approved of it, "in order that the German public be made aware of the horrors and suffering caused by Germans, and in order that the guilty parties be judged and punished."[22] Of those opposed to the trial, the highest percentage (45%) fell into the thirty-five- to fifty-four-year-old age group, that is, among people who had largely come of age under the Third Reich. These were not the people who had voted for Hitler, but they were the people who had fought for him. "As an argument, they said that the trial damaged our reputation abroad; it was all just a waste of money; it was time to finally be done with all this."[23]

Much of the heightened unpopularity of Nazi trials in 1964–65 can probably be accounted for by the large-scale debate on whether or not to extend the statute of limitations for Nazi crimes that was raging at the time.[24] This debate was explicitly concerned with the desirability of continuing such trials, rather than the validity of previous and/or ongoing trials. The wording of these survey questions – should such trials continue? – was clearly intended to evoke a response conditioned more by this debate than any specific trial. Nonetheless, it seems fair to say that at the very least the Auschwitz Trial did not have sufficient impact to convince a majority of Germans that such trials should be continued.

This impression is confirmed anecdotally by the statement made by the Federal Justice Minister Ewald Bucher (FDP), in an interview with *Der Spiegel* magazine in 1965. Arguing against the extension of the statute of

---

[21] FAZ, August 14, 1964.
[22] Ibid.
[23] FR, August 14, 1964.
[24] For the relationship between the Auschwitz Trial and the debate over the statute of limitations, see Marc von Miquel, " 'Wir müssen mit den Mördern zusammenleben!': NS-Prozesse und politische Öffentlichkeit in den sechziger Jahren," in Irmtrud Wojak, ed., *Gerichtstag halten über uns selbst ...": Geschichte und Wirkung des ersten Frankfurter Auschwitz-Prozesses* (Frankfurt: Campus Verlag, 2001), pp. 97–116.

limitations for Nazi crimes, and thus for the cessation of new Nazi prosecutions after 1965, Bucher said that adhering to the rule of law meant that "it is our fate to have to live with men like Kaduk too."[25] Similarly, in November 1964, the *Neue Rhein und Ruhr Zeitung* reported that the federal government opposed extending the statute of limitations because such an extension would violate the rule of law and itself constitute a "Lex Auschwitz."[26] In this regard, whatever impact the Auschwitz Trial had on the German public sphere, a substantial portion of the German public, and a number of high-ranking public officials as well, in fact used the trial to argue against holding further trials like it.[27]

Two conclusions emerge from the polling data. First, the polls all indicate that a large proportion of the population did not follow the trial at all closely (e.g., only 42% were able to even name the *city* in which the trial was being held). Second, a substantial minority of even those who did follow the trial remained hostile to it and similar trials. On this basis, it seems fair to say that there was indeed significant "inner resistance" to Nazi trials in general and to the Auschwitz Trial in particular, however difficult it is to measure this hostility with any precision.

This inner resistance is confirmed by more impressionistic accounts in the press. For example, near the end of the trial, one journalist asked fifty acquaintances to name one of the defendants in the trial; forty-five could not. Of the five who could, only the name of Wilhelm Boger, the notorious torturer, came to mind. And while thirty-eight of the fifty people asked were able to situate Auschwitz in Poland, almost none of them was able to state with any accuracy the number of victims estimated to have been killed there. Most spoke of several thousands, and one Bundeswehr soldier thought the victims numbered merely in the hundreds. The journalist concludes this rather sorry summary by noting with a certain bitterness that "the indictment charges 400,000 cases of murder. According to other sources, 2.5 of the 6 million Jewish victims of the Final Solution met their end in Auschwitz."[28]

Other journalists were able to find an equally bitter humor in the ignorance of so many Germans regarding the Auschwitz Trial. *Die Zeit*, for example, conducted a series of "man-on-the-street" interviews to asses what the residents of Frankfurt knew about the trial taking place in their midst.

[25] *Der Spiegel* 19 (1965): 23.
[26] Hans-Peter Moehl, "Bonn gegen Lex Auschwitz," *Neue Rhein und Ruhr Zeitung*, November 18, 1964.
[27] The opposition to the extension of the statute of limitations ultimately failed, and the Bundestag finally voted to extend the statute of limitations by setting the starting date not in 1945, as had previously been the case, but in 1949, with the constitution of the Federal Republic proper. The statute of limitations was extended for a further ten years in 1969, and then abolished altogether in 1979.
[28] Werner Diedrichs, "Mulka und die anderen: Drei Fragen vor dem Urteil im Auschwitz-Prozeß," *Ruhr-Nachrichten*, August 19, 1965.

Unsurprisingly, given the polling data, the answer was that they knew very little, and a series of awkward, embarrassing encounters ensued. For instance, the reporter asked an off-duty police officer for directions to some location in Frankfurt. The answer he received was "thorough and friendly." The reporter then asked the police officer how to find Messrs. Mulka, Klehr, and Kaduk. The officer responded that he did not know, but that if the reporter would simply ask at the Residency Registration Office (*Einwohnermeldeamt*), he could certainly get their addresses. But the reporter already knew their address. "The three men 'live' in Hammelsgasse, in the county jail." The officer "smiles... knowingly: 'Then they're in lock-up.'" The officer explained that if one wanted to visit someone in detention, it was necessary to get an official visitor's permit. The officer then asked what the charges against the three men were. "'Two of them allegedly killed several thousand people each and one of them is charged with accessory to mass murder.' Then, finally, it dawns on him: 'They're the defendants in the Auschwitz Trial. Naturally, it didn't occur to me....'"[29]

Whether with bitter regret or bitter irony, both of these reports indicate not only that ignorance of the Auschwitz Trial was widespread, but also that journalists themselves sensed a disconnect between their own fascination with the trial and the indifference or hostility of their readership, and it worried them. As one observer put it, "At the moment Nazi crimes are commanding considerable public attention in the form of the Auschwitz Trial. But it is unfortunately unclear whether they are receiving as much public as press attention."[30] More troubling still for reporters than even public apathy was the overt hostility emanating from at least some of their readers. "Damn it!" wrote one reader to the Frankfurt *Abendpost*, "give it a rest with your reporting about Auschwitz already. Do you seriously think that you can convince the world that you are interested in the truth? No, you and your dear compatriots are only interested in cheap thrills."[31]

A tone of superiority and contempt is palpable among journalists commenting on popular reactions to the trial, but so is a certain sense of futility. In the face of such inexcusable ignorance, what is to be done? This disconnect between the press and the "public" is the crux of the paradoxical public reaction to the Auschwitz Trial.

Emmi Bonhoeffer, widow of the martyred pastor Dietrich Bonhoeffer and one of the more astute observers of the trial, remarked in a letter to her friend Reche Jásli, "Naturally the Auschwitz Trial is unpopular. This makes it all the more peculiar that almost the entire press corps provides daily coverage,

[29] Horst Hachmann, "'Kennen Sie Wilhelm Boger?': Was Frankfurter über den Auschwitz-Prozeß wissen – Die traurige Bilanz einer Umfrage," *Die Zeit*, April 23, 1965.
[30] Günther Schultz, "Blick in die Zeit," *Monatsschrift für deutsches Recht* 19 (1964): 470.
[31] Gregor Splitt, "Nervenkitzel," *Abendpost*, December 22, 1964.

if not always very thoroughly. They write stories that nobody actually wants to read, certainly not those most in need of it."[32] The main reason the trial was so unpopular, according to Bonhoeffer, was that people worried that the trial might implicate them as well, directly or indirectly, legally or morally and thus disturb their "peace." As the theologian Helmut Gollwitzer put it, the trials put many Germans "in the same boat as the defendants," and thus people wanted to see an end to them, "for the sake of a quiet conscience."[33]

Similar observations can be found throughout the press coverage of the trial as well. For instance, Reiner Dederichs, reporting for the *Kölner Stadt-Anzeiger*, noted that there was a popular distaste for the trial, which was inexplicable simply in terms of the long time span between the trial and the events being judged. After all, he pointed out, no one protests that a child killer should be treated more leniently simply because his trial occurs shortly before the statute of limitations takes effect. Rather, he explained, people disliked such trials due to a "great unease," an unease at their own lack of opposition to the Nazis, their own uncertainty at how they might have behaved in Auschwitz, at the effortlessness with which the defendants had reintegrated into postwar German society.[34]

Such contemporary accounts of the "inner resistance" to the Auschwitz Trial share with more broadly psychoanalytic accounts of the politics of memory in West Germany what might be termed a repression hypothesis. This hypothesis, most famously articulated by Alexander and Margarete Mitscherlich in their 1967 book, *The Inability to Mourn*, holds that Germans, unable to confront their guilt after the war, repressed it instead.[35] In the classic Freudian manner, this repressed sense of guilt manifested itself in neurotic symptoms, in particular in a deformed political culture that adhered to the *forms* of democracy without truly internalizing democratic values.[36] The source of these neurotic symptoms, on such an account, is in effect an enduring social-psychological disposition rooted

---

[32] Emmi Bonhoeffer, *Zeugen im Auschwitz-Prozeß: Begegnungen und Gedanken* (Wuppertal-Barmen: Johannes Kiefel Verlag, 1965), p. 15.

[33] Helmut Gollwitzer, "Gleitwort," in ibid., p. 7.

[34] Reiner Dederichs, "Das große Unbehagen," *Kölner Stadt-Anzeiger*, March 10, 1964.

[35] Alexander Mitscherlish and Margarete Mitscherlich, *Die Unfähigkeit zu trauern: Grundlagen kollektiven Verhaltens* (München: Piper Verlag, 1967).

[36] In addition to the Mitscherlichs' work, see Ralph Giordano, *Die zweite Schuld oder Von der Last Deutscher zu sein* (Hamburg: Rasch und Röhring, 1987); Heinz Bude, *Bilanz der Nachfolge: Die Bundesrepublik und der Nationalsozialismus* (Frankfurt: Suhrkamp, 1992); Nadine Hauer, *Die Mitläufer, oder die Unfähigkeit zu fragen: Auswirkungen des National-sozialismus für die Demokratie von Heute* (Opladen: Leske & Budrich, 1994); and Gesine Schwan, *Politik und Schuld: Die zerstörerische Macht des Schweigens* (Frankfurt: Fischer Verlag, 1997).

in the experience of the Third Reich. Even those psychologists who trace the transmission of this neurotic complex to the "second generation" do so via the socialization process within families, such that the experience of the Third Reich remains a form of "original traumatism."[37] In other words, external events, such as the Auschwitz Trial, may occasion, but they cannot properly be said to cause, a neurotic defensive reaction.

Clearly, Germans have evinced a complex mix of fascination and denial with regard to the Nazi past that bears more than a passing resemblance to neurotic symptoms as described by psychoanalysis. Yet there is a historical specificity to the German reaction to the Auschwitz Trial that cannot quite be accounted for on the basis of a general, and hence historically undifferentiated, defensive reaction. In particular, given that 1965 represents a kind of "spike" in the unpopularity of Nazi trials, these defensive reactions clearly vary over time. Events matter for social psychology.

Furthermore, if public opinion theorists such as Walter Lippmann and Elisabeth Noelle-Neumann are at all correct that public opinion is largely created by the mass media, if it is comprised of what is and can be said publicly, then the public's ambivalence to the Auschwitz Trial must be accounted for in terms of what was said about it in the press, not just on the basis of extrinsic, enduring social psychological neuroses.[38] In fact, there was a complicated dialectical relationship in which the press's own fascination with the Auschwitz Trial helped to produce the public's ambivalence toward it, while that public ambivalence reinforced a sense among journalists that here above all they were fulfilling their role as democratic truth seekers.[39] The two positions, while perhaps emotionally antagonistic, were mutually reinforcing.

Reportage

The daily press reports on the Auschwitz Trial in both the national and regional press were governed by two imperatives: the hectic pace of daily

---

[37] The phrase is Simon Critchley's. See Simon Critchley, *Ethics-Politics-Subjectivity: Essays on Derrida, Levinas and Contemporary French Thought* (London: Verso, 1999), p. 183. For explicit consideration of the transmission to the second generation, see Anita Eckstaedt, *Nationalsozialismus in der "zweiten Generation": Psychoanalyse von Hörigkeitsverhältnissen* (Frankfurt: Suhrkamp, 1989), and Martin S. Bergmann and Milton E. Jucovy, eds., *Generations of the Holocaust* (New York: Basic Books, 1982).

[38] Walter Lippmann, *Public Opinion* (New York: Free Press, 1997 [1922]), and Elisabeth Noelle-Neumann, *The Spiral of Silence: Public Opinion – Our Social Skin*, 2nd ed. (Chicago: University of Chicago Press, 1993).

[39] On the origins of a self-consciously democratic press in postwar Germany, see Norbert Frei, *Amerikanische Lizenzpolitik und deutsche Pressetradition: Die Geschichte der Nachkriegszeitung Südost-Kurier* (Munich: Oldenbourg, 1986), pp. 7–8. For a more general overview, see also Harold Hurwitz, "Die Pressepolitik der Alliierten," in Harry Pross, ed., *Deutsche Presse seit 1945* (Bern: Scherz, 1965), pp. 27–55.

reporting and the ideology of journalistic objectivity. The former means that the "truth" is always provisional in the daily press, subject to revision tomorrow should events warrant it. The latter means that facts are taken to speak for themselves, that events are to be recalled without being directly interpreted, and that opinion is to be strictly segregated from information. These two imperatives – provisional truth and objectivity – are reconciled by means of a structural amnesia, in which one day's report only rarely makes any reference to the previous day's report. Each edition of the paper is an autonomous entity, a closed hermeneutic circle. This hermeneutic closure was noticeable in the Auschwitz Trial reports, for instance, in the common tendency for reporters to identify a person every time he or she was mentioned in the paper, even if that same person had been in every article for months.

Above all, the coverage of the Auschwitz Trial in the daily press can be characterized by a form of narrative fealty to the event which, in literature, would be referred to as "realism." There is the same general effort to immerse the reader in the occurrences, to "suture" any obvious narrative gaps and to thus foreclose any distantiation of the reader from the story.[40] This manifests itself particularly in two ways. First, there is a marked tendency to make extensive use of direct quotations, and where direct quotations are not used, paraphrases in the "voice" of the trial participants are the rule. Take the following report by the *Frankfurter Allgemeine*'s Bernd Naumann as an example:

The defendant Mulka declares in a haughty manner: "I do not feel implicated by Mr. Grabner's statements and have nothing to say in response."

He answers the questions of civil counsel Ormond in stereotypes and with a contemptuous expression: "That was after my time. –No, I had not received any orders. That was obviously after my time."

"Do you mean to say that during your time there were no public hangings?"

"I did not see any."

The beating of women?

"I can't recall. – I never visited the camp with Himmler."

The number of victims, the camp statistics?

"I know nothing about that."

Because: "As a matter of principle, I will only say what I know or what I became aware of."

He's not bad, this defendant Mulka, in the role of the honorable man.[41]

The reference to role playing at the end is revealing, since the entire exchange is structured very much like a play. Even when Naumann is not quoting, he speaks in the "voice" of the court. The emphasis on dialogue and on conveying character through gesture or expression lends a deliberately

---

[40] On the concept of suture, see Kaja Silverman, *The Subject of Semiotics* (Oxford: Oxford University Press, 1983), pp. 194–236.

[41] Bernd Naumann, "Boger: Keine Antwort – Mulka: Nicht betroffen," FAZ, June 26, 1964.

dramatic flare to the scene. Naumann was a master of this technique, but even less skilled writers in the daily press tried to dramatize the trial in similar ways. Take, for instance, the shouting match between the witness Ludwig Wörl and the defendant Kaduk. On the stand, Wörl testified that he had seen Kaduk drive a group of children into the gas chambers, using a drawn pistol to coerce them. Kaduk shouted denials in the strongest terms and refused to calm down, even when Judge Hofmeyer threatened to have him removed from the courtroom. Horst Hachmann, writing in the *Frankfurter Rundschau*, concluded the scene thus: "The witness however responds matter-of-factly though vehemently: 'Kaduk, you are no longer facing me with a pistol in your hand.' It was impossible to miss the cry from the audience during this heated exchange, 'Just kill him.' "[42]

We have already examined this exchange for what it reveals about the difficult position that witnesses found themselves in during the trial. In this context, what is interesting is the flair for the dramatic in the scene, not simply in the almost clichéd courtroom shouting match but in the highly ambiguous cry of outrage from the audience. The "him" to be killed is by no means clear from the syntax, and the reporter does nothing to clarify the matter. The trial audience here becomes a character in the drama on display for the newspaper audience, and the ambivalent emotions evoked by the scene are left unresolved – to heighten the dramatic tension? Or simply because the reporter can think of no proper resolution? The ideology of objectivity allows the reporter to evade such questions. He is merely reporting what happened. The highly constructed nature of such reports is veiled behind the apparent verisimilitude of "character."

In addition to such theatrical effects, the daily press also deployed what might be considered more novelistic techniques, in particular, atmospheric descriptions designed to set the scene. These served both to convey a kind of "you-are-there" sensibility and to provide the kind of moral commentary that the ideology of objectivity precluded at an explicit level. The *Ruhr-Nachrichten* provides one poignant example: "The witness abruptly interrupts his testimony, as the joyful cries of children playing at a nearby school suddenly intrude. For several seconds, dead silence reigns in the courtroom. But it is as if his final words nonetheless echo through the room: 'As Scherpe stopped and went drinking, Hantl took over and killed the remaining 30 children with phenol injections.' "[43]

Such techniques extended to the "characters" of the trial as well. Reporters tried repeatedly to convey something of their manner, their physiognomy, and ultimately, their personality. Wilhelm Boger's speech patterns, for instance, evoked the following description. "In a Swabian accent, at once

[42] Horst Hachmann, "Schwerer Zusammenstoß beim Auschwitz-Prozeß," FR, April 7, 1964.
[43] Max Karl Feiden, "Die Gefangenen in dem Arrestblock wurden zum Hungertod verurteilt," *Ruhr-Nachrichten*, May 2, 1964. The witness testifying was Dr. Czesław Głowacki.

exuberant and arrogant, his speech bubbles forth with such speed that the presiding judge has to interrupt repeatedly: 'Please speak more slowly, Mr. Boger!' "[44] Finally, even the courtroom itself was pressed into the service of narrative fealty. When the court moved from the Frankfurt City Council Chambers to the Gallus Haus civic center in April 1964, the *Frankfurter Neue Presse* commented: "Without anticipating the verdict, one can say that the defendants, some them charged with the most unbelievable bestiality, have been transferred to appropriate seats: their chairs are no longer fully upholstered but are now harder and narrower."[45]

Thus the daily press, specifically in its efforts to convey an objective sense of the conduct of the trial, tended to make use of the classic rhetorical techniques of realist fiction. One of the consequences of this was that at times, the press reports of the trial came perilously close to the clichés of the "courtroom drama." The cast of characters certainly fit the bill: the barbaric defendants (Boger, Klehr), the honorable defendant (Lucas), the strict but fair judge (Hofmeyer), the grandstanding lawyers (Laternser, Kaul). In some of these cases, the clichés stem as much from the actors as the reports. Laternser and Kaul *were* grandstanding lawyers, very deliberately playing out that role for propagandistic purposes. But in other cases, the tendency to portray *dramatic characters*, rather than real persons, obscured aspects of the trial that might otherwise have been more apparent. For example, the repeated characterization of Hofmeyer as a stern, resourceful, fair judge tended to conceal his sometimes very noticeable lack of sensibility toward the difficulties experienced by survivor witnesses during the trial. The very first witness in the trial, Dr. Otto Wolken, described the terrible condition the inmates in the infirmary were in, who were so stricken and emaciated that even the SS physician in charge was shaken. The *Frankfurter Allgemeine Zeitung* reported the following exchange between Wolken and Hofmeyer:

Wolken had been able to make notes regarding their [the patients'] condition: one, 180 cm tall, weighed 43 kg, an other, 175 cm tall weighed 39.5 kg, another, 180 cm tall, 36.5 kg.

"Well now," opines Presiding Judge Hofmeyer, with knowing resignation, "we don't want to read the entire list individually all the way through."

"Yes," agrees Wolken, and then adds after a short pause and a glance at his notes: "Here is one more, he weighed 28 kg."

"28 kg," repeated Hofmeyer quietly.[46]

Hofmeyer's "knowing resignation" is here portrayed positively, as if the reader too would share in it. It disguises the fact that his use of the phrase

[44] Horst Wolf, " 'Da hielten Deutsche zusammen,' " *Westdeutsche Allgemeine*, December 21, 1963.
[45] "Aufstand der Todeskandidaten," FNP, April 4, 1964.
[46] Bernd Naumann, "Aus dem Katalog der Ungeheuerlichkeiten," FAZ, February 28, 1964.

"well now" implies less a knowing resignation than an exasperated impatience, surely inappropriate under the circumstances.

Similarly, the noticeably strong desire to portray Dr. Lucas as representing the "good German," even in Auschwitz, made his eventual confession to participating in selections all the more shocking and disappointing.[47] He had been cast as a specific character. When it turned out that, in fact, his role was something quite different, the drama itself splintered. "Now the truth is out even for those of us who continue to believe that even among the concentration camp henchmen there were those who to an extent defended humanity."[48]

What might be termed the characterological style in objective newspaper reporting thus entailed both a concern with personality and a tendency to reduce it to monadic types. And in this, a strong homology existed with the juridical emphasis on the subjective disposition of defendants and the assumption of a causal nexus between motivation and action. The court's tendency to privilege atrocity over genocide, the juridical requirement for excessive brutality, the reduction of mass killing to a form of aiding and abetting rather than murder – all of these were reproduced in the characterology of the daily press. The "why" of murder, as a matter of personal character, became the predominant theme, and the historical event of genocide was reduced to the psychodrama of the courtroom suspense thriller.

At the same time, this characterological approach became one of the central vehicles in the daily press coverage for conveying the sense of the trial as a morality tale, with "good guys" and "bad guys" delineated more clearly than perhaps does justice to the actual historical situation in Auschwitz.[49] It is true that there were some exceptions to this rule, such as the reports on certain "ambivalent" characters, mostly so-called *Funktionshäftlinge* who collaborated with the Germans more or less actively.[50] But in the main the dramatic conventions of the press coverage of the trial tended to reduce the moral complexity of Auschwitz. In particular, with regard to the defendants, there was a very marked tendency to simplify the situation, not just in the way in which the most brutal perpetrators were, understandably, demonized to the point where it would be hard to recognize in them any trace of humanity, but in the way in which those few defendants who were not demonized

---

47 Bernd Naumann, "Dr. Lucas – Kamerad und Freund der Häftlinge. Zwei Zeuginen sagen für den Angeklagten aus: Tausende gerettet," FAZ, December 11, 1964; Bernd Naumann, " 'Dr. Lucas war uns eine Stütze': Der angeklagte Arzt wird von vier Zeugen entlastet," FAZ, January 12, 1965.

48 Marcel Schulte, "Die Ehrenmänner," FNP, March 12, 1965.

49 Cf., e.g., Primo Levi's discussion of the "gray zone" in the camps. Primo Levi, *The Drowned and the Saved* (New York: Vintage, 1989), pp. 36–69.

50 In particular, there was the case of Bunker-Jacob, the trustee in Bunker 11, who escorted inmates to executions and allegedly beat some inmates to death himself. See, e.g., "Gericht sucht 'Bunker-Jacob,' " FR, February 13, 1965.

were beatified to a degree that was even less justified. The defendants became devils (Boger) or angels (Lucas), rather than men.

The limited moral insight possible within this characterological approach reveals itself most clearly in the deep puzzlement expressed repeatedly in the press over how such monsters could revert to ordinary citizens after the war. On the one hand, the defendants were repeatedly, almost formulaically, referred to as "monsters," "demons," "devils," "beasts," or "barbarians." The tendency to portray them as the embodiment of pure, metaphysical evil was remarkably widespread in the daily press.[51] Given that these men were not even human, how much less did they have in common with the average reader?

Yet at the same time, the press recognized that these devils were also strikingly ordinary men. Thus, Ursula von Kardorff, writing in the *Süddeutsche Zeitung* noted, "Beneath the judges, next to the police, that must be the defendants. Grey haired men with small mouths and average faces. Is this the way that accomplices to murder look? But why are there women sitting in the row? It takes a while, but then I realize: those are not the defendants, those are the jurors....."[52] But it was precisely this typicality that made the defendants so morally incomprehensible to the press. "As [the defendant Bischoff] sits down again with difficulty, the judges and jurors examine him for a long time. The incomprehension shows in their eyes as well: that these defendants, who today stand before the jury like harmless citizens and honest men [*Biedermänner*], participated in crimes that are among the most terrible in human history."[53] Another report marveled that such "unimaginable horrors" had been perpetrated by such "philistines" (*Spießer*).[54]

The black-and-white logic of character, so typical of both German law and the German press, revealed itself to be incapable of grasping what Hannah Arendt so perceptively labeled the "banality of evil."[55] Indeed, the only solution the press could offer was one of sequence: These men *were* monsters and *became* ordinary citizens after the war. That they might have been ordinary citizens while they were monsters, indeed that the true core of their

---

[51] See, e.g., "Ihr werdet den Teufel kennenlernen," *Neues Deutschland*, August 26, 1964; Bernd Naumann, "'In mir werdet ihr den Teufel kennenlernen,'" FAZ, August 25, 1964; "'Ich bin Capesius – der Teufel,'" FR, August 25, 1964.

[52] Ursula von Kardorff, "Durchschnittsmenschen mit Jargon: Beobachtungen beim Auschwitz-Prozeß," SZ, March 6, 1964.

[53] Max-Karl Feiden, "Angeklagter mit dem guten Gedächtnis schweigt," *Ruhr-Nachrichten*, December 31, 1963.

[54] "2 Millionen Tote von Auschwitz klagen an," *Abendpost*, December 19, 1963.

[55] Hannah Arendt, *Eichmann in Jerusalem: A Report on the Banality of Evil*, rev. ed. (New York: Viking, 1964). Of course, Arendt herself missed this as well with regard to the Auschwitz Trial. See Hannah Arendt, "Introduction," in Bernd Naumann, *Auschwitz: A Report on the Proceedings against Robert Karl Ludwig Mulka and Others before the Court at Frankfurt* (New York: Frederick A. Praeger, 1966), pp. xi–xxx.

monstrosity might lay in their utter ordinariness, could not be fathomed. In this respect, the repeated claims about the typicality of the defendants, their very Germanness, did little to undermine the way they were nonetheless portrayed as nonhuman (and not just inhumane), as an alien species to be gaped at.

The subjectivism of German law abetted this marked proclivity of the daily press to reduce the various trial participants to "characters." Because the law was so heavily interested in the defendants as autonomous agents and willing subjects, the trial itself, even in its objective dimensions, tended to focus on their personalities. The question of "who" dominated the proceedings and the question of "why" was reduced to a common-sense psychology that could not but fail to distract from any answer to the question that was not a matter of personality. In this sense, there was an elective affinity between the German juridical concern for subjective dispositions and the daily press's efforts to create identifiable characters for their drama.

Of course the mainstream daily press, much less more narrowly targeted weekly publications such as the *Allgemeine Wochenzeitung der Juden in Deutschland* (AWJD) or even *Die Zeit* or *Der Spiegel*, was not the primary news source for most Germans in the 1960s.[56] A majority of people, to the extent that they followed the news at all, did so through the boulevard press, that is, illustrated magazines and tabloid newspapers. If a newspaper such as *Die Welt* had a circulation of 251,385 in 1964, a weekly illustrated such as *Quick* had a circulation of 1,486,437 (in 1965), while Axel Springer's daily tabloid, *Bild-Zeitung*, dominated all other periodicals in Germany with a circulation of 4,049,413.[57] Like the English tabloids (and unlike most of their American counterparts, such as the *National Enquirer*), the German boulevard press did not entirely ignore hard news, even if it was often reduced to gossip and "human interest" stories. Political events, foreign affairs, domestic policy debates, and even the Auschwitz Trial found their way into these publications, if in a limited and off-hand manner.

The boulevard press could hardly be said to have been more than sporadically interested in the Auschwitz Trial. Taken altogether, five boulevard

---

[56] It should be noted that while television was making major inroads, the press remained the dominant news medium in Germany through the mid-1960s. In the summer of 1963, only 51% of German households owned a TV set, while 79% of the population read a newspaper daily. Elisabeth Noelle and Erich Peter Neumann, *Jahrbuch der öffentlichen Meinung, 1958–64* (Allensbach: Verlag für Demoskopie, 1965), pp. 107, 93. Nonetheless, for TV coverage of the Auschwitz Trial, see Sabine Horn, "'Jetzt aber zu einem Thema, das uns in dieser Woche alle beschäftigt': Die westdeutsche Fernsehberichterstattung über den Frankfurter Auschwitz-Prozess (1963–1965) und den Düsseldorfer Majdanek-Prozess (1975–1981) – ein Vergleich," *1999: Zeitschrift für Sozialgeschichte des 20. und 21. Jahrhunderts* 17 (2002): 13–43.

[57] For *Die Welt* and *Bild* (both 1964), see Carlos Ossorio-Capella, *Der Zeitungsmarkt in der Bundesrepublik Deutschland* (Frankfurt: Athenäum, 1972), pp. 95, 97. For *Quick*, see Helmut Arndt, *Die Konzentration in der Presse und die Problematik des Verleger-Fernsehens* (Frankfurt: Alfred Metzner Verlag, 1967), p. 28.

publications (*Abendpost, Bild-Zeitung, Der Kurier, Der Mittag,* and *Quick*) published a mere forty-nine articles, twenty-eight of which were in the Frankfurt based *Abendpost,* where the story obviously had a "local angle." The nationally dominant *Bild-Zeitung* published a mere handful of articles about the trial (roughly six).

As always, in its coverage of the Auschwitz Trial, *Bild* kept its language simple, its stories short, and its politics conservative. Most of *Bild's* Auschwitz Trial stories were little more than shorthand summaries of the charges against the defendants.[58] On only one occasion did it discuss witness testimony, and then in the form of a series of one- or two-sentence excerpts from witness statements, almost exclusively focused on the most gruesome atrocity stories to emerge from the trial.[59] Overall, it would have been impossible to "follow" the trial from *Bild's* coverage, either as a trial or as a history lesson.

Furthermore, not only was the coverage in *Bild* superficial, it was also relentlessly trivializing in tenor. Two instances can be taken to exemplify this. In 1961, well before the trial itself officially convened, *Bild* published an article fretting over the retirement of one of Germany's athletic heroes. The Olympic bronze medal–winning yachtsman Rolf Mulka, son of the defendant Robert Mulka, had "sacrificed" his sailing career to aid his father in the preparation of his defense.[60] Mulka *fils* contended vehemently that his father was innocent of any crimes, as evinced by his exoneration in Denazification proceedings. "The trial will discover the truth. Until then, gloomy shadows will continue to darken the sparkle of an athletic career. There is no room anymore for sailing. Rolf Mulka has to lead the [family] firm by himself now, has to earn money. He has already sold property in order to cover initial legal fees." Clearly, on *Bild's* view, the real victim of the trial was Rolf Mulka. To be sure, it does pay lip service to the other side, with the stock phrases about dark shadows, but all of the pathos is on Mulka's side. Here was this glorious star in Germany's athletic pantheon, whose contributions to Germany's success were being hindered by these unfortunate accusations from the past. Of course the trial would find "the truth," but it was a pity that it had to come at the price of sporting success.

This trivializing impulse in *Bild's* coverage of the Auschwitz Trial is further revealed in a cartoon that accompanied the paper's article on the opening day.[61] Located in the center of the article, the cartoon depicts a man sitting in his easy chair in front of a Christmas tree, smoking a cigar (possibly in

[58] Gottfried Schemm, "Der Prozeß gegen die Massenmörder," *Bild,* December 20, 1963; Rudolf Winkler, "Nach 15 Tagen Gerichtsverhandlung: Nur 2 von 22 Angeklagten gaben ihre Verbrechen zu," *Bild,* February 10, 1964.
[59] Kurt Dittrich, " 'Der Hungertod dauert 15 Tage': 1 Jahr Auschwitz-Prozeß," *Bild,* December 11, 1964.
[60] Wolfgang Juckel, "Warum startet Deutschlands erfolgreichster Segler nicht mehr? Schwarze Schatten um Mulka," *Bild am Sonntag,* November 5, 1961.
[61] Schemm, "Prozeß gegen die Massenmörder."

reference to Chancellor Erhard, well known for his love of cigars). Out-side the window, literally whirling up from the ground like a tornado, is a dark figure in an SS uniform, labeled Auschwitz. The figure is reaching through the window to tap the contented Bürger on the shoulder. While at first glance, this cartoon might seem to be a warning against German com-placency regarding the past, such an interpretation is belied by the following statement from the article itself: "The 22 defendants on trial today were the closest helpers of that uncanny death machine which terrified an entire world, including us Germans once we found out about it after the war." Clearly, then, here the Nazi past is not something for which the Germans themselves are responsible, but rather a kind of natural disaster, like a tor-nado, something literally from outside the comfortable, Christian (hence, the Christmas tree), and undeniably German home.

A final note should be made regarding the press coverage of the Auschwitz Trial, which is that the centrality of the Jewish dimension of the mass murder at Auschwitz did not emerge with any great clarity. While terms such as "Judeocide" would be coined only much later to try to highlight the profound anti-Semitism of Nazi mass murder, the Auschwitz Trial itself provided all of the evidentiary resources necessary to grasp this, had any one at the time known to look for it.[62] It was not that Jews were never mentioned as Nazi victims in the daily press. They were. Rather, it was the particular place of Jews in the constellation of Nazi victims that was largely unrecognized. In general, Jews appeared as part of a more encompassing list of Nazi victims. More frequently even than that, only vague, quasi-anonymous terms such as "victim" or, most frequently of all, "inmate" (*Häftling*) were used to describe the persons killed at Auschwitz. In this, the press reiterated and amplified the trial's own internal tendencies. By de-emphasizing the witnesses' own experiences, it had also de-emphasized the Jewishness of the majority of the victims. Indeed, the cruelest irony of Auschwitz is, as Primo Levi noted, that it silenced its primary victims forever.[63] The press, in reporting faithfully the distorted image of the victims that emerged in the trial, merely replicated this aporia.

The press exacerbated this tendency, as can be most clearly seen in what reporters chose to leave out of their accounts. On January 9, for instance, the court questioned Mulka regarding the facts of the case. The Frankfurt *Abend-post* reported the scene thus: "The 68-year-old defendant Robert Mulka tilted his small, silver-haired head, as if he could not quite understand Presid-ing Judge Hofmeyer's question. 'Did you know that there were gas chambers, that people were killed there?' Mulka, the former adjutant for the Auschwitz extermination camp, reflected for several seconds before answering in a low

---

[62] Arno J. Mayer, *Why Did the Heavens Not Darken? The "Final Solution" in History* (New York: Pantheon, 1988), p. 3.

[63] Levi, *Drowned and the Saved*, pp. 83–84.

voice: 'I heard about them, but I never saw them personally.' During the tumult that broke out among the other twenty-one defendants, as some of them of them indicated their disbelief with their hands. . . . Mulka added, 'At night, one could see that something terrible was happening. I saw the pyres burning.'"[64]

The *Abendpost*, along with eight of thirteen other dailies reporting on the incident, made no mention of the following statement: "Previously, Presiding Judge Hofmeyer had backed Mulka into the corner with the question, what exactly he had thought about the delivery of Jews to the camp. Mulka explained with sweeping hand gestures that, in the Third Reich, the Jews were viewed as enemies of the state, and were therefore placed into concentration camps. 'One wanted to free the Third Reich from the Jews.'"[65]

If any publication could be expected to represent the Jewish position on the Frankfurt Auschwitz Trial, it would be the *Allgemeine Wochenzeitung der Juden in Deutschland* (AWJD). Although the paper's relations with the Central Council of Jews in Germany were complicated, the AWJD was the primary postwar German publication aimed explicitly and self-consciously at the Jewish community and comes as close as anything to having been the official voice of German Jews.[66] Not surprisingly, the AWJD provided more extensive coverage of the trial (forty-four articles) than any other weekly publication in Germany (e.g., seventeen articles in *Die Zeit*, nine articles in *Der Spiegel*, and thirty-six articles in the far-right *Deutsche National-Zeitung und Soldaten-Zeitung*). Clearly, the Jewish community took an active interest in the trial.

However, it would be a mistake to take this greater level of coverage as indicating that German Jews necessarily saw this trial as the proper forum for expressing *their* understanding of Nazism or its legacy for contemporary Germany. Of the AWJD's forty-four articles, thirty-six consisted of unsigned summary accounts of that week's trial events, very much in the "objective" style of the daily press. Given the constraints of a weekly paper, these were much less thorough than the coverage provided by the major dailies. More

---

[64] Paul Mevissen, "Der Adjutant des Teufels," *Abendpost*, January 10, 1964. Technically, the *Abendpost* is a boulevard paper, but its coverage of the trial was actually relatively extensive and conformed to the generic character of the rest of the daily press.

[65] "Keiner fühlt sich schuldig," AWJD, January 17, 1964. Two other papers reported this comment verbatim: "Mulka verwickelte sich in viele Widersprüche," *Neue Rhein und Ruhr Zeitung*, January 10, 1964, and Bernd Naumann, "Der ehemalige KZ-Adjutant: Für Häftlinge nicht verantwortlich," FAZ, January 10, 1964. The FR reported a similar but not identical quote. See Rudolf Eims, "Auschwitz-Adjutant Mulka kann sich nicht erinnern," FR, January 10, 1964. The following papers reported on Mulka's testimony without recording his comments regarding the desire to eliminate the Jews: *Der Tagesspiegel*, the *Rhein-Zeitung*, *Neues Deutschland*, the *Stuttgarter Zeitung*, the *Stuttgarter Nachrichten*, the *Abendpost*, *Die Welt*, the *General-Anzeiger*, and the *Westdeutsche Allgemeine* (all January 10, 1964).

[66] On the AWJD, see Michael Brenner, *After the Holocaust: Rebuilding Jewish Lives in Postwar Germany* (Princeton: Princeton University Press, 1997), pp. 125–30.

generally, it is virtually impossible to discern any significant differences in these reports, either stylistic or substantive, from the rest of the German media mainstream. It is true that the Jewish identity of the victims emerges somewhat more clearly in the AWJD coverage than it does in the daily press, but only slightly so. Thus, the AWJD was one of the few newspapers to report Mulka's unambiguous statement that people in the Third Reich wanted to be rid of the Jews.[67] But this quote was no more highlighted in the AWJD report than it was in either the *Frankfurter Allgemeine Zeitung* or the *Frankfurter Rundschau*. In the AWJD, the quote is buried right in the middle of the article, in the two other papers it comes at the very end. In none of the three reports is it presented as a pull-quote or sub-headline. In all three cases, a casual reader simply skimming the article over morning coffee would be more likely than not to miss this statement altogether.

In the final analysis, then, the AWJD's coverage of the Auschwitz Trial remains little different from that of much of the daily press, with one major exception. Ralph Giordano, half-Jewish, a victim of Nazi racial persecution, and one of the most consistent left-wing critics of the politics of memory in postwar West Germany, published a series of commentaries on the Auschwitz Trial in the AWJD in 1965. Unlike most other commentators on the trial, Giordano sought to situate the trial within a larger legal, cultural, and political framework. He traced the history of Nazi trials from Nuremberg to Ulm[68] and also analyzed the nationalist opposition to such trials.[69] Particularly interesting, however, is Giordano's interpretation of public reaction to the trial because he recognized with perhaps greater clarity than any other contemporary observer the risk that such trials might simply serve as an alibi for the general population. "The danger of these trials lies in the possibility that the national responsibility for that which took place between 1933 and 1945 will be reduced to that group of perpetrators who happen to be on trial today or tomorrow."[70] Furthermore, by largely eliminating the distinction between moral and legal guilt, such trials generated public animosity. Since most Germans were morally guilty but relatively few were strictly speaking criminally liable, this elision generated a tremendous public resentment, "a painful, unconscious confession of a larger conjuncture of guilt that seeks redemption."[71] Thus, within the context of a generally failed effort to remember and atone for the Nazi past, the trials of the 1960s were, according to Giordano, too little, too late, too isolated, and too narrowly focused to compensate adequately for the absence of a broader public engagement.

In the end, Giordano concluded that the Auschwitz Trial left behind "a single, overwhelming impression," that the only option was "to live – with

---

[67] "Keiner fühlt sich schuldig," AWJD, January 17, 1964.
[68] Ralph Giordano, "Auschwitz – und kein Ende (I)," AWJD, January 22, 1965.
[69] Ralph Giordano, "Auschwitz – und kein Ende (III)," AWJD, February 5, 1965.
[70] Ralph Giordano, "Auschwitz – und kein Ende (II)," AWJD, January 29, 1965.
[71] Ibid.

Auschwitz."[72] But the burden of living with Auschwitz was in no way divided equally. For Germans, Auschwitz might serve as a "contemporary compensatory object for a guilty conscience," but "we, the surviving victims of industrialized serial murder," would never again be able to see blood, feel pain, or behold a tattoo without thinking of Auschwitz. "To this day it has not set [us] free: living – with Auschwitz."[73]

Public Intellectuals and Trial Participants

If daily press reports sought principally to provide an account of the Auschwitz Trial, to narrate it in a way that made it compelling and accessible to the general public, this left largely open the question of how to interpret the trial. In particular, given the widespread public ambivalence toward the trial, a number of public intellectuals and trial participants felt it necessary to offer a justification for even having the trial.[74]

It was precisely because he was a survivor of nearly six years in Buchenwald and was the author of the first authoritative survey of the Nazi concentration camp system, as well as the fact that he was one of the leading Catholic intellectuals in postwar Germany, that Eugen Kogon was in a particularly good position to evaluate the significance of the Auschwitz Trial.[75] In particular, he represented that strand of German politics that, while to the left of official Christian Democracy, nonetheless felt that a rehabilitation of Christianity and its reintegration into the political consciousness of Germans was essential to the stabilization of a still tenuous democratic tradition in a country where it had always had trouble sinking deep roots.[76] Interestingly, given that he was not a legal scholar, Kogon's major commentary on the trial appeared in one of Germany's leading law

[72] Ralph Giordano, "Leben – mit Auschwitz: Epilog auf den Frankfurter Prozeß," AWJD, August 27, 1965.
[73] Ibid.
[74] The following account of the reaction to the Auschwitz Trial among public intellectuals leaves out any consideration of the *literary* response to the trial. See, e.g., Peter Weiss, *The Investigation: Oratorio in 11 Cantos*, trans. Alexander Gross (London: Marion Boyars, 1982 [1966]), and Horst Krüger, "Im Labyrinth der Schuld," *Der Monat* (May 1964), reprinted in Horst Krüger, *Das zerbochene Haus: Eine Jugend in Deutschland* (Frankfurt: Fischer Taschenbuch Verlag, 1980 [1976]), pp. 112–35. More generally, see Stephan Braese, " 'In einer deutschen Angelegenheit': Der Frankfurter Auschwitz-Prozeß in der westdeutschen Nachkriegsliteratur," in Wojak, ed., *"Gerichtstag halten,"* pp. 217–43, and Marcel Atze, "Der Auschwitz-Prozeß in der Literatur, Philosophie und in der Publizistik," in Irmtrud Wojak, ed., *Auschwitz-Prozeß 4 Ks 2/63* (Cologne: Snoeck, 2004), pp. 637–807.
[75] Eugen Kogon, *Der SS Staat: Das System der deutschen Konzentrationslager* (Munich: Karl Alber Verlag, 1946). In English, idem, *The Theory and Practice of Hell: The German Concentration Camps and the System behind Them*, trans. Heinz Norden (New York: Farrar, Straus, 1950).
[76] See, e.g., Eugen Kogon, "Der christliche Politiker," in idem, *Die unvollendete Erneuerung: Deutschland im Kräftfeld, 1945–1963* (Frankfurt: Europäische Verlagsanstalt, 1964), pp. 191–200.

reviews.[77] His was one of only three articles concerning the trial to appear in any of the major German law reviews.[78]

Kogon's article highlighted what he took to be Judge Hofmeyer's four main insights in his oral verdict, stressing that the judge's refusal to delve into historical questions represented not an abdication but an instance of "sovereign judicial self-restraint."[79] According to Kogon, Hofmeyer made it indisputably clear that (1) the criminal code of 1871 had remained in effect throughout the Nazi period, thus obviating any possible claim that the defendant's actions at Auschwitz had in some way been legalized, (2) that the National Socialist leadership knew full well that their orders were illegal (3) that these acts were not prosecuted at the time, not because they were legal but because the power structures of the Third Reich had de facto prevented any potential prosecutorial efforts and (4) that the subordinate ranks in the Nazi apparatus also knew their actions were illegal. Kogon's only caveat with regard to the trial was that, because the court was compelled to restrict itself to instances where murder could be proved beyond a doubt, the numbers of victims cited in the judgment were generally quite small, even if inevitably prefaced with the qualifying phrase "at least." As a result, Kogon feared that revanchists and deniers could point to the trial as "proof" that only a few thousand people ever died at Auschwitz.

As one can readily see from these four points, Kogon's concern with the verdict was two-fold. On the one hand, the emphasis on the *awareness* of illegality by perpetrators of all ranks had substantial legal implications, in that it ensured that in matters of "guilt," where it will be recalled that under German law the category of "will" was central, the defendants could not claim innocence on the basis of ignorance. On the other hand, the insistence on the ongoing validity of the 1871 criminal code and the merely de facto preclusion of prosecution for Nazi crimes during the Third Reich had historical implications at least as far reaching as its legal ramifications. In particular, it had profound exculpatory implications for the German judiciary, which was how Hofmeyer intended it. That Kogon, himself an ardent anti-Nazi liberal, approved of such a claim seems initially puzzling.

Once one recognizes, however, that any other argument would imply that the law itself, and not merely its application, could become perverted, Kogon's support for Hofmeyer's position becomes clearer. In a separate article situating Auschwitz and the Auschwitz Trial in the context of a

[77] Eugen Kogon, "Rechtsgrundsätze des Auschwitz-Urteils," *Neue Juristische Wochenschrift* 18, no. 41 (1965): 1901. Originally broadcast on August 21, 1965, as a radio commentary. Reprinted in Kogon's own journal, the *Frankfurter Hefte* a few months later. Kogon, "Kommetar nach dem Urteil," *Frankfurter Hefte* 20, no. 12 (1965): 838–39.
[78] The others were Rudolf Wassermann, "Die Prozesse gegen die nationalsozialistischen Gewaltverbrecher," *Juristische Rundschau* no. 1 (1964): 16–17, and Günther Schultz, "Blick in die Zeit," *Monatsschrift für deutsches Recht* 18 (1964): 470–71.
[79] Kogon, "Rechtsgrudsätze," p. 1901.

progressivist philosophy of history, Kogon argued that the entire history of mankind tended in the direction of the democratic rule of law. He defined "human uniqueness" as "the capacity for . . . deciding between possibilities, and therewith for responsibility."[80] This was the factor "on which the life or death of humanity depends." The western legal tradition, partially based in Kogon's view on the Christian tradition of emphasizing the dignity of all human beings in God's eyes, depended for its moral force on the presupposition of such free, rational choice. Consequently, any challenge to the law as such became a challenge to the "humane future" that Kogon sought so desperately to defend. Allowing Hofmeyer to get away with eliding the judiciary's own culpability was a small price to pay for defending the moral purity of law, given that the stakes were so high.

While most legal scholars remained silent on the Auschwitz Trial, at least one broke out of the legal ghetto to promote the same theme as Kogon: the inviolability of law as such. Writing in *Die politische Meinung*, Jürgen Baumann, after considering the hostility toward the Auschwitz Trial, argued that it was nonetheless imperative to continue prosecuting Nazi crimes until the statute of limitations set in for the same reason that it was imperative not to extend prosecutions beyond that point: "The reconstruction of the general legal consciousness is more important than that of the economy."[81] "Far worse," he continued, "than the National Socialist intrusions into existing law were the intrusions of this period into the general legal consciousness of the German people. It will take a long time yet before the German people once again develop a proper feeling for law and injustice. . . . Today, we must once again find a new middle, a new self-evident foundation for law and morality." And this more than anything else was the reason for continuing such trials. Thus Kogon and Baumann articulated what might be termed a legalistic justification for the Auschwitz Trial, one that also appeared in much of the conservative media as well. The trial was viewed primarily as an occasion for reflection on the meaning of law for postwar German society in general, for making the fundamental claim that Nazism represented not so much the legalization of illegality as the antithesis of legality, what Kogon referred to as "barbarism."[82]

For at least some of the participants, the Auschwitz Trial was too important, pedagogically, to be allowed to stand on its own. They worried, justifiably given the sometimes confusing and contradictory historical narratives that emerged in the trial, that mere reportage would fail to convey its real lessons adequately. Some, such as Fritz Bauer, were constrained by their

[80] Eugen Kogon, "Auschwitz und eine menschliche Zukunft," *Frankfurter Hefte* 19 (1964): 833.
[81] Jürgen Baumann, "Wozu noch Auschwitz-Prozesse? Verjährung ist Gesetz," *Die politische Meinung* 9 (1964): 63.
[82] Kogon, "Auschwitz," p. 832.

official positions from speaking out too unreservedly about the trial. Yet
Bauer, while not commenting much specifically on the Auschwitz Trial, made
it quite clear in a number of publications and interviews in the mid-1960s
that the point of the Auschwitz Trial, and all the others like it, was – as
Baumann and Kogon had said – to reintroduce law into Germany. In particular, Bauer wanted Nazi trials to reintroduce Germans to an understanding
of natural law that had been "banished from German law" by a nearly two-
hundred-year tradition of legal positivism. "It is a statement that one finds
in Socrates but also in the Bible: You should obey God more than men. At
its most basic, that is the Alpha and Omega of every law."[83]

Other trial participants, somewhat less constrained by their legal positions, sought to guide public interpretation of the trial even more directly.
First and foremost among these was Hermann Langbein, who not only was
actively involved in the preliminary investigation and a key background witness, but also served as the trial's chief documentarian and, in the 1960s,
its most prominent public interpreter. Langbein planned from the start to
document the trial, probably with an eye to publication. Indeed, there was a
minor controversy over Langbein's plan to document the trial shortly before
it started. Under German law, potential witnesses are not allowed to observe
the proceedings until after they have testified, the point being to avoid any
undue influence on their testimony. Since the prosecution intended Langbein
to serve as one of their key witnesses, this meant that he would not be able
to observe the trial until after his testimony. On December 12, 1963, the
Union Internationale de la Résistance et de la Déportation (UIRD) wrote to
judge Hofmeyer complaining about this fact.[84] The UIRD, with Langbein's
agreement, offered to withdraw Langbein's testimony, arguing that his ability to document the trial was more important than any testimony he might
give. Hofmeyer passed this letter on to the prosecution, who said that they
could not make do without Langbein's testimony.[85] In the end, a compromise was reached, where Langbein, in keeping with the court's plan to hear
background testimony first anyway, was called as one of the first witnesses.[86]
Langbein was then able to directly observe the remainder of the trial and,
in 1965, published his two-volume documentation of the trial.[87] Yet even

---

[83] Fritz Bauer, *Die Humanität der Rechtsordnung: Ausgewählte Schriften*, ed. Irmtrud Wojak
and Joachim Perels (Frankfurt: Campus Verlag, 1998), p. 113.

[84] See UIRD to Hofmeyer (December 12, 1963), FFStA HA 4 Ks 2/63, Bd. 18, Bl. 3643–44.

[85] Kügler to UIRD (December 19, 1963), FFStA HA 4 Ks 2/63, Bd. 18, Bl. 3641.

[86] Langbein to Großmann (January 6, 1964), FFStA HA 4 Ks 2/63, Bd. 18, Bl. 3707–8 and
Vermerk, Großmann (January 29, 1964), FFStA HA 4 Ks 2/63, Bd. 118, Bl. 3709.

[87] Hermann Langbein, *Der Auschwitz Prozeß: Eine Dokumentation*, 2 vols. (Frankfurt: Verlag Neue Kritik, 1995). Langbein was particularly well suited to this task, having also
written an excellent early history of German Nazi trials. See Langbein, *Im Namen des
deutschen Volkes: Zwischenbilanz der Prozesse wegen nationalsozialistischer Verbrechen*
(Vienna: Europa Verlag, 1963).

during the trial, Langbein worked tirelessly to interpret it publicly from a survivor's perspective.

Like Kogon, Langbein emphasized that the fundamental importance of the Auschwitz Trial was future-oriented. "It is a matter of the future when the judiciary tries to clear away all the rubbish of the past."[88] Specifically, the trial functioned "as a kind of social hygiene," helping to generate a "healthy climate" for the next generation, one in which "a repetition of all that we lived through becomes impossible, or at least as difficult as we can make it."[89] Langbein thus shared Baumann's understanding of the trial as a form of legal prophylaxis. "In the legal sphere, that means to revive the clear understanding that says: For every guilt which I incur, a punishment will follow."[90]

Unlike either Baumann or Kogon, however, Langbein saw this process as being more pedagogical than juridical. The main point of the trial was that through the large body of diverse witness testimony, a series of "mosaic stones" emerged, which helped to create a portrait of Auschwitz as a whole.[91] Above all, what Langbein hoped would emerge was a sense of Auschwitz as a site of bureaucratically organized mass murder, particularly through the testimony of the many *Funktionshäftlinge* who recounted the "paper war" waged against the inmates, making "individual murder...a trivial matter in comparison to this coldly administered apparatus" of mass murder.[92] It was this pedagogical potential of the trial that enabled Langbein to say, despite all the public ambivalence toward the trial, that it nonetheless had "a fundamental significance for political education."[93]

Civil counsel Henry Ormond likewise felt the need to provide public interpretations of the trial while it was still ongoing. Like many of his fellow commentators, Ormond stressed that the trial was, in general, a "model of judicial leadership."[94] It was particularly important that the court had rejected all of the legal arguments put forward by the defense either challenging the propriety of such trials or claiming that individual guilt could not be ascertained in organized mass crimes. Ormond also reiterated the central point he made in his *Plädoyer*, that the trial had destroyed many of the various myths that had grown up around the issue of guilt and responsibility in the Holocaust. He specifically stressed the trial's demolition of two myths. First, it was now clear that the defense of superior orders, the claim

---

[88] Hermann Langbein, "Probleme des Auschwitz-Prozesses," *Hessische Blätter für Volksbildung* 14 (1964): 27.

[89] Ibid., pp. 26–27.

[90] Ibid.

[91] Hermann Langbein, "Zwischenbilanz zum Auschwitz-Prozeß," *Das Beste aus Gestern und Heute*, no. 6 (June 1964): 162.

[92] Ibid., p. 160.

[93] Ibid.

[94] Henry Ormond, "Rückblick auf den Auschwitz-Prozeß," *Tribüne* 4 (1965): 1723.

that defendants in effect had acted under duress, was no longer tenable. Too many former SS men had testified that they knew of cases where people had refused to obey criminal orders without any severe disciplinary consequences, much less executions, for this claim to still be seen as plausible. Second, Ormond argued that the Auschwitz Trial had demolished the myth of a strict division between the Waffen and Totenkopf SS, that is, between a military and a camp SS. He stressed that all of the SS defendants still on trial at the end had been members of the Waffen SS and, moreover, that it had been the Waffen SS Construction Unit that had been responsible for building the gas chambers in Auschwitz.

The fact that Ormond chose to emphasize precisely these two myths in his publications reveals a fundamental tension that runs throughout his writings on the Auschwitz Trial. On the one hand, as a man acutely aware of the *historical* significance of Auschwitz, it was important to him that the trial reveal the camp's true dimensions and character. It was especially important that people hear this directly from survivors, because, "after their deaths, no one else will be able to bear witness. In a short while, no one in Germany would have any longer believed the unimaginable. In the not too distant future, Auschwitz would have become a legend."[95] Hence, it was highly significant, *historically and politically*, that it became widely known that the Waffen SS was every bit as implicated in the Nazi genocide as the Totenkopf SS.[96]

At the same time, however, as an attorney, he praised the court for insisting that what happened in Auschwitz was not war crimes or political crimes, "but rather criminal offenses in the statutory sense, whereby the perpetrators exercised their functions according to a division of labor within a well-organized, factory-like apparatus of murder."[97] He imputed personal greed as a primary motivator for many Auschwitz perpetrators, noting that members of execution squads got extra rations and that guards who shot inmates " 'trying to escape' " were given special leave. "The National Socialist *Unrechtsstaat* appealed from top to bottom . . . to the worst human instincts, an appeal which found ample echo."[98] The claim that Nazism appealed to the "worst human instincts" is, of course, hardly accidental, given that German law requires that killings be done on the basis of "base motives" in order to count as murder. But can we really dismiss out of hand the notion that at least some Nazi perpetrators may have acted in their particularly murderous manner based on some higher motive such as – as they themselves

---

[95] Ibid., p. 1728.

[96] Ormond seems to have been unaware of the fact that, organizationally, the Totenkopf SS was incorporated directly into the Waffen SS in 1940. See Charles W. Sydnor, Jr., *Soldiers of Destruction: The SS Death's Head Division, 1933–1945* (Princeton: Princeton University Press, 1977), p. 133. See also Gerald Reitlinger, *The SS – Alibi of a Nation, 1922–1945* (New York: Viking Press, 1957), pp. 168–69.

[97] Henry Ormond, "Zwischenbilanz im Auschwitz-Prozeß," *Tribüne* 3 (1964): 1188.

[98] Ibid.

repeatedly insisted – a sense of duty?[99] Ormond the historical pedagogue here took a back seat to Ormond the lawyer.

Here one sees the contours of one of the central *political* fault lines that ran through the coverage of the Auschwitz Trial: Which was more important, moral pedagogy or legal procedure? Other political conflicts emerged within the coverage of the Auschwitz Trial as well, because, of course, all ideological claims to the contrary, the press is never purely objective. There is always a political agenda, even if that agenda is merely to be thought of as having no agenda. And with such a highly charged topic as Auschwitz, politics mattered all the more.

Politics and the Press

To be sure, it is the nature of newspaper reporting to cover what actually happens in a given event, in this case the course of the trial. At the same time, such reportage is never "objective" in the strong sense of that term (though it can be more or less explicitly subjective and polemical). Obviously, the press came to the Auschwitz Trial with its own agendas. Above all, the press sought to tell a *story* about the trial, one with clear narrative boundaries, heroes with whom the reader could identify, as well as villains against whom they could root. These stories took two forms, creating a kind of story within a story. First, there was the story of the trial itself. Here the heroes and villains were lawyers and judges, witnesses and defendants. This narrative thrust legal maneuvers to the fore, and the obvious *denouement* was victory or defeat. At the same time, the trial was itself hardly devoid of content, nor was it a pure contest, but rather it was a juridical procedure for judging past crimes, with all the attendant historical and moral dimensions. The press was far from unaware of this. Thus, a second story emerged in the press coverage of the trial, the story of Auschwitz itself. This was, in the broadest sense, a historical narrative, a narrative concerned with past events and past actors. But precisely because the task of a trial is not necessarily to establish facts for their own sake, to narrate sequence, to identify causation, but to render judgment, to pass sentence, to enunciate *guilt*, this second story had a layer of moral significance that pulled the historical narrative of Auschwitz into the present narrative of the trial.

The press was placed in a difficult situation in trying to cope with these competing demands, that is, the demands of narrative fidelity to the events of the trial, on the one hand, and the claims of moral judgment, on the other. This dilemma was particularly acute given the trial's own difficulties

---

[99] In this regard, Ulrich Herbert's account of the peculiar sense of the propriety of racial mass murder felt by at least one high-ranking SS man, Werner Best, is instructive. Ulrich Herbert, *Best: Biographische Studien über Radikalismus, Weltanschauung und Vernunft, 1903–1989* (Bonn: Dietz Verlag, 1996).

in coping with the moral and historical dimensions of Auschwitz. This in turn helps to account for the difficulties that the press had in rendering coherent, morally adequate accounts of the trial; instead, it merely revealed what Lawrence Langer has called "a futile dispute between accusers and accused."[100] Langer decries the anecdotal nature of the testimony in the Auschwitz Trial, the lack of a clear historical narrative, and, above all, the agonistics of courtroom dispute, where the denials of the accused are given equal weight to the accusations of the victims. "Little," he continues, "in this bizarre courtroom drama leads to a unified vision of the place we call Auschwitz."[101] This results from the fact that the press was trapped between the need to take a moral stand and the constraints of reporting on a legal procedure that undermined from within any such moral stance.

In confronting this dilemma, the press resorted to a variety of rhetorical and representational strategies, which varied according to political orientation. The German press in the mid-1960s can be divided into four main political camps, although there is considerable overlap in the middle of the spectrum and it is by no means always clear where exactly a given paper falls.[102] Indeed, many papers cannot be placed firmly in any one camp, but rather must be analyzed as liminal cases that move between camps on various issues. The four camps were (1) on one extreme, a communist camp, most prominently represented by *Neues Deutschland* published in the GDR, as well as such minor fellow-traveler publications as the Düsseldorf magazine *Begegnung mit Polen*, (2) on the other extreme, was the nationalist camp, most prominently represented by the *Deutsche National-Zeitung und Soldaten-Zeitung*, (3) in the middle, a left-liberal camp including, for instance, the *Frankfurter Rundschau* or the *Süddeutsche Zeitung*, and (4) the conservative camp, containing, for example, the Springer newspapers (*Die Welt, Bild*, etc.) and, more ambivalently, the *Frankfurter Allgemeine Zeitung*.

Among the four political camps, the group that had perhaps the most difficult time in finding an adequate rhetorical strategy for representing the Auschwitz Trial was, somewhat surprisingly, the communist camp. The

---

[100] Lawrence L. Langer, *Admitting the Holocaust: Collected Essays* (Oxford: Oxford University Press, 1995), p. 89.

[101] Ibid.

[102] On political rhetoric in West Germany, see Wolfgang Bergsdorf, *Herrschaft und Sprache: Studie zur politischen Terminologie der Bundesrepublik Deutschland* (Pfullingen: Verlag Günther Neske, 1981). On the rise of a critical press, see Christina von Hoenberg, "Die Journalisten und der Aufbruch zur kritischen Öffentlichkeit," in Ulrich Herbert, ed., *Wandlungsprozesse in Westdeutschland: Belastung, Integration, Liberalisierung, 1945–1980* (Göttingen: Wallstein, 2002), pp. 278–311. Finally, on the mediatization of public political discourse in West Germany, see Bernd Weisbrod, ed., *Die Politik der Öffentlichkeit – Die Öffentlichkeit der Politik: Politische Medialisierung in der Geschichte der Bundesrepublik* (Göttingen: Wallstein, 2003).

Auschwitz Trial represented a challenge to the claims on which the GDR rested much of its legitimacy. One of the major pillars of East Germany's claim to represent the only truly anti-fascist German state was the alleged failure of the Federal Republic to prosecute Nazi criminals adequately. The very fact that West Germans were putting Nazis on trial – and prominently so, at that – thus jeopardized a central founding myth of the GDR. Under these circumstances, it is hardly surprising that the East Germans and their sympathizers reacted critically to the Auschwitz Trial. However, since the success of this anti-fascist myth depended, like all myths, on its remaining an unquestioned background assumption, the Auschwitz Trial could hardly be attacked directly. After all, what kind of anti-fascist would oppose putting Nazis on trial? A means had to be found whereby the efforts of the Frankfurt court could be made to seem not just inadequate or belated but more fundamentally in keeping with the purportedly fascist character of the Federal Republic itself. Therefore, the central rhetorical strategy in the communist press was what might be termed "cynical historicism."

The critique was made, accurately enough, that the Auschwitz Trial paid inadequate attention to the historical context of Auschwitz. But this critique was highly cynical, in that it itself promulgated a selective, one-sided understanding of history. Taking up the line pursued by Kaul in the trial itself, the East German press argued that IG Farben was almost solely responsible for Auschwitz, and the failure to prosecute any one of its board of directors represented a central failure of the trial.[103] Also following Kaul's lead, the East German press stressed that there was a fundamental continuity between the Third Reich and the FRG. "The Auschwitz Trial is over. But the guilt of Auschwitz remains unatoned. The system that gave birth to this guilt was not condemned. The foundations of this system remain untouched because they are also the foundations of Bonn."[104]

The success of such communist efforts to redirect attention away from the trial actually taking place to the trial that the East Germans alleged ought to be taking place is difficult to judge. Clearly, Kaul's efforts to highjack the trial itself failed. Furthermore, Kaul himself was highly critical of the coverage in the East German media, going so far as to write a series

---

[103] See, e.g., the claim that Hofmeyer was chosen because he would not pursue such questions. "Prozeß gegen SS-Henker von Auschwitz," *Neues Deutschland*, December 21, 1963. In a similar vein, the East Germans published a documentation during the trial, largely paralleling Kuczynski's findings, that emphasized the role of IG Farben in Auschwitz. See Arbeitsgruppe der ehemaligen Häftlinge des Konzentrationslager Auschwitz beim Komitee der Antifaschistischen Widerstandskämpfer in der Deutschen Demokratischen Republik, ed., *I.G. Farben, Auschwitz, Massenmord: Über die Blutschuld der I.G. Farben* (Berlin: Komitee der Antifaschistischen Widerstandskämpfer in der Deutschen Demokratischen Republik, 1964).

[104] Carlheinz v. Brück, "Schuld und Sühne," *Der Morgen*, August 21, 1965.

of pseudonymous articles for *Neues Deutschland* under the name of Otto
Frank.[105] Still, Kaul was a master at upstaging the proceedings for his own
purposes and became something of a media *bete noir* in the West German
press.[106] That the East Germans were thus able to make their case, not only
in their own state-controlled press, but also to an extent in the West German
media, is clear, although it should be recalled that the substantive content
of, for example, Kuczynski's testimony was not by and large reported in any
great detail in the West German press. It is similarly clear that East German
publications such as the *Braunbuch* paralleled the efforts of the emerging
Extra-Parliamentary Opposition in the Federal Republic to publicize the
failures of West German *Vergangenheitsbewältigung*.[107] While the degree of
direct influence exercised by such East German propaganda efforts on the
West German opposition was probably limited, there was a clear congruence
of interest between them.[108]

The Auschwitz Trial was an even more direct challenge to the
political pretensions of the nationalists in the newly reformed (1964)
Nationaldemokratischen Partei Deutschlands (NDP), who clustered around
Deutsche National-Zeitung und Soldaten-Zeitung (DNZ).[109] Claiming to
speak for the mass of Germans who had been demoralized by a postwar

---

[105] Nine of twenty-one of these are in Kaul's Nachlaß. See Otto Frank, "Impressionen vom
Auschwitz-Prozeß," BAB, Nachlaß Kaul, N 2503/1042. In October 1964, a very annoyed
Kaul wrote a letter to the editor in charge of West German reporting at *Neues Deutschland*,
complaining about the "bad level of reporting on the Auschwitz Trial" and noting that he
was not being treated with the proper respect by the paper in response to his articles. Kaul
to *Neues Deutschland* (October 12, 1964), BAB, Nachlaß Kaul, N 2503, Bd. 197.

[106] See Dietrich Strothmann's account of Kaul's ability to gain the sympathy of trial spectators by defending witnesses from the more egregious attacks by Laternser. Strothmann,
"Tribunal der Advokaten," *Die Zeit*, May 8, 1964.

[107] Michael Kohlstruck, "Das zweite Ende der Nachkriegszeit: Zur Veränderung der politischen
Kultur um 1960," in Gary S. Schaal and Andreas Wöll, eds., *Vergangenheitsbewältigung:
Modelle der politischen und sozialen Integration in der bundesdeutschen Nachkriegs-
geschichte* (Baden-Baden: Nomos, 1997).

[108] Thus Reinhard Strecker, who had organized the exhibit "Ungesühnte Nazi-Justiz" in 1959
with the support of the *Sozialistischen Deutschen Studienbunds* (SDS), complained to Kaul
in 1961 that the East Germans were making it difficult for him to get adequate access to
archival materials. See Kaul to ZK SED (June 21, 1964), BAB, Berlin, SAPMO DY 30/IV
2.2.028/57, Bl 205. At the same time, while Strecker's exhibit was clearly a product of
his own efforts and political engagement, it did correspond with an official East German
effort launched in 1957 to highlight the role of West German judges in the Nazi era. See
Klaus Bästlein, "Nazi-Blutrichter als Stützen des Adenauer-Regimes: Die DDR-Kampagnen
gegen NS-Richter und –Staatsanwälte, die Reaktionen der bundesdeutschen Justiz und ihre
gescheiterte 'Selbstreinigung' 1957–1968," in Grabitz et al., eds., *Die Normalität des Verbrechens*, pp. 408–43, and Marc von Miquel, *Ahnden oder amnestieren? Westdeutsche
Justiz und Vergangenheitspolitik in den sechziger Jahren* (Göttingen: Wallstein, 2004),
pp. 50–55.

[109] Thomas Assheuer and Hans Sarkowicz, *Rechtsradikale in Deutschland: Die alte und die
neue Rechte* (Munich: Beck, 1990).

history that deprived them of their proper national sentiments, this group felt the Auschwitz Trial was just one more example of what they called "National Masochism."[110] As one of the NDP leaders (and former Nazi party functionary) Otto Heß put it in an interview with *Der Spiegel*: "Our program is oriented toward the current political-psychological situation of the population, with their particular desire for self-respect, poise, common sense [*Besinnung*], and self-awareness...."[111] A central element in this effort to regenerate nationalist sentiments was generally to downplay and relativize Nazi crimes. For instance, the DNZ helped to sponsor the German visit of the American revisionist historian David Hoggan in 1964, whose book *Der erzwungene Krieg* (*The Forced War*) became something of a *cause célèbre* among German nationalists.[112]

In a certain sense, though, the nationalists had an easier time of it with their critique of Nazi trials than did the communists, since it was not necessary for them to defend such trials, even in principle. Their two general approaches to Nazi trials were to make the so-called *tu quoque* argument against the Allies and to call for a general amnesty for all "war crimes."[113] Thus, while the nationalists pretended to favor trials for *all* war crimes, including those of the Allies (their favorite example being the Allied air war against Germany), in reality this was simply a ploy used to demand a general amnesty for *German* "war crimes." The fact that they subsumed all instances of atrocity or genocide under the category of war crimes was itself a deliberate obfuscation of the unprecedented character of certain Nazi crimes, as well as an implicit critique of the distinctions drawn at Nuremberg among war crimes, crimes against peace, and crimes against humanity.

Naturally, this opposition to what they similarly always called "war crimes trials" also formed a central theme in the nationalist press coverage of the Auschwitz Trial. They deployed two strategies in representing the Auschwitz Trial: trivialization and cynical legalism (paralleling the cynical historicism of the communists). Trivialization here means the effort to

---

[110] Herbert Cysarz, "National-'Masochismus'?" *Deutsche National- und Soldaten-Zeitung* (DNZ), September 18, 1964.

[111] Cited in Kleßmann, *Zwei Staaten, eine Nation: Deutsche Geschichte, 1955–1970* (Göttingen: Vandenhoeck & Ruprecht, 1988), p. 210.

[112] David L. Hoggan, *Der erzwungene Krieg: Die Ursachen und Urheber des 2. Weltkriegs* (Tübingen: Verlag der deutschen Hochschullehrer-Zeitung, 1961), and, for the first English edition, published by the notorious revisionist press, see idem, *The Forced War: When Peaceful Revision Failed* (Costa Mesa: Institute for Historical Review, 1989). For Hoggan's popularity with the German far right in the 1960s, see "Einfach Schön," and "Spiegel-Gespräch: David Hoggan," in *Der Spiegel* 20 (1964): 28–48.

[113] See, e.g., "Deutschland braucht eine Generalamnestie: Die ungesühnte Kriegsverbrechen der Alliierten," DNZ, October 11, 1963; "Das Kardinalproblem im Auschwitz-Prozeß: Die unwiderlegbare Beweisführung der Verteidigung," DNZ, July 9, 1965; and Regina Dahl, "Auschwitz-Schauprozeß: Triumph der politischen Justiz?" DNZ, August 27, 1965.

relativize or minimize the crimes committed in Auschwitz. One of the main forms of this was to cast doubt on the number of Nazi victims. Thus the DNZ opined repeatedly that "the claim that more than 6 million Jews were murdered by Germans is untrue."[114] While stopping short of explicit Holocaust denial, in part no doubt because of the risk of legal sanctions, such efforts to minimize the number of victims, to deny the existence of any deliberate policy of genocide, and in general to deny *German* responsibility were part of a deliberate strategy to eliminate the Holocaust from the West German historical imagination as part of a more general strategy for neo-fascist restoration.[115]

The cynical legalism of the nationalists, on the other hand, paralleled the cynical historicism of the communists, in that it made use of certain common norms – in this case the legal protections of the rule of law – to cast doubt on the validity of the trial. For example, one of the nationalists' favorite tactics was to take up the defense's attacks on the accuracy of witness testimony. The DNZ would regularly point out contradictions that arose in the testimony of prosecution witnesses, claiming that the only point of such testimony was "to lay on all of us Germans the shame of crimes committed by individuals."[116] Even more disturbing were the occasional efforts at outright libel against witnesses, often bordering on the grotesque. For instance, a quasi-anonymous article (signed simply E.K.) in February 1964 charged that a purported witness in the Auschwitz Trial, one "Herr Aranyi," had been peddling "office supplies" in Munich, in an effort to extort money from Germans on the basis of their guilty feelings regarding Nazi crimes.[117] The unnamed author, aside from engaging in some egregious anti-Semitic stereotyping regarding the wealth and greed of the Jews, took the opportunity to state, as an aside, that "as long as power takes precedence over law, concepts like 'collective guilt' or 'war crimes' have no meaning for me."[118] The nationalist press also took up the defense's allegations of witness tampering and their accusations that the survivor witnesses were motivated primarily

---

[114] Dr. Gerhard Frey, "Die Wahrheit über die Judenmorde: Wie lange noch soll das deutsche Volk für Auschwitz büßen," DNZ, March 13, 1964. See also "Weihnachten 1963–1964: Auschwitz-Prozeß," DNZ, December 25, 1963.

[115] Prior to statutory reform in 1985, designed to make such cases easier to prosecute, Holocaust deniers could be prosecuted under §185 StGB ("Insult") or, from 1960, under §§130 and 131 StGB (Attacks on Human Dignity or Inciting Race Hatred). See Eric Stein, "History against Free Speech: The New German Law against the 'Auschwitz' – and Other – 'Lies,' " *Michigan Law Review* 85 (1986): 277–324, and Sebastian Cobler, "Das Gesetz gegen die 'Auschwitz-Lüge': Anmerkungen zu einem rechtspolitischen Ablaßhandel," *Kritische Justiz* 18 (1985): 159–70.

[116] "Im Auschwitz-Prozeß notiert: Die wiedersprechende Zeugenaussagen," DNZ, April 24, 1964.

[117] E.K., "Auschwitz-'Zeuge' auf Betteltour," DNZ, February 7, 1964. In point of fact, no witness named Aranyi or anything like it testified in the Auschwitz Trial.

[118] Ibid.

by a greedy desire for West German reparations.[119] "It is entirely obvious that the foreign witnesses, especially those from Poland, obtained financial advantages at the expense of the Frankfurt courts on the basis of their false testimony."[120]

On the other hand, the DNZ excused any seeming contradictions or errors in the testimony of defendants on the basis that, after so much time, anyone's memory would become a little vague. "Therefore, when a judge says during the interrogation of a defendant, 'Well, you claim to not be able to remember any more,' as if remembering were simply a matter of will-power, this shows *inter alia* not simply a lack of understanding or even a lack of good will, but also the difficulties inherent in trying to establish facts in such cases."[121] In other words, the vagaries of memory, which indicated malice on the part of witnesses, indicated innocence on the part of defendants.

The most striking feature of the extreme positions on the Auschwitz Trial is that not only were they explicitly political, but they also confronted the paradoxes of dealing with Nazi crimes in a juridical context by in effect rejecting the law entirely. Thus, if the law proved incapable of grasping the motivational interchangeability of perpetrators, the communists and the nationalists alike saw this as grounds for rejecting the law's claim to judge such perpetrators at all. This was the true point of both cynical historicism and cynical legalism. The former claimed that "bourgeois" law, itself a tool of monopoly capitalism, would never be able to get at the historical reality of Auschwitz. It recognized that the motives of the individual perpetrators were not the "cause" of Auschwitz, but rather than grasping this point in its true complexity, it merely substituted the greed of IG Farben as the monolithic foundation of Nazism, the Holocaust, and, by extension, the "Western Imperialism" of the Federal Republic. The only adequate response was a radical socialist transformation of society – á la the GDR, of course.

Cynical legalism equally rejected the law as a means for dealing with Auschwitz. It stressed the practical difficulties facing such trials and concluded that the legal rights of the accused demanded their being excused from judgment altogether. The cynicism of such a position can hardly be doubted in this instance, given the manifest one-sidedness of such legalism.

[119] See, e.g., "Nur Belastungszeugen durften kommen: Seltsamkeiten im Auschwitzprozeß [*sic*] um die polnischen Zeugen," DNZ, June 25, 1965; Regina Dahl, "So werden wir erpreßt: Die Wahrheit über den Auschwitz-Prozeß," DNZ, July 2, 1965; and "Der Sehn kamsah-konspirierte und – kassierte: Der Auschwitz-Prozeß wie ihn die Bundesbürger nicht kennen," DNZ, August 6, 1965.

[120] " 'Ein gerechtes Urteil einfach nicht möglich': Aufsehenerregendes Plädoyer Rechtsanwalt Dr. Laternser im Auschwitz-Prozeß," DNZ, June 18, 1965.

[121] Hans-Joachim Göhring, "Politische Justiz mit rechtsstaatlichem Denken nicht vereinbar," DNZ, December 11, 1964. This article is part of a four-part series which, taken together, present as coherent a version of the nationalist critique of Nazi trials as possible. See also DNZ, November 13 and December 11, 1964, and January 1, 1965.

It took the exculpatory tendencies of the law beyond their logical extreme, to the point where the perpetrators were presumed "innocent" not merely until proven guilty but in the face of all evidence. Then the revitalization of a Nationalist Germany could proceed without having to answer the terrible questions posed by Auschwitz. Thus for both the extreme camps, the limitations of the law in dealing with the historical reality of the Holocaust provide an excuse (and it was just an excuse) to reject the law altogether.

The liberals and conservatives of the mainstream press faced quite different challenges in reporting on the Auschwitz Trial. Both groups shared two fundamental political presuppositions, which profoundly influenced the rhetorical strategies they adopted. First, both agreed that the *Rechtsstaat*, the rule of law, was the only guarantor of a free society. Second, both groups formed part of the foundational Anti-Nazi consensus of the Federal Republic, which publicly rejected Nazi ideology, while actively reintegrating most individual Nazis back into society.[122] In this context, Nazi trials actually served a dual function, helping to draw the boundaries of what was considered politically and morally acceptable while not overly jeopardizing the reintegration or political loyalty of millions of former Nazis.

Yet this dual function posed a difficult challenge for both the liberal and conservative press in finding an adequate vocabulary for representing Nazi trials. How could one simultaneously stress the moral and political significance of such trials, yet not alienate an entire generation of readers?[123] Each political camp responded to this challenge by emphasizing a different aspect of the general postwar consensus; the liberals were more interested in delimiting anti-Nazism, while the conservatives emphasized the inviolability of the *Rechtsstaat*. This, more than anything, served as the political determinant of the rhetorical strategies adopted by the mainstream press in confronting the difficulties raised by the Auschwitz Trial.[124]

The main liberal rhetorical strategy might be called "didactic moralism." This approach tended to emphasize the moral lessons of the trial over the judicial outcome. Since the trial itself situated morality at the level of individual agency, the liberal press had to find a way to shift the moral focus onto more social terrain, if it wanted to draw general lessons from the trial.

---

[122] Norbert Frei, *Vergangenheitspolitik: Die Anfänge der Bundesrepublik und die NS-Vergangenheit* (Munich: C. H. Beck, 1996), p. 14.

[123] One historian has argued that this challenge was resolved via a public/private divide, in which public trials, through their "protective abstraction," sheltered private individuals from any need to confront directly the Nazi past. This explanation, however, is not fully persuasive, given that, if anything, the Auschwitz Trial suffered from a surfeit of concreteness, not abstraction. See Peter Graf Kielmansegg, *Lange Schatten: Vom Umgang der Deutschen mit der nationalsozialistischen Vergangenheit* (Berlin: Siedler Verlag, 1989).

[124] The boundaries between these two camps were by no means always clear. With the exception of papers with particularly rigid editorial policies, there was often variation between articles even in the same paper.

As a consequence, while the liberal press shared with the juridical arena an obsession with the motives of the perpetrators, it tended to recast these at a social rather than an individual level. For instance, the *Tagesspiegel* noted that the motives of the perpetrators were neither sadistic nor perverse but rather derived from an excessive sense of duty. As they drove their victims into the gas chambers, "they 'bravely' suppressed those feelings of pity that were not, they plausibly insist, unknown to them."[125] By emphasizing this sense of duty, an effort was made to escape the paradoxes of subjective motivation. The diverse motives of the perpetrators were subsumed under an all-consuming, stereotypically German love of duty. The problem is that this understanding still assumes a direct causal linkage between motive and act and cannot account for the fact that not all of the perpetrators necessarily had such an overdeveloped sense of obedience. One of the crucial features of the Holocaust was the motivational interchangeability of the perpetrators, that their strategic actions were bureaucratically coordinated without the necessity of their having a unitary motive for action. A sense of duty was certainly common among Holocaust perpetrators but was by no means their only motivation for killing. Anti-Semitism, greed, cowardness, peer pressure, and moral laziness were also at work.[126]

In the face of this dilemma, another dimension of the strategy of didactic moralism was simply to sidestep the issue of perpetrator motivation as best as possible, by emphasizing that the accused themselves were less significant than the moral and historical lessons of the trial. The *Frankfurter Neue Presse* noted: "The higher meaning of this trial will be to not identify the events of Auschwitz with the accused, to not rest content with the legal verdict alone, as if, finally, after months of trial (which does make certain amends) the chapter was closed because everything conceivable and possible had been done to satisfy the demands of justice."[127] The fate of the accused was seen as unimportant compared with the didactic purpose of the trial. The trial served as a memorial for future generations, teaching them to respect others and to resist demagoguery.

Gerhard Ziegler, writing in the *Frankfurter Rundschau*, made a similar point some months later, arguing that the point of the trial exceeded "the meaning of punishment."[128] Rather, the trial demanded that Germans recognize that they were "co-responsible" for Nazi crimes, given the popular support for the Nazi regime. Maybe the German people as a whole had not "selected, tortured, and serviced the gas chambers," but neither had this been "the solitary work of a few criminals." "There is no getting around it: This

[125] "Der Auschwitz-Prozeß," *Der Tagesspiegel*, December 20, 1963.
[126] See George C. Browder, "Perpetrator Character and Motivation: An Emerging Consensus?" *Holocaust and Genocide Studies* 17 (Winter 2003): 480–97.
[127] Friedrich Herzog, "Vor Gericht," FNP, December 20, 1963.
[128] Gerhard Ziegler, "Nicht selbst belügen," FR, May 18, 1964.

people cannot simply distance itself from concentration camp murderers – they too are unfortunately a part of us. We cannot lie to ourselves, because these proceedings are only ordinary criminal trials in their outward appearance. Their meaning lies in a general prevention for an entire people." For the liberal press, the Auschwitz Trial ought, in effect, to serve as a school for democracy.

Didactic moralism tried to avoid the problem of motivational interchangeability, first, by emphasizing the social character of perpetrator motives and, second, by downplaying the significance of the perpetrators themselves in favor of broad political lessons. Particular stress was laid on the collective responsibility of the German people for Nazi crimes. In this respect, the strategy of didactic moralism ran counter to the internal logic of the Frankfurt Auschwitz Trial, indeed can be seen as a deliberate effort to circumvent the subjectivism of German law. The problem with this strategy was twofold. On the one hand, the political lessons were so generalized as to have little impact on individual readers. The lessons that the *Frankfurter Neue Presse* drew from the Auschwitz Trial were extremely vague, to the point of being little more than platitudes. On the other hand, the effort to situate motives at the level of society itself failed to circumvent fully the subjectivism implicit in a concern with motives in the first place. Above all, because the trial itself did so little to unveil the social mechanisms at work in Auschwitz, assertions of collective responsibility remained at best accusatory imputations without concrete foundation.

In fact, as Eugen Kogon recognized, the subjectivism of the trial itself helped to generate the public's ambivalent reaction, thus undermining its pedagogical value. "The legal proceedings which so belatedly serve the cause of justice concentrate – how could they otherwise? – the causes on those who are guilty in the criminal sense. Since we follow the course of the proceedings in the press, the inhumanity of the event, which admittedly awakens a sense of horror in us but which remains at its foundation incomprehensible, is shifted away from us."[129] As didacticism shaded into moralism, and the psychopathology of the individual defendants substituted for social analysis, much of the German public rejected the lessons the liberal press insisted they should learn from the trial.

For their part, the conservatives also adopted a rhetorical strategy that suited their political orientation toward the rule of law. This was to emphasize repeatedly the inviolable nature of the *Rechtsstaat* as such. This strategy took two principal forms. First, it involved an explicit defense of the demands of the *Rechtsstaat* against the impositions of the public sphere. For example, the *Frankfurter Allgemeine Zeitung* remarked in a pretrial commentary that, while it was true that the scope and duration of the Auschwitz Trial alone

---

[129] Kogon, "Auschwitz," p. 831.

made it more than a "'normal' criminal trial," "extraordinary precautions" should be taken to ensure that the trial did not turn into a "stage," "because that would not serve the working through of this piece of the National Socialist past."[130] The article praised the court's decision to proceed with the trial before Christmas (1963), despite the fact that the intended location in the Gallus Haus, which would have had more room for spectators, was not yet available. While this decision might be disadvantageous for the public, it was only fair to the accused, many of whom had already been in custody for too long and deserved a speedy trial. "This [decision] is to be praised, no matter how justified efforts on behalf of the expected public interest might be. Nonetheless, the criminal proceedings alone stand in the foreground."[131]

The conservative weekly, *Christ und Welt*, made a similar point some months later, arguing that the only justification for the trial's enormous scope was that this provided the only way to assess accurately the guilt of each individual defendant. "After all, what is justice but the rendering unto each of us his due, even his due of guilt and punishment. This is the task of the trial, not to serve as an adult education program for *Vergangenheitsbewältigung*."[132] In this form, the defense of the *Rechtsstaat* became synonymous with the defense of the individuating character of law. Guilt, as a matter of will, was likewise a matter of the isolated, autonomous subject. The only purpose of contextualizing that subject was to view it all the more clearly in its isolation and autonomy.

Above all, the conservatives argued, the trial had to be protected from any contamination by "political" considerations, such as marred the Nuremberg Trials. As the *Münchner Merkur* complained, public discussions of the Auschwitz Trial suffered from a "particular misunderstanding." Rather than considering it a matter of individuals responsible for murder, it became a matter of people's "political past." "The 'murderer' is not important; the 'Nazi'-murderer is crucial." Such trials, then, came to serve merely as proof of the Federal Republic's commitment to "cleaning up the Nazi past," and as a result, "an ordinary criminal trial is made into a political issue."[133]

Therefore, the other form that the defense of the *Rechtsstaat* took in the conservative press was to decry the "politicization" of the trial by representatives of the two extreme camps. Writing in the CDU-oriented *Ruhr-Nachrichten*, Max Karl Feiden noted the enormous interest generated by Kaul's initial appearance.[134] He went on to note that only the nationalist defense attorney Hans Laternser seemed unsurprised by Kaul's appearance,

[130] "Der Auschwitz-Verfahren," FAZ, October 16, 1963.
[131] Ibid.
[132] Peter Jochen Winters, "Den Mördern ins Auge gesehen," *Christ und Welt*, May 29, 1964.
[133] Rainer Klose, "Bestraft wird lediglich die Tat," *Münchner Merkur*, August 20, 1965.
[134] Max Karl Feiden, "Einer der 21 Angeklagten im Auschwitz Trial ist noch Stolz auf seine niedrige SS-Nummer," *Ruhr-Nachrichten*, December 21, 1963.

establishing a theme that would become a leitmotif in the press coverage: the ongoing battle between Kaul and Laternser to appropriate the public agenda of the trial and the parallels between the two. Of the initial skirmish between Laternser and Kaul over the latter's admission, Feiden noted: "Thus the trial was swept up from the very start in a highly political current."[135] Feiden concluded by noting that Kaul was again, as he was in his efforts to intervene in the Eichmann Trial, less a representative of Auschwitz survivors than of the GDR. The assertion that Kaul did not belong in courtroom hardly needed to be added.

The conservative defense of the *Rechtsstaat* for its own sake thus sought to cloak itself in the mantle of a political neutrality and objectivity that is itself a defining feature of the *Rechtsstaat*. The problem with this rhetorical strategy was that, like the law itself, it tended to unravel in the face of the motivational interchangeability of perpetrators in the Holocaust. It propagated an emphasis on individual character that distorted the historical image of the Holocaust. One can take the following witness statement, reported in the *Frankfurter Allgemeine Zeitung*, as indicative of this focus: "Klehr could kill a few hundred or thousand people just like a cobbler ripping a decrepit sole from a shoe. He stalked and killed for the sheer joy of hunting, going from infirmary ward to infirmary ward in the process."[136] As powerful as this image is, it makes Klehr seem more like a Hollywood serial killer than a member of a highly organized killing organization. The defense of the *Rechtsstaat* thus entailed recapitulating the German law's own conceptual limitations in the face of state-sponsored genocide. Furthermore, by denigrating the pedagogical function of the trial, this focus on *Rechtsstaatlichkeit* contributed to an atmosphere of public uninvolvement. If the trial was completely "ordinary," then there was no reason for anyone to pay any more attention to it than they would to any other trial. The conservative defense of the *Rechtsstaat* was a central mechanism whereby the trial's reduction of the Holocaust to individual, subjective guilt was transmitted to the German public.

Conclusion

It would be fair to say that, with the relatively marginal exception of the nationalists, the West German press was broadly supportive of the Auschwitz Trial, whether as a form of moral pedagogy or as an embodiment of the *Rechtsstaat*, or simply because it made for good copy. Yet the West German public remained deeply ambivalent toward the trial, and all the press coverage not only failed to overcome this ambivalence but even helped to generate

---

[135] Ibid.
[136] Bernd Naumann, "'Er hat getötet aus Jagdleidenschaft': Klehr der Teilnahme bei Vergasungen beschuldigt," FAZ, September 19, 1964.

it. The trial, in seeking to judge Auschwitz in the terms of German law, repressed, distorted, or simply failed to elucidate certain vital historical and psychological "truths" about Nazi genocide. These limitations were then transmitted to the public via the press and tended to resurface as a "return of the repressed" rather than being consciously integrated into the political culture of the Federal Republic.

Most important, by focusing not just on the inhumane but on the almost literally inhuman aspects of Auschwitz, the press rendered it "infernal" in the strict sense, a living hell that had no connection to human experience or society. No court can plausibly lay claim to judging hell, and no audience can reasonably be expected to comprehend, much less applaud, such an effort.

In the end, then, one has to conclude that the assessment of one recent historian that, through Nazi trials, "Germans constructed a new identity based on a fresh start [and] a clean break with the past" is unfortunately over-optimistic.[137] Indeed, on the contrary, the striking tendency for West Germans repeatedly to encounter their own history with shock and surprise can at least partially be accounted for on the basis of the lessons they learned from the Auschwitz Trial and others like it, namely, that they too had been victims of Nazism, that the Holocaust was caused by the deviant motives of a few sadistic individuals, and that torture, not genocide, was the most important characteristic of Auschwitz.

---

[137] Claudia Koonz, "Between Memory and Oblivion: Concentration Camps in German Memory," in John R. Gillis, ed., *Commemorations: The Politics of National Identity* (Princeton: Princeton University Press, 1994), p. 262.

Conclusion

Genocide and the Limits of the Law

On one level, the central question that can be posed regarding the Frankfurt Auschwitz Trial is that of success or failure. Did the Auschwitz Trial succeed or fail? In asking this question, one must immediately also ask: On whose terms? The various actors in the trial each brought with them their own, often antithetical standards of success or failure. For some of the participants, this would largely have been a question of representational justice. Thus, for such consummate political figures as Kaul or Laternser, the trial would have been judged according to its propaganda features. For a man such as Fritz Bauer, who was no less political in his own way but whose understanding of politics was far less one-dimensional, the success or failure of the trial would have to have been evaluated in large part in pedagogical terms. On the other hand, there were other participants – Hofmeyer above all – whose primary, indeed perhaps exclusive concern, was for the juridical process and the strictly legal outcome of the trial.

As can be seen from this grouping, however, it is possible to step back from the immediate concerns of the participants, whether for propaganda or procedure, from their propensities for histrionic display or rigid sobriety, and to abstract out two distinct criteria by which the trial has been judged: its juridical propriety and its representational efficacy. These criteria can be articulated in terms of the claims of justice, on the one hand, and the claims of truth, on the other hand.

The Auschwitz Trial can be, and has been, judged to be both a success and a failure under both criteria. Not too surprisingly, those who had been most critical of the trial from the outset were most inclined to condemn it at its conclusion as well. Kaul, writing semi-anonymously in *Neues Deutschland*, declared that "the judgment is an insult to the dead of Auschwitz."[1] The fact that it took the Federal Republic twenty years to reach this verdict at all

---

[1] Dr. K [presumably Kaul], "Das Urteil von Frankfurt," *Neues Deutschland*, August 20, 1965.

was an indication of their fundamental reluctance to deal with the Nazi past. "In point of fact, how could the armaments millionaires allow their reliable assistants to be treated badly! After all, they still need helpers today and for the future who are willing to do anything, since their policies are aimed at a new war and a new mass murder."[2]

Others, however, viewed the trial in a much more favorable light. Henry Ormond, for one, was thoroughly satisfied with the trial as a juridical event. "When taken as a whole, the judgment can only be viewed as just. It was a fair judgment, just as it was a fair trial."[3] He was particularly pleased with the court's universal rejection of the defense's legal arguments concerning duress, higher orders, the validity of Nazi law, and the like. Ormond was also quite satisfied with the trial as a representational event. The massive publicity attracted by the trial was particularly beneficial. "Because the trial confirmed even more thoroughly what those familiar with the material have long known or suspected. It opened the eyes and sharpened the conscience of those of good will. And it brought to silence those powers who have tried for years to deny or trivialize what happened in the extermination centers."[4]

Most trial observers fell somewhere between these two poles. They expressed a degree of ambivalence about the trial. Shortly after the conclusion of the trial, the CIC issued its evaluation of the final judgment.[5] The CIC noted that, "if one expects penance for the mass murder of Jews, Gypsies and Slavs, then one must be bitterly disappointed."[6] But, the committee continued, it was hardly possible to expect a legal system designed for very different purposes to exact genuine penance for such enormous and widely organized crimes. "A collective verdict against all of those who served in an SS uniform in the extermination camps is impossible within the confines of the rule of law."[7] The judgment in the Auschwitz Trial was at least better than was typical in such trials, thanks particularly to Hofmeyer's effective leadership.

Nevertheless, the CIC was not fully satisfied with the verdicts in the trial. In particular, the committee was critical of the court's treatment of many of the accomplices in the trial.[8] It was troubling that only one SS officer was convicted as a perpetrator and even more troubling that in none of the cases where a defendant was convicted as an accomplice had he been given the maximum sentence. It was not unreasonable, according to the committee,

---

[2] Ibid.

[3] Henry Ormond, "Rückblick auf den Auschwitz-Prozeß," *Tribüne* 16, no. 4 (1965): p. 1724.

[4] Ibid., p. 1723.

[5] Eugen Kogon served as one of the vice presidents of the CIC and Hermann Langbein was one of its secretaries.

[6] *Bulletin des Comité International des Camps*, no. 10 (September 15, 1965), p. 1.

[7] Ibid., p. 2.

[8] "That is where a critique of German [Nazi] verdicts that is not based solely on emotion begins." Ibid., p. 3.

that defendants received milder sentences in those cases where, like those of Lucas, Scherpe, or Frank, there was evidence that the defendant had behaved in a "relatively humane manner."[9] But in other cases, particularly those of the two adjutants Mulka and Höcker, it was difficult to understand why they had not received the maximum sentence. While it might be accepted that, in light of his advanced age (he was seventy at the time), Mulka had received a milder sentence; his fourteen-year sentence was basically the equivalent of a life sentence anyway. But in Höcker's case, especially given that his prior duty in Majdanek demonstrated that he was "a specialist in mass murder," it was "inexplicable" that he had received a reduced sentence.[10]

The CIC was particularly irate that Capesius had been convicted as an accomplice and not a perpetrator. After all, he had personally enriched himself at the expense of his victims, even stealing their gold fillings to finance his own postwar prosperity as a pharmacist. "Anyone who did not shy away from profiting from mass murder clearly wanted and willed it."[11] The committee also chastised the prosecution for not bringing supplemental charges against Broad, Dylewski, and Schlage based on new allegations that arose during the proceedings, many of which were far more serious than the charges against them in the indictment. As a result, the court had been unable to convict them save as accomplices. On the CIC's account, then, the Auschwitz Trial would have to be judged a limited success in juridical terms. It was a better trial than most but hardly free of missteps and errors.

A similar critique was leveled by Karl Friedrich Kämper in the *Westfälische Rundschau*. "The judgment passed yesterday unfortunately demonstrates that, to an extent, the trial proceeded according to the motto: Only lock up the 'small' murderers behind prison walls for the rest of their lives, let the 'big' ones, who only dictated orders at their typewriters, get off easy."[12] Kämper was unwilling to conclude definitively that the judgment was unjust, however. "Of necessity, justice and law often diverge because the former is the goal toward which we strive but despite our best efforts, we can at best only ever realize the latter."

This general sense that the trial had done what it could but that it had not been able to do everything one might have liked was by far the most common evaluation of the Auschwitz Trial. Nor was it uncommon to note that the trial's limitations were those of law itself. "Everyone who has the least bit of good will," remarked the *Kölnische Rundschau*, "knows that state-organized mass murder of this magnitude cannot be atoned for by means of a criminal code designed to handle 'normal' crimes."[13] Similar considerations led the

[9] Ibid.
[10] Ibid., p. 4.
[11] Ibid.
[12] Karl Friedrich Kämper, " 'Unser' Auschwitz," *Westfälische Rundschau*, August 20, 1965.
[13] "Frankfurt und Jerusalem," *Kölnische Rundschau*, August 20, 1965.

Freie Presse to warn that "one should guard against overly quick judgments about the verdict, because these carry within themselves the risk of finishing with the past all too quickly as well."[14]

What these evaluations indicate is that it is more useful to think about the Auschwitz Trial in terms of limits and boundaries, rather than relying on the language of success and failure. In other words, rather than first choosing an evaluative criterion – truth or justice – and then applying this to the trial like a yardstick, it makes far more sense to examine what the trial actually *did,* in both the juridical and representational domains, where it drew the boundaries between these two and how the internal dynamic of tension and resolution between them unfolded.

Juridically, three factors are crucial for assessing the boundaries of the Frankfurt Auschwitz Trial. First and foremost, in keeping with the categories of German law, the trial was profoundly subjectivizing in character. In other words, it was concerned principally with the concrete guilt of the individual defendants; this guilt was, in turn, conceived largely in subjective terms, as a matter of the defendants' internal disposition toward their actions. While this orientation manifested itself most clearly in the court's discussion of the issue of perpetration in its final judgment, it was apparent throughout the proceedings. Even much of the apparently "objective" evidence served mainly to establish indices for evaluating the subjective motivations of the accused.

Second, the trial gave witnesses the opportunity to bear witness in their testimony, to speak the truth of their own subjective experiences of Auschwitz, only to repress those experiences immediately in the name of precision and judicial fair play. The fact that the court treated any evident emotion by witnesses during their testimony as a prima facie indicaton of their unreliability, combined with the repeated efforts by the defense to undermine the credibility of the witnesses in ways that at times bordered on the grotesque, indicates the extent to which the trial devalued the experiential truth of Auschwitz recounted by the survivor witnesses. The only truth that counted, that *could* count, was the juridical truth of individual agency, not the representational truth of the victim's suffering.

Finally, torture and other individual atrocities represented in many respects an "easy case," compared with the ambiguous domains of responsibility and obedience that characterized bureaucratically organized genocide. As a result, however much the prosecution and the court tried to place genocide at the center of both their juridical and historical narratives, atrocity tended to become the more palpably real crime. It was certainly the more rigorously punished infraction. Consequently, atrocity tended to occupy a privileged terrain compared with genocide. The disparity in the sentences

[14] Kh. Böhm, "Gerecht?" *Freie Presse*, August 20, 1965.

imposed for perpetrating torture as opposed to aiding and abetting genocide simply reinforced this privileged position.

In the representational arena, the trial produced several competing narratives of Auschwitz. Three factors in particular stand out in this process. First, the trial itself manifested a clear tension between atrocity and genocide, as the prosecution and the court sought to emphasize the importance of genocide yet ended up privileging atrocity; this tension was transformed in the press into an obsession. Genocide receded into the background, gore and sadism advanced to the fore. To read the press accounts of the trial, one might think that Auschwitz was first and foremost a school for torture, where genocide was merely an incidental byproduct. But of course this was the very opposite of the historical truth of Auschwitz.

Second, the juridically unavoidable focus on individual perpetrators and their subjective motivations became the dominant, though not the only, representation of Auschwitz to emerge from the trial. It is true that, in distinct ways, both the defense and civil counsel Kaul sought to highlight the social and structural dimensions of the Third Reich and, to a lesser extent, the Holocaust. For the defense, the Third Reich was a terrorist regime that controlled every aspect of people's lives, including especially the defendants. To hold them responsible for their actions under this regime was thus to blame men who were themselves victims. Whether the defense attorneys made this argument cynically, for purely tactical legal reasons, or whether they sincerely believed it cannot be known. What is certain is that their understanding of the social dimensions of the Third Reich was meant to restrict, not expand, the sphere of culpability. It was an instrumental counter-narrative designed to negate the prosecution's account of strong individual agency.

Similarly, Kaul stressed the social and structural dimensions of the Nazi regime, especially the role of IG Farben in the construction and maintenance of Auschwitz. His intention was quite the opposite of the defense's. He sought to expand the realm of responsibility to include particularly the leaders of German industry and the contemporary political and economic elites in West Germany. For him, what was crucial was the clear, direct, and unmediated line of continuity he perceived between Auschwitz and Bonn. Kaul's counter-narrative was every bit as instrumental as the defense's; its purpose was to legitimate the GDR's founding myth that it was the only truly anti-fascist German state.

In the final analysis, however, neither of these counter-narratives – in part, no doubt, because each was so transparently instrumental – was able to encroach very effectively on the dominant representation of Auschwitz as the murderous outcome of individual actions based on subjective motives. On this account, initially proposed by the prosecution and civil counsel Ormond and subsequently taken up by the court, the vast bureaucratic division of labor involved in the killing operations became simply a background condition for individuated morality plays. While it is true that the prosecution, the court, and, especially, the historians from the Institute for Contemporary History were at pains to demonstrate the interconnections among the SS, the concentration camp system, Nazi Polish policy, and Nazi anti-Jewish policy, none of these variables was ever accorded any real causal significance. At the end of the day, each of the defendants was considered – had to be considered under law – a radically autonomous subject of will. If Hitler's will, and Hitler's will alone, was the ultimate cause of Auschwitz, the individual wills of each of the defendants remained nonetheless *monadic,* in the sense that they bore no necessary relationship to anything but their own moral choices. This is inherent in the legal meaning of guilt under German law. If the defendants were guilty, it could be only in isolation.

Finally, although the defense failed in its attempts to construct a persuasive counter-narrative of structurally limited agency for the defendants, they were somewhat more successful in their endeavors to politicize the proceedings. If the trial necessarily re-presented the state's legitimate right to punish, it also necessarily opened up the possibility that parallel or alternative meanings could be appended as well. And by far the most prominent such emendation was the overlay of Cold War politics on the general narrative of subjective responsibility. The defense may have been the most diligent promulgators of this endeavor, but they were aided in their endeavors by Kaul's parallel efforts as well. And even the mainstream press was by no means immune from noting, if often with a certain unease, the ugly parallels between Nazism and what was happening in the "Soviet Occupied Zone." It was ultimately impossible to speak of the Nazi past in the Auschwitz Trial without at least implicitly comparing it to the contemporary communist dictatorships in Eastern Europe. Crude as they were, the defense's efforts to impugn the integrity of many East Block witnesses worked to a considerable degree. Moreover, Kaul's equally crude efforts to highlight the role of IG Farben were probably ultimately counterproductive for his propagandistic aims, generating a political defensiveness in the West German press that made them less, rather than more, likely to examine the deep social roots of the Holocaust.

So, what was the trial able to achieve within these boundaries? On the one hand, the trial produced remarkably nuanced treatments of the various defendants, perhaps a bit too nuanced in some instances. Certainly, none of them could be said to have been unfairly treated by the court, and in this sense, the trial was indeed a remarkable example of German legal procedure at its most conscientious. On the other hand, it was unable to articulate adequately a historical account of the Holocaust that fully incorporated or even sufficiently acknowledged the extent to which it was a "total social event," one in which every dimension of German society was implicated to one degree or another. It has been remarked by others that by punishing a few particularly egregious Nazi murderers trials such as this functioned as alibis for the remainder of German society, allowing them to in effect say, 'See, the guilty parties have been punished.'[15]

However, the problem is actually much more complicated than that. It was not simply that German Nazi trials provided an alibi for those disinclined to examine their own histories. More significant was the *kind of historical account* provided by the Auschwitz Trial. What was at stake was not just whether to think about the Nazi past but how to think about it. And in the Auschwitz Trial, the lens through which this past was viewed was carnivalesque, in the sense that like the mirrors in a carnival fun house, it greatly exaggerated one aspect of the truth, while simultaneously minimizing and distorting others. In this case, individual responsibility and individual atrocities were exaggerated and social structures and broader bureaucratic frameworks were diminished.

The fact is that, contra the assumptions of Daniel Goldhagen, within the context of the Holocaust, perpetrators acted on the basis of diverse motives.[16] While the question of perpetrator motivation in the Holocaust is enormously complicated, recent literature has generated what one scholar has called an "emerging consensus" on the issue.[17] This new literature points beyond the antithesis between brutal sadists, on the one hand, and banal bureaucrats, on the other hand. Above all, thanks in part to the impetus provided by Goldhagen's work, what has emerged is a renewed emphasis on the centrality of ideology to Holocaust perpetrators, though largely the empirical research here has focused on the planning elite behind the Holocaust.[18] Additionally, much of this literature points to an internal dynamic of radicalization within various Nazi organizations. "Relatively few perpetrators were 'willing and committed ideologues' before their radicalization."[19] Yet,

[15] This is the basic thesis of Jörg Friedrich's work. See Jörg Friedrich, *Die kalte Amnestie: NS-Täter in der Bundesrepublik*, rev. ed. (Munich: Piper, 1994).

[16] Daniel Jonah Goldhagen, *Hitler's Willing Executioners: Ordinary Germans and the Holocaust* (New York: Alfred A. Knopf, 1996). Goldhagen's thesis about the uniform anti-Semitic motivation of German perpetrators has, of course, come under considerable scholarly fire from various quarters as well. See, e.g., Norman G. Finkelstein and Ruth Bettina Birn, *A Nation on Trial: The Goldhagen Thesis and Historical Truth* (New York: Henry Holt, 1998), as well as the many (mostly critical) reviews reprinted in Julius Schoeps, ed., *Ein Volk von Mordern? Die Dokumentation zur Goldhagen Kontroverse um die Rolle der Deutschen im Holocaust* (Hamburg: Hoffman und Campe Verlag, 1996), or Robert R. Shandley, ed., *Unwilling Germans? The Goldhagen Debate* (Minneapolis: University of Minnesota Press, 1998).

[17] George C. Browder, "Perpetrator Character and Motivation: An Emerging Consensus?" *Holocaust and Genocide Studies* 17 (Winter 2003): 480–97.

[18] See, e.g., Yehuda Bauer, *Rethinking the Holocaust* (New Haven: Yale University Press, 2001); Michael Thad Allen, *The Business of Genocide: The SS, Slave Labor, and the Concentration Camps* (Chapel Hill: University of North Carolina Press, 2002); and Michael Wildt, *Generation des Unbedingten: Das Führerkorps des Reichssicherheitshauptamt* (Hamburg: Hamburger Edition, 2002).

[19] Browder, "Perpetrator Character," p. 495.

as Ruth Bettina Birn has argued, it is important, when discussing the question of perpetrator motivation in the Holocaust, to keep in mind that there are actually two distinct questions involved, which need to be addressed separately.[20] First, there is the question as to the origin of genocidal policy at the highest levels of the state apparatus. It is in this arena that many of the standard debates on the origin of the Holocaust have taken place, in particular the debate between "intentionalists" and "functionalists."[21] Second, there is the question as to the motives of the actual executioners in the various extermination centers, which has generally attracted more attention from social psychologists than historians.[22] No matter how apt the renewed interest in Nazi anti-Semitic ideology may be for the planning elite, at the level of the individual killers, what emerged most clearly in the Auschwitz Trial was the diversity of their motives. Some were passionate anti-Semites, some were cynical opportunists, some were sadists, and some were obedient fools. However central ideology was for the origins of the Holocaust, the radicalization of Nazi genocidal policy found its end point not in a monolithic "eliminationist anti-Semitism" but in a diverse set of executioners, each willing to kill for different reasons but all, nonetheless, willing.[23]

What matters most in the context of the Auschwitz Trial is not only that the diverse perpetrators of the Holocaust, operating on the basis of distinct motives, produced functionally identical results in the context of

---

[20] See Birn, *A Nation on Trial*, p. 134.

[21] See Ian Kershaw, *The Nazi Dictatorship: Problems and Perspectives of Interpretation*, 4th ed. (London: Arnold, 2000), pp. 93–133; Christopher Browning, "Beyond 'Intentionalism' and 'Functionalism': The Decision for the Final Solution Reconsidered," in idem, *The Path to Genocide: Essays on Launching the Final Solution* (Cambridge: Cambridge University Press, 1992), pp. 86–121, or Tim Mason, "Intention and Explanation: A Current Controversy about the Interpretation of National Socialism," in Gerhard Hirschfeld and Lothar Kettenacker, eds., *Der Führerstaat: Mythos und Realität* (Stuttgart: Klett-Cotta, 1981), pp. 21–40. For the most penetrating recent scholarship on these issues, see Saul Friedländer, *Nazi Germany and the Jews*, vol. 1 (New York: Harper Collins, 1997); Henry Friedlander, *The Origins of Nazi Genocide: From Euthanasia to the Final Solution* (Chapel Hill: University of North Carolina Press, 1995); and especially Christopher Browning and Jürgen Matthäus, *The Origins of the Final Solution: The Evolution of Nazi Jewish Policy, September 1939–March 1942* (London: Arrow, 2005).

[22] For historical analyses, see Christopher Browning, *Ordinary Men: Reserve Police Battalion 101 and the Final Solution in Poland* (New York: Harper Perennial, 1992), and Gerhard Paul, ed., *Die Täter der Shoah: Fanatische Nationalsozialisten oder ganz normale Deutsche?* (Göttingen: Wallstein, 2002). For more social psychological approaches, see Israel W. Charny with Chanan Rapaport, *How Can We Commit the Unthinkable: Genocide, the Human Cancer* (Boulder: Westview, 1982); Robert Jay Lifton, *The Nazi Doctors: Medical Killing and the Psychology of Genocide* (New York: Basic Books, 1986); Leonard S. Newman and Ralph Erber, eds., *Understanding Genocide: The Social Psychology of the Holocaust* (New York: Oxford University Press, 2002); and Eric A. Zillmer et al., *The Quest for the Nazi Personality: A Psychological Investigation of Nazi War Criminals* (Hillsdale, N.J.: Lawrence Erlbaum, 1995).

[23] Goldhagen, *Hitler's Willing Executioners*, pp. 14–15.

296 The Frankfurt Auschwitz Trial, 1963–1965

state-organized mass murder, but also that, as a consequence, these perpetrators themselves became functionally interchangeable. Or as the jurist
Peter Noll puts it: "The psychological and therefore, in light of the principle of guilt, the jurisprudential problem is that, in the case of organized
mass crimes, every single participant can, quite properly, see himself as fully
replaceable and, consequently, in the final analysis as not responsible for his
actions."[24] The central problem confronting the Auschwitz Trial was how
to judge a unitary crime – the genocide of the Jews – on the basis of a legal
system that defined crimes differently based on distinct perpetrator motives.

There were those in the Federal Republic who recognized the difficulties,
both jurisprudential and historiographical, posed by this functional interchangeability among Holocaust perpetrators. Claus Roxin, for instance,
argued forcefully that the existing theory of perpetratorship was inadequate to such state-organized mass crimes. He claimed that it was necessary
to reconceptualize perpetratorship in such cases to include what he called
"mastery over the will by virtue of an organizational power apparatus."[25]
Such a concept of perpetratorship would allow for both high-ranking officials and their various subordinates to be viewed as exercising simultane-
ous mastery over the act of murder. The high-ranking officials, despite their
absence from the scene, still controlled the action by virtue of the organized
character of the activity. The low-ranking executioners exercised mastery
over the act by virtue of their direct involvement in the killing. "Such
an organization, for instance, takes on a life of its own, independent of
the changing composition of its membership. It functions without depending on the individual personality of those carrying out orders, essentially
'autonomously.'"[26] The defining feature of this kind of mastery of the will
is the "fungibility of the executioners."[27]

Such voices, however, had little impact on legal practice in the Federal
Republic and certainly not on the course of the Auschwitz Trial. Even Henry

---

[24] Peter Noll, "Die NS-Verbrecherprozesse strafrechtsdogmatisch und gesetzgebungspolitisch
betrachtet," in Peter Schneider and Hermann J. Meyer, eds., *Rechtliche und politische
Aspekte der NS-Verbrecherprozesse: Gemeinschaftsvorlesung des studium generale Wintersemester 1966/67* (Mainz: Gutenberg-Universität Mainz, 1968), p. 46.

[25] Claus Roxin. "Straftaten im Rahmen organisatorischer Machtapparate," in *Goltdammer's
Archiv für Strafrecht* (1963), pp. 193–207. Interestingly enough, and in marked contrast
to the situation in Germany, Roxin's theories in this regard later exercised considerable
influence over the legal procedures put in place in Argentina for the trials resulting from the
"dirty war" of the 1970s. See Carlos Santiago Nino, *Radical Evil on Trial* (New Haven: Yale
University Press, 1996), pp. 84–85.

[26] Roxin, "Straftaten," p. 200. Roxin argues that in general, there are three ways to control
the actions of others: force, deception, or the willing interchangeability of the actors.

[27] Ibid. It is worth noting that Roxin explicitly argued that such a form of perpetratorship by
high-ranking officials did not preclude the culpability of their lower ranking subordinates.
In such cases, "there is no lack of freedom and responsibility on the part of the immediate
executioner, who is to be punished as a culpable perpetrator by his own hands." Ibid., p. 201.

Ormond declared that the atrocities committed at Auschwitz did not represent some special kind of crime like political crimes or war crimes. They were "rather criminal offenses in the statutory sense, whereby the perpetrators exercised their functions according to a division of labor within a well-organized, factory-like apparatus of murder."[28] On this view, the criminal division of labor had no impact per se on the nature of the individual crime. It was simply the context of the crime in the same way that a wife's affair might be the context of her murder by a jealous husband. And of course, the Auschwitz court itself and especially presiding judge Hofmeyer were even more insistent on the normalcy of both the Auschwitz Trial and the crimes of Auschwitz.

Thus, the court saw the actions of the accused as criminal actions, pure and simple, as German law and precedent mandated. The law dictated what did and did not constitute murder, did and did not constitute perpetration. As legal actors, the members of the court were strictly limited in their room for maneuver in interpreting such matters. Still, the court had to acknowledge that these actions took place as functional elements within a larger state apparatus, which organized and directed them. As Hofmeyer put it in an essay written shortly after the trial, every effort must be made to "fit Nazi trials into the framework of [ordinary] criminal procedure – that is, if we do not view these trials as political trials but as murder trials in the sense of the criminal code, though admittedly ones in which the political situation which led the defendants to their actions cannot be lost from view but dare not become the centerpiece of the proceedings either."[29] It is in this context that the court's rejection of the prosecution's attempt to apply the doctrine of ideal concurrence to Auschwitz must be understood. Hofmeyer, presumably mindful of the risks of having the verdict overturned on appeal, adopted a cautious approach to interpreting the issue of perpetration.[30] Consequently, for the Auschwitz Trial court, in keeping with prevailing judicial practice, Nazi crimes were viewed as having taken place as part of a criminal division of labor but also as having remained, despite that, ordinary crimes.

[28] Henry Ormond, "Zwischenbilanz im Auschwitz-Prozeß," *Tribüne* 3, no. 11 (1964): 1188. Translation note: Ormond here contrasts *Verbrechen* with *Delikte*, where *Verbrechen* means crimes in the broadest sense, and *Delikte* are confined to more specific, statutory offenses. Cf. Henry Ormond, "Gedanken zum Problem der Schreibtischmörder," *Tribüne* 4 (1965): 1511–17.

[29] Hans Hofmeyer, "Prozessrechtliche Probleme und praktische Schwierigkeiten bei der Durchführung der Prozesse," in Ständigen Deputation des deutschen Juristentages, ed., *Probleme der Verfolgung und Ahndung von nationalsozialistischen Gewaltverbrechen: Sonderveranstaltung des 46. Deutschen Juristentages in Essen*, vol. 2 (Munich: C. H. Beck'sche Verlagsbuchhandlung, 1967), p. 44.

[30] Hofmeyer's caution in this regard proved justified. The BGH rejected the prosecution's appeal on the issue of ideal concurrence. See StA Revisionsbegründung (August 25, 1965), FFStA 4 Ks 2/63, Bd. 123, Bl. 19607. For the BGH's rejection, see BGH Urteil in Rüter, *Justiz und NS-Verbrechen*, pp. 881–82.

They still had to be conceptualized as individual actions originating in the psychological disposition of individual perpetrators.

However, it is precisely this relationship between personal motivation and criminal action that state-sponsored bureaucratic mass murder disrupts. As Max Weber pointed out some eighty years ago, one of the central character- istics of bureaucracy is that it renders subjective motivation irrelevant to the accomplishment of tasks.[31] This structural irrelevance of personal motives is no less characteristic of Nazi genocide than of any other form of for- mally rational bureaucratic activity. This is the true significance behind the terrifying exchange in Primo Levi's memoir, *Survival in Auschwitz*, where the inmate Levi asks one of his guards the simple question: "Why?" To which the guard replies, "There is no why here."[32] The point is not that the Holocaust did not have causes, but rather simply that these cannot be ade- quately explicated solely at the level of the individual perpetrator.

The whole character of German criminal law is designed to individuate and specify criminality and criminals, to prioritize the significance of their individual, subjective motives for action. But such distinctions can be mis- leading, if not perverse, when applied to the Holocaust, since it is a crime that makes sense only in its totality. And as a totality, this crime presup- posed diverse perpetrator motives, some of which may not even have been "base" at all except in their mode of application at Auschwitz. This is not to say that the Holocaust presupposed any specific set of diverse motives. Rather, like any large-scale public enterprise, it presupposed that one could achieve the relevant action coordination on the basis of diverse (perhaps even divergent), formally irrelevant motives. This is the essence of strategic action coordination. But differentiating the perpetrators of the Holocaust on the basis of presumed motivation means necessarily to fragment the Holocaust into a series of distinct, often unconnected crimes or half-crimes, none of which begins to add up to the whole crime of genocide. This belies the true character of the Holocaust as a total social act, like war, one that can only be fetishized or ideologized when not identified as such. This is why the Auschwitz Trial could sincerely strive for justice on one level – the level of criminal punishment – while simultaneously generating a kind of injustice on another level – the level of historical consciousness.

In a very real sense, one could say that German law's insistent focus on the subjective motivations of the defendants aided and abetted that distortion of memory already inevitable in the face of long-past, deeply traumatic events.

---

[31] "Decisive is that this 'freely' creative administration (and possibly judicature) would not constitute a realm of *free*, arbitrary action and discretion, of *personally* motivated favor and valuation, such as we shall find to be the case among pre-bureaucratic forms." Max Weber, *Economy and Society: An Outline of Interpretive Sociology*, vol. 2 (Berkley: University of California Press, 1978), p. 979.

[32] Primo Levi, *Survival in Auschwitz*, trans. Stuart Woolf (New York: Collier, 1960), p. 29.

As Primo Levi has stated: "One must note that the distortion of fact is often limited by the objectivity of the facts themselves, around which there exists the testimonies of third parties, documents, *corpora delicti,* historically accepted contexts. It is generally difficult to deny having committed a given act, or that such an act was committed; it is, on the contrary, very easy to alter the motivations which led us to an act and the passions within us which accompanied the act itself. This is an extremely fluid matter, subject to distortion even under very weak pressure; to the questions Why did you do this? Or What were you thinking as you did it? No reliable answer exists, because states of mind are by nature labile and even more labile is the memory of them."[33]

Yet the Frankfurt court had no choice but to shift the focal point of its proceedings to this slipperiest of terrain. That this was to the advantage of the defendants in the trial is quite apparent; it allowed many deeply impli-cated defendants (Mulka springs to mind) to escape the life sentence they would surely have received based solely on their "objective" actions. What is worse, in a sense, is that this subjectification of legal narration constituted a distraction from other possible questions, those that would have pointed in deep and profound ways *beyond Auschwitz,* to the broader, more disturbing problematic of the social conditions of possibility for genocide. This would necessarily have implicated almost the whole of German society, at least in moral and political terms.

Tzvetan Todorov's proposed solution to this dilemma, that judges simply eschew history in favor of universal law, is unfortunately no more adequate, nor would it even be possible.[34] When judges are asked to render verdicts on historical events or, more precisely, individual contributions to historical events, history can never be absent from the courtroom. Any attempt to omit it would produce distortions at least as misleading, if not more so, than the attempt to construct historical narrative in legal terms. As much as Judge Hofmeyer's instincts told him to leave history and politics to others, he could not help but recognize the need to situate the crimes of the Auschwitz Trial defendants in their historical context, or at least the juridical version of that context. Actions whose scope and impetus extend directly and immediately beyond the individual actor cannot be judged merely by the application of universal law but only in terms of an understanding of contextual culpability. All of the various actors in the Auschwitz Trail were aware of this to some

---

[33] Primo Levi, *The Drowned and the Saved,* trans. Raymond Rosenthal (New York: Vintage, 1989), p. 30.

[34] Todorov wrote of the dismissal of charges against Paul Touvier in France that "what is especially worth criticizing is not that they [the court] wrote bad history, it's that they wrote history at all, instead of being content to apply the law equitably and universally." Tzvetan Todorov, "The Touvier Affair," in Richard J. Golsan, ed., *Memory, the Holocaust, and French Justice* (Hanover: University Press of New England, 1996), p. 120.

extent, which is why they all constructed competing historical narratives. But in the end, each of these narratives either returned to the juridical framework of personal responsibility or failed to have any significant impact on the trial.

In other words, German courts, in confronting the Holocaust, were caught on the horns of a dilemma. To omit history from the trial altogether was an impossibility, given the nature of the crimes involved, but to construct that history in the normative vocabulary of German law was to distort the events of the Holocaust in ways that profoundly minimized its radicality and socio-structural scope, although it is doubtful that the legal actors in the trial could even have been aware of this distortion at the time, given the state of the historiography of the Holocaust in the mid-1960s. The tragedy of the Auschwitz Trial is not that it distorted an established historical understanding of Nazi genocide but that, in attempting to render criminal justice on that genocide, it failed to understand the full import of its own evidence.

The principle exceptions to this rule were, ironically enough, the defense counsel. In particular, they were keenly aware that the prosecution's legal narrative of Nazi criminality in effect misled itself with regard to both the legal status of Nazi actions and the degree and character of agency exercised by the defendants in Auschwitz. Many of these actions were, under the legal standards of the Third Reich, and in terms of positive law, *legal*. That the German judiciary had subsequently declared them, *ipso jure,* to have in fact been illegal the whole time was itself an ex post facto stipulation. For the defense attorneys, of course, this fact was one they tried to put to tactical use in exculpating their clients. One cannot be convicted of a crime if the action was not illegal. The greater historical and moral truth, that the Holocaust was a crime not because it was illegal in the positive sense but *despite the fact that it was not,* eluded the Auschwitz Trial defense counsel.[35] Their prosecution and judicial colleagues grasped the moral truth that the Holocaust had to be viewed as a criminal act, if the term "criminal" was to have any but a purely expedient meaning, but missed the more challenging dilemma of a criminality of, not against, law.

Similarly, the prosecution's vehement insistence that the defendants had exercised decisive, voluntary control over the course of events in Auschwitz, were directly "masters over life and death" there, was at best partially true. However perverse the conclusions he drew from this fact, Laternser was quite right to point out that by the time the deportees arrived at Auschwitz, their fate was sealed. While the defense's often cynical, sometimes crudely ideological efforts to stress their clients' limited scope for agency proved to

---

[35] Gerhard Werle and Thomas Wandres, *Auschwitz vor Gericht: Völkermord und bundes-deutsche Strafjustiz* (Munich: C. H. Beck, 1995), pp. 38–40.

be their most tactically savvy maneuver, leading as it did to many of the defendants being convicted as accomplices, rather than perpetrators, it also rendered their insight dubious. For the nationalist right, this argument merely confirmed that only Hitler was to blame (if even that). For the mainstream of German political culture, the fact that it had been the *defense* that stressed the limited autonomy of the defendants, their embeddedness in a larger state apparatus of murder, rendered this insight too politically suspect even to engage. And rightly so, because to claim that the Holocaust was a total social event, one that can be understood adequately only in terms of the structural lineaments of German society during the Third Reich, is decidedly *not* to assert that individual participants ought not be held criminally liable for their actions. It is rather to argue that such findings of individual guilt must be embedded within a larger framework that adequately situates them in the social context of genocide. To claim otherwise is to manipulate the truth for dubious purposes.

In the final analysis, then, the Auschwitz Trial could construct only an account of Auschwitz that isolated it from German society, from much of German history, and from its very conditions of possibility. Individuals were held responsible for Auschwitz, not as social actors, but as atomized monads. Torture was found to be the more egregious crime than genocide. Nazi law and the judicial state apparatus that sustained it were arbitrarily wished out of existence. None of these conclusions was capable of grasping the Holocaust as such. Consequently, the lessons learned by the West German public from the Auschwitz Trial failed to integrate an understanding of the Holocaust into the political culture of the Federal Republic in such a way that it ceased to be "shocking." This was precisely because so long as Auschwitz was explained at the level of individual motivation, it could not be understood at the level of political and social history.

All of which, then, raises the question posed by James Boyd White in his work on legal poetics: What makes some legal stories adequate and others not? When legal narratives are adequate, as in the *Oresteia* on White's reading, they integrate the competing, conflicting, overwhelming forces that afflict human life into a coherent, manageable pattern. "These forces are here integrated into a new form of life and activity, an institution that will tell stories with authority, so that they will remain the same and not slide into other intolerable and mysterious meanings. The law will thus rescue us all from the unbearable incoherence of the world that has been presented to us – an incoherence of story, of intellect, of action, of the very self."[36] In this sense, adequate legal narratives "work" because they *work socially.*

[36] James Boyd White, "Telling Stories in the Law and in Ordinary Life: The *Oresteia* and 'Noon Wine,'" in *Heracles' Bow: Essays on the Rhetoric and Poetics of the Law* (Madison: University of Wisconsin Press, 1985), p. 180.

In other words, not only do legally effective narratives organize the incoherent "noise" of social life, as Niklas Luhmann would have it;[37] they also
represent this new coherence back to society in a plausible and *meaningful*
manner. The inverse is true as well. Inadequate legal narratives fail because
they *fail socially.* According to White, Katherine Ann Porter's story "Noon
Wine" provides a valuable example of such failure. In this story, the pro-
tagonist, Mr. Thompson, commits suicide after being acquitted of murder
in a trial. The acquittal is inadequate to rehabilitate Mr. Thompson in his
own eyes, as evinced by his compulsive need to re-narrate the killing to his
neighbors after the trial and, ultimately, by his suicide. As such, White sees
this as a classic example of a failed legal narrative.

There are two reasons for this inadequacy on White's reading. First, the
verdict failed to rehabilitate Mr. Thompson despite acquitting him because
the trial's narrative was incomplete: It told not Thompson's version of events
but the court's. "The acquittal is not a judgment about what really happened
in the world, but about what happened in court."[38] Second, this *merely* legal
verdict did not meet Mr. Thompson's social needs (the good will and esteem
of his neighbors) because it was not and could not be "self-validating." The
verdict, like any legal document, could be assigned alternative meanings
outside the courtroom. "The text of a judicial judgment, like the text of a
contract or a statute, is in its own terms purely authoritative, but it is always
a question what role any such text will have in the community that it seeks
to govern."[39]

Here, then, the issue of success and failure returns, no longer in terms of
abstract truth or justice but in terms of social consequences. In confronting
Nazi genocide, German criminal law came up fundamentally against the
limits of its capacity to generate socially meaningful judgments. I would
argue that, as a legal and historical narrative, the Auschwitz Trial *failed
socially.* The story that it told did not organize the incoherent "noise" of
the Holocaust adequately. By reducing the complexity and systematicity of
the Holocaust to the dynamics of individual psychology, by relegating history to the status of a background condition for individual agency, and by
bracketing the experiential truth of the Auschwitz survivors, the trial helped
to fragment, rather than to conceptually organize, the Holocaust. True to
Hofmeyer's word, the trial remained, at the end of the day, a trial of "Mulka
and others," not an Auschwitz trial, much less a Holocaust trial in any strong
sense. This was in large part because, while the Holocaust itself was hardly
incoherent, the trial was incapable of articulating an understanding of its
coherence, which would have required a confrontation with the structural

---

[37] Niklas Luhmann, *Social Systems*, trans. John Bednarz, Jr., with Dirk Baecker (Stanford:
Stanford University Press, 1995), p. 214.
[38] White, "Telling Stories," p. 185.
[39] Ibid.

dimensions of systematic genocide that was beyond the bounds of German criminal law.

As Hannah Arendt has argued, "the fundamental problems posed by crimes of this kind...[is] that they were, and could only be, committed under a criminal *law* and by a criminal *state*."[40] Obviously, then, this poses a crucial dilemma for any court presuming to try such crimes. The law is first and foremost a dimension of the state, as the defense team in the Auschwitz Trial pointed out. This is different from merely being the state's instrument. The law is not so much a tool that the state uses as it is one of the essential media through which the state exists. The law derives its power from the state, and the (modern) state, its power from the law. This is what any trial represents at its core. The message is that the state retains the right (and has the capacity) to seal any breach in the social order. This is why trials are the form of redressive action *par excellence* in social dramas. Therefore, when it is the state itself that is criminal, is itself the source of the breach in the social order, it becomes difficult to see how the state can sit in judgment on itself. "Physician heal thyself!" may be sound advice, but its execution is in this context cumbersome at best. Such a cure becomes all the more difficult with regard to the Holocaust, where what is at stake is not simply a state-sponsored breach of social order but a state-enacted negation of the very possibility of social order. The Holocaust was not simply the murder of millions of individuals; it was the abolition of the very principle of social solidarity. How can any *single* state then claim to reconstitute the very foundation of social solidarity, which is the prerequisite for the existence of the state itself? This paradox led Karl Jaspers, among others, to argue that only an International Tribunal could render justice to such crimes.[41]

Instead, German law held that Nazi crimes, although state-sponsored, had always been *illegal* under existing law. The notion that law itself could become an instrument of illegality was thus made simply to "vanish" in an act of tremendous hubris and wishful thinking. As with all such vanishing acts, however, the legerdemain remained an illusion. The German refusal to accept the profound implications of state-implemented mass murder did not, in fact, eliminate those implications. Rather, it drove them underground, whence they reemerged with alarming regularity.

Indeed, these two dimensions of the social failure of the Auschwitz Trial – its inadequate theory of individual agency and its incomplete understanding of state criminality – form the central mechanism whereby this trial and

---

[40] Hannah Arendt, *Eichmann in Jerusalem: A Report on the Banality of Evil* (New York: Penguin, 1963), p. 262.

[41] For Jaspers's critique of Israel's claim to jurisdiction in the Eichmann case, see Hannah Arendt and Karl Jaspers, *Correspondence, 1926–1969*, ed. Lotte Kohler and Hans Saner (San Diego: Harcourt, Brace, 1992), pp. 410–14.

others like it helped to generate the recurring crises of memory that characterize postwar West German history. Because the understanding of the defendants as individual agents disguised the way in which the vast majority of German *society,* that is, Germans as an *organized* collectivity, were implicated in that same process of genocide, they could quite plausibly insist that they did not know of their own involvement. Most Germans had not, by and large, killed any Jews directly. And this fact was reinforced by the law as a kind of innocence. So, when some cultural event, some mode of discourse, some form of representation called their attention to this dimension of social responsibility in one way or another, their reaction was quite literally hysterical.

Similarly, the fundamental failure to confront *state-legitimated* mass criminality in German Nazi trials represented to Germans a portrait of their past that left them unimplicated. All they had done was to obey the law. If the law was innocent, then so too were they. This dynamic revealed itself with acute clarity and startling disingenuousness in Hofmeyer's defense of the German judiciary under the Third Reich. The law itself became a shield against culpability because culpability was reduced to individual criminal responsibility under law. In the press accounts of the Auschwitz Trial, the defendants were sometimes identified as in some ways "typically German," particularly in their proclivity for obedience. But this was obedience to an aberration, to a monstrous criminal regime that barely deserved the term "government." There was no way to derive from this depiction either the vast popularity of that regime among its German subjects or the strong lines of continuity connecting it to the Federal Republic. Legal continuity was continuity with the Imperial Reich and the Weimar Republic, not the Third Reich.

What then was the relationship between truth and justice that emerged in the Auschwitz Trial? The trial strove to find both justice and truth in the only terms available under the circumstances, those of German law. The result was indeed "fair" in these terms, though, as many commentators noted, one would be hard pressed to call it "justice" in the broadest sense of that term. The competing historical narratives that accompanied this quest for juridical justice were in no case truly adequate to the task at hand. However beneficial it may have been to have the "facts" of Auschwitz authoritatively determined in a court of law, these facts alone hardly spoke for themselves. And the various interpretive frameworks that emerged from the trial distorted the truth of the Holocaust at least as much as they revealed it. In particular, the form of "guilt" that emerged was so strictly delimited and so strongly rooted in individual psychology that the multifaceted complexity of guilt as a social category disappeared; in its rush to discern individual culpability, the trial displaced and eliminated the dimension of collective responsibility. Justice without truth or, more aptly, with the wrong kind of truth ultimately provides neither truth nor justice. In the end, the two can exist only in a symbiotic relationship of mutual dependence. What would ultimately be needed to satisfy the demands of both truth and justice would be a form of law, juridical and representational, that encompassed both individual responsibility and systematic, state-organized collective action. That the Auschwitz Trial was unable to attain this synthesis is hardly surprising given the character of German law. Whether a more adequate legal framework can be developed in future remains to be seen.

Bibliography

Archives

Archiv des Presse- und Informationsamtes der Bundesregierung, Bonn
Bundesarchiv, Berlin Lichterfelde
    Nachlaß Kaul, N2503/190
    Stiftung Archiv der Parteien und Massenorganizationen der DDR (SAPMO)
    DY 30/IV 2/2.028/57
    DY 30/IV 2/2.028/125
    DY 30/J IV 2/2 A-999
Bundesarchiv, Koblenz
    Bundesministerium des Innern, B 106
    Bundeskanzleramt, B 136
    Bundesministerium der Justiz, B 141
    Bundespresse- und Informationsamt, B 145
Frankfurt Staatsanwaltschaft, 4 Ks 2/63
    Hauptakten, 88 vols.
    Handakten, 27 vols.
Fritz Bauer Institute, Frankfurt am Main
    Sammlung Auschwitz Prozeß
Hessisches Hauptarchiv, Wiesbaden
    Hessische Minister der Justiz:
    Komplex KZ Auschwitz. Az. III (IV – 1076/59), 3 vols.
    Abt. 631a, Nr. 100
    Abt. 503. Nr. 1161
Institut für Zeitgeschichte, Munich
    House Archiv
Stadtarchiv, Frankfurt am Main
    Magistratsakten, Zugang III/2/1979, Sig. 61

Periodicals

Abendpost
Allgemeine Wochenzeitung der Juden in Deutschland

Allgemeine Zeitung/Neuer Mainzer Anzeiger
Augsburger Allgemeine
Badische Zeitung
Begegnung mit Polen
Berliner Morgenpost
Das Beste aus Gestern und Heute
Bild
Blätter für deutsche und internationale Politik
Bonner Rundschau
Bremer Nachrichten
Christ und Welt
Deutsch-Polnische Hefte
Deutsche Außenpolitik
Deutsche Nachrichten
Deutsche National-Zeitung und Soldaten-Zeitung
Deutsche Tagespost
Dokumentation der Zeit: Informations-Archiv
Frankfurter Allgemeine Zeitung
Frankfurter Hefte: Zeitschrift für Kultur und Politik
Frankfurter Neue Presse
Frankfurter Rundschau
Freie Presse
Die Freiheit
General-Anzeiger
Gestern und Heute
Hamburger Abendblatt
Hamburger Abendecho
Hamburger Echo
Handelsblatt
Hannoversche Allgemeine Zeitung
Hannoversche Presse
Hefte von Auschwitz
Hessische Allgemeine
Hessische Blätter für Volksbildung
Kieler Morgen
Kölner Stadt-Anzeiger
Kölnische Rundschau
Der Kurier
Lübecker Nachrichten
Main-Post
Mannheimer Morgen
Der Mittag
Der Monat
Der Morgen
Münchner Merkur
Nachtausgabe
National-Zeitung
Neue Juristische Wochenschrift

Neue Justiz
Neue Rhein und Ruhr Zeitung
Neue Tagespost
Neue Zeit
Neues Deutschland
Das Parlament
Die politische Meinung
Quick
Rhein-Neckar-Zeitung
Rhein-Zeitung
Rheinische Post
Rheinischer Merkur
Die Rheinpfalz
Ruhr-Nachrichten
Saarbrücker Zeitung
Schwarzwälder Bote
Sonntagsblatt
Spandauer Volksblatt
Der Spiegel
Stuttgarter Nachrichten
Stuttgarter Zeitung
Süddeutsche Zeitung
Der Tagesspiegel
Die Tat
Telegraf
Tribüne
Vorwärts
Die Welt
Welt am Sonntag
Welt der Arbeit
Weser-Kurier
Westdeutsche Allgemeine
Westfälische Nachrichten
Westfälische Rundschau
Wiesbadener Kurier
Die Zeit

Secondary Sources

Abel, Charles F., and Frank H. Marsh. *In Defense of Political Trials*. Westport, Conn.: Greenwood, 1994.

Allen, Michael Thad. *The Business of Genocide: The SS, Slave Labor, and the Concentration Camps*. Chapel Hill: University of North Carolina Press, 2002.

Aly, Götz. *"Final Solution": Nazi Population Policy and the Murder of the European Jews*. London: Arnold, 1999.

Aly, Götz, and Susanne Heim. *Vordenker der Vernichtung: Auschwitz und die deutschen Pläne für eine neue europäische Ordnung*. Frankfurt: Fischer Verlag, 1997.

Arbeitsgruppe der ehemaligen Häftlinge des Konzentrationslagers Auschwitz, ed. *I.G. Farben-Auschwitz-Massenmord: Über die Blutschuld der I.G. Farben.* Berlin: Komitee der Antifaschistichen Widerstandkämpfer in der DDR, 1964.

Arendt, Hannah. *Eichmann in Jerusalem: A Report on the Banality of Evil.* New York: Penguin, 1963.

Arendt, Hannah. *The Life of the Mind.* New York: Harcourt, Brace, Jovanovich, 1978.

Arendt, Hannah, and Karl Jaspers. *Correspondence, 1926–1969,* ed. Lotte Kohler and Hans Saner. San Diego: Harcourt, Brace, 1992.

Arndt, Helmut. *Die Konzentration in der Presse und die Problematik des Verleger-Fernsehens.* Frankfurt: Alfred Metzner Verlag, 1967.

Assheuer, Thomas, and Hans Sarkowicz, *Rechtsradikale in Deutschland: Die alte und die neue Rechte.* Munich: Beck, 1990.

Balzer, Friedrich-Martin, and Werrner Renz, eds. *Das Urteil im Frankfurter Auschwitz-Prozess, 1963–1965.* Bonn: Pahl-Rugenstein, 2004.

Barkan, Elazar. *The Guilt of Nations: Restitution and Negotiations for Historical Injustices.* New York: Norton, 2000.

Bartov, Omer. *Hitler's Army: Soldiers, Nazis, and War in the Third Reich.* Oxford: Oxford University Press, 1992.

Bassiouni, M. Cherif. *Crimes against Humanity in International Law.* Dordrecht: Martinus Nijhoff, 1992.

Bastian, Till. *Furchtbare Soldaten: Deutsche Kriegsverbrechen im Zweiten Weltkrieg.* Munich: C. H. Beck, 1997.

Bauer, Fritz. *Die Humanität der Rechtsordnung: Ausgewählte Schriften,* ed. Irmtrud Wojak and Joachim Pereles. Frankfurt: Campus Verlag, 1998.

Bauer, Fritz. "Ideal- oder Realkonkurrenz bei nationalsozialistischen Verbrechen?" *Juristenzeitung* 22 (1967): 625–28.

Bauer, Fritz. *Das Verbrechen und die Gesellschaft.* Munich: Ernst Reinhardt Verlag, 1957.

Bauer, Fritz. *Wir aber wollen Male richten euch zum Gedächtnis.* Dortmund: Schul- und Kulturamt der Stadt Dortmund, 1960.

Bauer, Yehuda. *Rethinking the Holocaust.* New Haven: Yale University Press, 2001.

Baumann, Jürgen. "Beihilfe bei eigenhändiger voller Tatbestandserfüllung." *Neue Juristische Wochenschrift* 16, no. 13 (1963): 561–65.

Baumann, Jürgen. "Die Tatherrschaft in der Rechtsprechung des BGH." *Neue Juristische Wochenschrift* 15, no. 9 (1962): 374–77.

Benton, Wilbourn E., and Georg Grimm, eds. *Nuremberg: German Views of the War Trials.* Dallas: Southern Methodist University Press, 1955.

Berg, Nicolas. *Der Holocaust und die westdeutschen Historiker: Erforschung und Erinnerung.* Göttingen: Wallstein, 2003.

Bergmann, Martin S., and Milton E. Jucovy, eds. *Generations of the Holocaust.* New York: Basic Books, 1982.

Bergmann, Werner. "Die Reaktion auf den Holocaust in Westdeutschland von 1945 bis 1989." *Geschichte in Wissenschaft und Unterricht* 21 (1992): 327–50.

Bergsdorf, Wolfgang. *Herrschaft und Sprache: Studie zur politischen Terminologie der Bundesrepublik Deutschland.* Pfullingen: Verlag Günther Neske, 1981.

Binding, Karl. *Die Normen und Ihre Übertretung: Eine Untersuchung über die rechtmässige Handlung und die Argen des Delikts,* 2nd ed. 4 vols. Leipzig: Felix Meiner, 1914 [1877].

Blackstone, William. *Commentaries on the Laws of England.* 4 vols. Chicago: University of Chicago Press, 1979 [1769].

Bloxham, Donald. *Genocide on Trial: War Crimes Trials and the Formation of Holocaust History and Memory.* Oxford: Oxford University Press, 2003.

Bockelmann, Paul. *Schuld und Sühne,* 2nd ed. Göttingen: Vandenhoeck & Ruprecht, 1958.

Bonhoeffer, Emmi. *Zeugen im Auschwitz-Prozeß: Begegnungen und Gedanken.* Wuppertal-Barmen: Johannes Kiefel Verlag, 1965.

Braese, Stephan, ed., *Rechenschaften: Juristischer und literarischer Diskurs in der Auseinandersetzung mit den NS-Massenverbrechen.* Göttingen: Wallstein, 2004.

Brechtken, Magnus. *Madagaskar für die Juden: Antisemitische Idee und politische Praxis, 1885–1945.* Munich: Oldenbourg, 1997.

Brenner, Michael. *After the Holocaust: Rebuilding Jewish Lives in Postwar Germany.* Princeton: Princeton University Press, 1997.

Breyer, Stephen. "Crimes against Humanity: Nuremberg, 1946." *New York University Law Review* 71 (1996): 1161–63.

Brink, Cornelia. *Auschwitz in der Paulskirche: Erinnerungspolitik in Fotoausstellungen der Sechziger Jahre.* Marburg: Jonas Verlag, 2000.

Brochhagen, Ulrich. *Nach Nürnberg: Vergangenheitsbewältigung und Westintegration in der Ära Adenauer.* Hamburg: Junius Verlag, 1994.

Broszat, Martin. *Nationalsozialistische Polenpolitik, 1939–1945.* Frankfurt: Fischer, 1961.

Broszat, Martin. "Siegerjustiz oder strafrechtliche 'Selbstreinigung' – Vergangenheitsbewältigung der Justiz, 1945–1949." *Vierteljahrshefte für Zeitgeschichte* 29 (1981): 477–544.

Browder, George C. "Perpetrator Character and Motivation: An Emerging Consensus?" *Holocaust and Genocide Studies* 17 (Winter 2003): 480–97.

Browning, Christopher. *Nazi Policy, Jewish Workers, German Killers.* Cambridge: Cambridge University Press, 2000.

Browning, Christopher. *Ordinary Men: Reserve Police Battalion 101 and the Final Solution in Poland.* New York: Harper Perennial, 1992.

Browning, Christopher. *The Path to Genocide: Essays on the Launching of the Final Solution.* Cambridge: Cambridge University Press, 1992.

Browning, Christopher. "Wehrmacht Reprisal Policy and the Mass Murder of Jews in Serbia." *Militärgeschichtliche Mitteilungen* 33 (1983): 31–47.

Browning, Christopher, and Jürgen Matthäus. *The Origins of the Final Solution: The Evolution of Nazi Jewish Policy, September 1939–March 1942.* London: Arrow, 2005.

Bruns, Hans-Jürgen. *Strafzumessungsrecht: Gesamtdarstellung,* 2nd ed. Cologne: Carl Heymans Verlag, 1974.

Buchheim, Hans, et al. *Anatomie des SS-States.* Munich: DTV, 1994 [1967].

Bude, Heinz. *Bilanz der Nachfolge: Die Bundesrepublik und der Nationalsozialismus.* Frankfurt: Suhrkamp, 1992.

Bundesministerium der Justiz. *Die Verfolgung nationalsozialistischer Straftaten im Gebiet der Bundesrepublik Deutschland seit 1945.* Bonn: Bundestagsdrucksache IV/3124, 1964.

Buruma, Ian. *The Wages of Guilt: Memories of War in Germany and Japan.* New York: Farrar Straus Giroux, 1994.

Buscher, Frank M. *The U.S. War Crimes Trial Program in Germany, 1945–1949.* New York: Greenwood, 1989.

Charny, Israel W., with Chanan Rapaport. *How Can We Commit the Unthinkable: Genocide, the Human Cancer.* Boulder: Westview, 1982.

Conot, Richard E. *Justice at Nuremberg.* New York: Carroll & Graf, 1984.

Clay, Lucius D. *Decision in Germany.* New York: Doubleday, 1950.

Cobler, Sebastian. "Das Gesetz gegen die 'Auschwitz-Lüge': Anmerkungen zu einem rechtspolitischen Ablaßhandel." *Kritische Justiz* 18 (1985): 159–70.

Cohen, Robert. *Understanding Peter Weiss.* Columbia: University of South Carolina Press, 1993.

Conradt, David P. "Changing German Political Culture." In Gabriel A. Almond and Sidney Verba, eds., *The Civic Culture Revisited.* Boston: Little, Brown, 1980, pp. 212–72.

Cornelissen, Christoph, Lutz Klinkhammer, and Wolfgang Schwentker, eds. *Erinnerungskulturen: Deutschland, Italien und Japan seit 1945.* Frankfurt: Fischer Verlag, 2003.

Cover, Robert. *Narrative, Violence, and the Law: The Essays of Robert Cover,* ed. Martha Minow et al. Ann Arbor: University of Michigan Press, 1995.

Critchley, Simon. *Ethics-Politics-Subjectivity: Essays on Derrida, Levinas and Contemporary French Thought.* London: Verso, 1999.

David, René, and John E. C. Brierley. *Major Legal Systems in the World Today: An Introduction to the Comparative Study of Law,* 2nd ed. New York: Free Press, 1978 [1968].

Davidson, Eugene. *The Trial of the Germans: An Account of the Twenty-two Defendants before the International Military Tribunal at Nuremberg.* New York: Collier, 1966.

de Certeau, Michel. *The Practice of Everyday Life.* Trans. Steven Rendall. Berkeley: University of California Press, 1984.

Demant, Ebbo, ed. *Auschwitz – "Direkt von der Rampe weg...": Kaduk, Erber, Klehr: Drei Täter geben zu Protokoll.* Reinbeck: Rowohlt Taschenbuch Verlag, 1979.

Doering-Manteuffel, Anselm. "Dimensionen von Amerikanisierung der deutschen Gesellschaft." *Archiv für Sozialgeschichte* 35 (1995): 1–35.

Doering-Manteuffel, Anselm. *Wie westlich sind die Deutschen? Amerikanisierung und Westernisierung im 20. Jahrhundert.* Göttingen: Vandenhoeck & Ruprecht, 1999.

Douglas, Lawrence. *The Memory of Judgment: Making Law and History in the Trials of the Holocaust.* New Haven: Yale University Press, 2001.

Dower, John W. *Embracing Defeat: Japan in the Wake of World War II.* New York: W. W. Norton, 1999.

Dressler, Joshua. *Understanding Criminal Law,* 2nd ed. New York: Matthew Bender, 1995.

Ducklau, Volker. "Die Befehlsproblematik bei NS-Tötungsverbrechen: Eine Untersuchung anhand von 900 Urteilen deutscher Gerichte von 1945 bis 1965." Ph.D. diss., Universität Freiburg, 1976.

Duff, R. A. *Intention, Agency and Criminal Liability: Philosophy of Action and the Criminal Law.* Oxford: Basil Blackwell, 1990.

Eckstaedt, Anita. *Nationalsozialismus in der "zweiten Generation": Psychoanalyse von Hörigkeitsverhältnissen.* Frankfurt: Suhrkamp, 1989.

Entscheidungen des Bundesgerichtshofes in Strafsachen. 36 vols. Berlin: Carl Heymanns Verlag, 1951–90.
Entscheidungen des Reichsgerichts in Strafsachen. 77 vols. Leipzig: Verlag von Beit und Comp, 1880–1944.
Fabréguet, Michel. "La Commission des Nations Unies pour les Crimes de Guerre et la Notion de Crimes contre l'Humanité (1943–1948)." *Revue d'Allemagne* 23 (Fall 1991): 519–53.
Federal Rules of Evidence Handbook. Cincinnati: Anderson, 2001.
Feldman, Lily Gardner. *The Special Relationship between West Germany and Israel.* Boston: George Allen & Unwin, 1984.
Ferencz, Benjamin B. *Less than Slaves: Jewish Forced Labor and the Quest for Compensation.* Published in Association with the United States Holocaust Memorial Museum. Bloomington: Indiana University Press, 2002 [1979].
Finkelstein, Norman G., and Ruth Bettina Birn. *A Nation on Trial: The Goldhagen Thesis and Historical Truth.* New York: Henry Holt, 1998.
Finkielkraut, Alain. *Remembering in Vain: The Klaus Barbie Trial and Crimes against Humanity.* Trans. Roxanne Lapidus with Sima Godfry. New York: Columbia University Press, 1992.
Fletcher, George P. *Basic Concepts of Criminal Law.* Oxford: Oxford University Press, 1998.
Foucault, Michel. *Discipline and Punish: The Birth of the Prison.* Trans. Alan Sheridan. New York: Vintage, 1977.
Frank, Reinhard. *Über den Aufbau des Schuldbegriffs.* Giessen: Alfred Töpelmann, 1907.
Frei, Norbert. *Amerikanische Lizenzpolitik und deutsche Pressetradition: Die Geschichte der Nachkriegszeitung Südost-Kurier.* München: R. Oldenbourg, 1986.
Frei, Norbert. "Der Frankfurter Auschwitz-Prozeß und die deutsche Zeitgeschichtsforschung." In Fritz Bauer Institut, ed., *Auschwitz: Geschichte, Rezeption und Wirkung.* Frankfurt: Campus Verlag, 1996, pp. 123–38.
Frei, Norbert. *Vergangenheitspolitk: Die Anfänge der Bundesrepublik und die NS-Vergangenheit.* Munich: C. H. Beck, 1996.
Frei, Norbert, Dirk van Laak, and Michael Stolleis, eds. *Geschichte vor Gericht: Historiker, Richter und die Suche nach Gerechtigkeit.* Munich: C. H. Beck, 2000.
Freudiger, Kerstin. *Die juristische Aufarbeitung von NS-Verbrechen.* Beiträge zur Rechtsgeschichte des 20. Jahrhunderts, vol. 33. Tübingen: Mohr Siebeck, 2002.
Friedlander, Henry. *The Origins of Nazi Genocide: From Euthanasia to the Final Solution.* Chapel Hill: University of North Carolina Press, 1995.
Friedländer, Saul. *Nazi Germany and the Jews,* vol. 1: *The Years of Persecution, 1933–1939.* New York: HarperCollins, 1997.
Friedländer, Saul, ed. *Probing the Limits of Representation: Nazism and the "Final Solution."* Cambridge: Harvard University Press, 1992.
Friedrich, Jörg. *Die kalte Amnestie: NS-Täter in der Bundesrepublik,* rev. ed. Munich: Piper, 1994 [1984].
Fröhlich, Claudia. "Die Gründung der 'Zentralen Stele' in Ludwigsburg – Alibi oder Beginn einer systematischen justitiellen Aufarbeitung der NS-Vergangenheit?" In Gerhard Pauli and Thomas Vormbaum, eds., *Justiz und Nationalsozialismus – Kontinuität und Diskontinuität: Fachtagung in der Justizakademie des Landes NRW, Recklinghausen, am 19. und 20. November 2001.* Berlin: Berliner Wissenschafts-Verlag, 2003, pp. 213–50.

Fulbrook, Mary. *German National Identity after the Holocaust*. Cambridge: Polity, 1999.

Gabriel, Oscar W. "Demokratiezufriedenheit und demokratische Einstellungen in der Bundesrepublik." *Aus Politik und Wissenschaft* 22 (1987): 32–45.

Gellately, Robert. *Backing Hitler: Consent and Coercion in Nazi Germany*. Oxford: Oxford University Press, 2001.

Geyer, Michael. "Germany, or, The Twentieth Century as History." *South Atlantic Quarterly* 96 (Fall 1997): 663–702.

Gilbert, G. M. *Nuremberg Diary*. New York: Signet, 1947.

Ginsburgs, George, and V. N. Kudriavtsev, eds. *The Nuremberg Trials and International Law*. Dodrecht: M. Nijhoff, 1990.

Ginzburg, Carlo. *The Judge and the Historian: Marginal Notes on a Late-Twentieth-Century Miscarriage of Justice*. London: Verso, 1999.

Giordano, Ralph. *Die zweite Schuld oder Von der Last Deutscher zu sein*. Hamburg: Rasch und Röhring Verlag, 1987.

Gnielka, Thomas. "Die Henker von Auschwitz: Ein Prozeß und seine Vorgeschichte." *Metall* 16 (1961).

Goldhagen, Daniel Jonah. *Hitler's Willing Executioners: Ordinary Germans and the Holocaust*. New York: Alfred A. Knopf, 1996.

Gotto, Klaus ed. *Der Staatssekretär Adenauers: Persönlichkeit und politisches Wirken Hans Globkes*. Stuttgart: Klett-Cotta, 1980.

Götz, Albrecht. *Bilanz der Verfolgung von NS-Straftaten*. Cologne: Bundesanzeiger Verlag, 1986.

Grabitz, Helga, et al., eds. *Die Normalität des Verbrechens: Bilanz und Perspektive zu den nationalsozialistischen Gewaltverbrechen. Festschrift für Wolfgang Scheffler zum 65. Geburtstag*. Berlin: Edition Hentrich, 1994.

Greve, Michael. *Der justitielle und rechtspolitische Umgang mit den NS-Gewaltverbrechen in den sechziger Jahren*. Europäische Hochschulschriften: Reihe III Geschichte und ihre Hilfswissenschaften, vol. 911. Frankfurt: Peter Lang, 2001.

Grewe, Wilhelm. *Nürnberg als Rechtsfrage*. Stuttgart: Ernst Klett, 1947.

Gutman, Yisrael, and Michael Berenbaum, eds. *Anatomy of the Auschwitz Death Camp*. Bloomington: Indiana University Press, 1994.

Habermas, Jürgen. *The Theory of Communicative Action*, vol. 2: *Lifeworld and System: A Critique of Functionalist Reason*. Boston: Beacon, 1987.

Hardwig, Werner. "Über den Begriff der Täterschaft: Zugleich eine Besprechung der Habilitationsschrift von Claus Roxin 'Täterschaft und Tatherrschaft.'" *Juristenzeitung* 20, no. 21 (1965): 667–71.

Harris, Whitney. *Tyranny on Trial: The Trial of the Major German War Criminals at the End of World War II at Nuremberg, Germany, 1945–1946*. Dallas: Southern Methodist University Press, 1999 [1954].

Hart, H. L. A. *The Concept of Law*, 2nd ed. Oxford: Oxford University Press, 1994.

Hart, H. L. A. *Punishment and Responsibility: Essays in the Philosophy of Law*. Oxford: Clarendon, 1968.

Hart, H. L. A., and A. M. Honoré. *Causation in the Law*, 2nd ed. Oxford: Clarendon, 1985.

Hartman, Geoffrey H., ed. *Holocaust Remembrance: The Shapes of Memory*. Oxford: Blackwell, 1994.

Hauer, Nadine. *Die Mitläufer, oder die Unfähigkeit zu fragen: Auswirkungen des Nationalsozialismus für die Demokratie von Heute.* Opladen: Leske & Budrich, 1994.

Hayes, Peter. *Industry and Ideology: IG Farben in the Nazi Era,* new ed. Cambridge: Cambridge University Press, 2001.

Heinemann, Hugo. "Die Binding'sche Schuldlehre: Ein Beitrag zu ihrer Widerlegung." In *Abhandlungen des kriminalistischen Seminars zu Marburg,* ed. Franz von Liszt. Freiburg: J. C. B. Mohr, 1889.

Henkys, Reinhard. *Die nationalsozialistischen Gewaltverbrechen: Geschichte und Gericht,* ed. Dietrich Goldschmidt. Stuttgart: Kruez-Verlag, 1964.

Herbert, Ulrich. *Best: Biographische Studien über Radikalismus, Weltanschauung und Vernunft, 1903–1989,* 2nd ed. Bonn: Dietz Verlag, 1996.

Herbert, Ulrich, ed. *Wandlungsprozesse in Westdeutschland: Belastung, Integration, Liberalisierung, 1945–1980.* Göttingen: Wallstein, 2002.

Herbst, Ludolf. *Wiedergutmachung in der Bundesrepublik Deutschland.* Munich: R. Oldenbourg, 1989.

Herf, Jeffrey. *Divided Memory: The Nazi Past in the Two Germanys.* Cambridge: Harvard University Press, 1997.

Hey, Bernd. "NS-Gewaltverbrechen: Wissenschaft und Öffentlichkeit. Anmerkungen zu einer interdisziplinären Tagung über die Vergangenheitsbewältigun." *Geschichte in Wissenschaft und Unterricht* 9 (1984): 86–91.

Hey, Bernd. "NS-Prozesse: Versuch einer juristischen Vergangenheitsbewältigung." *Geschichte in Wissenschaft und Unterricht* 6 (1981): 51–70.

Hilberg, Raul. *The Destruction of the Jews,* rev. ed. 3 vols. New York: Holmes and Meier, 1985.

Hilberg, Raul. *Sonderzüge nach Auschwitz.* Frankfurt: Ullstein, 1987.

Hirsch, Rudolf. *Um die Endlösung: Prozeßberichte über den Lischka-Prozeß in Köln und den Auschwitz-Prozeß in Frankfurt/M.* Rudolstadt: Greifenverlag, 1982.

Hockerts, Hans Günter, and Christiane Kuller, eds. *Nach der Verfolgung: Widergutmachung nationalsozialistischen Unrechts in Deutschland?* Göttingen: Wallstein, 2003.

Hoffmann, Christa. 'Die justitielle 'Vergangenheitsbewältigung' in der Bundesrepublik Deutschland: Tatsachen und Legenden." In Uwe Backes, Eckhard Jesse, and Rainer Zitelmann, eds., *Die Schatten der Vergangenheit: Impulse zur Historisierung des Nationalsozialismus.* Frankfurt: Ulstein, 1992.

Hoffmann, Christa. *Stunden Null? Vergangenheitsbewältigung in Deutschland 1945 und 1989.* Bonn: Bouvier, 1992.

Hoffmann, Friedrich. *Die Verfolgung der nationalsozialistischen Gewaltverbrechen in Hessen.* Baden-Baden: Nomos, 2001.

Hofmeyer, Hans. "Prozessrechtliche Probleme und praktische Schwierigkeiten bei der Durchführung der Prozesse." In *Probleme der Verfolgung und Ahndung von nationalsozialistischen Gewaltverbrechen: Sonderveranstaltung des 46. Deutschen Juristentages in Essen,* ed. Standigen Deputation des deutschen Juristentages. Munich: C. H. Beck'sche Verlagsbuchhandlung, 1967.

Hoggan, David L. *Der erzwungene Krieg: Die Ursachen und Urheber des 2. Weltkriegs.* Tübignen: Verlag der deutschen Hochschullehrer-Zeitung, 1961.

Hoggan, David L. *The Forced War: When Peaceful Revision Failed.* Costa Mesa: Institute for Historical Review, 1989.

Horn, Sabine. " 'Jetzt aber zu einem Thema, das uns in dieser Woche alle beschäftigt':
Die westdeutsche Fernsehberichterstattung über den Frankfurter Auschwitz-
Prozess (1963–1965) und den Düsseldorfer Majdanek-Prozess (1975–1981) – ein
Vergleich." *1999: Zeitschrift für Sozialgeschichte des 20. und 21. Jahrhunderts* 17
(2002): 13–43.

Höß, Rudolf. *Commandant of Auschwitz.* Trans. Constantine FitzGibbon. London:
Weidenfeld and Nicolson, 1959.

Höß, Rudolf. *Kommandant von Auschwitz: Autobiographische Aufzeichnungen.*
Stuttgart: Deutsche Verlags-Anstalt, 1958.

Hurwitz, Harold. "Die Pressepolitik der Alliierten." In Harry Pross, ed., *Deutsche
Presse seit 1945.* Bern: Scherz, 1965, pp. 27–55.

International Military Tribunal. *The Trial of the Major War Criminals before the
International Military Tribunal, 14 November 1945–1 October 1946.* 42 vols.
Nuremberg: Secretariat of the Tribunal, 1947–49.

Jackson, Robert H. *The Nuremberg Case.* New York: Cooper Square, 1971.

Jacobs, Norbert. "Der Streit um Dr. Hans Globke in der öffentlichen Meinung der
Bundesrepublik Deutschland, 1949–1973: Ein Beitrag zur politischen Kultur in
Deutschland." Ph.D. diss., University of Bonn, 1992.

Jäger, Herbert. *Verbrechen unter totalitärer Herrschaft: Studien zur nationalsozialistischer Gewaltkriminalität.* Frankfurt: Suhrkamp, 1982.

Jakobs, Günther. *Das Schuldprinzip.* Opladen: Westdeutscher Verlag, 1993.

Jarausch, Konrad H., and Michael Geyer. *Shattered Past: Reconstructing German
Histories.* Princeton: Princeton University Press, 2003.

Jasper, Gotthard. "Wiedergutmachung und Westintegration: Die halbherzige justizielle Aufarbeitung der NS-Vergangenheit in der frühen Bundesrepublik." In
Ludolf Herbst, ed., *Westdeutschland, 1945–1955: Unterwerfung, Kontrolle, Integration.* Munich: R. Oldenbourg Verlag, 1986.

Jaspers, Karl. *Wohin treibt die Bundesrepublik? Tatsachen, Gefahren, Chancen.*
Munich: Piper, 1966.

Johnson, Eric A. *Nazi Terror: The Gestapo, Jews, and Ordinary Germans.* New
York: Basic Books, 1999.

Kant, Immanuel. *The Metaphysics of Morals.* Trans. Mary Gregor. Cambridge: Cambridge University Press, 1996.

Kant, Immanuel. *Religion within the Limits of Reason Alone.* Trans. Theodore M.
Greene and Hoyt H. Hudson. New York: Harper Torchbooks, 1960.

Kárný, Miroslav. "Waffen-SS und Konzentrationslager." *Jahrbuch für Geschichte* 33
(1986): 231–61.

Katz, Leo. *Bad Acts and Guilty Minds: Conundrums of the Criminal Law.* Chicago:
University of Chicago Press, 1987.

Kaul, Friedrich Karl. *Auschwitz Trial in Frankfurt-on-Main: Summing up and reply of
Professor Dr. Friedrich Karl Kaul, legal representative of the co-plaintiffs resident
in the German Democratic Republic in the criminal proceedings against Mulka
and others before the criminal court at the Provincial Court in Frankfurt-on-Main.*
N.p., 1965.

Kaul, Friedrich Karl. *Schlußvortrag und Erwiderung des Prof. Dr. Friedrich Karl
Kaul Prozeßvertreter der in der Deutschen Demokratischen Republik ansässigen
Nebenkläger im Strafverfahren gegen Mulka u.a. vor dem Schwurgericht beim
Frankfurt am Main.* Herausgegeben von der Arbeitsgruppe der ehemaligen

Häftlinge des Konzentrationslagers Auschwitz beim Komitee der Antifaschistischen Widerstandskämpfer in der Deutschen Demokratischen Republik und dem Nationalrat der Nationalen Front des demokratischen Deutschlands, 1965.

Kempner, Robert M. W. *Ankläger einer Epoche: Lebenserinnerungen.* Frankfurt: Ullstein, 1983.

Kershaw, Ian. *The Nazi Dictatorship: Problems and Perspectives of Interpretation,* 4th ed. London: Arnold, 2000.

Kenny, Anthony. "Intention and *Mens Rea* in Murder." In *Law, Morality, and Society: Essays in Honour of H. L. A. Hart,* ed. P. M. S. Hacker and J. Raz. Oxford: Clarendon, 1977.

Kielmansegg, Peter Graf. *Lange Schatten: Vom Umgang der Deutschen mit der nationalsozialistischen Vergangenheit.* Berlin: Siedler Verlag, 1989.

Kimball, Warren F. *Swords or Ploughshares? The Morgenthau Plan for Defeated Germany, 1943–1945.* Philadelphia: Lippincott, 1976.

Kirchheimer, Otto. *Political Justice: The Use of Legal Procedure for Political Ends.* Princeton: Princeton University Press, 1961.

Kittel, Manfred. *Die Legende von der "Zweiten Schuld": Vergangenheitsbewältigung in der Ära Adenauer.* Berlin: Ullstein, 1993.

Kleßmann, Christoph. *Zwei Staaten, eine Nation: Deutsche Geschichte, 1955–1970.* Göttingen: Vandenhoeck & Ruprecht, 1988.

Klotz, Johannes. "Die Ausstellung 'Vernichtungskrieg. Verbrechen der Wehrmacht 1941 bis 1944': Zwischen Geschichtswissenschaft und Geschichtspolitik." In Detlef Bald, Johannes Klotz, and Wolfram Wette, eds., *Mythos Wehrmacht: Nachkriegsdebatten und Traditionspflege.* Berlin: Aufbau Taschenbuch Verlag, 2001, pp. 116–76.

Kochavi, Arieh J. *Prelude to Nuremberg: Allied War Crimes Policy and the Question of Punishment.* Chapel Hill: University of North Carolina Press, 1998.

Kogon, Eugen. *Der SS Staat: Das System der deutschen Konzentrationslager.* Munich: Karl Alber Verlag, 1946.

Kogon, Eugen. *The Theory and Practice of Hell: The German Concentration Camps and the System behind Them.* Trans. Heinz Norden. New York: Farrar, Straus, 1950.

Kogon, Eugen. *Die unvollendete Erneuerung: Deutschland im Kräftfeld, 1945–1963.* Frankfurt: Europäische Verlagsanstalt, 1964.

Kohlstruck, Michael. "Das zweite Ende der Nachkriegszeit: Zur Veränderung der politischen Kultur um 1960." In Gary S. Schaal and Andreas Wöll, eds., *Vergangenheitsbewältigung: Modelle der politischen und sozialen Integration in der bundesdeutschen Nachkriegsgeschichte.* Baden-Baden: Nomos, 1997.

Komitee der Antifaschistischen Widerstandskämpfer der Deutschen Demokratischen Republik, ed. *SS im Einsatz: Eine Dokumentation über die Verbrechen der SS,* 3rd ed. Berlin: Kongress-Verlag, 1957.

Koonz, Claudia. "Between Memory and Oblivion: Concentration Camps in German Memory." In John R. Gillis, ed., *Commemorations: The Politics of National Identity.* Princeton: Princeton University Press, 1994.

Korn, Hans-Joachim. "Täterschaft oder Teilnahme bei staatlich organisierten Verbrechen." *Neue Jurisitische Wochenschrift* 18, no. 27 (1965): 1206–10.

Kröger, Ulrich. "Die Ahndung von NS-Verbrechen vor Westdeutschen Gerichte und ihre Rezeption in der deutschen Öffentlichkeit 1958 bis 1965 unter besonderer

Berücksichtigung von 'Spiegel,' 'Stern,' 'Zeit,' 'SZ,' 'FAZ,' 'Welt,' 'Bild,' 'Hamburger Abendblatt,' 'NZ' und 'Neuem Deutschland.'" Ph.D. diss., University of Hamburg, 1973.

Krüger, Horst. *Das zerbochene Haus: Eine Jugend in Deutschland*. Frankfurt: Fischer Taschenbuch Verlag, 1980 [1976].

Kuczynski, Jürgen. "Die Verflechtung von sicherheitzpolizeilichen und wirtschaftlichen Interessen bei der Einrichtung und im Betrieb des KZ Auschwitz und seiner Nebenlager." *Dokumentation der Zeit: Informations-Archiv* 16 (1964): 36–42.

Küsters, Gerd-Walter. *Kants Rechtsphilosophie*. Darmstadt: Wissenschaftliche Buchgesellschaft, 1988.

LaCapra, Dominick. *Representing the Holocaust: History, Theory, Trauma*. Ithaca: Cornell University Press, 1994.

Landeszentrale für Politische Bildung NRW, ed. *Vereint Vergessen? Justiz- und NS-Verbrechen in Deutschland*. Düsseldorf: Landeszentrale für Politische Bildung Nordrein-Westfalen, 1993.

Langbein, Hermann. *Der Auschwitz Prozeß: Eine Dokumentation*. 2 vols. Frankfurt: Verlag Neue Kritik, 1995 [1965].

Langbein, Hermann. *Im Namen des deutschen Volkes: Zwischenbilanz der Prozesse wegen nationalsozialistischer Verbrechen*. Vienna: Europa Verlag, 1963.

Langbein, John H. *Comparative Criminal Procedure: Germany*. St. Paul: West Publishing, 1977.

Langer, Lawrence L. *Admitting the Holocaust: Collected Essays*. Oxford: Oxford University Press, 1995.

Laternser, Hans. *Die andere Seite im Auschwitz-Prozeß, 1963/65*. Stuttgart: Seewald Verlag, 1966.

Laternser, Hans. *Verteidigung deutscher Soldaten: Plädoyers vor alliierten Gerichten*. Bonn: Rolf Bohnemeier, 1950.

Lavy, George. *Germany and Israel: Moral Debt and National Interest*. London: Frank Cass, 1996.

Lemke, Michael. "Kampagnen gegen Bonn: Die Systemkriese der DDR und die West-Propaganda der DDR, 1960–1963." *Vierteljahrshefte für Zeitgeschichte* 41 (1993): 153–74.

Lemke, Michael. "Der Lange Weg zum 'geregelten Nebeneinander': Die Deutschlandpolitik der DDR Mitte der fünfziger bis Mitte der siebziger Jahre." In Christoph Kleßmann, Hans Misselwitz, and Günther Wichert, eds., *Deutsche Vergangenheiten – eine gemeinsamen Herausforderung: Der schwierige Umgang mit der doppelten Nachkriegsgeschichte*. Berlin: C. Links, 1999: 61–86.

Levi, Primo. *The Drowned and the Saved*. Trans. Raymond Rosenthal. New York: Vintage, 1989.

Levi, Primo. *Survival in Auschwitz*. Trans. Stuart Woolf. New York: Collier, 1960.

Lifton, Robert Jay. *The Nazi Doctors: Medical Killing and the Psychology of Genocide*. New York: Basic Books, 1986.

Lippmann, Walter. *Public Opinion*. New York: Free Press, 1997 [1922].

Lipstadt, Deborah E. *Denying the Holocaust: The Growing Assault on Truth and Memory*. New York: Free Press, 1993.

Longerich, Peter. *Politik der Vernichtung: eine Gesamtdarstellung der Nationalsozialistische Judenverfolgung*. Munich: Piper, 1998.

Lozowick, Yaacov. *Hitler's Bureaucrats: The Nazi Security Police and the Banality of Evil.* Trans. Haim Watzman. London: Continuum, 2000.

Lübbe, Hermann. "Der Nationalsozialismus im politischen Bewußtsein der Gegenwart." *Historische Zeitschrift* 236 (1983): 579–99.

Lübbe, Hermann. "Verdrängung? Über eine Kategorie zur Kritik des deutschen Vergangenheitsverhältnisses." In Hans-Hermann Weibe, ed., *Die Gegenwart der Vergangenheit: Historikerstreit und Erinnerungsarbeit.* Bad Segeberg: C. H. Wässer, 1989: 94–106.

Luhmann, Niklas. *Social Systems.* Trans. John Bednarz, Jr., with Dirk Baecker. Stanford: Stanford University Press, 1995.

Maguire, Peter. *Law and War: An American Story.* New York: Columbia University Press, 2001.

Marrus, Michael R. "The Holocaust at Nuremberg." In *Yad Vashem Studies*, vol. 26. Ed. David Silberklang. Jerusalem, 1998.

Marrus, Michael R. *The Nuremberg War Crimes Trial, 1945–46: A Documentary History.* Boston: Bedford, 1997.

Maser, Werner. *Nürnberg: Tribunal der Sieger.* Düsseldorf: Econ Verlag, 1977.

Mason, Tim. "Intention and Explanation: A Current Controversy about the Interpretation of National Socialism." In Gerhard Hirschfeld and Lothar Kettenacker, eds., *Der Führerstaat: Mythos und Realität.* Stuttgart: Klett-Cotta, 1981, pp. 21–40.

Mayer, Arno J. *Why Did the Heavens Not Darken? The "Final Solution" in History.* New York: Pantheon, 1988.

Mazower, Mark. "Military Violence and National Socialist Values: The *Wehrmacht* in Greece, 1941–1944." *Past and Present* (February 1992): 129–58.

Meusch, Matthias. *Von der Diktatur zur Demokratie: Fritz Bauer und die Aufarbeitung der NS-Verbrechen in Hessen (1956–1968).* Wiesbaden: Historische Kommission für Nassau, 2001.

Meyrowitz, Henri. *La Répression par les Tribunaux Allemands des Crimes contre L'Humanité et de L'Appartenance a une Organisation Criminelle en Application de la Loi No. 10 du Conseil de Contrôle Allié.* Paris: Librairie Générale de Droit et de Jurisprudence, 1960.

Mitscherlich, Alexander, and Margarete. *Die Unfähigkeit zu trauern: Grundlagen kollektiven Verhaltens.* München: Piper Verlag, 1967.

Moeller, Robert G. *War Stories: The Search for a Usable Past in the Federal Republic of Germany.* Berkeley: University of California Press, 2001.

Müller, Ingo. *Furchtbare Juristen: Die unbewältigte Vergangenheit unserer Justiz.* Munich: Knaur, 1987.

Naimark, Norman M. *Fires of Hatred: Ethnic Cleansing in Twentieth-Century Europe.* Cambridge: Harvard University Press, 2001.

Nationalsozialismus und Justiz: Die Aufarbeitung von Gewaltverbrechen damals und heute. Münster: agenda Verlag, 1993.

Naucke, Wolfgang. "Über den Einfluß Kants auf Theorie und Praxis des Strafrechts im 19. Jahrhundert." In J. Blühdorn and J. Ritter, eds., *Philosophie und Rechtswissenschaft: Zum Problem ihrer Beziehung im 19. Jahrhundert.* Frankfurt: Vittorio Klosterman, 1969.

Naumann, Bernd. *Auschwitz: A Report on the Proceedings against Robert Karl Ludwig Mulka and Others before the Court at Frankfurt.* Trans. Jean Steinberg. New York: Frederick A. Praeger, 1966.

Naumann, Bernd. *Auschwitz: Bericht über die Strafsache gegen Mulka und andere vor dem Schwurgericht Frankfurt.* Frankfurt: Athenäum Verlag, 1965.

Naumann, Bernd. *Auschwitz: Bericht über die Strafsache gegen Mulka und andere vor dem Schwurgericht Frankfurt,* abridged and revised by the author. Frankfurt: Fischer Bücherei, 1968.

Naumann, Bernd. *Auschwitz: Bericht über die Strafsache gegen Mulka und andere vor dem Schwurgericht Frankfurt.* Berlin: Philo Verlag, 2004.

Newman, Leonard S., and Ralph Erber, eds. *Understanding Genocide: The Social Psychology of the Holocaust.* New York: Oxford University Press, 2002.

Nino, Carlos Santiago. *Radical Evil on Trial.* New Haven: Yale University Press, 1996.

Noelle, Elisabeth, and Erich Peter Neumann. *Jahrbuch der öffentlichen Meinung, 1958–64.* Allensbach: Verlag für Demoskopie, 1965.

Noelle-Neumann, Elisabeth. *The Spiral of Silence: Public Opinion – Our Social Skin,* 2nd ed. Chicago: University of Chicago Press, 1993.

Ormond, Henry. "Gedanken zum Problem der Schreibtischmörder." *Tribüne* 4, no. 14 (1965): 1511–17.

Ormond, Henry. "Plädoyer im Auschwitz-Prozeß." *Sonderreihe aus Gestern und Heute* 7 (1965): 1–63.

Ormond, Henry. "Rückblick auf den Auschwitz-Prozeß." *Tribüne* 4, no. 16 (1965): 1723–28.

Ormond, Henry. "Zwischenbilanz im Auschwitz-Prozeß." *Tribüne* 3, no. 11 (1964): 1183–90.

Orth, Karin. *Die Konzentrationslager-SS: Sozialstrukturelle Analysen und biographische Studien.* Göttingen: Wallstein, 2000.

Osiel, Mark. *Mass Atrocity, Collective Memory and the Law.* New Brunswick: Transaction, 1997.

Ossorio-Capella, Carlos. *Der Zeitungsmarkt in der Bundesrepublik Deutschland* Frankfurt: Athenäum, 1972.

Ostendorf, Heribert. "Die – wiedersprüchlichen – Auswirkungen der Nürnberger Prozesse auf die westdeutsche Justiz." In Gerd Hankel and Gerhard Stuby, eds., *Strafgerichte gegen Menschheitsverbrechen: Zum Völkerstrafrecht 50 Jahre nach den Nürnberger Prozessen.* Hamburg: Hamburger Edition, 1995: 73–95.

Paul, Gerhard, ed. *Die Täter der Shoah: Fanatische Nationalsozialisten oder ganz normale Deutsche?* Göttingen: Wallstein, 2002.

Pauli, Gerhard. *Die Rechtsprechung des Reichsgerichts in Strafsachen zwischen 1933 und 1945 und ihre Fortwirkung in der Rechtsprechung des Bundesgerichtshofs.* Berlin: W. de Gruyter, 1992.

Pendas, Devin O. "The Historiography of Horror: The Frankfurt Auschwitz Trial and the German Historical Imagination." In Jeffrey Diefendorf, ed., *Lessons and Legacies VI: New Currents in Holocaust Research.* Evanston: Northwestern University Press, 2004.

Pendas, Devin O. "'I didn't know what Auschwitz was': The Frankfurt Auschwitz Trial and the German Press, 1963–1965." *Yale Journal of Law and the Humanities* 12 (Summer 2000): 101–50.

Pendas, Devin O. "Truth and Its Consequences: Reflections on Political, Historical and Legal 'Truth' in West German Holocaust Trials." *traverse: Zeitschrift für Geschichte/Revue d'Histoire* 11/1 (2004): 25–38.

Persico, Joseph. *Nuremberg: Infamy on Trial.* New York: Viking, 1994.

Peschel-Gutzeit, Lore Marie. *Zur rechtlichen Auseinandersetzung mit der NS-Gewaltherrschaft und dem SED-Regime.* Berlin: Walter de Gruyter, 1995.

Peters, Karl. *Strafprozeß: Ein Lehrbuch*, 4th rev. ed. Heidelberg: C. F. Müller Juristischer Verlag, 1985.

Postone, Moishe. *Time, Labor, and Social Domination: A Reinterpretation of Marx's Critical Theory.* Cambridge: Cambridge University Press, 1993.

Presse- und Informationsamt der Bundesregierung. *Die Verfolgung nationalsozialistischer Straftaten in der Bundesrepublik.* Flensburg: Christian Wolff, 1963.

Radlmaier, Steffen, ed. *Der Nürnberger Lernprozeß: Von Kriegsverbrechen und Starreportern.* Frankfurt: Eichborn Verlag, 2001.

Ratz, Michael, et al. *Die Justiz und die Nazis: Zur Strafverfolgung von Nazismus und Neonazismus seit 1945.* Frankfurt: Röderberg-Verlag, 1979.

Redaktion Kritische Justiz, ed. *Der Unrechts-Staat: Recht und Justiz im Nationalsozialismus.* 2 vols. Baden-Baden: Nomos Verlagsgesellschaft, 1983–84.

Reitlinger, Gerald. *Die Endlösung: Hitlers Versuch der Ausrottung der Juden Europas, 1939–1945.* Berlin: Colloquium Verlag, 1956.

Reitlinger, Gerald. *The Final Solution: The Attempt to Exterminate the Jews of Europe, 1939–1945.* New York: A. S. Barnes, 1953.

Reitlinger, Gerald. *The SS-Alibi of a Nation, 1922–1945.* New York: Viking Press, 1957.

Renz, Werner. "Auschwitz als Augenscheinsobjekt: Anmerkungen zur Erforschung der Wahrheit im ersten Frankfurter Auschwitz-Prozess." *Mittelweg 36* 1 (2001): 63–72.

Renz, Werner. "Der erste Frankfurter Auschwitz-Prozess: Völkermord als Strafsache." *1999: Zeitschrift für Sozialgeschichte des 20. und 21. Jahrhunderts* 15 (2000): 11–48.

Renz, Werner. "Der I. Frankfurter Auschwitz-Prozess: Zwei Vorgeschichten." *Zeitschrift für Geschichtswissenschaft* 50 (2002): 622–41.

Renz, Werner. "Opfer und Täter: Zeugen der Shoah: Ein Tondbandmitschnitt vom ersten Frankfurter Auschwitz-Prozess als Geschichtsquelle." *Tribüne* 41 (2002): 126–36.

Renz, Werner. "Tatort Auschwitz: Ortstermin im Auschwitz-Prozess." *Tribüne* 40 (2001): 132–44.

Robbers, Gerhard. *An Introduction to German Law.* Trans. Michael Jewell. Baden-Baden: Nomos Verlag, 1998.

Robertson, Geoffrey. *Crimes against Humanity: The Struggle for Global Justice.* New York: New Press, 1999.

Rondholz, Eberhard. "Die Ludwigsburger Zentrale Stelle zur Aufklärung nationalsozialistischer Verbrechen." *Kritische Justiz* 20 (1987): 207–13.

Rosenbaum, Alan S. *Prosecuting Nazi War Criminals.* Boulder: Westview, 1993.

Roxin, Claus. *Täterschaft und Tatherrschaft*, 6th ed. Berlin: Walter de Gruyter, 1994 [1963].

Roxin, Claus. "Straftaten im Rahmen organisatorischer Machtapparate." In Heinrich Grüntzer, ed., *Goltdammer's Archiv für Strafrecht.* Hamburg: R. v. Decker's Verlag 1963: 193–207.

Roxin, Claus, Gunther Arzt, and Klaus Tiedemann. *Einführung in das Strafrecht und Strafprozeßrecht*, 3rd rev. ed. Heidelberg: C. F. Müller Juristischer Verlag, 1994.

Rückerl, Adalbert. *Die Strafverfolgung von NS-Verbrechen, 1945–1978: Eine Dokumentation.* Heidelberg: C. F. Müller, 1979.

Rückerl, Adalbert. *NS-Verbrechen vor Gericht: Versuch einer Vergangenheitsbewältigung.* Heidelberg: C. F. Müller Juristischer Verlag, 1984.

Rüter, C. F., et al., eds. *Justiz und NS-Verbrechen: Sammlung Deutscher Strafurteile wegen nationalsozialistischer Tötungsverbrechen, 1945–1966.* 23 vols. Amsterdam: University Press Amsterdam, 1979.

Sandkühler, Thomas, and Hans-Walter Schmuhl. "Noch Einmal: Die I.G. Farben und Auschwitz." *Geschichte und Gesellschaft* 19 (1993): 259–67.

Schabas, William A. *Genocide in International Law.* Cambridge: Cambridge University Press, 2000.

Schildt, Axel, and Arnold Sywottek, eds. *Modernisierung im Wiederaufbau: Die westdeutsche Gesellschaft in der 5oer Jahre.* Bonn: Dietz, 1998.

Schildt, Axel, Detlev Siegfried, and Karl Christian Lammers, eds. *Dynamische Zeiten: Die 6oer Jahre in den beiden deutschen Gesellschaften.* Hamburg: Christians, 2000.

Schmidt, Regina, and Egon Becker. *Reaktionen auf politische Vorgänge: Drei Meinungsstudien aus der Bundesrepublik.* Frankfurter Beiträge zur Soziologie, vol. 19, with a preface by T. W. Adorno and L. v. Friedenburg. Frankfurt: Europäische Verlagsanstalt, 1967.

Schneider, Peter, and Hermann J. Meyer, eds. *Rechtliche und politische Aspekte der NS-Verbrecherprozesse: Gemeinschaftsvorlesung des studium generale Wintersemester 1966/67.* Mainz: Gutenberg-Universität Mainz, 1968.

Schneider, Ulrich, ed. *Auschwitz – Ein Prozeß: Geschichte-Fragen-Wirkungen.* Cologne: PapyRosssa Verlag, 1994.

Schoeps, Julius H., ed. *Ein Volk von Mördern? Die Dokumentation zur Goldhagen-Kontroverse um die Rolle der Deutschen im Holocaust.* Hamburg: Hoffmann und Campe Verlag, 1996.

Schoeps, Julius H., and Horst Hillerman, eds. *Justiz und Nationalsozialismus: Bewältigt-Verdrangt-Vergessen.* Stutgart: Burg Verlag, 1987.

Schönke, Adolf, and Horst Schröder. *Strafgesetzbuch: Kommentar,* 10th ed. Munich: C. H. Beck'sche Verlagsbuchhandlung, 1961.

Schönke, Adolf, and Horst Schröder. *Strafgesetzbuch: Kommentar,* 11th ed. Munich: C. H. Beck'sche Verlagsbuchhandlung, 1963.

Schönke, Adolf, and Horst Schröder. *Strafgesetzbuch: Kommentar,* 12th ed. Munich: C. H. Beck'sche Verlagsbuchhandlung, 1965.

Schrafstetter, Susanna. "The Diplomacy of *Widergutmachung*: Memory, the Cold War, and the Western European Victims of Nazism, 1956–1964." *Holocaust and Genocide Studies* 17 (Winter 2003): 459–79.

Schwan, Gesine. *Politik und Schuld: Die zerstörerische Macht des Schweigens.* Frankfurt: Fischer Verlag, 1997.

Schwarz, Otto, and Theodor Kleinknecht. *Strafprozeßordnung, Gerichtsverfassungsgesetz, Nebengesetze und ergänzende Bestimmungen.* Beck'sche Kurzkommentare, vol. 6. Munich: C.H. Beck'sche Verlagsbuchhandlung, 1963.

Scott, James C. *Weapons of the Weak: Everyday Forms of Peasant Resistance.* New Haven: Yale University Press, 1985.

Seifert, Karl-Heinz, and Dieter Hömig, eds. *Grundgesetz für die Bundesrepublik Deutschland: Taschenkommentar,* 4th ed. Baden-Baden: Nomos, 1991.

Sewell, William H., Jr. "A Theory of Structure: Duality, Agency, and Transformation." *American Journal of Sociology* 86 (July 1992): 1–29.

Shandley, Robert R., ed. *Unwilling Germans? The Goldhagen Debate*. Minneapolis: University of Minnesota Press, 1998.

Shklar, Judith N. *Legalism: Law, Morals and Political Trials*. Cambridge: Harvard University Press, 1964.

Silverman, Kaja. *The Subject of Semiotics*. Oxford: Oxford University Press, 1983.

Smith, Bradley F. *Reaching Judgment at Nuremberg*. New York: Basic Books, 1977.

Staff, Ilsa. "Fritz Bauer (1903–1968): 'Im Kampf um des Menschen Rechte.'" In *Streitbare Juristen: Eine andere Tradition*, ed. Redaktion Kritische Justiz. Baden-Baden: Nomos Verlag, 1988.

Stein, Eric. "History against Free Speech: The New German Law against the 'Auschwitz' – and Other – 'Lies.'" *Michigan Law Review* 85 (1986): 277–324.

Stolleis, Michael. *The Law under the Swastika: Studies on Legal History in Nazi Germany*. Chicago: University of Chicago Press, 1998.

Stolting II, Hermann. *Plädoyer im Auschwitz-Prozess*. N.p., n.d.

Syndor, Charles W., Jr. *Soldiers of Destruction: The SS Death's Head Division, 1933–1945*. Princeton: Princeton University Press, 1977.

Taylor, Telford. *The Anatomy of the Nuremberg Trials: A Personal Memoir*. New York: Knopf, 1992.

Taylor, Telford. *Final Report to the Secretary of the Army on the Nurnberg [sic] War Crimes Trials under Control Council Law No. 10*. Buffalo: William S. Hein & Co, 1997 [1949].

Todorov, Tzvetan. "The Touvier Affair." In Richard J. Golsan, ed., *Memory, the Holocaust, and French Justice*. Hanover: University Press of New England, 1996.

Tolstoy, Leo. "The Raid." In *The Raid and Other Stories*. Trans. Louise Maude and Aylmer Maude. Oxford: Oxford University Press, 1982.

Tusa, Ann, and John Tusa. *The Nuremberg Trial*. New York: Atheneum, 1986.

van Pelt, Robert Jan. *The Case for Auschwitz: Evidence from the Irving Trial*. Bloomington: Indiana University Press, 2002.

Varon, Jeremy. *Bringing the War Home: The Weather Underground, the Red Army Faction, and Revolutionary Violence in the Sixties and Seventies*. Berkeley: University of California Press, 2004.

Vogel, Rolf. *Der demokratische Staat im Kampf gegen radikale Ausdrucksformen in der Bundesrepublik Deutschland: eine Dokumentation der Deutschland-Berichte*. Bonn, 1968.

Vogel, Rolf. *Ein Stempel hat gefehlt: Dokumentation zur Emigration deutsche Juden*. Munich: Droemer Knauer, 1977.

Vogel, Rolf. *Israel: Staat der Hoffnung*. Stuttgart: Schwabenverlag, 1957.

von Miquel, Marc. *Ahnden oder amnestieren? Westdeutsche Justiz und Vergangenheitspolitik in den sechziger Jahren*. Beiträge zur Geschichte des 20. Jahrhunderts, vol. 1. Göttingen: Wallstein, 2004.

Wachs, Phillip-Christian. *Der Fall Theodor Oberländer (1905–1998): Ein Lehrstück deutscher Geschichte*. Frankfurt: Campus Verlag, 2000.

Wagner, Bernd Christian. *IG Auschwitz: Zwangsarbeit und Vernichtung von Häftlingen des Lagers Monowitz, 1941–1945*. Munich: K. G. Sauer, 2000.

Warburg, Justus R. G. *Die anwaltliche Praxis in Strafsachen*. Stuttgart: Verlag W. Kohlhammer, 1985.

Weber, Jürgen, and Peter Steinbach, eds. *Vergangenheitsbewältigung durch Strafver-fahren? NS-Prozesse in der Bundesrepublik Deutschland.* Munich: Günter Olzog Verlag, 1984.

Weber, Max. *Economy and Society: An Outline of Interpretive Sociology.* 2 vols. Berkeley: University of California Press, 1978.

Weinke, Annette. "Der Kampf um die Akten: Zur Kooperation zwischen MfS und osteuropäischen Sicherheitsorganen bei der Vorbereitung antifaschistischer Kampagnen." *Deutschland-Archiv* 32 (1999): 564–77.

Weinke, Annette. "Strafverfolgung nationalsozialistischer Verbrechen in den frühen Sechzigern: Eine Replik." *Mittelweg 36* 3 (2001): 45–48.

Weinke, Annette. *Die Verfolgung von NS-Tätern im geteilten Deutschland. Vergangenheitsbewältigung 1949–1969 oder: Eine deutsch-deutsche Beziehungsgeschichte im Kalten Krieg.* Paderborn: F. Schöningh, 2002.

Weisbrod, Bernd, ed. *Die Politik der Öffentlichkeit – Die Öffentlichkeit der Politik: Politische Medialisierung in der Geschichte der Bundesrepublik.* Göttingen: Wallstein, 2003.

Weiss, Peter. *Die Ermittlung: Oratorium in elf Gesängen.* Frankfurt: Suhrkamp, 1965.

Weiss, Peter. *The Investigation: Oratorio in 11 Cantos.* Trans. Alexander Gross London: Marion Boyars, 1982 [1966].

Welzel, Hans. *Das deutsche Strafrecht: Eine systematische Darstellung,* 9th ed. Berlin: Walter de Gruyter, 1965.

Welzel, Hanz. *Um die finale Handlungslehre: Eine Auseinandersetzung mit ihren Kritikern.* Tübingen: J. C. B. Mohr (Paul Siebeck), 1949.

Werle, Gerhard, and Thomas Wandres. *Auschwitz vor Gericht: Völkermord und bundesdeutscher Strafjustiz.* Munich: C. H. Beck, 1995.

Wette, Wolfram. *Die Wehrmacht: Feindbilder, Vernichtungskrieg, Legenden,* 2nd ed. Frankfurt: Fischer Verlag, 2002.

White, James Boyd. *Heracles' Bow: Essays on the Rhetoric and Poetics of the Law.* Madison: University of Wisconsin Press, 1985.

Wildt, Michael. *Generation des Unbedingten: Das Führerkorps des Reichssicherheitshauptamt.* Hamburg: Hamburger Edition, 2002.

Wilke, Jürgen, Brigit Schenk, Akiba A. Cohen, and Tamar Zemach. *Holocaust und NS-Prozesse: Die Presseberichterstattung in Israel und Deutschland zwischen Aneignung und Abwehr.* Cologne: Böhlau Verlag, 1995.

Williams, Raymond. *Marxism and Literature.* Oxford: Oxford University Press, 1977.

Wittmann, Rebecca Elisabeth. *Beyond Justice: The Auschwitz Trial.* Cambridge: Harvard University Press, 2005.

Wittmann, Rebecca Ellisabeth. "Holocaust on Trial? The Frankfurt Auschwitz Trial in Historical Perspective." Ph.D. diss., University of Toronto, 2001.

Wittmann, Rebecca Elisabeth. "Indicting Auschwitz? The Paradox of the Frankfurt Auschwitz Trial." *German History* 21 (2003): 505–32.

Wittmann, Rebecca Elisabeth. "Telling the Story: Survivor Testimony and the Narration of the Frankfurt Auschwitz-Trial." *Bulletin of the German Historical Institute,* no. 32 (Spring 2003): 93–101.

Wittmann, Rebecca Elisabeth. "The Wheels of Justice Turn Slowly: The Pretrial Investigation of the Frankfurt Auschwitz Trial 1963–1965." *Central European History* 35 (2002): 345–78.

Wojak, Irmtrud. "Herrschaft der Sachverständigen? Zum ersten Frankfurter Auschwitz-Prozeß." *Kritische Justiz* 32 (1999): 605–16.

Wojak, Irmtrud, ed. *Auschwitz-Prozeß 4 Ks 2/63, Frankfurt am Main*. Cologne: Snoeck Verlagsgesellschaft, 2004.

Wojak, Irmtrud, ed. *"Gerichtstag halten über uns selbst...": Geschichte und Wirkung des ersten Frankfurter Auschwitz-Prozesses*. Fritz Bauer Institut Jahrbuch 2001 zur Geschichte und Wirkung des Holocaust. Frankfurt: Campus Verlag, 2001.

Wojak, Irmtrud, and Susanne Meinl, eds. *Im Labyrinth der Schuld: Täter-Opfer-Ankläger*. Fritz Bauer Institut Jahrbuch 2003 zur Geschichte und Wirkung des Holocaust. Frankfurt: Campus Verlag, 2003.

Young, James E. *Writing and Rewriting the Holocaust: Narrative and the Consequences of Interpretation*. Bloomington: Indiana University Press, 1988.

Young, Robert M. "Marxism and the History of Science." In R. C. Olby et al., eds., *Companion to the History of Modern Science*. London: Routledge, 1996: 77–86.

Zillmer, Eric A., et al. *The Quest for the Nazi Personality: A Psychological Investigation of Nazi War Criminals*. Hillsdale, N.J.: Lawrence Erlbaum, 1995.

Index

Cäsar, Joachim, 159
Central Office for the Investigation of
    National Socialist Crimes (Ludwigsburg),
    15, 20, 21, 28, 35, 36, 42, 45, 47, 57, 102,
    195
Certeau, Michel de, 80–81, 102
Christ und Welt, 285
Churchill, Winston, 8
Clausen, Wilhelm, 115
Clay, Lucius D., 10
Cold War: as context for Auschwitz Trial, 2,
    23, 25, 27, 28, 123–24, 128, 182–91; as
    impediment to prosecution, 40–42;
    manipulation of by defense counsel, 142,
    182, 187, 188–89, 293; role in
    "Auschwitz: Pictures and Documents"
    exhibition, 183–86
Comité International des Camps, Brussels
    (CIC), 41, 126, 185, 289–90
concurrence, *See* guilt
Corrin, Charles, 165
Cover, Robert, 72
crimes against humanity: annullment in the
    Grundgesetz, 14; application in Nazi
    trials, 11–12; critique of notion by German
    nationalists, 279; definition of, 9–10;
    disavowal by German courts, 12–13,
    53

Dachau, 92, 157, 243
Dassendorf, 48
defendants, Auschwitz Trial, 99; acquittal for
    lack of evidence, 236; alleged aid to camp
    inmates, 205, 214–15, 225; anti-Semitism
    of, 206; assertion of individual guilt of in
    verdict, 230, 234–35; benefits of Auschwitz
    service, 206; categories of, 98–100, 234;
    characterization as "good Germans," 247,
    262, 263; cooperation among, 161;
    hostility to survivors by, 163; Nazi
    membership of, 133–34, 197, 205; press
    depictions of, 260, 261, 262–64, 281;
    remorselessness of, 207; representation as
    accomplices, 138–39, 212–14, 247;
    representation as perpetrators, 113, 158,
    196–97, 204, 206–208, 209;
    representation as victims, 212, 221, 224,
    292; sense of duty as motivation for, 283;
    SS service of, 131–33, 197, 205–206, 230;
    trial's consequences for, 96, 232
defense counsel, Auschwitz Trial: argument
    of duress by higher orders

(*Befehlsnotstand*), 33, 50, 137, 157, 193,
    198–99, 203, 209, 213, 274; argument of
    inability to issue orders, 135; argument of
    insufficient evidence of personal
    culpability, 216; argument of legality of
    Nazi law, 220, 225, 228–29, 231, 300;
    argument of limited agency, 212–16, 242,
    247, 300; argument of nonjurisdiction of
    German courts, 218–19, 228, 229, 231;
    argument of perceived legality of orders,
    137, 139, 193, 220, 221–22; argument of
    personal disapproval of orders, 43, 44,
    137, 139; argument of service at Auschwitz
    as involuntary, 132–33, 139, 205–206,
    247; argument of "surpassed causation,"
    213, 242, 300; attacks on legitimacy of
    trial, 142, 189, 212, 231; attempts to
    reclaim moral self-worth of defendants,
    97; attribution of responsibility for
    genocide to Nazi leadership, 215, 224;
    challenges to eyewitness credibility, 38,
    142, 163–64, 193, 216–17, 231–32, 244,
    280, 293; challenges to role of outside
    parties, 222; charges of press bias, 223;
    charges of procedural irregularity, 222–26;
    charges of prosecutorial misconduct, 223;
    charges of witness tampering, 40, 190–91,
    200, 223–24, 232, 280; closing arguments,
    211–26; complaints of excessive publicity,
    222, 223; cross-examination of Kuczynski,
    153–54; cynicism of, 225; distinction of
    ends from means, 44–45; Laternser as
    "star," 94; objections to "Auschwitz:
    Pictures and Documents" exhibition, 183,
    223; objections to general allegations, 117;
    objections to prosecution theory of
    "concurrence," 198, 213, 215, 244;
    objections to testimony of Kuczynski, 148,
    150, 154; obligations to clients, 95–96;
    personnel, 93–95; political tactics, 94, 142,
    183, 188–91, 193, 220, 293; representation
    of survivors as vengeful, 216; role of Baer's
    absence for, 50; rudeness of, 162; use of
    animosity amongst survivors, 38, 190; use
    of military law by, 221–22
democratization, 6; and denazification, 10,
    16–17
denazification, 10, 19, 33, 84, 265
deterrence, as goal of criminal sanctions, 73,
    224
*Deutsche National-Zeitung und
    Soldaten-Zeitung*, 267, 276, 278–79

For EU product safety concerns, contact us at Calle de José Abascal, 56–1°, 28003 Madrid, Spain or eugpsr@cambridge.org.

www.ingramcontent.com/pod-product-compliance
Ingram Content Group UK Ltd.
Pitfield, Milton Keynes, MK11 3LW, UK
UKHW042145130625
459647UK00011B/1188